Confederate
Emancipation

Confederate Emancipation

Southern Plans to Free and Arm Slaves during the Civil War

BRUCE LEVINE

OXFORD

UNIVERSITY PRESS

2006

OXFORD

UNIVERSITY PRESS

Oxford University Press, Inc., publishes works that
further Oxford University's objective of excellence
in research, scholarship, and education.

Oxford   New York
Auckland   Cape Town   Dar es Salaam   Hong Kong   Karachi
Kuala Lumpur   Madrid   Melbourne   Mexico City   Nairobi
New Delhi   Shanghai   Taipei   Toronto

With offices in
Argentina   Austria   Brazil   Chile   Czech Republic   France   Greece
Guatemala   Hungary   Italy   Japan   Portugal   Singapore
South Korea   Switzerland   Thailand   Turkey   Ukraine   Vietnam

Published by Oxford University Press, Inc.
198 Madison Avenue, New York, NY 10016
www.oup.com

Library of Congress Cataloging-in-Publication Data
Levine, Bruce C., 1949–
Confederate emancipation: southern plans to free and arm slaves during
the Civil War/Bruce Levine.
p. cm.
Includes bibliographical references and index.
ISBN 978-0-19-531586-8

1. Slaves—Emancipation—Confederate States of America.
2. Confederate States of America—Politics and government.
3. Slaves—Confederate States of America—History—19th century.
4. Slaves—Southern States—History—19th century.
5. United States—History—Civil War, 1861–1865—African Americans.
6. Confederate States of America—Race relations—Political aspects.
I. Title.
E453.L48 2005
973.7'14—dc22
2005047746

Printed in the United States of America
on acid-free paper

To my sister, Nancy,
With love and appreciation

CONTENTS

4
"We Can Devise the Means"
The Long-Term Plan

5
"On the Footing of Soldiers"
Enacting and Implementing New Policy, 1864–1865

6
"Like a Drowning Man Catching at Straws"
Could It Have Worked?

Conclusion
From Black Troops to Black Codes
"Confederate Emancipation" in War and Peace

Confederate Emancipation

INTRODUCTION
The Puzzle of Confederate Emancipation

orthern Georgia can be bitterly cold in winter, and so it was on the evening of January 2, 1864. Sleet fell as a bearded soldier in his mid-thirties rode into the troop encampment in the woods outside the hill town of Dalton.[1] The rider was General Patrick R. Cleburne, an Irish-born division commander in the Confederate Army of Tennessee. He was not physically prepossessing, was often shabbily dressed, and was only a mediocre horseman. But he was also an energetic, courageous, cool-headed, and thoughtful man whose brilliant combat record had steadily propelled him up the ranks from private to general officer, twice won him the thanks of the Confederate Congress, and earned him the nickname of "the Stonewall of the West."[2]

Cleburne had come into Dalton to attend a momentous meeting, one to which all corps and division commanders had been invited. But the young general had not been summoned out into that inclement evening; the meeting was his idea. He had spent much of the previous month sitting in his tent at nearby Tunnel Hill considering the requirements of Confederate victory in the war. Cleburne seemed admirably suited to that task. His immediate superior, Lt. Gen. William J. Hardee, who knew the Irishman well, later eulogized his "highly logical cast" of mind. "Before expressing an opinion upon a subject, or coming to a decision in any conjuncture of circumstances," Cleburne "wore an expression as if solving a mathematical proposition," and the conclusion he reached "was always stamped with mathematical correctness."[3]

An engraving of Major-General Patrick R.
Cleburne of the Confederate Army of Tennessee. (The Library of Congress)

In December 1863, those analyti-
cal powers led the general to make a
proposal that startled and shocked
many. Employing the debater's skills
he had acquired as an attorney in civilian life, Cleburne produced a
lengthy memorandum on the plan's
behalf. It called on the Confederacy to
"immediately commence training a large
reserve of the most courageous of our
slaves" to become soldiers. And, Cleburne
added, "If we arm and train him and make
him fight for the country in her hour of dire dis-
tress, every consideration of principle and policy demand [*sic*] that we should
set him and his whole race who side with us free."[4] When Cleburne circulated
this document among the officers of his division, four brigade commanders,
ten regimental commanders, and one cavalry division commander promptly
added their signatures to his. Some other senior officers in the army who had
not signed the memorandum reportedly sympathized with its contents.[5]

Tonight Cleburne would present this proposal to the rest of his army's
leadership. By a few minutes past 7, nearly a dozen generals had gathered in
the quarters of their newly appointed commander, Joseph E. Johnston. After
brief preliminaries, Cleburne began to read his memo aloud and continued
for more than half an hour. When he finished, an old friend, Gen. Thomas
C. Hindman, expressed his broad agreement. Then Maj. Calhoun Benham,
Cleburne's chief of staff, who had earlier seen the text, presented a prepared
rebuttal. Thereafter Gens. James Patton Anderson, William B. Bate, and
William H. T. Walker attacked Cleburne's proposal with considerably greater
heat.[6] A few days later the memorandum encountered another unapprecia-
tive reception in Richmond, where Jefferson Davis and his cabinet summarily
rejected Cleburne's suggestions.[7]

Although those negative reactions evidently took Cleburne aback, they
were quite predictable.[8] During the war's first months, the Confederate president had identified slavery and its preservation as central to the secessionists'
cause. The vast wealth and impressive development of the southern states,
Davis reminded the Confederate Congress, were achievements "for the full
development and continuance of which the labor of African slaves was and is
indispensable." The ascendant Republican party "menaced" that labor sys-

tem, and "with interests of such overwhelming magnitude imperiled," Davis recalled, "the people of the Southern States were driven . . . to the adoption of some course of action to avert the danger" posed.[9] Just a month earlier, Vice President Alexander Stephens of Georgia had proudly identified white supremacy and black bondage as together forming the very "cornerstone" of Confederate rule. In fact, Stephens had enthused, "our new Government" was "the first in the history of the world" to base itself squarely upon the "great physical, philosophical, and moral truth" that "the negro is not equal to the white man" and that "slavery—subordination to the superior race—is his natural and normal condition."[10]

Not surprisingly, therefore, the Davis administration not only dismissed Cleburne's proposal to emancipate and arm black southerners in January of 1864; it also ordered all further discussion of that explosive subject suppressed in the Army of Tennessee. Patrick Cleburne's death a few months later at the battle of Franklin helped enforce that seal of silence.[11] But Cleburne's idea refused to die with its author. Quite the contrary, in fact. By early November of 1864, the Confederate president had reversed himself and was readying public opinion for a decision to arm and emancipate able-bodied male slaves. Before long, his secretary of state, Judah P. Benjamin, was urging the white South to tell its bondsmen, "Go and fight; you are free."[12]

The Richmond government's dramatic turnabout and embrace of this idea triggered a fierce, broad-based, and wide-ranging public dispute that dominated political life during the Confederacy's final six months of existence. It was, in fact, precisely the kind of explosive controversy about slavery's place in the South's economy, race relations, ideology, and political life that Davis had sought to suppress when he squelched Patrick Cleburne's proposal—and that planters and their advocates had been working hard to avoid for more than thirty years. Not only should "the proposition itself . . . never have been made," an Alabaman now lamented, but "the arguments for and against the proposition ought never to have been made public."[13] "We are sorry that so much has been said about it," one North Carolina editor agreed. "It is a matter that cannot be handled too delicately. We beg of our legislators to beware, to be cautious. They cannot be too much so."[14]

Too late. Government officials, journalists, plantation owners and small farmers, army officers and common soldiers, slaves and free blacks, all were now pulled into the discussion's powerful vortex. The arch-secessionist Virginia planter Edmund Ruffin complained that the notion of arming and emancipating slaves now "enters the resolutions of public meetings, & the speeches there delivered, as well as in private conversations & arguments."[15] It was "the great question now stirring the public mind," a Virginia state senator affirmed.[16] It soon preoccupied the soldiers of Lee's Army of Northern

Virginia, too. "[A]ll the talk now," as one of its privates wrote his sister, "is about putting 200,000 nigroes [*sic*] in the army."[17]

The dispute extended far beyond Virginia's borders. "The subject," as one Deep South politician observed, "is now before the country, in all its length, and breadth, and depth."[18] Throughout the Confederacy newspaper editors threw themselves into (and their columns open to) the raging debate. From Alabama soldier Douglas J. Cater reported that "the question of whether or not we should place negroes in the field seems to be the topic of conversation in all social circles."[19] A Raleigh, North Carolina, editor was amazed to "hear people talking on the street corners in favor of the measure," and Tar Heel plantation mistress Catherine Edmondston marveled at her neighbors' fixation on it.[20] South Carolina senator James L. Orr claimed the topic "had excited the public mind more than any other."[21] "Every one I talk to," Georgia's Mary Akin found, had a strong opinion on the subject.[22] Indeed, noted another Georgian, the issue had "swallowed up all other matters of public interest."[23] Col. Richard L. Maury summed up the matter accurately: "This Negro soldier question is the great one of the day."[24]

This "Negro soldier question" dominated public discussion for good reason. It raised in an especially stark and dramatic way key questions not only about the southern war effort but also about the southern cause more generally. "No question of more serious import has been agitated," Virginia congressman Thomas S. Gholson thought, "since the commencement of the present war."[25] "No question has arisen during this war," a Georgia newspaper editor agreed, "so much affecting the very principles for which we contend."[26] For precisely that reason, artillery captain Thomas J. Key believed, the measure "will make or ruin the South."[27]

To many, ruin seemed by far the likelier outcome. This suggestion was "opposite to all the sentiments and principles which have heretofore governed the Southern people," warned the Richmond *Examiner*.[28] Virginia's Robert M. T. Hunter, president pro tempore of the Confederate Senate, a former Confederate secretary of state, and one of the most politically powerful men in the South, demanded, "What did we go to war for, if not to protect our property?"[29] An incredulous North Carolina legislator questioned the sanity of the measure's sponsors; had "despair made them lose all their reason"?[30]

No one put this objection more sharply than Robert Barnwell Rhett, Jr., the fire-eating editor of the Charleston *Mercury*, an early advocate of secession. "The mere agitation in the Northern States to effect the emancipation of our slaves largely contributed to our separation from them," Rhett reminded his readers. "And now, before a Confederacy which we established to put at rest forever all such agitation is four years old, we find the proposition gravely submitted that the Confederate Government should emancipate slaves in the States."[31] On the floor of the Confederate congress, Tennessee's Henry S. Foote crossed the t's and dotted the i's, asking "If this Government is to destroy slavery, why fight for it?"[32]

In the midst of (and despite) this uproar, the proposal received potent public endorsement from none other than Robert E. Lee, the Confederacy's newly designated Confederate general in chief and its most popular public figure. In February 1865, Lee declared the arming of slaves to be "not only expedient but necessary," adding that "those who are employed [under arms] should be freed."[33] The following month Jefferson Davis signed and began implementing a law authorizing the induction of hundreds of thousands of black soldiers into his armies. Lee's headquarters issued instructions about mustering and training those troops, and hand-picked recruiters fanned out across the Confederacy.

In the end, this dramatic controversy and its upshot produced little in the way of practical results. Nevertheless, what some have called "Confederate emancipation"[34] and the far-reaching debate that it triggered have attracted the attention of generations of writers (including both professional and amateur historians) anxious to determine what this remarkable chapter in Confederate history signified about the South, about secession, and about the ferocious war that secession begat.

The questions they have raised are manifold. First, why were black troops proposed in the first place? Why was such a policy ultimately adopted? How did various sectors of the population and army react to the idea? Were southern white soldiers willing to serve alongside black troops?

Second, what did these proposals reveal about the motives behind secession and the Confederacy's formation? Did they make it necessary to re-evaluate these subjects? More specifically, did they undermine the belief that the Confederacy formed and fought to preserve slavery and white supremacy?

Third, would slaves welcome this offer and fight willingly and effectively on the Confederacy's behalf? And did this plan contain the potential to alter the course and outcome of the war?

These last questions point to a fourth set: Had this plan succeeded in rescuing the Confederacy from defeat, what would it have meant for the future structure and functioning of the South's economy? How could the plantation system have survived such a policy's adoption? Did this policy, then, signal a readiness to abandon the economic interests of the slave masters? And did the Cleburne-Davis proposal contain the seeds of a postwar southern history dramatically different from the one that actually occurred?

Historian Robert F. Durden launched the modern reexamination of this intriguing episode with a documentary collection published more than thirty years ago. Deeply informed, carefully annotated, interpretively provocative, that volume has remained the principal resource on the subject ever since then. In fact, although Durden never considered his volume to be the last word on this matter, it has until now remained the *only* published book-length study of it.[35]

The present work aims to carry the investigation forward. It draws on several different types of evidence, including both the words and actions of the principal architects of the emancipate-and-recruit policy and those of their leading critics. Letters and petitions that Confederate military officers, enlisted men, and civilians sent to one another and to the Richmond government (many of which Union forces captured following the fall of Richmond and are now held at the National Archives) also receive considerable attention. So does the voluminous newspaper record, including the news columns, editorials, and numerous letters through which members of the citizenry joined the public debate.[36]

Perhaps most importantly of all, the present account strives to set the whole story squarely in the context of the war's progress, its impact upon on the social and political psychology of the Confederate leadership, soldiers, and citizenry, the evolution of Union policy toward the slaves and slavery, and especially the conduct of the South's black population. Little about this episode makes much sense, I am convinced, except in the light of the way millions of slaves responded to the new conditions that war created. That response constitutes a textbook example of how the "inarticulate" and "powerless" can intervene decisively in the historical process. During the last three decades, scholars have learned a great deal about that and other aspects of the war; their discoveries now make it possible to view and evaluate the story of Confederate emancipation in clearer perspective.

For most postwar partisans of the Confederacy, Richmond's bid to arm emancipated slaves posed no great interpretive challenge, represented no puzzle at all. As such people saw it, this measure grew out of—and conclusively proved the validity of—three axioms basic to their view of the war as a whole. First, that chattel slavery was a mild, benign institution that instilled contentment and therefore loyalty in southern blacks. Second, that southern masters therefore could and did place great confidence in slaves' loyalty, enough to serenely place weapons in black hands. Third, that despite slavery's many virtues as an institution, it was never central to the Confederate cause; the Confederacy was not formed and did not fight in order to preserve the South's "peculiar institution." It fought instead for the South's right to govern itself, a goal for which white southerners were willing to sacrifice all else, *including* slavery.

The first of these three axioms—that bondage was a blessing to both blacks and whites—was a pillar of the most militant line of proslavery argument in the antebellum era. God had made Africans to serve the white population, it held, and masters respected their obligations to treat those servants humanely and fairly. Georgia's Robert Toombs put the case in classical terms in an 1853 speech, asserting that "the African is unfit to be intrusted [*sic*] with political power and incapable as a freeman of securing his own happiness or contributing to the public prosperity." Therefore "whenever the two races co-exist a state of slavery is best for him and society. And under it in our country he is in a better condition than he has ever attained in any other age and country, either in bondage or freedom."[37] An Atlanta editor only enlarged upon the point when he called the slaves' position "an enviable one" and insisted that "they constitute a privileged class in the community." Indeed, this writer added, he thought often of "how happy we should be were we the slave of some good and provident owner," since in that case "simple daily toil would fill the measure of duty, and comfortable food and clothing would be the assured reward."[38]

In this view, furthermore, the great majority of black southerners understood and respected the divine order of things. Bondspeople were satisfied with their lot in life and were firmly devoted to their masters. On the eve of secession, Edmund Ruffin mused about the slaves' "cheerful contentment" and their "affectionate loyalty to their superiors."[39] Secretary of War James A. Seddon affirmed in November of 1864 that during the current conflict "the feelings . . . of the great mass of the negroes have been conclusively manifested to be with their protectors and masters."[40] "[T]he slaves of the South," a South Carolina legislative committee proudly reported at the end of that year, "have diligently, faithfully and loyally discharged their duties" and thereby "proved their attachment" to us. They have "performed every work in which it has been our interest to direct and employ them," whether on "the fortifications, in the hospitals, on the field with their masters," and they have done it all "cheerfully."[41]

The loyalty of slaves to the Confederacy remained an article of faith in much of the white South long after the war's conclusion. It became central to the so-called "Lost Cause" belief system, according to which slavery had been merely an excuse for northern hostility toward and aggressions against the South. The war, in this view—far from revealing black resentment of slavery—had in fact pitted a virtually united South against a predatory North intent upon conquest for other, selfish reasons. In 1881, Jefferson Davis repeated this appraisal in his memoirs, as did Jubal A. Early, the Confederate major general who played a central role in shaping the white South's semi-official memory of those times.[42]

Surely such contented, obedient, disciplined, and loyal slaves would make dependable Confederate soldiers. So argued some supporters of the measure both before, during, and after the war. After all, such things had been done successfully before. "Ancient masters," the classicist J. L. Reynolds pointed out in 1860, "assured of the fidelity of their slaves, employed them for the defence of their persons, their families, and their country."[43] And doubtless confidence in slave loyalty was even more justified in the American South than in old Greece and Rome. "Our slaves will be found loyal to their masters," a Tennessee editor predicted during the war's first month, "and if necessary, we will arm such of them as we can spare from our fields to resist our foes, who will find in these pretended objects of their philanthropy the ugliest customers they will have to encounter."[44]

Once this idea became a practical proposal, predictions like these multiplied. Yankees could deny it all they wished, a Missourian trumpeted, but all knew that already "thousands of slaves follow their masters . . . through the dangers of the battle-field" and that "many have laid down their lives" as proof of "their love." It followed that the same "relation, affection, and sympathy between himself and master" would induce the slave "to play the part of a faithful soldier to the rebellion."[45] "Let them be armed and marshaled for our defence," a Virginia newspaper editor promised, "and the whole world will confess that they have been altogether mistaken in their estimate of Southern slavery and the feelings of the inferior race toward their masters."[46]

Robert E. Lee gave this claim his blessing. "Long habits of obedience and subordination," he assured a fellow Virginian, "coupled with the moral influence which in our country the white man possesses over the black, furnishes an excellent foundation for that discipline which is the best guaranty of military efficiency."[47] Although Albert Taylor Bledsoe, an early chief of the Confederate War Bureau, opposed the policy, he had no doubt "that almost every slave would cheerfully aid his master in the work of hurling back the fanatical invader."[48] More than three years later, Secretary of War James A. Seddon, who shared Bledsoe's distaste for the proposal, also declared his faith in slaves' loyalty to their masters. "No fear is entertained of their fidelity," Seddon advised Jefferson Davis in early November 1864, "for the feelings, as the interests of the great mass of the negroes have been conclusively manifested to be with their protectors and masters." And "under the leadership of those whites to whom they have been habituated and in whom they have confidence," they would certainly fight with both "steadfastness and courage" against the Yankee foe.[49]

Those ultimately assigned the task of recruiting slaves to the Confederate armies sounded the same note.[50] And Lt. Gen. Richard Taylor fondly reported the testimony of a former slave who had been recruited during the war by the Union army and who had then been taken prisoner by Confederate troops. The man's captors had quickly put him to work as a military laborer. One day, Taylor later recalled, the black prisoner approached him and offered to take up arms for the Confederacy. "We would rather fight for our own white folks," he declared, in Taylor's account, "than for strangers."[51] Secretary of State Judah P. Benjamin and other Confederate notables told similar stories.[52]

Barely two years after Appomattox, J. D. B. De Bow, one of the antebellum South's most prominent journalists and an early and enthusiastic secessionist, fashioned the template for much postwar reflection on wartime proposals to arm slaves. Black southerners, De Bow wrote, had "adhered in general with great fidelity to the cause of their masters during the struggle." That fact, he added, "was a great surprise to the enemy, who had supposed that at the first signal the whole slave population would be in arms, and would rush at every hazard to their standards." Instead, however, the slaves "followed their masters to the field without desertion, and were proud of the service. They worked cheerfully upon the fortifications and earth-works in sight of the enemy, and without thought of desertion. They adhered to the duties of the farm and plantation when all police system was at an end, and maintained obedience, docility and respect."

That proud record stood, De Bow asserted, as "evidence of the mild, paternal and patriarchal nature of the institution of slavery as it existed at the South." Confidence in such unflinching black loyalty had also made it possible for the South to put muskets in its slaves' hands. "So firmly fixed did our people remain in the faith that the negro would be true to his master," De Bow concluded, "that it was finally proposed to receive him into the ranks of the army as a soldier." And "so popular was the idea, that enlistments began to take place, and had the war continued the negro must have formed a large element of our military strength." In fact, De Bow was sure, if the war had lasted longer, "three or four hundred thousand" black troops could have "been thrown into the field." And then "the whole aspect of affairs might have been changed."[53]

As noted, images of benevolent masters and grateful slaves obtained and retained a powerful grip on both popular and scholarly imaginations long after the war concluded. Those images conveyed a positive view of antebellum slaveowners and encouraged readers to reflect sympathetically about why thoughts of seeing "modifications" imposed upon their "gracious" system "might easily be lamented" and "regarded with a shudder."[54] But such ardent assertions of slavery's merits raise a major interpretive problem. If lamentations and shudders about slavery's possible demise lay behind secession and armed resistance to Union armies, then how can the project of Confederate emancipation be explained? If the southern states had left the old Union to preserve gracious slavery—and if they had warred since 1861 for the same purpose—why would they agree in 1865 to sacrifice their central war aim for the sake of military success? Wasn't this illogical—indeed, irrational?

Supporters of the project then and later replied by pointing to the third pillar of their view of the war—that it was *not* a war about slavery. Although slavery was a relatively benign (if not positively virtuous, efficient, and enlightenment-spreading) institution, they claimed, its preservation was never uppermost in the minds of secessionists. The South fought, instead, in defense of state's rights against the all-consuming appetite of the federal government. It fought to defend a distinctive regional way of life and set of values against the cultural imperialism of northerners, especially New Englanders. It fought to safeguard the southern population's right to govern itself without outside interference. As one Georgian put it in 1865, "mere property in negroes" was not "considered as a matter of any practical moment." Instead "independence and Constitutional Government" were "the great principles for which we are fighting."[55]

The Richmond *Enquirer*, standing in the front ranks of the plan's latter-day proponents, insisted that "slavery has nothing whatever to do with this war" and that therefore the South would without a second thought "sweep the institution from before us the moment it stands in the way of the accomplishment of our liberty."[56] Yes, the *Enquirer* continued, "the people of these States believe slavery right, permitted and sanctioned in the word of God, proper for the white man, good for the black, economical as a system of labor, and necessary to the proper cultivation of the great staples of this country." "But, notwithstanding all this, the people of these States are willing and prepared to surrender all for liberty from Yankee dominion, for independence and nationality."[57] Implementing this measure, moreover, would show as much to the world, would prove conclusively that "the slaveholder prefers nationality and free government to negroes and negro property."[58]

In the hands of the Confederacy's champions, antebellum and wartime southern attempts to reform the peculiar institution—to ease restrictions on slaves' religious practice and access to education, and to recognize and reinforce their marriages and family lives—became further evidence that the South's attachment to slavery was already on the wane before Sumter fell.[59] Indeed, many contended, it had only been outside interference that had slowed that process down. The average slave, claimed a North Carolina newspaper editor in early 1865, had "long ago discovered that his condition was rapidly improving before abolitionists began to meddle with his affairs."[60] Absent northern meddling, a like-minded Texan added, the bondsman's "state of slavery would be gradually improved. Laws would be passed protecting him in the married relation and preventing the separation of husband and wife and parents and young children, and gradually, in the long lapse of ages, he would come forth elevated, redeemed, and prepared for freedom."[61] "When once delivered from the interference of Northern abolitionism," South Carolina's Mary Jones told herself, "we shall be free to make and enforce such rules and reformations as are just and right."[62]

Surely a South ready to radically reform and even abandon slavery would not have gone to war to preserve it. Edward A. Pollard, who had served as assistant editor at the fiercely secessionist Richmond *Examiner*, presented slavery's place in the Civil War in just that light shortly after the war's conclusion. The peculiar institution, he affirmed, had been merely "an inferior object of the contest." That was apparent, he continued, in both the Confederate program of "Negro enlistments and consequent emancipation" and "the easy assent which the South gave to the extinction of Slavery at the last."[63] Robert E. Lee, too, did what he could to reinforce this latter-day view of the war and its meaning. "So far from engaging in a war to perpetuate slavery," Lee told one postwar interviewer, "I am rejoiced that slavery is abolished."[64] Going further still, Lee assured another writer that slavery had already been moving toward extinction by the time that war broke out. Lee insisted that he, like other Confederate leaders, "had always been in favor of emancipation of the negroes," albeit on a gradualist basis. "The best men of the South," he added, "have long desired to do away with the institution and were quite willing to see it abolished."[65]

In the postwar era, both Jefferson Davis and Alexander Stephens stoutly denied that slavery had brought on the war. From his postwar prison cell and again in an authorized biography, Stephens claimed that the published version of his famous "Cornerstone" speech of 1861 had been based upon "reporter's notes which were very imperfect" and only "hastily corrected by me" before being set in type. As a result his meaning had been "grossly misinterpreted."[66] In his own subsequent retrospective, Stephens dubbed the war "a strife between the principles of Federation, on one side, and Centralism, or Consolidation, on the other. Slavery, so called, was but the question on which these antagonistic principles . . . were finally brought into actual and active collision with each other on the field of battle."[67] Jefferson Davis used his memoirs to make a similar case. "The existence of African servitude was in no wise the cause of the conflict," he wrote, "but only an incident." Hostility between North and South "was not the consequence of any difference on the abstract question of slavery. It was the offspring of sectional rivalry and political ambition. It would have manifested itself just as certainly if slavery had existed in all the states, or if there had not been a negro in America."[68]

Such depictions of the Confederacy's aims and concerns laid the basis for explaining the meaning of "Confederate emancipation." Precisely because slavery was at most a subordinate issue in the hearts and minds of Confederate leaders, those leaders were quite prepared to sacrifice slavery in the interests of the higher goal of southern liberty and independence. And during the following decades, this version of history became common currency among Lost Cause defenders.[69] Thus Lt. William M. Polk, son and wartime subordinate of Gen. Leonidas Polk, claimed that among "a large number of southern men of the class to which . . . General Polk belonged" their "individual preferences undoubtedly favored ultimate freedom of the negro." Why, then, had they so furiously resisted Republican rule and fought for southern independence? Simply because they considered the decision to initiate emancipation to be "one belonging exclusively to themselves, and one in which they should be free to act without outside dictation or interference."[70]

This way of presenting the matter eventually crossed over into mainstream scholarship. Professor Thomas Robson Hay repeated the younger Polk's assertion nearly verbatim in his seminal article of 1919, "The South and the Arming of the Slaves."[71] Historian Allan Nevins decades later reaffirmed the same view. "Most informed men" in the Confederacy, wrote Nevins, had "realized that slavery was not an institution which would last forever," that "its utility was nearing an end," and that "soon it would have to be modified, and eventually, relinquished." They had fought the Union merely because they "wished . . . to choose the hour and method by which they should decree its gradual extinction."[72]

Since the 1960s, however, a scholarly revolution has repudiated sepia-tinged nostalgia for the Old South and most apologetic depictions of the Confederate cause. Professional historians today generally acknowledge that slaver's preservation was central both to antebellum southern politics and to the South's withdrawal from the federal Union. Whatever the personal motives of individual southern citizens and soldiers, those who led the secession movement, formed the Confederacy, and oversaw its war for independence did all those things principally because the Republican Party's rise threatened the future of bondage.[73]

But how can this modern consensus account for the fact that central leaders of the Confederacy eventually sought to win the war with a measure involving large-scale emancipation? Most scholars who address that question argue that Confederate war aims changed during the course of the war. Slavery, they say, was central to secession and the Confederacy's formation. But as the blood-letting continued and escalated, simply achieving political separation from the hated northern foe replaced the requirements of the plantation system in the Confederacy's hierarchy of values and aims. In this view, national independence for the South thus did eventually become an end in itself for much of the Confederate leadership—and an end worth achieving even at the expense of the original reason for founding the Confederacy. Champions of arming and freeing slaves, conclude scholars who take this ground (as Charles H. Wesley did in 1937), were so "intent on winning" that they "were willing to accept any expedient; even to reverse themselves on the theories upon which the Confederacy had predicated its existence."[74] As another put it in 1960, this legislation "meant that there was a class of men in the South" that was "willing to sacrifice a principle of long standing, slavery, to attain . . . the independence of the Confederate States of America." In the words of a third, those who proposed to arm and free slaves in 1865 "had but one goal: independence, the ability to exist as a people."[75] From this angle, the black-soldier measure looks like only the most extreme example of how the war eventually turned white southerners' goals and values on their heads: "ultimately, the Confederacy was willing to give up her 'peculiar institution,' just as she had forsaken other cherished institutions, for the sake of independence."[76]

Some recent writers have taken a still more positive view of the Confederate proposal to arm slaves, seeing in it a critical reevaluation of both slavery and the South's racial order more generally. While Jay Winik grants that the South took this step "more for utilitarian reasons than for reasons of conscience," he adds that "the decision itself was ultimately also a testament to the abomination of the institution itself," which "many Southerners" had "belatedly recognized."[77] To Ervin L. Jordan, Jr., white Confederate soldiers who volunteered to officer black units were "by implication supporters of racial equality."[78] Robert F. Durden saw in the proposal to arm and emancipate slaves proof "that there was yet a reservoir of good will between the white and black races in the South" that might have inaugurated an era of more equitable and amicable black-white relations there.[79] And some professional historians hold that enlisting black troops was a viable option for the Confederacy, one that could have elicited the cooperation of numerous slaves, thereby potentially altering the outcome of the war.

Adamant "neo-Confederates" go considerably further. The war, they still insist, had *never* been fought on behalf of slavery; loyalty to the South, southern self-government, southern culture, or states rights—rather than to slavery and white supremacy—fueled the southern war effort.[80] Their insistent celebration these days of "Black Confederates" (the thousands and thousands of slaves and free blacks who supposedly served the Confederate cause freely and enthusiastically) seeks to legitimate that claim.[81] So does a particular rendition of the Confederacy's 1865 black-troops policy. One modern champion of the Confederate tradition thus asserts that "if southerners had been primarily fighting to preserve slavery, as some have argued, then they would not have considered emancipation" as a policy, "nor would they have assented to the raising of black Confederate regiments during the final months of the war."[82] But that, the Sons of Confederate Veterans triumphantly declares, is exactly what did occur: "The CSA eventually freed slaves who would join the army and did recruit and arm black regiments."[83]

This book takes a fresh look at southern arm-and-emancipate proposals, their origins and justifications, the objections and resistance that they provoked, the final form they took, and the practical results that they produced. Chapter 1

follows the early rise and changing fortunes of the idea of arming and emancipating Confederate slaves during the three and a half years between the
war's beginning and the Davis government's about-face in the fall of 1864. It
identifies both the ideological and practical grounds on which Richmond
first stoutly resisted the idea as well as the reasons for its later reconsidera-
tion. Chapter 2 examines the firestorm of opposition that greeted Davis's
November 1864 proposal. In exploring that opposition, this chapter also clari-
fies the ways in which key sectors of the white South identified their central
values and goals, and especially how they viewed the relationship between
slavery and secession. A crucial but often neglected part of the story, one that
powerfully influenced the way in which the debate in the Confederacy unfolded, is the subject of chapter 3. It compares the white southern leadership's
expectations and claims about wartime slave conduct with what slaves actually did between 1861 and 1865. In the process, it shows how the beliefs and
actions of black southerners became a major military factor, not only helping
to reshape Union policy but also limiting the options and influencing the
choices of the Confederacy's leaders. Chapter 4 asks how plans to free and
arm large numbers of slaves for the Confederacy's defense could square with
a commitment to preserving the South's plantation system, unfree black labor, and white supremacy. To help answer that question, it compares "Confederate emancipation" with parallel historical situations elsewhere in the world,
other occasions in which social and political elites strove to avoid utter ruin
by modifying the ways in which they held and exercised power.

   With these pieces of the puzzle in place, chapter 5 then picks up the
narrative thread of chapter 1. It traces the growth of support for and the
eventual enactment of a black-troops law between the end of 1864 down
through March and April of 1865. It examines the changes wrought in public
opinion and in the minds of the soldiery by the military developments of
those final six months. It looks closely at the provisions of the law that Congress finally and narrowly passed and then evaluates the Confederacy's attempts to implement that law by actually recruiting and training black
troops—and at the very meager results that those attempts yielded. In light
of those results, chapter 6 then asks whether—and under what circumstances—
the original project of arming and emancipating slaves might have proven
viable, might even have altered the outcome of the war. The book's conclusion, finally, offers a balance sheet for this experience and what it reveals
about slavery, secession, the southern war effort, and the connections that
bound these things together. Finally, it suggests the significance of this episode for subsequent southern history—and especially for the southern elite's
attempt to regain its footing in a postwar, post-slavery nation.

   The argument that informs and structures these chapters differs in important respects from the way that this subject has most often been under-

stood in the past. Proposals to arm and emancipate slaves, it holds, arose because the Confederate war effort was plagued by an increasingly critical complex of military, political, and morale problems. Individual southern army officers and political leaders began to contemplate the use of black troops only because (and only when) they recognized the depth of the crisis into which these difficulties had plunged the southern war effort. Both Confederate armies and the institution of slavery were in serious jeopardy by the second half of 1863. Those developments—and the interrelationship between them—argued in favor of offering freedom to bondsmen in exchange for service as southern soldiers.

From 1863 through 1865, however, the key authors and supporters of such stratagems planned to grant no more than the most limited, circumscribed form of freedom to the black soldiers they expected to recruit. By sharply restricting the rights and liberties accorded to those former slaves, they hoped to maintain their hold over the black population and keep it available as a cheap and malleable plantation labor force. Although the war certainly stirred southern white hatred of the North, that hatred did not eclipse the defense of planter interests in the Confederate leadership's calculations. Cleburne's and Davis's proposals did *not* signify a radical revision or repudiation of the basic goals for which southern leaders went to war. Those proposals aimed to salvage not only southern national independence but also (and *thereby*) as much of the Old South's economy and basic social structure as could now be saved.

Nevertheless, most slaveowners (as well as most non-slaveholding white Confederates) continued to oppose and resist such measures right down to the Confederacy's collapse. They did that especially out of fear that any significant weakening of slavery's bonds would lead to the collapse of both the plantation system and white supremacy more broadly. Few slaves were willing to respond positively to this overture, meanwhile, because by then most recognized where their interests lay in the Civil War, recognized that the Confederacy's defeat would bring them a fuller form of freedom, and much more swiftly, than would a Confederate victory achieved on any basis. The combined (if very differently motivated) opposition of masters and slaves consigned this long and hotly debated black-troops plan to impotence and oblivion. But during the years and decades following the war, some of the principal considerations that had shaped the "Confederate emancipation" plan continued to guide the white South's policy toward the African American population—testifying once again to the larger meaning and long-term significance of the subject of this book.

I

"A DESPERATE EXPEDIENT"
The Heresy and its Origins, 1861–1864

W e are going to make soldiers of some of our negroes if the war
continues," a South Carolina secession leader warned a Phila-
delphian in January 1865. And that, John A. Inglis added, would
make possible an "invasion from our side and a distribution of the fair lands
of Ohio, Indiana and Illinois, among our conquering and wasting African
legions." His correspondent would doubtless "think this is a desperate expedient," Inglis anticipated, but "our people do not so regard it." To emphasize
his own enthusiasm for the project, Inglis prayed that heaven would "speed
the day."

On the subject of desperation vs. enthusiasm, however, Inglis protested
too much, as the same letter inadvertently revealed. The Confederacy had
for years refused to consider this course of action precisely because (as he
now put it) it had "shocked all our habits of thoughts and feelings." That is
why "the mind of the people" had become "reconciled" to it only at the eleventh hour.[1] Compelling this change of heart was a complex of serious military and political ills that manifested themselves vividly in mid-1863 and
that—while fluctuating in intensity during the next year and half—reached
fever pitch during the Confederacy's last six months of life. As War Department clerk John B. Jones candidly noted in his private diary in March 1865,
the black-soldier plan was "the desperate remedy" for a "very desperate case."[2]

In fact, suggestions that the South place slaves in uniform arose at the very
outset of the conflict. When Jefferson Davis exulted over the Confederate

victory at First Manassas in 1861 and declared it a harbinger of ultimate triumph, brigade commander Richard S. Ewell shook his head in dissent. The South, he cautioned, was only at "the beginning of a long, and, at best, doubtful struggle." But there was one measure, he added, that would secure the defense of southern independence. When Davis asked what that might be, Ewell replied, "Emancipating the slaves and arming them."[3]

Ewell here referred to a simple reality known to everyone. The Union contained approximately three times as many military-age white males as did the Confederacy.[4] But the Confederacy contained three and a half million slaves, who made up almost 40 percent of the Confederacy's total population.[5] At the level of simple arithmetic, therefore, arming them was a common-sense solution to the South's manpower problem.

During 1861, Confederate officials began to hear on this subject from some residents of the Deep South, where slaves made up the highest proportion of the total population. Nowhere was it clearer (as three Mississippi petitioners noted) that "the population of the Southern States is a complex one, consisting of two races." That biracial population was "not far from being equally divided, and indeed in this State the slave element preponderating." It was therefore foolish "to attempt the defense of the country with only one of these elements of its power."[6] In January 1861, just a few days after Mississippi left the Union, one of its planters urged the governor to repeal the state law that forbade slaves to bear arms so that "masters may on their own premises drill and practice their own slaves" in their use. Otherwise "our lives, and property may be greatly imperilled."[7] Jefferson Davis's government soon received similar suggestions from Georgia, Alabama, and South Carolina.[8] In July, W. S. Turner, a plantation owner in the black-belt district around Helena, Arkansas, approached his old friend Leroy Pope Walker, the recently-named Confederate secretary of war, in order to "get negro regiments received for Confederate service." Turner claimed to speak for "many others in this district," including "one man that will furnish and arm 100 of his own" slaves and provide his own son to lead them.[9]

A string of Union victories during the winter and spring of 1862 seemed to underscore the need for such a policy. The western war theater's topography left the Confederacy especially vulnerable there to incursion by numerically superior Union forces.[10] In February, Tennessee's strategically located Forts Henry and Donelson fell, followed by the city of Nashville; by the end of April, New Orleans, too, had been lost. "In view of the late reverses to our arms and in the belief they were occasioned for the most part by the superiority of the enemy in numbers," three Mississippi slaveowners now urged Governor John J. Pettus to authorize "the employment of the slave population or of a portion thereof in the military service of the country." Those slaves could not only erect and maintain fortifications but might also "on occasions of great exigency be relied on in the ranks." The slaves' masters should receive "just compensation" from the government.[11]

Some notables began to suggest that emancipation could prove useful in yet another way. Throughout the war, many southerners hoped that England and France might formally recognize the Confederacy diplomatically, challenge the Union's steadily tightening blockade of southern ports, attempt to mediate between the warring parties, or in some other manner aid the secessionist cause.[12] One of the few impediments to such aid, they believed, was the European population's by now well-known hostility to slavery. Perhaps the Confederacy could purchase European intervention with a promise to emancipate its own slaves? One of those nursing such hopes was Duncan F. Kenner, a wealthy Louisiana sugar cane planter and Confederate congressman. The fall of New Orleans deeply shook Kenner's confidence in the Confederacy's future; so, in all likelihood, had Lincoln's Emancipation Proclamation. Right after its announcement Kenner began to press his friends Jefferson Davis and Judah P. Benjamin to adopt a plan of gradual emancipation in order to win British and French diplomatic recognition.[13] Mobile congressman Edmund S. Dargan seconded the idea after the fall of Vicksburg and "the disastrous movement of Lee into Pennsylvania."[14]

Davis's government firmly rebuffed all such suggestions. Why? Partly, especially at first, out of excessive confidence in southern military prowess.[15] But by the end of the war's first year, Richmond had begun to awaken to the dimensions of its difficulties and especially of its manpower problem. In April 1862 the Confederate government enacted conscription, and before long Davis also staked a claim to the labor of southern blacks. In 1863, the Confederate army obtained broad powers to impress civilian private property "for temporary use." Such property included slaves needed to build and maintain fortifications or to perform other types of military-support labor. A supplemental law of February 1864 specifically authorized the War Department to assign such tasks to free black males generally and up to 20,000 male slaves.[16] The Confederate government, then, was not averse on principle to using slave labor in support of the war effort.[17]

To all talk about using slaves as *soldiers*, however, Richmond stubbornly turned a deaf ear. In July 1861, Albert Taylor Bledsoe, then chief of the Bureau of War, bluntly informed Arkansan W. S. Turner that his department was "not prepared to accept" Turner's offer to raise a black regiment.[18] And when General Richard S. Ewell urged the Confederate president to enlist slaves during the war's first summer, an appalled Jefferson Davis dismissed the idea out of hand. It was "stark madness," Davis exclaimed, that "would revolt and disgust the whole South."[19] Davis and his cabinet knew that those who urged such a course early in the war represented a distinct minority of the South's white population and an even smaller proportion of its slaveholders.

Reflecting the views of the overwhelming majority, the Confederate government would tolerate no slaves—indeed, no men at all who were not certifiably white—under arms. Yes, a few individual southern communities (such as New Orleans and Mobile) permitted some free people of color to serve in home guard and other local-defense units. In March of 1862, Louisiana's governor commended "the loyalty of the free native colored population" of New Orleans and called upon its standing militia unit to remain at the ready. The Alabama legislature authorized Mobile's mayor to enroll free black males there into locally assigned militia companies.[20] But these localized exceptions to the rule would not be permitted to overthrow the rule itself. That much became clear just a month later, when a prominent Mobile citizen offered to raise "a battalion or regiment of creoles" to serve in the regular Confederate army. These men, this gentleman testified, were "mostly property-owners," including slaveowners, and were "as true to the South as the pure white race" even though they "are mixed blooded." But that last detail constituted reason enough for the War Department to spurn the offer.[21]

The subject came up again in late 1863. This time it was Maj. Gen. Dabney H. Maury, of the Confederate Department of the Gulf, who proposed enlisting a unit of Mobile "creoles." It was true, Maury acknowledged, that these men "have, many of them, negro blood in the degree which disqualifies other persons of negro race [*sic*] from the rights of citizens." But because of the peculiarities of local history, he explained, "they do not stand here on the footing of negroes." Under the terms by which the United States originally acquired this part of the continent, such creoles had been "guaranteed all the immunities and privileges of the citizens of the United States, and have continued to enjoy them up to this time." Mobile's congressman endorsed Maury's initiative.[22] Yet Secretary of War James A. Seddon remained adamant. If Mobile's creoles could be "naturally and properly" distinguished from blacks, then they could be allowed to don the gray. If, however, they could not be thus "disconnected from negroes," General Maury could employ them only as military laborers ("as 'navies,' to use the English term") or for some other types of "subordinate working purposes."[23]

There was, to be sure, both regional and national precedent for placing blacks under arms. African American soldiers had fought in the American revolution. In 1775, the British governor of Virginia had promised freedom to slaves who would abandon Patriot masters and join the royal army. The threat that this offer posed—plus a shortage of Patriot volunteers—finally induced the Continental army and many state militias to enlist free blacks and slaves into their own ranks as well. Most slaves who fought as soldiers for the United States eventually received their freedom.[24]

But much had changed in North America since those days. The rise of King Cotton beginning in the 1790s had dramatically increased both slavery's profitability and its geographic reach. Proslavery ideology had grown more confident and more aggressive, especially in the cotton states, increasingly depicting African American bondage not as the necessary evil that Thomas Jefferson had described but as the unadulterated blessing that John C. Calhoun praised ("a good, a positive good" that was "indispensable to the peace and happiness of both" races).[25] Slavery's ideological justification had meanwhile come to rest more than before on arguments about the intrinsic inequality of blacks and whites.[26] Simultaneously the northern states had turned away from and against chattel slavery, first abolishing it within their own borders and eventually supporting a major new party (the Republicans) pledged to blocking slavery's expansion into any territories or new states.[27]

It was, of course, the election of that party's presidential candidate that had precipitated secession in 1860–61. The lower-South states that founded the Confederacy had explained their practical concerns and ideological imperatives rather forthrightly. Alabama left the Union to protect its "domestic institutions." A Mississippi spokesman indignantly pointed to Republican attempts to "subvert the rights of the South"—more specifically, the right "by which one man can own property in his fellow man." Georgia left the Union out of "a deep conviction . . . that a separation from the North was the only thing that could prevent the abolition of her slavery." Texas walked out denouncing "the debasing doctrine of the equality of all men, irrespective of race and color—a doctrine at war with nature, in opposition to the experience of mankind, and in violation of the plainest revelations of Divine Law."[28]

For the authors of such words, more than for the eighteenth-century colonials who fought the British Empire, the color line was far too dear and far too central to their cause to permit its blurring by the enlistment of black troops. The sanctity of slave property and white supremacy, most believed, should certainly not be questioned by the very government created to protect those institutions. Or, as Secretary of War James A. Seddon tersely explained in 1863, the stance that the Confederacy had taken both before "the North and before the world will not allow the employment as armed soldiers of negroes."[29] Anyone attempting to change that stance (as a Virginia legislator subsequently observed) would collide with "a mountain of prejudices" directly arising from "the institution of Southern slavery."[30] In any case, the Davis government long denied that it had the constitutional power to do what Cleburne and others asked.[31]

This rigid rejectionist stance had been easiest to justify early in the war, when the South's supply of white soldiers still seemed sufficient—when, as Albert Taylor Bledsoe put it in mid-1861, the Confederate government happily found itself surrounded by "a superabundance of our own color rendering their services to the Government."[32] Richmond continued to insist that black troops were unnecessary over the next three years. When an anonymous "Native Georgian" urged enlisting slaves as soldiers in October 1864, thus, the secretary of war repeated his opinion that southern whites could still supply as many troops as the Confederacy could usefully employ.[33]

But reality had begun to diverge from such sunny assessments at least as early as mid-1863. The Union's Emancipation Proclamation and its simultaneous decision to recruit blacks into its army had further highlighted—and soon worsened—the South's numerical inferiority in population. Then, in July of that year, both Vicksburg, Mississippi, and Port Hudson, Louisiana, fell to enemy forces, completing the Union's conquest of the Mississippi river. That achievement physically split the Confederacy, turned its main inland water route into a Union artery, and opened the way for the enemy's deep penetration into the Confederate heartland. Almost simultaneously, Robert E. Lee's Army of Northern Virginia suffered its staggering repulse at Gettysburg. Lee had entertained great expectations for his Pennsylvania campaign, hoping to pull Union troops away from both Richmond and points west, encourage European involvement in the American war, demoralize the North, and politically strengthen the Peace Democrats in the Union's impending congressional elections. The defeat at Gettysburg dashed all those hopes, and the 28,000 Confederate casualties sustained there (amounting to fully a third of Lee's effectives on the eve of battle) imposed a manpower loss from which Lee's army never fully recovered.[34]

The role of public morale in shaping the Civil War's outcome is very controversial. Some believe that the white South's population was from the outset too internally divided and insufficiently committed to the Confederacy to achieve military victory. Others insist that battlefield reverses caused most of the South's morale problems (rather than vice versa) and that these problems reflected declining confidence in ultimate military victory far more than any basic alienation from the Confederate cause. But whatever its sources (and these were certainly varied), the growth of defeatism was apparent by the summer of 1863, and that mood—although it fluctuated in strength—eventually contributed significantly both to Confederate military difficulties and to increasing public and official receptivity to suggestions that black troops be employed to ease those difficulties.

In the aftermath of Vicksburg and Gettysburg, a chill of foreboding passed through sectors of the Confederate elite, military and political alike.[35] Robert Garlick Hill Kean, the staunch Alabama secessionist who by then headed the War Bureau, noted that "steadfastness is yielding to a sense of hopelessness of the leaders."[36] The chief of the Confederate Ordnance Department, Josiah Gorgas, wrung his hands as well. Vicksburg's fall was "a terrible blow to our cause" that "apparently sets us back indefinitely," Gorgas wrote in his journal, and the bleak news from Pennsylvania was driving spirits even lower.

"Yesterday we rode on the pinnacle of success—to-day absolute ruin seems to be our portion. The Confederacy totters to its destruction."[37] The well-connected Lt. Gen. Richard Taylor reached equally ominous conclusions. Peering through the smoke hanging over Mississippi and Pennsylvania battle-fields, Taylor and "one or two of our ablest and most trusted generals" saw portents of eventual Confederate defeat.[38] After Gettysburg, Robert E. Lee offered to resign his command. Jefferson Davis, who felt duty-bound to issue optimistic prognoses throughout the war, privately acknowledged that "the clouds are dark over us" and that he felt "shrouded" in "the depths of . . . gloom."[39] Word of the president's dejection circulated through official Richmond. So did rumors that Robert E. Lee feared that without additional troops, the South would have "to make peace on the best terms we can."[40]

The military setbacks of the summer of 1863 ate even more corrosively into the resolve of the Confederate public. The "terrible blow" suffered in Mississippi "has produced much despondency" among civilians, War Department clerk John B. Jones observed, while the "appalling" bulletins from Pennsylvania had spread "sadness and gloom throughout the land!"[41] A prominent Alabama planter judged the spreading despondency "unequaled since the Formation of our Government."[42] Mobile's congressman reported that news about Vicksburg and Gettysburg had "so broken down the hopes of our people that even the little strength yet remaining can only be exerted in despair." Already "Mississippi is very nearly subdued and Alabama is nearly exhausted," and it seemed likely to "end in the ruin of the South."[43] "Vicksburg is gone and as a consequence Mississippi is gone," a planter of that state declared in July, "and in the opinion of allmost [sic] every one here the Confederacy is gone."[44] "The people," reported Trans-Mississippi commander Gen. E. Kirby Smith, "particularly in Arkansas and Louisiana, lukewarm, dispirited, and demoralized," were now "to a great extent prepared for returning to their allegiance" to the old Union.[45]

The methods employed to overcome the Confederacy's problems did little to relieve this despondency. In October 1862, the Congress had voted to exempt from the military draft one able-bodied male for every plantation containing twenty or more slaves. Advocates of those exemptions considered it necessary to keep white supervisors at home to ensure that slaves would continue to grow essential crops rather than rebel or escape to the enemy.[46] But as the war's costs grew, so did popular resentment of anything that smacked of special privilege and special pleading.

The belief that secession and war would serve the interests of slaveowners and only slaveowners had already been widespread in some southern locales in 1860. A prominent North Carolina planter and politician recorded at Christmastime that year that "the people who did not own slaves were swearing that they 'would not lift a finger to protect rich men's negroes,'" adding that "this sentiment prevails to an extent you do not imagine." Sadly, he added, many among "the ignorant poor" had accepted "the idea that there is an antagonism between poor people and slave-owners."[47] James Bell, a small-scale non-slaveholding Alabama farmer, expressed precisely that opinion to his son four months later. The elder Bell had no use for the South's big "Negroholders." "All they want," he warned, "is to git you pupt up and go fight for there infurnal negroes and after you do there fighting you may kiss there hine parts for o they care."[48] In 1860–61, however, a combination of political conviction, racial doctrine, and local loyalties bound most southern whites together across the lines of partisanship and social class. And many, soldiers and civilians alike, remained loyal and steadfast to the end.

But over time the sheer weight of the lengthy and brutal war strained, frayed, and then in many cases snapped the bonds of Confederate unity. Sentiments ranging from political disaffection through war weariness, defeatism, and hopelessness sapped resolve and, more tangibly, manpower. Thus did military reverses beget morale problems and morale problems aggravate military difficulties. Historian Gary W. Gallagher, who argues forcefully against underestimating the commitment of southern whites to Confederate independence, nonetheless acknowledges "the admittedly impressive evidence of disaffection and disillusionment from the summer of 1863 forward" that "indicate a complex mood of deepening gloom punctuated by desperate bursts of hope."[49]

Exempting planters and overseers from conscription antagonized many who had initially rallied to the Confederate cause but who increasingly resented being forced to make what they saw as disproportionate sacrifices on its behalf. Robert E. Lee's aide-de-camp, Col. Charles Marshall, later recalled this exemption's "very injurious" effect "upon the army and upon the people." The Union had done its best "to inculcate the idea that the war was a slaveholders' war, in which the non-slaveholding people of the South had no interest." And most southerners did in fact believe, Marshall added, "that the object of the war was to defend slavery." What else but "surprise, not to say indignation" could average Confederate citizens and soldiers feel as they watched "part of the class of slaveholders" being spared "the common burden of the country"?[50] "[W]hat does the poor soldier say," South Carolina farmer William McNeely similarly wondered, "trudging[,] suffering[,] and fighting through this war [M]y family at home suffering while my rich neighbor with his thirty or forty negroes and fine plantations faring sumptuously every day . . . and has never as much as lifted a finger in support of this cruel war to my knowledge."[51]

A soldier in the 51st North Carolina regiment was ready with an answer. Private O. Goddin informed Gov. Zebulon Vance at the end of 1863 that "when he *volunteered* he left a wife with four children to go to fight for his country." But the planter-exemption and other laws had shown him that "the Govt. has made a distinction between the rich man (who had something to fight for) and the poor man who fights for that he never will have." Now, as a result, the "poor soldiers who are fighting for the 'rich mans negro'" had grown "tired of the rich mans war & poor mans fight."[52] Early in September 1864 Jefferson Davis received another such a protest written by "many soldiers" in "the ditches" of Georgia who were "ask[ing] ourselves what we are fighting for." They, too, were "tired of fighting for this negro aristockracy [sic]," tired of fighting "for them that wont fight for themselves." "This war and the hardships and dangers must fall on all classes alike or we are determined it shall cease as far as we are concerned," these soldiers warned.[53]

The battlefield reverses and erosion of popular morale of mid-1863 aggravated the Confederacy's manpower problem. Southern troops in both war theaters began to abandon their ranks in growing numbers.[54] The assistant secretary of war estimated that from fifty to a hundred thousand southern soldiers were absent without leave after the fall of Vicksburg and the Gettysburg defeat.[55] "The Confederacy wants more men," wrote Captain Samuel T. Foster, of the 24th Texas Cavalry, of Patrick Cleburne's division. "Lee wants men. Bragg wants men. They are wanted everywhere; but where are they to come from?"[56]

Those questions focused attention upon untapped human resources. "I myself see but one chance, but one course to pursue" in order to save the Confederacy, wrote Mississippi planter Dr. Oliver G. Eiland in July 1863; that was to mobilize and arm all male slaves between sixteen and fifty years of age.[57] Georgia slaveholder J. H. M. Barton thought it now apparent that "the Confederacy must *go down*, or our army must be increased and that largely." Since "the patriotic men of the south have given up their sons," he reasoned, why would they "not give up their negroes," especially since "there is no other help" available.[58] Benjamin Bolling concurred. A prosperous slaveholding farmer in west-central Alabama, Bolling claimed to have long favored such a step. But especially now that "it seems we are about to be overrun" it was "time we was up and doing, and that with all our might." There was in any case no alternative, he agreed with Barton, "because our material for an army of white men is so much exhausted."[59]

Some eighty miles to Bolling's east, Alabama planter and manufacturer Benjamin H. Micou penned an elaborate, four-page plan for the military mobilization of male slaves and sent it to the secretary of state (who had once been the law partner of Micou's brother). Micou thought such a measure urgent not only on military grounds but also to improve the political temper of the country. Local elections in 1863 in Alabama (as elsewhere) were registering "a feeling of doubt and distrust" toward the Davis regime and its supporters. "Some of our best men have been defeated," and most of the victors seemed willing to seek peace through reunion. Meanwhile a spirit was spreading that was "gradually bringing into antagonism the rich & the poor. Some poor men talk that the war is killing up their sons & brothers for the protection of the slaveholder." Micou thought this resentment quite unfounded, since "this I consider is emphatically the people's war." But the political dangers posed by such resentment must nonetheless be taken seriously. Draft exemptions must be tightened and better justified, Micou believed, and the government's previous refusal to enroll slaves in the army must be reconsidered. "The people are clamoring . . . for the Slaves to be brought into service for defence of our rights and liberties."[60]

Perhaps the Richmond regime was growing accustomed to such confidential advice by the summer of 1863. (The secretary of state noted on J. H. M. Barton's letter that "several of such papers have been rec'd."[61]) But Jefferson Davis was not prepared for the more public and more politically potent prodding that he now received. At the end of August, Alabama's state legislature resolved that since Union forces were already "enlisting and drafting the slaves of the people of the South," Richmond should consider "using in some effective way a certain percentage of the male slave population of the Confederate States, and to perform such services as Congress may by law direct."[62] The vague language seemed chosen to invite an inclusive definition of those services. A public meeting in west central Alabama's Greene County employed less ambiguous phrases: "The North having armed a portion of our slaves to fight against us, we, in turn, should arm enough of them to at least counterbalance the force of insurgent blacks arrayed against us."[63] An influential Deep South newspaper editor whose city had recently fallen to Union troops now explicitly called for placing slaves under arms. The government, argued the Jackson *Mississippian*, must "proceed at once to take steps for the emancipation or liberation of the negroes itself. Let them be declared free, placed in the ranks, and told to fight for their homes and country."[64] Influential editors in Lynchburg, Virginia, as well as both Montgomery and Mobile, Alabama, were soon drawing the same conclusions.[65]

So did an anonymous open letter published in Georgia in December 1863. The letter was signed "Culloden," evidently to invoke the 1746 battle in which Scots Highlanders led by "Bonnie Prince Charlie" Stuart succumbed to a much larger and better equipped English army. The overmatched Confederate forces, Culloden warned, also found themselves in desperate straits. "The enemy holds nearly half our territory," he pointed out. "His guns are thundering and his vast armies pressing upon us all along the seaboard and the land-frontier, from the Rappahannock to the Rio Grande." Southern armies "resist, but we fall back, or we do not advance." Nor was the situation about to improve. The enemy, after all, had made all the aforementioned gains when Confederate forces were stronger than they were now. Worse still, by the time spring weather allowed combat to resume "the Yankee Government will have greatly added to its troops."[66]

The resulting emergency, Culloden advised, demanded a far more thorough mobilization of the white male population than had yet been undertaken. But even that would not suffice at this juncture. The South must tap an even more important reservoir. "Over half a million male negroes and mulattoes are inside our lines. Cannot they afford their quota of soldiers?" To induce them to do so, let the South give the slave "the 'chances of a white man' as against the Yankee—put him by the side of a white Southern soldier, allow him a little monthly pay, assure him of freedom for good conduct, his State consenting; let him feel that he defends his own country as well as ours." In combat, this black soldier would act as "the subordinate of the white soldier"; between battles, the same black soldier could serve as "a servant in camp, to cook and wash" for the white troops. [67]

Culloden said little that others had not said before him. This letter's principal significance derived from its author's real identity. Wielding Culloden's pen was Gen. Thomas C. Hindman of the Army of Tennessee, a former Arkansas congressman and Patrick Cleburne's prewar law partner.[68] The publication of Hindman's letter marked the first time that a high-ranking Confederate officer had decided not merely to bring such views to the attention of government officials (as Richard S. Ewell had done in the summer of 1861) but to place them directly before the Confederate public.

Looming behind both Hindman's letter and Cleburne's subsequent memorial lay the Confederate military debacle in November 1863, when Braxton Bragg's 45,000-strong Army of Tennessee, its ranks already dispirited and its officer corps riven with dissension by its lengthy string of prior defeats, had once more proved unable to cope with a numerically superior foe. A few months earlier Bragg had managed to score his single major success of the war, routing Rosecrans's Army of the Cumberland at the battle of Chickamauga and then besieging Rosecrans within the city of Chattanooga. But the fruits of the Chickamauga victory proved meager. Union forces soon reinforced to some 75,000 simply broke the siege of the city and hurled south-

Gen. Thomas C. Hindman of the Confederate Army of Tennessee. (The University of Arkansas Libraries)

ern troops from atop nearby Missionary Ridge, a position that had seemed impregnable.[69] Two Yankee divisions came swarming over the crest of the ridge so quickly and forcefully that they nearly trampled the startled defenders, who fled in inglorious disarray down the ridge's opposite slope.[70] A southern journalist on the scene thought it "the most ignominious defeat of the whole war" and found it hard to explain "how a defeat so complete could have occurred on ground so favorable."[71] A southern veteran of that encounter described it as "the greatest disaster sustained by the Confederate arms in pitched battles."[72] "If we cannot hold as good a place as the Misherary [*sic*] ridge," wrote a disgusted W. A. Stephens of the 46th Alabama regiment, "we had as well quit." The humiliation plunged the Army of Tennessee's morale to new depths and forced Bragg to resign his command.[73]

The calamity at Chattanooga once again threw the South's manpower problem into stark relief. Patrick Cleburne's December 1863 memo frankly assessed that problem and the military and political ills linked to it. "We have now been fighting for nearly three years," the general reminded his colleagues, and "have spilled much of our best blood, and lost, consumed, or thrown to the flames an amount of property equal in value to the specie currency of the world." But "the fruits of our struggles and sacrifices have invariably slipped away from us and left us nothing but long lists of dead and mangled. Instead of standing defiantly on the borders of our territory or harassing those of the enemy, we are hemmed in today into less than two-thirds of it, and still the enemy menacingly confronts us at every point with superior forces." The effect of all this on troop *esprit* was corrosive. "Our soldiers can see no end to this state of affairs except in our own exhaustion; hence, instead of rising to the occasion, they are sinking into a fatal apathy." Symptoms of a generalized moral breakdown in the ranks had become obvious, and desertion was increasing even among sections of the army previously immune to its lure. "If this state continues much longer," the general bluntly concluded, "we must be subjugated."

At the root of the crisis, Cleburne emphasized, was the fact that "the enemy already opposes us at every point with superior numbers, and is endeavoring to make the preponderance irresistible." Unlike the Union, however, the Confederacy contained no still-untouched reserves of white males.[74] There was therefore no choice but to turn to the able-bodied male slave, place him under arms, and reward him with his freedom. In the meantime, to demonstrate good intentions, "we must immediately make his marriage and parental relations sacred in the eyes of the law and forbid their sale."[75] Surely no true southern patriot would refuse to make these sacrifices, Cleburne added. For "as between the loss of independence and the loss of slavery, we assume that every patriot will freely give up the latter—give up the negro slave rather than be a slave himself."[76]

Cleburne's presentation received a mixed reception in northern Georgia. While some officers evidently agreed with it, others responded with shock and fury. Gen. William B. Bate spurned the proposal as "infamous" and "hideous and objectionable," "beneath which the serpent of Abolitionism coiled."[77] Gen. James Patton Anderson dismissed Cleburne's "monstrous proposition" as "revolting to Southern sentiment, Southern pride, and Southern honor." Gen. William H. T. Walker damned Cleburne as a leader of an "abolition party" and a traitor. Gen. Braxton Bragg agreed that the memo's author and his allies were "abolitionist men" who "should be watched."[78] Cleburne and his associates had hoped to win the support of the army's officer corps for the proposal and then, with their hand thus strengthened, to bring the matter before the Davis administration. But the uproar provoked at Dalton led newly appointed Army of Tennessee commander Joseph E. Johnston to refuse to submit Cleburne's memorandum to the government and to order the discussion closed.[79]

In the event, it was one of Cleburne's bitterest critics who conveyed the Irishman's views to Jefferson Davis. Anxious to warn the Confederate president of the sedition brewing in Georgia, General Walker ignored Johnston's wishes and proceeded on his own authority to forward Cleburne's memorandum to Richmond in mid-January via a trusted intermediary, Georgia congressman Herschel V. Johnson.[80] Davis received and read Cleburne's memo and brought it before his cabinet, where the reaction was overwhelmingly negative.[81] The president then quickly sent word to Johnston that Cleburne's views were misguided and that "the dissemination or even promulgation of such opinions under the present circumstances of the Confederacy, whether in the Army or among the people can be productive only of discouragement, distraction, and dissension." Johnston was therefore ordered to suppress "not only the memorial itself, but likewise . . . all discussion and controversy respecting or growing out of it."[82]

Davis's instructions reached northern Georgia at the end of January. Johnston immediately (and disingenuously) assured Richmond that "none of the officers to whom the memorial was read favored the scheme" and promptly agreed to shut down the discussion. So did Cleburne, who ordered an aide to destroy all copies of the controversial memo but one. Then that copy, too, was apparently destroyed, shortly after which the memo's audacious author died at the battle of Franklin.[83]

Davis and Seddon thus had good reason to hope, at least initially, that they had successfully contained the explosive debate begun at Dalton. In fact, however, the proposals and arguments of Hindman, Cleburne and their allies had reached more eyes and ears than was generally realized at the time. Hindman had written up his proposal as a legislative bill, and had asked a congressman to introduce it into the House of Representatives. That congressman did submit it informally to a House committee.[84] The same congressman or one of his colleagues reportedly described the proposal to another "party of gentlemen in Richmond" on Christmas day of 1863.[85] Before he learned of the government's gag order, Patrick Cleburne, too, had shared his opinions with some politicians and "many of the wealthy men" of both Atlanta and Mobile during a brief January furlough.[86] Still others present at Dalton also confided what they had seen and heard there to third parties.[87] Meanwhile, Jefferson Davis's closest adviser, Judah P. Benjamin, began to reconsider the merits of Cleburne's proposal.[88]

In the short term, nevertheless, the discussion ebbed, partly because Confederate fortunes improved early in the 1864 campaign season. Joseph E. Johnston appreciably slowed Sherman's progress through northwestern Georgia, and Union forces in Virginia sustained outsized casualties in return for apparently paltry gains at the Wilderness, Spotsylvania Court House, Cold Harbor, and Petersburg. The sense of urgency that earlier had driven Hindman, Cleburne, and others to press the Confederacy to revise its policy against slave soldiers correspondingly eased.[89]

But while the Union armies' frustratingly slow and costly progress depressed northern morale, the long arc of the South's military trajectory still pointed downward, a trajectory apparent especially to Georgians who found themselves in Sherman's path in the autumn of 1864. In September, Atlanta's fall brought home to a much larger public that the scales of war had tilted more decisively than ever in favor of the North.[90] Then, in mid-November, Sherman's army began its almost 300-mile, month-long march to the Georgia coast, leaving a fifty- to sixty-mile-wide swath of desolation in its wake. At the end of the month, Gen. George H. Thomas dealt Johnston's Army of Tennessee a severe beating at Franklin, Tennessee, and then all but destroyed it two weeks later at Nashville. Sherman's occupation of Savannah in December only deepened the gloom in the Confederacy.

Once again Richmond heard warnings about popular demoralization. "The people talk as if they were already subjugated," worried a private then stationed in west-central Georgia, and "a strong union sentiment exists" here.[91] Another report from Georgia claimed that "more than half the state militia" sympathized with calls to end the war through peaceful reconstitution of the Union on its prewar basis.[92] A Georgia farmer believed popular longing for peace was stronger still, that "if the question were put to the people of this state, whether to continue the war or return to the union, a large majority would vote for a return"—and would do so even "if *emancipation* was the *condition*."[93] "Demoralization is rife in our armies," the Confederate president heard from a friend in the same state. "Among the people at home the sign of succumbing may be seen," and "treason is stalking the land."[94]

Things were scarcely better in Davis's own Mississippi. "A general discontent and loss of confidence in the administration and our success" prevailed there, and steadfast Confederates had dwindled to a mere "'Spartan band,' while the timid, the traitor, and the time-server are 'legion.'"[95]

As in the past, the military setbacks and declining morale of mid-1864 both reflected and aggravated the South's chronic manpower shortage. Desertion spiked after the fall of Atlanta, and by the end of June the Confederacy had about seventy thousand (or 30 percent) fewer troops in the field than it had just months earlier.[96] During an emergency visit to Georgia at the end of September 1864, Jefferson Davis publicly conceded that "two thirds of our [army] men are absent—some sick, some wounded, but most of them absent without leave."[97] Mississippi too "literally swarms with deserters," according to that state's former senator, James Phelan, as a result of a general belief in the "hopelessness of success."[98] Some left the ranks because they had come to oppose the Confederate cause. More did so out of a generalized resentment of the burdens that the war imposed upon them or out of anxiety about the fate of family members back home. Still others left because victory had come to seem impossible.[99] Whatever the reason, the effect was the same—to reduce southern troop levels and increase the need to find a new source of able-bodied manpower.

By the end of 1864, the situation had become desperate. The South now had only a quarter as many soldiers present for duty as the North, and War Bureau chief R. G. H. Kean, contemplating the Union armies' next levy of conscripts, found it "hard to see" how the South could face them. "The truth is," Kean wrote on Christmas day, "we are prostrated in our energies and resources. The conscription has been pressed to its utmost limits, and beyond any reasonable ones."[100] In that period, Assistant Secretary of War John A. Campbell later recalled, "the hospitals, workshops, factories, plantations; the rolls of exempts, and of men detailed, were diligently examined to find persons to perform military duty without accomplishing any effective result."[101] In fact, the head of the conscription bureau had already reported many months earlier that the population no longer contained any potential "fresh material for the armies" and that therefore "the functions of this Bureau may cease with the termination of the year 1864."[102]

By many accounts, furthermore, southern armies had declined qualitatively as well as quantitatively.[103] Stationed near Petersburg, Virginia, thus, Sgt. Alexander W. Cooper informed his president that "the element from which you have heretofore drawn your armies is exhausted," leaving behind "the mere dreggs [sic] of the noble armies that have so far sustained the Confederacy."[104] "Our poor harrowed and overworked soldiers are getting worn out with the campaign," ordnance chief Josiah Gorgas judged, unconsciously echoing sentiments that Patrick Cleburne had expressed considerably earlier. "They see nothing before them but certain death and have I fear fallen into a sort of hopelessness, and are dis-spirited. Certain it is that they do not fight as they fought at the Wilderness and Spotsylvania." Indeed, Gorgas believed, "they begin to look upon themselves as doomed men." The South desperately needed more soldiers, and Gorgas privately concluded now that "there is no help except to use negroes, giving them their freedom."

As Gorgas knew, he was not alone in drawing such conclusions now. "The common sentiment of the country," he thought, "is rapidly verging to this point."[105] Letters now reaching Davis and the War Department suggested that much and more.[106] This chorus, moreover, had not only increased in volume; it had also begun to change in tone. Earlier in the war, such counsel had generally arrived couched in highly respectful, deferential language. Growing anguish and anxiety transformed respect into impatience and deference into incredulity that the government had still not utilized so obvious a source of military manpower. "I have been amazed to see that no one thus far has conceived, or if conceived had the boldness to present, in my judgment, the only solution of all these perils and difficulties," one Virginian exclaimed.[107] "Had the negroes in this state been called out when Sherman was passing through, armed even with clubs, axes, spades, and hoes," a Georgian lectured Davis, "we could have annihilated his army." But now that Savannah had fallen and Sherman was heading northward, "prompt action on your part is imperative."[108] "Is it not time now to enlist the negroes?" demanded another correspondent, who wondered acidly if "congress & the authorities" had "even had this subject under consideration." If not, it would certainly seem that "this subject is well worthy [sic] your consideration"— assuming that "it is not now too late to do anything."[109]

More important than the change in tone was the increasingly public form that such calls now took. In late 1863, the Davis administration had managed to muffle the discussion that began in and around the beleaguered Army of Tennessee. A year later, however, the South's manifestly deeper crisis made containment flatly impossible. The debate now burst open again, this time with far greater force and before a far larger audience. Simultaneously, it reached much more deeply into the nation's central governing circles.

At the end of September 1864, Louisiana Gov. Henry W. Allen opened this latest and final round of debate with a confidential letter to Secretary of War Seddon. Union forces intercepted the message, which was quickly published. "I have long been convinced," Allen's letter advised, "that we have in our negro slaves the means of increasing the number of available fighting men." Now, he continued, "the time has come to put into the army every able-bodied negro man as a soldier" and to do so "immediately."[110] Soon afterward, Allen and five other Confederate governors (those of Virginia, North Carolina, South Carolina, Georgia, and Alabama) conferred in Augusta and resolved that "the course of the enemy, in appropriating our slaves who happen to fall into their hands, to purposes of war, seems *to justify a change of policy on our part*." It was therefore time for "authorities, under proper regulations, to appropriate such part of them [the slaves] to the public service as may be required."[111] As with the Alabama legislature's pronouncement a year earlier, the language was general—vague enough, in this case, to allow some of the signatories later to deny any intention of placing slaves under arms. But many who read the governors' communiqué certainly thought such an intention evident.[112]

By early October 1864, Nathaniel Tyler's Richmond *Enquirer* was ready to press the matter more forthrightly. Surely "the question of making soldiers of negroes, of regularly enlisting them and fighting them for their safety as well as our own," he editorialized, "must have presented itself to every reflecting mind." The proper way to frame the matter, the *Enquirer* continued, was this: ". . . whenever the subjugation of Virginia or the employment of her slaves as soldiers are alternative propositions, then certainly we are for making them soldiers, and giving freedom to those negroes that escape the casualties of battle."[113] At the end of the month, the Charlotte, North Carolina, *Democrat* flatly declared that the threshold specified by the *Enquirer* had already been crossed. "It will be necessary to take negroes" into the army, insisted the *Democrat*, "or abandon the struggle for independence."[114] Charles Button's Lynchburg *Virginian* and John Forsyth's Mobile *Advertiser*, both of which had first raised the idea in 1863, now returned to it more aggressively.[115]

At last, Jefferson Davis publicly embraced manumission as a war measure. In a November 7 message to Congress he characteristically depicted the military situation as hopeful—more favorable, in fact, than it had been a year earlier. But the overall manpower problem, he conceded, was quite serious. And to address that problem successsfully, Davis asserted, would require "a radical modification in the theory of the law."[116]

Heretofore, Davis explained, the Confederate government had sought to meet its manpower requirements partly by impressing slaves and using them in

Mississippi's Jefferson Davis, President of the Confederate States of America. (The Library of Congress)

noncombat military-support roles. The results, however, had proven smaller than anticipated. There were other problems with impressment as well. It allowed the government to use the private property of its residents for the common defense, as in the construction and maintenance of fortifications— but it allowed the government to mobilize such slaves only temporarily, only for "a certain term of service," only for "short periods." During that period, the slaves' legal owners retained title, and they reasserted direct control when the specified period elapsed. This arrangement did not satisfy the government's need to have men serve for more protracted periods and in capacities that would expose them to great "hazard." To meet these needs, the government must "acquire for the public service the entire property in the labor of the slave, and to pay therefor due compensation rather than to impress his labor for short terms." Such slave laborers must, that is, become the property of the government.

The government had the right to do this, Davis continued, because the slave was not merely property like any other property. The slave also "bears another relation to the State—that of a person." In times of emergency, the government had as much right not only to the labor but also to the very lives of such persons as it did of any other resident. It was now time for the government to assert that right. To do so, Davis wished to purchase 40,000 slaves outright and prepare them to serve indefinitely as front-line military laborers.[117]

And now Davis dropped the other shoe. Service of this kind would not only require protracted terms of duty. It would also require the slaves to display "loyalty and zeal." How could such loyalty and zeal be elicited? Should such a slave "be retained in servitude, or should his emancipation be held out to him as a reward for faithful service, or should it be granted at once on the promise of such service"? Davis replied that such slave laborers should be promised eventual freedom and the right to enjoy that freedom within the Confederacy after the war had been won.

The Confederate president did not yet request the power to arm and employ those slaves as combatants. Indeed, he pointedly took his distance "from those who advise a general levy and arming of the slaves for the duty of soldiers." White recruits, Davis claimed, were still numerous enough to fill "the armies we require and can afford to keep in the field." But he did open the door to employing black troops in the future, should the need arise. In defining that need, he borrowed a formula already used by Patrick Cleburne and the Richmond *Enquirer*. "Should the alternative ever be presented of subjugation or of the employment of the slave as a soldier," Davis said, "there seems no reason to doubt what should then be our decision."[118]

Perhaps Davis really believed that black troops were as yet unnecessary. Many others, supporters and opponents alike, presumed that his rhetorical caution was just political theater—that he had, in fact, already decided to place blacks under arms but wished to accustom the public to the idea before actually proposing it. If Davis intended his words to mislead and disarm potential critics, however, he underestimated them. "The President is initiating the very scheme against the adoption of which he pretends to argue!" raged Mobile politician Charles C. Langdon. "His whole argument is intended to prepare the public mind for its adoption. It is the entering wedge." It was "nothing more nor less than the negro conscription policy of the Richmond *Enquirer*, but far more objectionable, because presented insidiously."[119]

Others, though, faulted Davis for excessive caution, for moving too slowly. "I see the President dissents from arming the negro," wrote Archie Livingston, a sergeant in the 3rd Florida Infantry. But "why not do it? Our ranks need filling up, and something ought to be done, to encourage our already [wearied?] soldiers to still continue his [*sic*] exertions for Southern independence."[120] "Why endeavor to hug the delusion, that the arming of the negroes will not become necessary," the Richmond *Enquirer* wanted to know, "when the march of events steadily progresses toward that measure?" In fact, "it would *now* be very proper to begin to arm the negroes," since "before six months have passed" it might very well be too late.[121] The titular Confederate governor of Kentucky, Richard Hawes, privately conveyed the same opinion to Davis a few weeks later.[122]

By then, a much more influential governor—Virginia's William Smith—had already sought to accelerate the pace of developments. "A man must be blind to current events," Smith told his state's legislature on December 7, "to the gigantic proportions of this war, to the proclamations of the enemy," not to see that the alternatives of victory or defeat were already "presented *now*." The time had already come, therefore, to "arm such portion of our able-bodied slave population as may be necessary, and put them in the field, even if it resulted in the freedom of those thus organized."[123] A close Davis ally who communicated regularly with the Confederate president, Smith probably expressed these views with Davis's approval.[124]

In any case, the president and his cabinet were moving in the same direction, as another exchange of letters would shortly reveal. Upon reading Smith's message in the press, Frederick A. Porcher, a professor of history and literature at the College of Charleston, decided to pursue the governor's point with his old friend, Judah P. Benjamin. The course that Smith advocated, Porcher assured Benjamin, was "our true policy," even though it was "palpable that this is the entering wedge of a quiet plan of emancipation." Only such a plan seemed likely to enlist the aid of England and France on the Confederacy's behalf—which aid, Porcher hoped, would sufficiently gratify the South "to overcome the old fashioned prejudices and feelings of our people" against tampering with the institution of slavery. But one thing was certain: the initiative must come immediately or it would prove useless. "Now is the time for our govt. to act," Porcher urged. "A short time hence and it may be too late," because by then "the power of action may be taken away from us."[125] Benjamin's late-December reply to Porcher showed that he was way ahead of his old college chum. "The policy foreshadowed in the President's message" of November 7, Benjamin confidently predicted, would soon be implemented. That would entail not only emancipating slave soldiers "as a reward for good services" but also new state laws that would ultimately free the black soldiers' families as well. The secretary of state sought Porcher's aid in rallying support for such a policy.[126]

On February 9, Benjamin used a major public meeting in Richmond to appeal directly to the populace on behalf of the administration's policy. "I came here to say disagreeable things," Benjamin told the crowd. "I tell you, you are in danger unless some radical measure be taken . . . I tell you there are not enough able bodied white men in the country." But "war is a game that cannot be played without men," he went on. So "where are the men" to come from? According to Benjamin, the Confederacy contained some 680,000 military-age black men; surely it was time to call on their aid. "Look to the trenches below Richmond," he exhorted the crowd. "Is it not a shame that the men who have sacrificed all in our defenses should not be reinforced by all the means in our power?" Did it really matter at this stage whether such reinforcements were "white or black?" When someone in the audience shouted, "Put in the niggers!" others raised a cheer. Taking his cue, Benjamin proposed, "Let us say to every negro who wishes to go into the ranks on condition of being made free—'Go and fight; you are free.'"[127] Do this, he assured his listeners, and "in less than thirty days the army would be reinforced by twenty thousand men."[128] Evidently encouraged by the mostly positive response he had received there, Benjamin two days later sought the open political support of the Confederacy's most revered figure, Gen. Robert E. Lee. He also asked of the Army of Northern Virginia "an expression of its desire to be reenforced by such negroes as for the boon of freedom will volunteer to go to the front."[129]

Judah P. Benjamin, who served successively as the Confederacy's attorney general, secretary of war, and secretary of state. (The Library of Congress)

An 1863 photograph of Gen. Robert
E. Lee. (The Library of Congress)

Years later, Lee claimed to have
pressed Jefferson Davis to adopt such
a policy "often and early in the
war."[130] There is no record of Lee's
having done so, at least before the
fall of Atlanta. Thereafter, however,
the general did urge such a step. He
did so in a late-October letter to congressman William Porcher Miles,
chairman of the House's military affairs committee.[131] Then, in January
1865, Lee recommended to Virginia
state senator Andrew Hunter that
the South employ slaves as combat
troops "without delay." Emancipation was also a necessity, the general
added, for the families of those who enlisted. Like Patrick Cleburne before
him (and Frederick A. Porcher more recently), Lee then carried this reasoning
a major step further. "The best means of securing the efficiency and fidelity of
this auxiliary force," he thought, "would be to accompany the measure with a
well-digested plan of gradual and *general* emancipation."[132]

Lee's letter to Andrew Hunter was never published during the war (nor,
it seems, for another twenty years).[133] But a large section of the Confederate
cognoscenti quickly learned its contents, and newspapers were soon referring knowingly to Lee's views.[134] And then, within a week of hearing from
Benjamin, Lee wrote a third letter on the subject, one that did promptly
reach print, as Lee surely intended that it should. On February 18, he told
Mississippi congressman Ethelbert Barksdale both that arming slaves was
"not only expedient but necessary" and that "those who are employed should
be freed."[135]

Although the principal impetus behind such thinking was the search for additional soldiers, desperate dreams of obtaining foreign assistance also re-
emerged during the war's last six months. The South's dire straits now renewed
hopes (voiced earlier by Duncan Kenner) that a Richmond-initiated emancipation policy could strengthen Europe's sympathy for the Confederacy and
thereby facilitate British or French intervention in the war on the South's
side. One southern expatriate assured his brother back in Charlotte that "if
the negroes should be armed and do their duty" on behalf of secession "you

may confidently count on the South taking active possession of European sympathy in this quarrel."[136] Patrick Cleburne had promised his fellow officers that such a measure "will at one blow strip the enemy of foreign sympathy and assistance, and transfer them to the South."[137] The Montgomery *Mail* was just as sure that this step "would at once thaw the icy hearts of foreign nations, and warm them to active sympathy in our struggle to attain it."[138] "Our cause, stripped of the prejudices which slavery has thrown around it," the Richmond *Enquirer* agreed, would finally stand revealed for what it really was, "the cause of a people struggling for nationality and independence, and the United States would stand before the world as the oppressor, denying the principles by which its own struggle for liberty was justified."[139] In emancipating its new black soldiers, the Confederacy would thus strengthen itself not only militarily but also diplomatically.

Perhaps it might also mollify mounting domestic resentment of a planter elite that seemed to many insufficiently ready to sacrifice for the sake of a war fought principally on its behalf. John Forsyth's Mobile *Register* sounded that note when it blamed Vicksburg's fall partly on local masters who had refused to provide slave laborers to build needed siege fortifications. "Men who had sent their sons, brothers and friends off to find a bloody grave, would not permit their negroes to work on the defenses," Forsyth seethed in a refrain that would re-echo down through the rest of the war. Such men "cling to the negro with the tenacity of death, because forsooth, he may be worth a few hundred dollars to them."[140]

Masters who opposed using slaves as soldiers thus touched some already sensitive nerves. One Georgia woman demanded of her governor that "rich speculators and extortioners should be compelled to send a part of their negroes to fight" rather than keeping the latter at home where they "uphold their aristocratic owners who are nothing but vampires."[141] Another Georgian denounced "the rich planters" who preferred to "stay at home undisturbed" and surrounded by their chattels. And then, the writer continued, "if it is hinted cuffey [*sic*] is wanted to help defend his country and property, we see a great howl set up about it, and more fuss made than if 1000 white men were sacrificed."[142]

In early December 1864, a letter appeared in the Richmond *Enquirer* that shrewdly invoked this resentment in support of Davis's proposal. Signed "Barbarossa," the letter was evidently authored by an able, thoughtful, and legally trained mind. Perhaps it was the work of the secretary of state, who was known to write anonymous letters to the press in support of administration policy.[143] "Some of the non-slaveholders," Barbarossa warned Confederate masters, would take great exception "if the negro is not allowed to bear his part of the common burden." They would indignantly demand of the nation's leaders, "What! Shall we go to war to defend slavery, and then be informed by a slaveholding Congress that the father, the husband, the apprentice and the minor have all been turned over to the conscript officer . . . *but that they will not disturb the right of property in a slave*?[144] Even a critic of Davis's proposal grieved that, by evading their proper share of war burdens, some masters had created "dissatisfaction in the mind of the soldier that owns no slave"—the very dissatisfaction, he believed, that "has been the instigating cause of the effort now making to arm our slaves."[145] What better way to soothe such dissatisfaction, asked some administration supporters, than to place slaves in the army, thereby visibly sacrificing the property of the rich on the altar of national independence? Maybe doing that, Virginia's Gov. William Smith suggested, would "effectually silence the clamor of the poor man about this being the rich man's war."[146]

In early 1864, when Patrick Cleburne read his memo to the generals assembled in Dalton, Georgia, the kind of measure that he and Thomas Hindman advocated could not find a single congressional sponsor. A year later it could—and did. On February 6, 1865, Kentucky congressman James W. Moore took the first step. He asked to have the Military Affairs Committee consider and advise the House about whether to endow the president with the power to "call into the Military service of the Confederate States, all able bodied negro men" in the land, "to be used in such manner and for such purposes" as Jefferson Davis judged necessary and "on such terms" as he "may think will render them most effective." The House did, in fact, refer the proposal to the committee named.[147] In the Senate the next day, Mississippi's Albert Gallatin Brown called for legislation placing up to 200,000 slaves in the army "by voluntary enlistment with the consent of their owners, or by conscription, as may be found necessary." Owners of those slaves would be compensated, and the slaves themselves would go free "in all cases where they prove loyal and true to the end of the war."[148]

Recognizing that the Confederacy was outnumbered and outgunned from the start, a few individuals had suggested the arming (and sometimes the freeing) of slaves even in the spring of 1861. Over time, they grew in number. But during the war's first three and a half years, Richmond refused to consider this policy because it seemed to threaten both slavery and white supremacy, the twin pillars of southern economy, social relations, culture, and ideology. Having seceded from the Union and gone to war to protect those institutions, few southern political and community leaders were ready to seek military victory through a policy that apparently abandoned the original purpose of the struggle.

The core Confederate leadership's adamant opposition dictated that the proposal's first proponents would necessarily arise from outside its ranks. As one congressman belatedly conceded, "We, who sit here . . . have, perhaps too often sealed our lips or closed our doors—until the people, ceasing to look to us for instruction or sympathy, at last" set out to find "conclusions without our assistance."[149] Initial support for the idea came from individual army officers, journalists, and private citizens who most clearly perceived the significance of the Confederacy's manpower shortage and who were prepared to address that peril soberly. Some of them also hoped that such a measure could increase the Confederacy's diplomatic leverage while simultaneously reducing popular resentment of the planter elite and boosting support for the war effort.

As that war effort entered its final, most desperate phase following the fall of Atlanta in September 1864, some key political and military leaders finally acknowledged that arming slaves was necessary. Even now, however, the Davis administration felt constrained to raise the subject only gingerly and hesitantly. That hesitancy was justified; the president's November 7 message provoked a torrent of protest in Richmond and throughout the South from both slaveowners and non-slaveowners. Those objections spelled out in greater detail the very concerns that had led the Confederacy's military and political leadership to reject the same proposal for so long. In doing so, they illuminated a range of issues central to southern (and especially Confederate) history, including the purpose of secession, the goals of the southern war effort, and the place that African Americans occupied in the lives and outlooks of white Southerners.

2

"WHAT DID WE GO TO WAR FOR?"
The Critics' Indictment

The war's growing demands had driven first Richard S. Ewell, then Thomas C. Hindman and Patrick R. Cleburne, and at last Benjamin, Davis, and Lee to accept the unwelcome idea of arming and freeing slaves. By no means all Confederate partisans agreed with them about the doleful state of the southern war effort, so that subject became one focus of the ensuing debate. But this proposal's manifold and dramatic implications also aroused much deeper concerns and passions.

In the eyes of its opponents, the suggestion that the Confederacy emancipate and mobilize blacks challenged much that white southerners had come to believe about race, law and government, and the most basic demands of their economy. "Its propositions contravene principles upon which I have heretofore acted," Gen. William B. Bate proclaimed grandly concerning Patrick Cleburne's memo. It proposes "to discard our recieved [*sic*] theory of government, destroy our legal institutions and social relations."[1] North Carolina congressman J. T. Leach declared that "the use of negro soldiers in the Confederate Army would be wrong in principle, disastrous in practice, an infringement upon states rights, an endorsement of the principle contained in President Lincoln's emancipation proclamation, an insult to our brave soldiers and an outrage upon humanity."[2]

This head-on collision between proposed policy and traditional wisdom guaranteed that criticism of the proposal would be both heated and global. Elaborating such an indictment led critics to restate, elaborate, and defend fundamental tenets of Old South social and economic life, ideology, and politics. The blistering language that so many opponents employed reflected the size of the stakes involved. Generals W. H. T. Walker and Braxton Bragg had denounced Patrick Cleburne as an abolitionist and impugned his loyalty to the South. Similar reactions greeted more highly placed individuals who came to the measure later on. Jefferson Davis's proposal to manumit slave conscripts indicated to North Carolina congressman Josiah Turner, Jr., that "all the abolitionists were not in the North."[3]

Not even the nearly sainted Robert E. Lee was spared such treatment. When Lee endorsed arming and freeing slaves, Robert Barnwell Rhett, Jr.'s Charleston *Mercury* accused him of being "an hereditary Federalist, and a disbeliever in the institution of slavery," the latest in a long line that had included "some of the strongest and most influential names and individuals in Virginia."[4] But Lee did not have to send for a copy of the *Mercury* to find his loyalty to southern values impugned. The same challenge confronted him in a journal published much closer to home. The Richmond *Examiner* (edited by John M. Daniel and Edward A. Pollard) declared that Lee's opinion "suggests a doubt whether he is what used to be called a 'good Southerner'; that is, whether he is thoroughly satisfied of the justice and beneficence of negro slavery as a sound, permanent basis of our national polity."[5]

As prominent Confederates went, Rep. Josiah Turner, Jr., shared relatively little with editors Rhett and Daniel. Before the war Turner had been a Whig and then a Unionist until his state joined the Confederacy. Rhett and Daniel were ardently, even precociously, pro-secession Democrats. Those differences did not prevent early fire-eaters and crypto-Unionists from employing many of the same arguments and approvingly quoting one another's words.[6] As that cooperation suggests, opposition to the proposal was not only powerful but also broadly based, attracting support from across the Confederacy's political spectrum. Vociferous opponents included founders of the Confederacy, prominent army officers, state governors, members and former members of the president's cabinet, and leaders of both the Senate and House of Representatives. It embraced former Whigs, such as Charles C. Langdon, the ex-mayor of Mobile, and congressmen Thomas S. Gholson of Virginia, James T. Leach of North Carolina, and William G. Swan of Tennessee. It also boasted a great many long-time Democrats, including Mississippi congressman Henry C. Chambers and Georgia's Howell Cobb, who at one time or another served as governor, speaker of the U.S. House of Representatives, U.S. secretary of the treasury, chairman of the February 1861 convention that founded the Confederate government, and general in the Confederate army.

The opposition included both prewar secessionist firebrands and people who had resisted secession until the last minute. Among the former were a number of influential newspaper editors, such as Rhett, J. Henly Smith of the Atlanta *Southern Confederacy*, A. D. and Richard G. Banks, Jr., of the Montgomery *Mail*, and Willard Richardson of Galveston's *Tri-Weekly News*. At their side stood such powerful political figures as William Porcher Miles, who represented Charleston in both the U.S. and Confederate House of Representatives and who chaired the latter's military affairs committee; Georgia's Robert Toombs, a former U.S. senator who became the Confederacy's first secretary of state, a member of its House of Representatives, and then one of its brigadier generals; and Virginia's R. M. T. Hunter, who had served as speaker of the U.S. House of Representatives, a U.S. senator, the Confederacy's second secretary of state, and then president pro tempore of the Confederate Senate. Among outspoken opponents of arming slaves who had also resisted secession until the last minute were John J. Seibels, a diplomat who supported Stephen A. Douglas in 1860 and became military adjutant to Alabama's governor when the war broke out; Benjamin F. Dill, editor of the *Memphis Appeal*; and North Carolina Whig and wartime governor Zebulon B. Vance, as well as his quondam political opponent, William H. Holden, editor of the *North Carolina Standard*. The political breadth of this opposition testifies that plans to arm and free slaves seemed to challenge assumptions and principles dear to most white Southerners.

The least politically charged way to challenge black-soldier plans was to dispute their necessity. The plan's advocates acknowledged, after all, that it was an extreme measure, one that no good southerner would favor under circumstances less dire. Opponents simply denied that the situation was dire at all. "We are not & cannot be whipped," Gen. William B. Bate declared categorically at the start of 1864.[7] Florida congressman Samuel St. George Rogers agreed. "There is nothing in the present aspect of our military affairs," Rogers insisted, "to justify the hazardous experiment of placing slaves in our armies as soldiers."[8] Tennessee's William G. Swan was even more categorically optimistic. A resolution that he brought into the Confederate House of Representatives in November 1864 adamantly insisted that "no exigency now exists, nor is likely to occur in the military affairs of the Confederate states, to justify the placing of negro slaves in the army as soldiers in the field."[9]

Swan was not alone in making such cheerful prognoses. The Richmond *Dispatch* insisted that same month that "our affairs are in a better condition, and our prospects are brighter, than they have *ever* been since the commencement of the war."[10] "There was a time," the Richmond *Examiner* conceded nearly two months later, "when there was a danger that the Southern Confederacy would be overpowered by the violence and superior power of its enemy." But fortunately "that time is passed."[11] Just five days before Appomattox, a prominent Mississippi planter reassured his governor that "God never permitted nor never will permit such a people [as ours] to be subjugated or deprived of their freedom."[12] A writer in Georgia remained certain even two weeks later that "subjugation is an impossibility."[13]

Such sunny assessments could often be justified by citing the government's own communiqués. In rejecting the administration's proposed measures, Mississippi congressman Henry C. Chambers specifically cited Jefferson Davis's resolutely optimistic status report of November 7.[14] How could the president "tell us we are [too] strong to conquer," a Texan asked and then in the same breath recommend a policy predicated on "our weakness"? Or, this writer demanded pointedly, had those citizens who had taken government war reports at face value "been deceived"?[15] Tellingly, the region in which opponents of arming slaves clung most tenaciously to an optimistic view of the war's progress was the Trans-Mississippi department, and especially Texas, where little fighting occurred, where the war's burdens were lightest, and where access to grimmer war news from the rest of the Confederacy was limited by both distance and Union control of the Mississippi.[16] Elsewhere in the South it grew ever more difficult to deny the Confederacy's military decline during the war's final autumn, winter, and spring.

But, skeptics still demanded, how could the Confederacy take any appreciable number of young male slaves out of the fields without thereby weakening the country and the war effort even further? Wouldn't doing that perilously reduce the South's crucial agricultural work force, thereby depriving either the populace or the army (or both) of the food they required? This danger was hardly speculative. Even in 1863 the South's fragile and frequently ruptured transportation network was often leaving urban dwellers and soldiers hungry. No solution to the problem had arisen, congressman Thomas S. Gholson pointed out, except to urge "every section to raise as large crops as its means will allow." But could such advice be followed if the country simultaneously placed the tillers of the soil into the army? "How vain it would be," Gholson exclaimed, "to marshal a large army, and then be compelled to disband it for the want of food" even as "we heard the cries of women and children begging for bread?"[17] Food shortages and consequently high food prices had already triggered angry rioting in a number of urban centers. In Richmond, notoriously, authorities had managed to disperse a crowd of angry women demanding flour only by threatening them with muskets.[18] To aggravate the subsistence problem under those circumstances, said the Wilmington *Journal*, would "be worse than a blunder—it would be a political crime."[19]

Even more serious and immediate, many critics feared, would be this policy's impact on army morale. Virginia's R. M. T. Hunter did not believe "that our troops would fight with that constancy which should inspire troops in the hour of battle, when they knew that their flanks were being held by negroes."[20] Placing black companies among white ones, Rep. Henry C. Chambers predicted, would dissolve the firm bond of identification and trust that had previously held regiments together, leaving only "a chain which the electric spark of sympathy and mutual confidence can no longer traverse." Then "the answering smile, the triumphant glance, the understood pledge of mutual devotion, heretofore transmitted from company to company" will be "all interrupted and destroyed."[21]

Worse yet, opponents warned, the measure would offend the white troops' racial pride. The *North Carolina Standard* declared that "our soldiers" regard the proposal "as an insult."[22] "Do you think that our brave men will consent to be placed upon the same footing with our own slaves," a Virginian demanded, or with "the slaves of their neighbors" who had now been "converted into freemen?"[23] "If negro soldiers go into the army," predicted a letter published in a Georgia newspaper, "freemen and white men will come out of it."[24] "The soldiers of South Carolina will not fight beside a nigger," promised the Charleston *Mercury* more bluntly."[25]

Such forecasts were easy to believe. Race consciousness in the Confederate army was high. Soldiers accused by their comrades of being mulattoes had to prove the purity of their blood on pain of ejection from the ranks.[26] And there seemed no dearth of evidence that such feelings were deep-seated and widespread among the troops. Charley Baughmann of the Otey Battery, Virginia Light Artillery, had no quarrel with blacks serving as military laborers or menials, but "I never want to see one with a gun in his hand" and "I never want to fight side by side with one." Nor, Baughmann was sure, would any of his comrades. "The army would not submit to it, half if not more than half would lay down their guns if they were forced to fight with negroes." In fact, "they were nearly unanimous in saying that they would desert rather than serve with them."[27] Maj. Jedediah Hotchkiss expressed almost identical sentiments to his wife the following month. "I think the soldiers are opposed to arming them [slaves]," he said. "They want them used as wagoners etc but are unwilling to see arms put in their hands."[28] Capt. M. E. Sparks of the 9th Georgia Regiment cautioned the public not to believe published reports of soldier support; the latter "do not . . . reflect or give a true expression of the sentiment of the army."[29] In late 1864, troops stationed in Florida resolved "that the position of soldier is honorable, responsible, and dignified, and should not be degraded by placing the negro by his side."[30] A group of soldiers from Tennessee and Missouri announced flatly that "we are not willing to fight with them."[31] Even advocates of black troops granted that the army's initial reaction to the proposal "would be great objection. Officers would declare their intention to resign—they would feel degraded."[32]

Some opponents of the black-soldier plan acknowledged that nonslaveholder support for the Confederacy was *already* wavering, but suggested an alternate way of using slaves to solidify that support. The Alabamian Theodore Nunn urged Richmond in the fall of 1864 to "give each soldier in the confederacy a negro man to be his property [and] let that slave be his servant in camp & in batle [*sic*] to be a soldier by his masters [*sic*] side." Doing this would have not only a military value but also a political one because "it would interest many of our soldier [*sic*] in slavery & they too would feel better & fight better & stop deserting & stragling."[33] In the Confederate House of Representatives, Tennessee's John DeWitt Clinton Atkins urged in early February 1865 that the government "at once put a hundred thousand slaves, between the ages of 17 and 45, in the field." Rather than promise liberty to those slaves, however, Richmond should "purchase all the slaves thus put into service, and give to each white soldier in the army, a slave" as the soldier's personal "property in his own absolute right." That would serve "to interest all our soldiers in the institution of slavery."[34] J. W. Ellis suggested the same thing to Jefferson Davis and brought such a measure into the North Carolina State Senate.[35] In their own way, counterproposals like these also reflected broader concerns that differences of interest between southern masters and non-slaveowners were undermining the Confederate war effort.[36] Lt. T. M. Muldrow of the 19th South Carolina regiment proposed an even more ambitious variation on this solution. Let the Confederate government "offer a bounty of land and negroes to all of the *enemy* who will desert and join our armies. Say four negroes and fifty acres of land." "This plan would not only give us present strength but future security by greatly increasing the number of Slave-holders—a great desideratum . . . "[37]

Those who advocated *using* slaves as bounties with which to encourage loyal military service by slaveless whites continued to oppose the *arming and freeing* of slaves as very bad policy. Seeking to obtain European aid in exchange for emancipation struck critics as equally misguided. True, many believed that popular antislavery sentiment in both England and France restrained government officials there from actively taking the Confederacy's side. But just as influential was the fear of backing a loser. London and Paris might risk the wrath of Washington (and of their own people) by backing Richmond *if* Richmond seemed capable of waging a successful military struggle. At this late date, however, any Confederate promise to free slaves would surely look to Europeans like a desperate confession of weakness and despair. Furthermore, the Richmond *Examiner* argued, since actually instituting such a measure would both demoralize the army and effect "the destruction of our labour [*sic*] power," it would in fact "leave us of no use to them, ourselves, or to anybody else." It therefore followed as night the day, the *Examiner* continued, that just "when we should have made this graceful concession to the publick [*sic*] opinion of Europe," that same Europe "would very certainly cheat us." Upon "seeing that we were whipped, and the pluck taken out of us," London and Paris would decide not to aid the South but rather to "make friends of our enemies at our expense."[38]

In any case, critics contended, the whole question was really moot; the Davis government simply had no legal right to emancipate such would-be slave soldiers. "If we admit the right of the Government to impress and pay for slaves to free them," Georgia governor Joseph E. Brown objected, "we concede its power to abolish slavery."[39] No such legal right existed. "No slave can ever be liberated by the Confederate Government without the consent of the States."[40] The Richmond *Whig* agreed, as did R. M. T. Hunter, who insisted that "the Government had no power under the Constitution to arm and emancipate the slaves, and the Constitution granted no such great powers by implication."[41]

The implied power to impress private property could certainly not be stretched this far. That constitutional provision, Georgia Governor Joseph E. Brown argued, "only authorizes the use of the property during the existence of the emergency which justifies the taking." A wartime government thus could and did temporarily take possession of a citizen's building and use it as an army warehouse. But the impressment power could not transfer permanent ownership of that building to the government. As soon as the military emergency had passed, the government was obliged to return the building to its original owner. In just the same way, Brown claimed, "the Government may impress slaves to do the labor" it requires for the successful prosecution of the war. But it "can vest no title to the slave in the Government for a longer period than the emergency requires the labor." And the government *surely* "has not the shadow of right to impress and pay for a slave" in order then "to set him free." On the contrary, "the moment it ceases to need his labor the use reverts to the owner who has the title."[42]

It was, of course, just these legal impediments that Davis now wanted to remove with new law. But legislation of that type, critics warned, would overthrow both the constitution and slaveowning principle. It would "trample on State rights."[43] The North Carolina House of Representatives "denie[d] the constitutional power of the Confederate government to impress slaves for the purpose of arming them, or preparing them to be armed, in any contingency, without the consent of the States being freely given, and then only according to State law."[44] Even the constitution of the United States, critics added, had barred legislation of the kind that Davis now proposed. And "we are not aware," the Richmond *Dispatch* added drily, "that the Confederate Government has any power which the Federal Government had not."[45] How could it? Was not the Confederate constitution specifically designed to afford slavery more protection than had the U.S. Constitution? Wasn't that the point of the Confederate document's Article 1, Sec. 9, paragraph 4, which provided that "no . . . law denying or impairing the right of property in negro slaves shall be passed" by the Confederate government?[46] Florida planter and politician David Yulee warned his friend Jefferson Davis, furthermore, that "whenever the Confederate government treats Slaves in the States otherwise than *as property* a social revolution is begun in the South, the end of which may not be foreseen."[47]

It was not difficult to refute at least some of these legal arguments, at least on the plane of formal logic. Yulee's horror at treating slaves as anything but property suggested a surprising ignorance of important precedent. Many decades earlier, for example, in the *Federalist Papers*, Virginia's James Madison had justified including slaves in the population count to determine representation in the House of Representatives precisely on the grounds that those slaves were not only property but also people.[48] More germane still was the argument that national emergencies necessarily altered the status of individual rights. In December 1864 a lengthy and able brief on that theme appeared in the Richmond *Enquirer*; it took the form of an open letter signed "Barbarrossa." (As already noted, the anonymous author may well have been the Confederate secretary of state.) While the individual has a right to his private property, Barbarossa argued, the state—charged with the task of defending that individual and all others—had a right to lay hands upon such property for that purpose. And "when these two rights . . . are brought by the circumstances of the country in conflict, the less important and the less exalted gives way."[49] Here, in fact, was the doctrine that the greater end (defense of the nation and its citizens) justified necessary if unpleasant means (infringing on some property rights). However troubling to believers in timeless moralities and absolute rights, this doctrine unavoidably guided all statecraft, but most obviously in times of war, whose extraordinary requirements inevitably altered peacetime procedures and restricted peacetime liberties.

But invoking this general principle in this way and in this case only contributed to raising the stakes of the debate by focusing it upon matters of national values, ideology, and purpose. Exactly *what* larger good was served, critics demanded, by threatening the key institutions and principles (slavery and white supremacy) for which the Confederacy had been founded and in defense of which it had gone to war? Even more to the point: *was* the defense of the Confederacy still a greater good if it required destroying the very thing that the Confederacy had been created to save? Destroy these things and what would be left of the Old South that was worth saving? The entire project of slave enlistment and emancipation, the Macon *Telegraph and Conservative* protested, was "contrary to all our hereditary opinions, policy, and traditions."[50]

Some who eventually endorsed the proposal had opposed it only recently on some of these same grounds; they now found it hard to hide their discomfort. Such a man was Mississippi congressman Ethelbert Barksdale,

who granted a bit sheepishly that the subject was "not free from embarrassing considerations."[51] An angry Col. John J. Seibels, the Alabama governor's
sometime military adjutant, put the matter less delicately. Prior to the
present debate, he pointedly recalled, for a southerner even to "hint at the
propriety of emancipation . . . would have secured the individual a coat of
tar and feathers."[52]

To emancipate slaves and place them in the army conflicted in many
ways with the elaborate ideology that justified African American bondage, an
ideology that white southerners had for generations imbibed with their mothers' milk. For one thing, the idea of enlisting black soldiers flew in the face of
what every right-thinking southerner had been taught about what the African was and could and could not do. He was excellently suited for the role of
servant or laborer. But, as South Carolina's William Porcher Miles declared
at one point, "the negro was unfit by nature for a soldier."[53] He belonged,
Raleigh's *North Carolina Standard* agreed, to "an unwarlike and comparatively innocent race."[54] "Of great simplicity of disposition, tractable, prone
to obedience and highly imitative," Mississippi's Henry C. Chambers elaborated, "he is easily drilled; but timid, averse to effort, without ambition, he
has no soldierly quality."[55] The Richmond *Examiner* was happy to share its
expertise on the subject with its readers. "[W]e happen to know the negro
race—it is not a fighting, conquering, military race—it has never been so in
any country, in any time, in the faintest, most problemmatical degree. Never
did negroes win battles and they never will." While they might "be put in a
state of frantick [*sic*], but emphatically blind and senseless excitement" and in
that state could "make a brutal and frenzied *rush*—not a *charge*," black soldiers would inevitably "be cut down themselves in vast numbers by troops of
another race in whom the intelligence always subserves, if it does not direct,
the passions."[56]

Yes, it was true that the Union had placed free blacks and emancipated
slaves in its army. But Confederate journals had repeatedly assured their readers that the results to date were paltry and pathetic. This demonstrated, asserted the Memphis *Appeal* in October 1864, that "they are a timid race" that
"will not fight even for their own freedom."[57] If black soldiers had proved
useful to the North at all, one Virginian suggested, they had done so not as
combatants but as vandals—only when set loose as "plundering parties" after
the real battles had ended. "This," he added, "is in fact the only species of
warfare for which the African is fitted."[58] Surely such a sorry martial record
was enough to demonstrate the bankruptcy of the whole idea. Virginia soldier Charley Baughman thought so; everyone knew that "one white soldier is
worth a regiment of blacks."[59]

But poor battlefield performance would prove the least of the South's
woes if it enlisted "African" troops, critics warned. As soon as they were armed,

they would desert. Worse, they would carry their weapons, ammunition, and military intelligence with them.[60] "They would," congressman Josiah Turner, Jr., warned, "prove the enemy's best allies in accomplishing our overthrow and destruction."[61] Such predictions could not have amazed members of the Confederate government; at least some of them had only recently expressed the same misgivings. In August of 1863, Judah P. Benjamin confided to Benjamin H. Micou, the brother of his former law partner, that "the collection and banding together of negro men in bodies, in the immediate neighborhood of the enemy forces[,] is an experiment of which the results are far from certain. The facility which would be thus afforded for their desertion in mass might prove too severe a test for their fidelity when exposed to the arts of designing emissaries of the enemy who would be sure to find means of communicating with them."[62] The Davis government's Comptroller and Solicitor, Louis Cruger, still worried about "the danger of the negroes, when in distinct companies & Battalions, marching over to the Enemy."[63]

Black deserters who did *not* flock to the Union army might prove even more dangerous to the South. "If there should be any possessing an aptitude for command or war, (and there might be some although incapacitated as a race)," Benjamin F. Dill of the Memphis *Appeal* contended, "they would incite and lead servile insurrections"—or at the very least "incite discontent and insubordination"—among those blacks still in bondage.[64] Advocates of slave troops often referred to the example of ancient Sparta's helots, who fought for their owners and were elevated in status as a reward. "Yet these Helots, thus 'elevated' . . . by the use of arms," Dill noted, "rose several times against their masters, and were with difficulty reduced to subjugation." It was also worth recalling that the Spartacus revolt in Rome "was one of the results of the 'elevation' of white slaves by placing arms in their hands."[65] The specter of another slave revolt, one much closer in time and place, also hovered over the Confederacy's wartime debate—the slave revolt of the 1790s in Saint Domingue that eventually renamed the country Haiti. North Carolina's James T. Leach foresaw that placing arms in the hands of freed slaves "would make a San Domingo of our land."[66] After all, Henry C. Chambers reminded his colleagues, "it was the free negroes of old Saint Domingo, who had been trained to arms, that excited the insurrection of the slaves."[67]

But even these practical perils created by arming blacks only touched on the largest issues involved—the ideological impact and the practical cost of any policy involving large-scale emancipations. The main justification for slavery in the United States based itself on the supposed inequality of the white and black races. Many proslavery ideologues liked to dilate upon the benefits of enslaving society's manual laborers rather than leaving them free (much less granting them full citizenship rights). But lest such elitist effusions frighten or anger the South's huge population of manually laboring slaveless whites, those ideologues rarely failed to add that slavery was right and proper only when those enslaved belonged to an inferior race.[68] Providentially (as John C. Calhoun had phrased it), such a race was present in the American South.[69] Whites were by nature superior, blacks intrinsically inferior, and the only kind of society that could viably include both must enforce the supremacy of the former over the latter. God had made blacks to serve and work for whites; whites, reciprocally, accepted the responsibility of directing the lives and efforts of all in the common interest of all. As one Texan reminded advocates of manumission in February 1865, "African slavery is founded on the principle that the man or the race which is morally and intellectually inferior, must be subordinate. This we hold to be the great moral law which has governed the world, and must always govern it; and gover[n]s it, too, for the greatest benefit of both classes."[70]

By recognizing and respecting this great moral law and basing their social relations upon it, southern whites claimed to have created a land of abundance, culture, and harmony. They also boasted of creating a black producing class that was better off and happier than any other laboring population in the world.[71] To violate this racial order, to overturn this divinely sanctioned hierarchy, would defy God and topple society itself into the abyss of anarchy, poverty, barbarism, and race war. It would consign the black race in particular to oblivion, since all knew that blacks could neither govern nor sustain themselves if left to their own devices nor survive a direct contest with whites.[72]

Most white southerners had heard and repeated such assertions from childhood and could now only greet Confederate talk about large-scale emancipation with open-mouthed amazement. As one soldier typically protested, the suggestion was "a virtual abandonment of the long contested question . . . of the negroe's [sic] capacity for self-government and for freedom."[73] We have always held, recalled the Richmond *Whig*, "that servitude is a divinely appointed condition for the highest good of the slave, is that condition in which the negro race especially may attain the highest moral and intellectual advancement of which they are capable." Far from being an act of kindness, the *Whig* added, it would therefore "be an act of cruelty to deprive the slave of the care and guardianship of a master."[74] "[L]et us beware of giving any consent or adhesion," the Richmond *Examiner* urged, "to the doctrine that people of that race gain by being turned wild—or 'made free,' if we are to use that improper Yankee cant."[75] "By the adoption of this scheme," therefore, Mobile politician Charles C. Langdon agonized, "we stand convicted before the world of deliberately promulgating a tissue of monstrous falsehoods."[76] In short, critics objected, the proposal put the lie to bedrock racial justifications of both slavery and white supremacy.

The proposal's supporters flatly denied this accusation. They were conceding nothing in principle by making this practical suggestion. They continued to stand by what they had always said concerning the African's real nature and true interests. The only change was the unfortunate necessity to humor the African's erroneous views about those subjects. In order to save their society from destruction, they would indulge the blacks' misguided yearnings for freedom. Doing this represented no radical innovation in either policy or law. After all, the Richmond *Enquirer* noted, most Confederate states already permitted individual manumission. Did granting such legal permission imply that blacks were better off free? Of course not; it only made error legal. "We hold the belief that the negro is best off, is in 'the right place,' when he has a good master; but the negro may think otherwise." To secure his fidelity as a soldier, we are willing to offer him what he mistakenly desires. "Nothing is yielded to the ignorant prejudices of the world; a simple bargain is struck. The negro wants his freedom; whether a boon or a curse, he wants it, and for it may be willing faithfully to serve in the army of his country."[77]

This agile rationalization, however, required acknowledging two discomfiting facts. The first was that, contrary to so many of the South's previous assertions, the slaves did indeed wish to be free. The second was that southern masters would now have to *permit* those slaves to choose freedom over bondage—and to that extent, at least, to take their own fates into their own hands. And this, railed the Richmond *Examiner*, was the most dangerous development of all. It accepts that "we, the white race, are no longer to judge for negroes, but leave them to judge for themselves." It conceded the white race's loss of mastery; it abdicated whites' proper, divinely ordained control over black life. It surrendered whites' long and tenaciously maintained role as shapers not only of white but also of black history. Surely, such a concession was intolerable to any true southerner. Still less tolerable was the bargain's upshot. For no matter how cleverly worded or rationalized, the result still "is abolition."[78]

And there, truly, was the rub. All the other objections—that the measure was unnecessary, was impractical, was dangerous, would fail to elicit European aid, would demoralize white soldiers, would violate the constitution, would starve the South, or would compromise it ideologically—all paled beside the last and most fundamental item on the indictment. "Great and insurmountable as they are," wrote Charles C. Langdon of those and other criticisms, they "sink into insignificance, are really but 'dust in the balance'" compared to the fact that arming and emancipating slaves "would inevitably" bring about "the destruction of the institution of slavery, and the consequent ruin and degradation of the South."[79]

That manumission of individual black soldiers must end in a "universal emancipation" seemed perfectly obvious to critics. On this point, at least, they agreed with Cleburne, Lee, and others. The genie of emancipation, once out of the bottle, would not be forced back into it. To the Lynchburg *Republican* it seemed only logical that "if 250,000 negro men are entitled to their freedom because they fight for it, then their wives, children and families are also entitled to the same boon, just as the wives, children and families of the white men who fight the same battles."[80] Soon nothing at all would remain of the South's peculiar institution. How can we allow this terrible process of dissolution and degeneration to begin, when (as the Memphis *Appeal* put it) "it is our obvious interest, industrially and economically, to hold on to slavery as a cardinal question, one to which our very political and social being and destiny are involved"?[81]

The *Appeal*'s words—and the debate as a whole—revealed that plans to arm and emancipate slaves had forced the Confederate nation and its leaders back to basics. The plan raised anew, and in the sharpest imaginable way, the question of why the southern states had left the Union, why they had formed the Confederacy, why they had gone to war, and to what fundamental aims they were pledged.

Many justifications of secession, both in 1860–61 and especially after the war, emphasized legal-constitutional generalities and the right of southerners to rule themselves. Jefferson Davis did just that, for example, in his inauguration speech of February 18, 1861.[82] But many others explicitly cited the need to defend slavery against northern attacks. In 1861 both Davis and Alexander Stephens had boldly identified the new Confederacy with the defense of bondage. Stephens had called it the cornerstone of the South's new government. The same kind of assertions had resounded in debates over secession in much of the South during the previous six months.[83]

In 1864–65, the call to salvage southern independence at slavery's expense threw the great mass of Confederate masters into opposition and provoked outbursts of indignation and abuse from across the Confederacy's political spectrum.[84] Patrick Cleburne's adjutant, Capt. Irving A. Buck, had foreseen that reaction at the end of December 1863, when the general had discussed his own proposal with the captain prior to presenting it to the rest of his army's high command. Buck had then warned Cleburne that "the slave holders were very sensitive as to such property, and were totally unprepared to consider such a radical measure."[85] The intervening year, disastrous as it had been for the Confederacy, had disposed few southern masters to look upon that kind of measure with any greater sympathy.

Slavery was the economic, social, and political foundation of the antebellum South. The black slaves' status as racial pariahs and as private property allowed landowners to work them harder, longer, and at a lower cost than they could with free white workers. When urged to replace his slaves with wage workers, South Carolina's James Henry Hammond replied in 1845 that if he could obtain wage workers as cheaply he "would, without a word, resign my slaves . . . But the question is, whether free or slave labor is the cheapest to use in this country, at this time, situated as we are. And [that issue] is decided at once by the fact that we cannot avail ourselves of any other than slave labor. We neither have, nor can we procure, other labor to any extent on anything like the [inexpensive] terms mentioned."[86] Now to sacrifice slavery for the sake of military advantage would mean (in the words of War Bureau chief R. G. H. Kean) "a dislocation of the foundations of society."[87] Here, thundered Mississippi congressman Henry C. Chambers, was "a proposition to subvert the labour system, the social system and the political system of our country."[88] This policy, warned Henry L. Flash of the Macon *Telegraph and Confederate*, would "put a final end to an institution, to which the South is indebted for *all* that makes her superior . . . to the descendants of the puritans of New England."[89] This, because—as both of Charleston's principal newspapers asserted—"African slave labor is the only form of labor whereby our soil can be cultivated, and the great staples of our clime produced." If we "free the negro . . . he would scorn such drudgery," Texan Caleb Cutwell assured his neighbors, and as soon as he left the fields "our fine farms in the Southern low-grounds" would become barren "and our rich staples of cotton, rice and sugar would depart from the commerce of the world."[90] If the South were to take Robert E. Lee's advice, plantation mistress Catherine Edmondston stormed, we would "destroy at one blow the highest jewel in the Crown . . . Our Country is ruined if [we] adopt his suggestions."[91] "Who would live in such a country as ours," the Charleston *Mercury* wanted to know, "without slaves to cultivate it?"[92]

Nor, critics continued, was slavery's demise a problem for slaveowners alone. Defenders of the peculiar institution had long represented it as the only way to enforce the prized privileges and dominant position of the white race as a whole. Slavery's breakdown therefore threatened the vast numbers of whites who never owned a slave. Jefferson Davis, then a U.S. senator from Mississippi, had captured the argument neatly in an 1851 speech. "No white man, in a slaveholding community, was the menial servant of any one," Davis had asserted, because the "distinction between him and the negro . . . elevated, and kept the white laborer on a level with the employer." Emancipation would cast the poor white man down to the level of the poor black. "Free the negroes, however, and it would soon be here, as it is in the countries of Europe, and in the North, and everywhere else, where negro slavery does not exist. The poor white man would become a menial for the rich, and be, by him, reduced to an equality with the free blacks, into a degraded position."[93]

Opponents of placing blacks in the army now turned Davis's own 1851 argument against the Confederate president. Not the planter but "the poor man" would reap the bitterest fruits of Davis's new legislative harvest, the

Charleston *Mercury* intoned. In the new South created by this new policy, the poor white man "is reduced to the level of a nigger, and a nigger is raised to his level. Cheek by jowl they must labor together as equals."[94] Gen. William Bate had protested in response to Cleburne's proposal that it "would result in breaking down all barriers between the black and white races."[95] Florida's David Yulee now issued a similar warning to the Confederate president, predicting that white supremacy's days would be numbered as soon as the first black soldier was mustered into service. "To associate the colors in the [army] camp is to unsettle castes; and when thereby the distinction of color and caste is so far obliterated that the relation of fellow soldiers is accepted, the mixture of races and toleration of equality is commenced."[96] That innovation would not only dissolve the army; it would ruin the entire society, because legal freedom for the slave could only lead to complete racial equality. "In a social sense," a Georgia editor explained, "there is no intermediate point between freedom and citizenship."[97] "If the negroes are to be free," the Lynchburg *Republican* agreed, they would become "equally free with the master."[98] One of the *Republican*'s readers hurried to second that view: "If they are to be emancipated, of course they are to be invested with all the immunities of freedom—including the elective franchise, the right to hold land, inherit and transmit property and all the privileges of citizenship."[99] A manifesto signed by ten Confederate soldiers simply equated the black-soldiers bill with "Negro equality."[100]

The link between freedom and equality, critics claimed, was not merely rhetorical. It rested on tangible political realities. Placing arms in the hands of blacks would deprive whites of the power to define what freedom would mean for the former slaves. If whites then tried to deny that freedom meant equality, critics added, the blacks themselves would certainly assert the connection, and forcefully. They would use their newly won freedom precisely to press for that equality, a pressure that whites would find very difficult to resist. For "if that claim is ignored or denied, they will attempt to establish it by the means which you place in their hands."[101] The *North Carolina Standard* spelled it out less squeamishly: "If we denied them this right they would be apt to fight for it; and with arms in their hands, and accustomed as they would be to the use of them, they would be formidable foes."[102]

The white South's recurring nightmare now threatened to play itself out during waking hours to its melodramatic conclusion. The end of slavery for some blacks would bring freedom to them all. Freedom would necessarily produce equality. Equality would level all social (including sexual) barriers between blacks and whites. And then, one Texan inevitably continued, "the black, having political equality with his former owner, would soon aspire to be the husbands [*sic*]of our daughters and sisters."[103] "Just give this large body of free negroes to understand that they are freemen," Mobile's Charles

C. Langdon agreed, " . . . and there will be no end to their demands, until they are placed on a perfect equality with the white man, socially and politically." They will then demand "the right to sit at the same table, to attend our social parties, to marry our daughters."[104] "The [black] conscript must be sometimes furloughed," a Virginian warned, "and I forebear to depict the state of things which will exist when the furloughed conscripts return to the home" and there encounter young white women, whose "father . . . is a conscript [still] in the camp."[105]

Robert Barnwell Rhett, Jr., forbore to depict nothing, publicly imagining the consequences in lurid detail. The white man, Rhett wrote, will have to submit to seeing "his wife and his daughter . . . bustled on the street by black wenches, their equals," even as "swaggering buck niggers are to ogle them, and to elbow him." "Gracious God!" the horrified Rhett cried out. "Is this what our brave soldiers are fighting for?" Surely not, and just as surely no true southern soldier would submit to it. "The brave soldier who is fighting for the supremacy of his race will have none of it—no, none of it. He wants no Hayti here—no St. Domingo—no mongrels in his family—no miscegenation with his blood."[106] As so often in the past and future, raising the specter of miscegenation aimed both to stiffen the masters' resistance and to give them a rhetoric with which more effectively to address the non-slaveholding white majority.[107]

Was it not to prevent the destruction of slavery and its manifold economic, political, and social consequences, the Macon *Telegraph and Confederate* asked, that the South had opted first for secession and then for war? "This terrible war and extreme peril of our country," its editor recalled, were "occasioned . . . more by the institution of negro slavery" than "by any other subject of quarrel."[108] "For it and its perpetuation," affirmed the Memphis *Appeal*, "we commenced and have kept at war."[109] In fact, added the Charleston *Mercury*, "the mere agitation in the Northern States to effect the emancipation of our slaves largely contributed to our separation from them." But now, incredibly, "before a Confederacy which we established to put at rest forever all such agitation is four years old, we find the proposition gravely submitted that the Confederate Government should emancipate slaves in the States."[110]

William W. Holden's *North Carolina Standard* wholeheartedly agreed with Rhett about very little, but it did concur that this "proposition surrenders the great point upon which the two sections went to war."[111] Where was the logic in defending slavery with measures that dissolved it? Should we not wage this war, a Georgian asked in mock innocence, in a way calculated "to secure and not destroy the objects for which it was inaugurated"?[112] Virginia's Robert M. T. Hunter reportedly asked in amazement, "What did we go to war for, if not to protect our property?"[113]

Here at last was the most basic, the most compelling, the most oft-repeated and widely circulated argument against the plans of Cleburne, Davis, and Lee: Those plans "throw away what we have toiled so hard to maintain," as planter James Wingard objected.[114] "Quite a sensation" was "being created in our ranks by the report that the slaves are to be armed and put in the field," a Missouri soldier recorded in his diary, because "the men think [it would be] yielding that for which they have fought for the last four years."[115] Another army diarist, this one in neighboring Arkansas, growled that "It is virtually giving up the principle on which we went to war."[116] To Senator August E. Maxwell of Florida, too, the proposal meant abandoning "the cause we have been defending."[117] "To say that we are ready to emancipate our slaves," wrote a Texas editor, "would be to say, that we are ready to relinquish what we commenced fighting for."[118] How can we "yield up the institution for which we have been battling so long and so obstinately," a Georgian asked in wonder.[119] "There never was, in the history of the world," Col. John J. Seibels exclaimed, "a more complete abandonment of a cause . . . than this proposition to free the negroes and make soldiers of them."[120]

Advocates of the black-soldier plan commonly responded to outraged protests like these with public expressions of bafflement. What could their opponents possibly mean? How could they so grotesquely distort the noble and high-minded premises and purposes of secession and the war waged to enforce it? Had they not been listening to the South's leaders? Did they really not know what the war was about—that it was a struggle not for slavery but for self-determination? If they did not, it was high time that they learned. On the South's part, the Mobile *Register* instructed, this was simply "a war for constitutional liberty, and the rights of self-government."[121] The Richmond *Sentinel*, whose editor, Richard M. Smith, now most closely hewed to the line of the Davis administration, added a dash of sarcasm. "We are told by some horrified individuals," Smith noted, "that this is 'giving up the cause.'" To which Smith replied, "What cause? We thought that *independence* was, just now, the great question."[122]

With these words the *Sentinel* editor echoed a line of argument pioneered by Patrick Cleburne and later repeated by Jefferson Davis. No one invoked it with greater persistence during this debate than the Richmond *Enquirer*. "Negro slavery," it tirelessly repeated, "was the mere occasion, and is not the object or end of this war."[123] It was the North that dishonestly depicted slavery as the casus belli in order to discredit the South in the eyes of a credulous world. But the North's tragic success in that effort only made it more urgent to set the record straight, to "dispel this . . . delusion" that in the Confederacy "slavery is preferred to nationality—negroes to liberty— cotton to freedom."[124] Fortunately, fate had now provided the opportunity to dispel this delusion once and for all. Let the South move expeditiously to free slaves and enlist them as soldiers. By doing this, it will teach "to the world the lesson that, for national independence and freedom from Yankee domination, in addition to sacrifices already made, the people of these States are ready and willing, when the necessity arises, to sacrifice any number or all of the slaves to the cause of national freedom."[125] Or in thus justifying our cause, the *Enquirer* challenged its opponents, "have we drifted farther than we desired, and said more than we meant? Have we been playing the game of brag, with the blood of our sons and brothers mere counters? Have we sacrificed hundreds of thousands of our best and noblest citizens in merely bullying our enemy and playing upon the credulity of the world?"[126]

To all such high-flown phrases critics commonly replied with a bored yawn or an impatient snort. "Slavery" and "aggressions upon it by the North, apprehensions for its safety in the South, was alike the mediate and immediate cause of Secession," a Georgian lectured, and "all other questions were subordinate to it." All of us understood in 1860–61 that "the principle of State Sovereignty, and its [con]sequence, the right of secession, were important to the South principally, or solely, as the armor that encased her peculiar institution."[127] Charleston's principal newspaper editors took the same ground. The *Courier* fairly rolled its eyes at attempts to elevate states' rights above slavery when those two causes were, of course, inseparably intertwined. "Slavery, God's institution of labor, and the primary political element of our Confederation of Government, state sovereignty . . . must stand or fall together. To talk of maintaining our independence while we abolish slavery is simply to talk folly."[128] "*We want no Confederate Government without our institutions,*" the *Mercury* roared. "And we will have none."[129] Correct, North Carolina's peace faction chimed in. It, too, "want[s] no such independence as that."[130] And Tar Heel Gov. Zebulon Vance could only agree that "our independence . . . is chiefly desirable for the preservation of our political institutions, the principal of which is slavery."[131] From the trans-Mississippi theater came the same refrain. "Independence without slavery, would be valueless," wrote Texan Caleb Cutwell, because "the South without slavery would not be worth a mess of pottage."[132] "Of what value is 'self-government' to the South," one of Cutwell's neighbors demanded, "when the very fabric of Southern prosperity has tottered to its fall!"[133]

The answers to these questions were presumed obvious. Ominously, however, more than a few opponents of arming and freeing slaves addressed that rhetorical question directly. Should the Confederacy abandon the defense of slavery, they would swiftly abandon the Confederacy. Should talk of freeing slaves "meet with any considerable favor at the South," the Lynchburg *Republican* declared, then the Confederacy will have proven "not worth one drop of the precious blood which has been shed in its behalf."[134] "We are fighting for our system of civilization," declared South Carolina's Robert

Barnwell Rhett, Jr. "We intend to fight for *that*, or nothing." And since Confederate soldiers agreed, the *Mercury* warned, "to talk of emancipation is to disband the army."[135] Brig. Gen. Clement H. Stevens of the Army of Tennessee had already told a subordinate that "if slavery is to be abolished then I take no more interest in our fight."[136]

All these ex-Unionists and ex-fire-eaters agreed that arming and freeing slaves was wrong. This practical agreement did not prevent either of them, however, from depicting the idea as only the logical extension of the other's basic political program. The radical secessionists who published the Charleston *Mercury* and the Richmond *Examiner* were sure that the proposal bespoke insufficient loyalty toward the institution of slavery, a vacillation that the *Mercury* identified with the Upper South, where soil and climate made bound labor merely one of several economic options for the landholder. In the cotton states, however, African slavery was the *sine qua non* of wealth and civilization. Here, editor Rhett asserted, was the key to both Robert E. Lee's enthusiasm for emancipation and the *Mercury*'s firm opposition to it.[137] This argument expressed a distrust by South Carolina of Virginia that was by 1865 already many decades old.[138]

As we have already seen, however, many of the earliest calls to use black troops came not from the Upper South but from the cotton kingdom, and in 1864–65 quite a few of its most prominent champions (including Ethelbert Barksdale, Albert Gallatin Brown, Judah P. Benjamin, and of course Jefferson Davis) did, too. Such facts led one Confederate soldier to sneer that the same "fellows of the extreme South who were *first* to plunge into the struggle" were also now "the *first* to be willing to accept terms of dishonor and humiliation."[139] Some especially fierce opponents of the plan, conversely, hailed from the Confederacy's northern tier.

Reluctant secessionists who opposed Confederate emancipation saw in that proposal evidence of a political malady quite different from the one that the Charleston *Mercury* diagnosed. William W. Holden, editor and publisher of the Raleigh *North Carolina Standard*, attributed responsibility for the slave-soldier scheme to the secessionist fire-eaters who (he charged) had irresponsibly lured the South into first one and then another reckless, costly, foredoomed scheme. "First, peaceable secession was to give us independence; then King Cotton was to do it; then foreign intervention was to do it; next, we should *certainly* whip the enemy when we got him away from his gunboats; and now, all these expectations having failed, we are to get our independence through the negro."[140] This last panacea, Holden continued, highlighted another crippling symptom of the secessionist monomania—a foolhardy readiness to sacrifice everything, even slavery, on the altar of southern independence. In 1861 "the people were told that the only course to *prevent* emancipation, and the placing [of] the slaves on an equality with the whites, was to secede from the old government," Holden recalled. And now "we are . . . called upon to do the very thing which it was said the enemy intended to force upon us."[141]

If the Confederacy really *was* prepared to sacrifice slavery in a vain attempt to win this unwinnable war, Holden continued, it could certainly put that sacrifice to more productive, viable use. Why not offer it as a means of achieving a peace settlement and easing reentry into the Union? "The people of this State," the *North Carolina Standard* asserted, "might be willing to part with their slaves" if there were no other way "to end the war; but they are not willing to part with them in order to prolong the war," by turning those slaves into soldiers.[142]

Despite their genuine and important differences with one another, the South's Rhetts and Holdens, like most other opponents of the Davis administration's last-minute plan, agreed on one central and fundamental point, one that they considered nearly self-evident—that the South had withdrawn from and made war upon the old Union primarily to safeguard its "peculiar institution." As Confederate black-soldier plans attested, however, the war's actual impact upon slavery proved to be quite different from the one that secession's architects had foreseen. The causes of this unanticipated development were numerous, but probably the most important and least expected were the actions of the slaves themselves. During the four years of sectional war, southern bondspeople took a series of bold initiatives that confounded their masters, deeply influenced Union policies and military fortunes, and helped dictate the terms of the Confederacy's agonizing struggle over whether to arm and emancipate them.

3

BLACK AND GRAY
Slaves and the Confederate War Effort

Edmund Ruffin, the prominent Virginia planter, agricultural innovator, and political fire-eater, in 1860 published a work of fantasy meant to encourage the slave states to withdraw from the federal Union. More specifically, it aimed to convince timorous neighbors that the South could secede with relative ease and at small cost—that "its means for safe and perfect defence . . . , for achieving independence, and for securing the subsequent preservation of peace, and unprecedented prosperity" would all be as certain "as the most ardent southern patriots would desire."[1]

Entitled *Anticipations of the Future, To Serve as Lessons for the Present Time*, Ruffin's book described an imagined future set in the era 1864–1870, a future in which the slave states seceded from a Republican-controlled Union and then successfully repelled attempts to force their return. In Ruffin's account, written in the form of newspaper dispatches, all of the South's efforts were crowned with success and nearly all those of the Union with failure. In this perfect world, the border states of Kentucky, Missouri, and Maryland joined the states in secession. The slaveless whites of western Virginia conducted themselves as "sound and true southerners." Attempts to blockade the southern coast failed. Attempts to seize the Mississippi river were repulsed. Washington, D.C., fell to southern arms.

Ruffin's optimistic oracle included an especially reassuring description of "the zealous feelings of patriotism evinced by negro slaves" during this imagined North-South conflict. The Union, he wrote, had "relied on in advance . . . the seduction and incitement of the slaves to desert their masters and seek freedom in the camp or country of the invaders." And, indeed, with the entry of Union troops into the South, indeed, "every slave had it completely in his power to desert his master's plantation, and join the invaders." But while "a few slaves, and especially in the beginning," did do that, "in general, and with few exceptions," slaves proved to be "more alarmed at, and more fearful of the invading forces than were the masters." In Ruffin's tale, faithful slaves labored in great numbers on southern fortifications, "enjoy it greatly, and soon become as zealous partizans [*sic*], and as hostile in feeling to the northern enemy, as any citizens." Confident that such scenes accurately depicted basic realities, Ruffin concluded that his story "ought to have shown to all reasoning abolitionists of the northern states that there is little aid to their cause to be expected from negro deserters and allies." On the contrary, the South's loyal black retainers "might well be relied upon as soldiers" by the slaveowners themselves. Even "their natural and constitutional cowardice" would be "perhaps compensated" by the "implicit obedience and perfect subordination of negroes to the authority of white men, as masters and commanders."[2]

By the time Ruffin's *Anticipations* appeared, proslavery writers had been stoutly proclaiming the military superiority of slavery-based society for decades. In support of that claim they invoked thousands of years of history, from the ancient world down through the American Revolution and the War of 1812. Although "it has commonly been supposed that this institution will prove a source of weakness in relation to military defence against a foreign enemy," South Carolina's Chancellor William Harper wrote in 1838, "in a slave-holding community, a larger military force may be maintained permanently in the field, than in any state where there are not slaves." This, James Henry Hammond explained in 1845, because the same slave population that "remained peaceful on our plantations and cultivated them in time of war under the superintendence of a limited number of our citizens" would allow the South to "put forth more strength in such an emergency, at less sacrifice, than any other people of the same numbers."[3] The southern journalist, J. D. B. De Bow, confidently expounded the same view in the summer of 1861. "History furnishes abundant proof," he declared, "that the institution of domestic slavery conduces to national strength; and the events of the day are about to confirm the lessons of history." Like Greece and Rome, the American South would "turn out every citizen as a soldier, with slaves to attend the camp and wait on the soldiery, and yet leave slaves enough at home to carry on the ordinary routine of industry."[4] Seven months into the war, the Montgomery *Advertiser* boasted that "the institution is a tower of strength to the South" and "really one of the most effective weapons employed against the union by the South."[5] Two years later, Major Samuel W. Melton, the Confederacy's assistant adjutant general, was still affirming that "it is in our system of slave labor that our great strength consists; that it is which makes our 8,000,000 productive of fighting material equal to the 20,000,000 of the North."[6]

Slave labor did, in fact, prove essential to the Confederate war effort. It could hardly have been otherwise. After all, as William Harper had observed, "in general the labor of our country is performed by slaves."[7] Nearly 40 percent of the Confederacy's population were unfree, and those people included much of the South's work force. During peacetime, their labor yielded most of the South's wealth, in the form especially of rice, sugar, tobacco, and cotton. The work required to sustain the same society during war naturally fell disproportionately on black shoulders as well. By drawing so many adult white men into the army, indeed, the war multiplied the importance of the black work force. Slave labor produced much of what southern troops ate and most of the cotton that the South attempted to sell (at least during the second half of the war) in order to obtain the exchange needed to purchase what it did not produce.

Slaves also performed a range of tasks more directly connected with the war effort. They mined iron ore, coal, salt, and saltpeter (niter). They made horseshoes, nails, harnesses, bridles, collars, saddles, guns, and ammunition. They maintained roads, canals, and railroads, and they shod and tended army horses and mules. They loaded and unloaded military cargoes, drove wag-

A team of black laborers mounting cannon in the works for the attack on Fort Sumter, March, 1861. (The Library of Congress)

ons, and piloted vessels that carried such cargoes to Confederate armies. They built and maintained fortifications, emplaced artillery, and obstructed rivers to slow Union naval progress along them. They served as stretcher bearers, ambulance drivers, hospital attendants, and nurses.[8] As Georgia's governor Joseph E. Brown accurately noted in the spring of 1863, "the country and the army are mainly dependent upon slave labor for support."[9]

Many southern soldiers brought slaves with them into the army as personal servants, especially in the war's earlier stages. Those servants' storied loyalty became a source of special pride to the white soldiers. "Thousands of slaves follow their masters," a Missourian boasted, "be they in the ranks or at the head of armies, through the dangers of the battle-field, and many have laid down their lives" as proof of "their love" for those masters.[10] Some of those servants took occasional pot-shots at the enemy, much to the delight of the Confederate soldiers around them. A typical newspaper portrait of one such man concluded that "this faithful Confederate negro, though a slave, . . . has made many Yankees bite the dust."[11] Decades later, George Baylor, a southern cavalry veteran, fondly reminisced about this type of "Army Negro." With the Confederacy's defeat, Baylor recalled, he had informed one of them, a man named Phil, that "he was now free and at liberty to go where he pleased." In reply, however, the still-faithful Phil "inquired if he could not live at his old home, and when assured he could, if he wished, a great burden seemed lifted from his heart, and he moved on cheerfully."[12]

To Confederate partisans, such accounts proved that the South's slaves were devoted to their masters and satisfied with their status and condition. They showed, a Texan argued, "that the slave is contented with his lot; and far more happy therein than in the freedom which the Yankees have given him."[13] The *Southern Presbyterian* exulted that such slaves had proven "so faithful, so docile, so true to their only friends on earth, [to] the masters God has given to them."[14] The typical slave, editorialized the Raleigh *Confederate*, had "long ago discovered that his condition was rapidly improving before abolitionists began to meddle with his affairs." As a result, "he distrusts an abolitionist, and a yankee, while he confides in the Southern man."[15] The Yankees, a Virginia editor gloated, "stand aghast at the evidence which our colored population give of affection for our people and attachment to our soil." "The experience of this war," a Missourian agreed, "has pretty well dissipated the false idea, inculcated in the minds of the Northern people by teaching of abolition—fanaticism—that Nat Turner embodied the representative characteristics of the Southern slaves."[16] "Look at the thousands who have had every chance of escape and with safety," a North Carolinian wrote. "Of those who have followed their masters to the war, or who have been employed as teamsters, cooks, &c., &c., how wonderfully few have deserted!"[17]

In the aftermath of the 1859 John Brown raid at Harpers Ferry, Virginia illustrator David Hunter Strother warned against any more such attempts by depicting a master arming his slaves to resist attacks on his plantation. The illustration appeared in *Harper's Weekly*, November 19, 1859. (The New York Public Library)

To some these stories seemed to demonstrate still more—that slaves would serve well as Confederate soldiers. This oft-demonstrated "relation, affection, and sympathy between himself and master" would make the slave "a faithful soldier to the rebellion."[18] Three Mississippians reasoned that, since "instances are not wanting in this war" in which slaves displayed "the most courageous loyalty and devotion to their masters," doubtless the same kind of "devotion would attach them, in the hour of peril, to the side of their master" if they were placed under arms.[19] "If similar promises were held out to him to-morrow, by us and the Yankees," the Raleigh *Confederate* predicted, "nine hundred and ninety-nine negroes, out of a thousand, will prefer to trust their own home people."[20] "Let them be armed and marshaled for our defence," the Lynchburg *Virginian* assured its readers, "and the whole world will confess that they have been altogether mistaken in their estimate of Southern slavery and the feelings of the inferior race toward their masters."[21] In fact, slaves's actual conduct during the war confounded such expectations and predictions, thereby immensely complicating the plans of their masters and of their masters' military and political representatives. The more far-sighted Confederate leaders eventually understood that they would have to base viable plans on more realistic assessments of slave values and loyalties.

The logical link between asserting slaves' fidelity to their owners and predicting their dependability as Confederate soldiers seemed simple enough.

The next step in the argument advanced by most supporters of the slave-soldier idea, however, was less obvious. If slaves were so satisfied with their status—and both grateful and loyal to their masters—why offer to sever their bonds? Why alter their status at all? Didn't emphasizing their fidelity and contentment suggest that manumission was an unnecessary—even a wrong-headed, if not positively destructive—reward? Why not simply muster southern blacks into the army as slaves?

The pro-Confederate London *Times* certainly thought it could be done that way. There was, the *Times* declared in early November 1864, "no reason to doubt that the negro will fight just as bravely in support of the cause of slavery, which is the cause of the master, as he will in the cause of liberty."[22] Some white southerners strongly agreed. By all means place blacks in uniform, urged one North Carolina farmer in January 1865. But banish all thought of freeing them in the process. "Giving our negro soldiers their liberty," this man thought, could "only be the idea of a visionary and thoughtless enthusiast."[23] "We should fight," a Texan insisted, and "make our slaves fight" not for the blacks' freedom but *"for Southern slavery,* knowing that in this contest God is on our side."[24] The Richmond *Whig,* too, thought it only "right" that the slave "should assist in defending the blessings he himself enjoys" as the property of a southern master. "We may accomplish all that we desire by using the negroes simply as slaves."[25] When Mississippi governor Charles Clark finally endorsed the use of slaves as soldiers in February 1865, he too insisted on removing manumission from the plan. For one thing, "freedom would be a curse to them and to the country." But in any case offering the slaves freedom was unnecessary, since "few of them aspire to this, or covet it."[26]

A number of military men approved this way of posing the matter.[27] The most prominent among them was Brig. Gen. Francis A. Shoup, a veteran artillerist with the Army of Tennessee who became its chief of staff in the summer of 1864. During the next winter Shoup wrote a letter to Confederate Kentucky senator Gustavus Henry that then circulated in pamphlet form. In that document the general stoutly denied "that to make good soldiers of these people, we must either give or promise them freedom. On the contrary, it is my firm conviction that to do either would be to impair their efficiency and tractability." Instead he proposed simply "to let the slavery question remain just where it is." That proposition boasted the added attraction that, once the war was won, slave soldiers could be returned immediately to the fields. As Shoup saw it, "Their service as soldiers would in no way unfit them for their former duties." It would, on the contrary, only prepare them to be "the better servants" after the war had been won.[28]

Whatever else it was, this recommendation was at least logically consistent with ringing affirmations that slaves were both loyal to their masters and content to remain in bondage. But both propositions were refuted by slave conduct during the war and the war's impact on slavery. It was certainly true that slaves attempted no large-scale uprisings behind Confederate lines during the war. Black South Carolinians later told Union Col. Thomas Wentworth Higginson why. Attempting an insurrection when nearly all white men were not only armed but also militarily organized—while the slaves themselves "had no knowledge, no money, no arms, no drill, no organization" and no confidence that their plans would not be betrayed—would have been suicidal.[29] Nevertheless, as an insightful white Georgia writer reminded his countryfolk early in 1865, "Evidences are not wanting to illuminate the ill suppressed discontent of many of our slaves." Whites should not feel "over secure" merely because that discontent had not exploded in open revolts. Rather, "they should remember that the whole white population being under arms, any uprising of the negroes was more than ever impracticable." The South, he admonished, should not mistake the slaves' understandable caution for contentment.[30] By the end of 1863, in fact, it was slaves' increasingly manifest and well-documented *dis*content and *dis*loyalty that fueled much of the determination to place them in the Confederate army. And it was this dawning acknowledgment that slaves ardently desired to be free—and were prepared to act upon (and fight for) that goal—that prompted the offer of liberty as a reward for Confederate military service.

Slave loyalty and contentment had been easier to believe in during the prewar era, when prudent blacks had carefully concealed their deepest thoughts and strongest feelings from the whites around them. But the Republican party's first presidential campaign, in 1856, had begun to encourage and embolden members of the South's black population.[31] Lincoln's election four years later, the secession movement that followed, and then the outbreak of armed hostilities did much more; they inaugurated a radically and explosively new stage in the country's history. Slaves strove to understand and exploit those developments for their own purposes.[32] "The slaves, to a man, are on the alert," the black newspaper correspondent George E. Stephens discovered as he traveled through northern Virginia during the war's early months. They "are watching the events of the hour, and . . . hope lights up their hearts."[33] On a tobacco plantation located far to the south and west, "miles from any railroad or large city or daily newspaper," the young Booker T. Washington awoke early one morning to find "my mother kneeling over her children and fervently praying that Lincoln and his armies might be successful, and that one day she and her children might be free." The boy subsequently heard his mother and other slaves join in "many late-at-night whispered discussions that . . . showed that they understood the situation, and that they kept themselves informed of events by what was termed the 'grape-vine' telegraph."[34] In Georgia and South Carolina, authorities punished slaves for singing hymns that anticipated the coming of freedom.[35]

Making sense of the war era's news was a complex, difficult undertaking, however, especially for a slave population successfully maintained in a state of near-total illiteracy. Slaveowners did their best to mislead bondspeople about the war's nature and its implications for them. They assured them that the North had no chance to defeat the Confederacy militarily. Moreover, they admonished, a Union victory would leave slaves worse off than before, for in that case they would share the doleful lot of wretched northern blacks. "The white folks would tell their colored people not to go to the Yankees," the former slave Susie King Taylor later remembered, "for they would harness them to carts and make them pull the carts around, in place of horses." Or else, masters warned, the Republicans would sell slaves away from their homes, friends, and family members—to New Orleans, for example, or, even worse, to the reputed hell-hole of Cuba. One former slave thus typically recalled (in the Gullah accents of the Carolina Sea Islands), our masters "tell we dat de Yankees would shoot we, or would sell we to Cuba, an' do all de wust tings to we, when dey come." At the very least, slaves heard, the Yankees would simply return them to their vengeful owners. Union troops' often hostile treatment of fugitives, particularly during the first year of the war, lent credence to admonitions like these. In light of all this, it is hardly surprising that some slaves and southern free blacks made ostentatious displays of loyalty to the Confederacy, hoping thereby marginally to improve their own conditions or, at least, avoid the wrath of aroused southern whites.[36]

But slaves heard their owners say contradictory things. Since the 1850s, masters and their spokesmen had been loudly equating Republicans and abolitionists and depicting Republican ascendancy as the overture to mass emancipation. Ultimately, the accumulated weight of such pronouncements made a deeper impression on southern blacks than the masters' more recent attempts to frighten their chattels. Harry, a slave foreman on a Sea-Islands plantation, later recounted his master's attempt to induce the blacks to join him in taking flight when Union troops arrived. "He tell we dat de Yankees would shoot we, when dey come. 'Bery well, Sar,' says I. 'If I go wid you, I be good as dead. If I stay here, I can't be no wust; so if I got to dead, I might's well dead here as anywhere. So I'll stay here an' wait for de 'dam Yankees.'" Harry concluded, "I knowed he wasn't tellin' de truth all de time." Instead he and most others had heard that "de Yankees was our friends, an' dat we 'd be free when dey come, an' 'pears like we believe *dat*."[37] A similar account comes from South Carolina's Combahee River, where a group of slaves, advised to fear approaching Yankee gunboats, had then watched their overseer flee. "Good-by, ole man," they later remembered calling after him. "That's right. Skedaddle as fas' as you kin. When we cotch you ag'in, I 'specs you'll know it. We's gwine to run sure enough; but we knows the Yankees, an' we runs that way," gesturing toward the Union ships.[38]

Some slaves had seized the initiative even before Fort Sumter fell. On March 12, 1861, eight black Floridians escaped from their masters and presented themselves before Fort Pickens, one of the few federal installations in the Deep South that secessionists had not already confiscated. The fort's commander, Lt. Adam J. Slemmer, was amused to find the fugitives "entertaining the idea" that the garrison's troops "were placed here to protect them and grant them freedom." Lieutenant Slemmer "did what I could to teach them the contrary," arranging to have them returned to their legal owners.[39] A couple of months later, however, a similar scene unfolded in a different way at Ft. Monroe, on the Yorktown peninsula. At the end of May, three fugitives sought sanctuary there. The fort's commander was Gen. Benjamin Butler, who was no abolitionist and not even a Republican. He had, in fact, campaigned in 1860 for the candidate of the southern Democrats, Kentucky's John C. Breckinridge. But Butler bitterly condemned secession and proved ready to think creatively and act audaciously in order to put it down.

The fugitives reaching Ft. Monroe gave him that opportunity. "We had heard it since last Fall," one of them explained, "that if Lincoln was elected, you would come down and set us free . . . the colored people have talked it all over; we heard that if we could get in here we should be free, or at any rate, we should be among friends."[40] Butler hardly regarded these ragged-looking people as friends. But he was struck by the ironies and possibilities that their presence symbolized. Should the rebels "be allowed the use of this property against the United States," Butler wondered, "and we not be allowed its use in aid of the United States?" At length, he refused to return the refugees to their owners. Declaring them confiscated as "contraband of war," he put them to work under the direction of his own quartermaster—and under his protection.[41] Word of Butler's decision spread rapidly along the slave grapevine. Two days later, eight more runaways made their way to "Freedom Fort." Another fifty-nine men and women joined them the following day. Over the next couple of months, the total number seeking sanctuary there reached nine hundred.[42] Lincoln recognized Butler's ingenuity and endorsed his action as a legitimate tactic of war.

By reacting shrewdly to the initiative of the slaves themselves, by recognizing how that initiative served the military needs of the Union, Butler and Lincoln began fashioning a winning policy. In August 1861, Congress passed the first Confiscation Act, which provided that any master using a slave (or permitting that slave to be used) in aid of the Confederate war effort "shall forfeit all right" to that slave. In July 1862, Congress approved the second Confiscation Act, which declared that slaves belonging to rebels would, upon falling into Union hands, "be deemed captives of war, and shall be forever free of their servitude and not again held as slaves."[43] Within a few months more, Lincoln had issued his preliminary emancipation proclamation, announcing that on January 1, 1863, all slaves within the Confederacy's domain would become, in the eyes of the U.S. government, "then, thenceforward, and forever free."[44]

Once again, the slave grapevine spread the news, most swiftly in areas closest to the Union or Union army encampments. One federal official asked some Confederate prisoners of war "what effect the President's Proclamation of Freedom had produced in the South." They responded that "it had played hell with them." The official then expressed surprise, since he knew that few slaves could actually read the proclamation's text. To which one of the southerners replied "that one of his negroes had told him of the proclamation five days before he had heard it in any other way." Some of the other prisoners confirmed that "their negroes gave them their first information of the proclamation" as well. A South Carolina fugitive supplied the solution to the seeming mystery: "We'se can't read, but we'se can listen."[45] By the end of the war, it is estimated, between five and seven hundred thousand slaves had managed to enter Union lines.[46] Soon after reaching that sanctuary, some fugitives began laying plans to return home in order to liberate friends and

In this 1864 engraving by J. W. Watts, a Union soldier reads the Emancipation Proclamation to a slave family. (The Library of Congress)

family members. A Georgian named Nat reportedly helped between seventy and a hundred other bondspeople reach freedom during the war years before a Confederate soldier shot and killed him. Such expeditions could carry former slaves hundreds of miles back into the Confederate interior, sometimes bringing Union troops in their train.[47]

Patrick Cleburne's Army of Tennessee, the principal Confederate force west of the Appalachians, had witnessed slavery's disintegration firsthand during 1863 as it campaigned across the state whose name it bore. Gen. Braxton Bragg, the army's commander until early December, was the proud owner of a Louisiana sugar plantation and fancied that he knew what slavery looked like when it functioned properly. "The very plantation is a small military establishment, or it ought to be," he had written just before the war. At its heart was "discipline, by which we secure system, regularity, method, economy of time, labor and material." And it was discipline, too, that kept such "a large class of our population in subordination."[48] In fact, that discipline and subordination was never as complete as Bragg and others like him wanted to believe.[49] But cracks in the facade widened considerably after the outbreak of war. Reports of runaway slaves were soon increasing in the Mississippi valley.[50] Some Union forces pushed southward into the valley, from Kentucky into Tennessee, in January–February 1862; others began driving northward from the Gulf of

A wagon full of "contrabands" crosses the Rappahannock River to reach Union troops in 1862. (The Library of Congress)

Mexico through lower Louisiana in April and May. By summer, federal troops controlled two-thirds of Tennessee and parts of northern Alabama and Mississippi as well as southern Louisiana and Alabama. The conquest of the big river culminated a year later in the taking of Vicksburg and Port Hudson. Some of the South's largest and richest plantations and some of its densest slave populations were to be found in that region.

At first slowly and unevenly, but before long dramatically and on an even larger scale than in the East, the federal military presence in the western war theater eroded slavery's bonds.[51] "There is a great disposition among the negroes to be insubordinate, and to run away and go to the federals," a provost marshal in Natchez informed Mississippi's governor in the summer of 1862, before Lincoln issued his preliminary emancipation proclamation. "Within the last 12 months we have had to hang some 40 for plotting an insurrection, and there has been about that number put in irons."[52] Union army chaplain John Eaton, of the 27th Ohio Infantry Volunteers, accompanied Ulysses S. Grant's troops that fall as they for the first time "enter[ed] a region densely populated by the Negroes." Just after the October battle of Corinth, as Mississippi cotton planters fled, field laborers "flocked in vast numbers—an army in themselves—to the camps of the Yankees," Eaton reported. It was an arresting sight. "With feet shod or bleeding, individually or in families," this virtual "army of slaves and fugitives" was "pushing its way irresistibly" forward, in numbers so large it seemed "like the on-coming of cities."[53]

Jefferson Davis had a personal window on such developments. Throughout his life, he had sung slavery's praises and extolled the close relationship it fostered between master and man. "Their servile instincts rendered them contented with their lot," he was still affirming decades later, and "a strong mutual affection was the lasting effect of this lifelong relation . . . Never was there happier dependence of labor and capital on each other."[54] His older brother Joseph ran the family's cotton plantations in Davis Bend, Mississippi, about thirty miles south of Vicksburg. For decades, Joseph had sought to secure the loyalty and cooperation of his human property by raising their living standards somewhat, offering material incentives for superior work, and allowing for a degree of community self-policing greater than the norm.[55]

But the ravages of war were unkind both to the Davis family's plantations and to its confidence in the slaves' happiness and affection. In the spring of 1862, as Union forces approached, Joseph Davis fled from his home. His attempt to take the family's labor force with him failed, however, as most of the blacks disappeared into the surrounding countryside—along with articles of furniture and clothing they had appropriated from the Davis big house.[56] Even the presidential mansion in Richmond felt the impact of slave disaffection. In January 1864, Jefferson Davis's personal servant and Varina Davis's maid "decamped" toward the Yankees. Later the same month another servant tried to burn the mansion down.[57]

Slavery's breakdown also dealt hard blows to Confederate Arkansas, home to Gens. Thomas C. Hindman, Patrick Cleburne, and many of their men. Union Gen. Samuel R. Curtis, headquartered in Helena, applied the provisions of the first Confiscation Act with energy and enthusiasm, distributing certificates of freedom to slaves covered by the terms of that law. As they learned of Curtis's welcoming attitude, black laborers began "throwing down their axes and rushing in for free papers" in what Curtis called a "general stampede." By the summer of 1863, many thousands had reached his lines; by the end of the war, more than 5,500 black Arkansans had become Union soldiers.[58]

The soldiers of the Confederate Army of Tennessee, in which a frank discussion of this subject had first erupted, could hardly miss slavery's dissolution; it was taking place under their noses.[59] In the early summer of 1863, Union Gen. William S. Rosecrans's army brought freedom to tens of thousands of Tennessee slaves.[60] The emancipation of so many slaves deprived Cleburne and his comrades of the military laborers that they required.[61] And in the fall of 1863, Maj. George L. Stearns (a long-time abolitionist instrumental in organizing the 54th Massachusetts Regiment) began recruiting black men in Tennessee into the U.S. army. At a public meeting of black residents of Nashville that fall, a community leader exhorted his neighbors to "rally to arms, for arms alone will achieve our rights. God will rule over our destinies. He will guide us, for He is the friend of the oppressed and down-trodden. The God of battles will watch over us and lead us. We have nothing to lose, but everything to gain."[62] Some twenty thousand black Tennesseans served in the Union army over the next two years.[63]

When Sherman's army advanced from southeast Tennessee into northwest Georgia in early 1864, it carried the same dynamic across the Appalachians. Black refugees swarmed toward the advancing Union forces.[64] Typical was the scene that greeted Sherman's troops as they entered the town of Covington, Georgia. William T. Sherman despised blacks, and the same sentiment pervaded much of his army. Nevertheless, as one of Sherman's generals noted, "Every day, as we marched on we could see, on each side of our line of march, crowds of these people coming to us through the roads and across the fields, bringing with them all their earthly goods, and many goods which were not theirs."[65] At one plantation, Sherman himself later recalled, he came upon an elderly black man and "asked him if he understood about the war and its progress." The man told Sherman that "he did; that he had been looking for the 'angel of the Lord' ever since he was knee-high, and, though we professed to be fighting for the Union, he supposed that slavery was the cause, and that our success was to be his freedom." Sherman then asked if "all the negro slaves" there held the same opinion, and the old man "said they surely did."[66]

The approach of Union troops quickly undermined the plantation discipline that Braxton Bragg so prized. "The negroes . . . say they *are* free," complained Mrs. Clement C. Clay, Sr., the mother of an Alabama senator, in September 1863, and as a result "we cannot exert any authority" and must "beg ours to do what little is to be done."[67] A year and a half later, as Union troops moved into South Carolina, a plantation overseer reported that "two yankeys come up and turnd the People [the slaves] loose to distribet the house which they did, taking out every thing & then to the smoke hous & Store Room doing the same as in the house . . . the hogs in the Pen is Kild & all the Stock is taken a way the horses is all taken a way. Some of the People owns some of them."[68]

This pattern was by then quite familiar in Louisiana, where owners and supervisors found themselves already in 1862–63 unable to enforce the old work rules and rhythms. Field hands began appropriating food supplies, firewood, farm implements, and livestock, and whatever else they could use or sell for cash.[69] Governor and planter Thomas O. Moore heard from a neighbor in mid-1863 that a Union raid into the area "turned the negroes crazy. They became utterly demoralized at once and everything like subordination and restraint was at an end." (As these words implied, a "demoralized" slave was one whom whites could no longer control.) "All business was suspended and those that did not go on with the [Union] army remained at home to do *much worse*." As an example of the latter, the neighbor added, "your boy Wallace and two others . . . forcibly put a Confederate soldier in the stocks at your place on Saturday night a week ago. They abused him too, very much."[70]

William J. Minor, one of the wealthiest planters in the Natchez region, had presciently opposed secession in 1860 on the grounds that "it would lead to war and war to emancipation."[71] Two years later, when federal troops approached, he abandoned his holdings but then returned in January 1863 to attempt to live under occupation. At one of his three sugar plantations, Minor found "the negroes . . . completely demoralised—They are practically free—going, coming, and working when they please." "They destroy every thing on the plantation. In one night they killed 30 hogs . . . they ride the mules off at night and at all times." Indeed, he noted in amazement, "The most of them think, or pretend to think that the plantation and every thing on it belongs to them."[72]

Things were no better on Minor's other estates. "Found all the negroes at home but many working badly," he reported in January.[73] "But few of the negroes went to work today," he complained one day in February. "Many concealed themselves in their houses. Several . . . refused to go to work when I ordered them. Isaac Simpson went off some distance [and] got out his knife—

began to sharpen it on a piece of brick." When Minor "went up to him and asked him what he was doing," Simpson "said he was sharpening his knife to *cut his nails.*" (The ironic emphasis was Minor's.)[74] A few months later another bondsman "broke into the house [and] stole some money and other articles" and subsequently threatened two white men on the plantation.[75]

Masters had always known that slavery required active enforcement by government. They now watched as experience confirmed that belief. Replacing the political and military power of the Confederacy with that of the Republican-led Union, even in those places where the Emancipation Proclamation was not supposed to apply, therefore meant destroying the old social and economic order as well. Opponents of slavery had often claimed that free workers would serve southern landowners as well as slaves. Masters and their spokesmen had replied that only an enslaved labor force could be made to work as hard, as obediently, and as cheaply as plantation profits required. Proslavery newspapers now trumpeted that southern agriculture in Union-occupied districts was confirming their darkest predictions. "An Old Planter" complained at length about the "new system of negro labor" that had sprung up in the Union-occupied Louisiana sugar districts. Black laborers showed little "concern about what is their duty to do," he grumbled, but cared a great deal about "by what means they can most easily escape doing." And now "there is no police, no watch, no guards to arrest them," or otherwise compel them to do the planter's will. As a result, no planter "ever knows what to do," either. "No one can tell if they have labor on terms to justify going on with business, or that such control of it will be given as to entitle proprietors or lessees to continue the struggle."[76] "The crying evil, which may be heard on every plantation down in [Union-occupied] Mississippi," according to another newspaper account, "is the incorrigible indolence of the negroes, and with it the lack of power to make the niggers work."[77]

The implications should the Union conquer the South were thus clear. The Republicans would not permit us, R. M. T. Hunter predicted at a February 1865 public meeting in Richmond, "to regulate or restrain them [the former slaves], so as to make them useful or correct their viciousness." Instead, "the United States Congress is to have the power to regulate those questions, and would be continually interfering between the white and black; and this power of regulation would be in the hands of those who, for one generation at least, would be extremely hostile to us."[78]

The old order changed most dramatically in areas that Union troops occupied. But Confederate masters discovered slave discipline breaking down even in districts that Union troops had not yet occupied. Black field laborers began to demand improvements in their conditions and implicit but no less momentous alterations in their status—and threatened to withhold their labor unless such demands were met. Owners thus found themselves forced to bargain more and more explicitly for the services of those who were nominally still their property.[79] As northern forces approached Fredericksburg, Virginia, in April of 1862, Betty Herndon Maury (Col. Richard Maury's sister) noted that "the negroes are going off in great numbers and are beginning to be very independent and impudent." She soon reported that "matters are getting worse and worse here every day with regard to the negroes. They are leaving their owners by the hundreds and demanding wages."[80] A Louisiana overseer added that of those field workers who had *not* made their way to Union lines "very few are faithful—Some of those who remain are worse than those who have gone."[81]

In truth, some southern whites had begun to worry considerably earlier than that about what their slaves intended and how they would act as military-age white men left plantation districts to join the army. How would slave laborers behave when so many masters and overseers were gone? Just weeks after the fall of Ft. Sumter, a militia officer in Jasper County, Mississippi, reported "rumours [that] are rife, that the Negroes of the surrounding neighborhoods are making preparations to raise an insurrection, headed by white men, as soon as our volunteers leave" for camp.[82] Shortly afterward, the Tennessee legislature provided for the raising of "a Home Guard of Minute Men" who were "to see that all the slaves are disarmed; to prevent the assemblage of slaves in unusual numbers; to keep the slave population in proper subjection; and to see that peace and order is observed."[83] Around the same time, visiting English journalist William Howard Russell marked the glaring contradiction on this subject lodged within southern white consciousness. "There is something suspicious in the constant never ending statement that 'we are not afraid of our slaves,'" Russell noted in his diary. "The curfew and the night patrol in the streets, the prisons and watch-houses, and the police regulations prove that strict supervision, at all events, is needed and necessary."[84] Neither these fears nor the strict supervision of slaves that they inspired melted away. "Many plantations have a large number of negroes and no white man on the place," a worried Brig. Gen. W. N. R. Beall noted in late July 1862. "The negroes show very marked sign of discontent and Danger is apprehended."[85]

Concerns about home front security, as already noted, helped enact draft exemptions for planters or overseers. They also informed many calls to place slaves in the army. "Some of our people are fearful that when a large portion of our fighting men are taken from the country," the War Department heard from Athens, Georgia, in May 1861, "that large numbers of our negroes aided by [northern] emissaries will ransack portions of the country, kill numbers of our inhabitants, and make their way to the black republicans." To allay such fears and "lessen the dangers at home," John J. Cheatham asked, could some of these negroes "not be incorporated into our armies?"[86] In July

1864, Georgia's James D. Lennard endorsed this concern. The declining number of white males on the home front, Lennard advised James A. Seddon, was making "our negroes . . . more impudent," and "on the part of our families and our crops we may well dread the consequences."[87]

The Lynchburg *Virginian* grasped the argument and echoed it, if with obvious discomfort, at the end of December 1864. The alternative to placing slaves in uniform was to leave them at home to form what in the following century would be called a fifth column. "Do we wish to be exposed in front and rear?" the *Virginian* asked. "Would it not be better to have a portion of this force removed to the front, than to leave it all behind when every able-bodied white man is in the ranks? We prefer not to discuss this point, but every intelligent mind can comprehend our meaning, and perceive the propriety of accepting the alternative we have presented."[88] The next conscription call-up of white men, Alabama's Benjamin Bolling worried, "will drain certain locations so close that the slaves might do a great deal of harm, in fact a great many is already alarmed on this subject Especially women and children."[89]

Some white women did indeed feel themselves particularly vulnerable to this menace.[90] One of them was a Mrs. L. Cassels of South Carolina, whose husband and two sons were serving in the Confederate army. Mrs. Cassels advised Jefferson Davis on the eve of his November 1864 message to Congress that drafting any more white men from her area would leave "thousands of families . . . with no one but a woman and her little children." Everyone knew that "the negro is not going to mind his mistress when his master and the neighboring men are gone" but will instead "burn out and pillage and rob the neighborhood of everything to eat." In that light, Mrs. Cassels asked, "would it not be best . . . to put a portion of our negroes in the service and leave white men at home to oversee the balance"?[91]

Mary F. Akin felt the same kind of jitters but presented the solution in more bloodthirsty terms. In January 1865 she wrote to her congressman husband "in favor of putting negros [sic] in the army and that *immediately*." "The negro men," she specified, "ought to be put to fighting and where some of them will be killed," since "if it is not done there will soon be more negroes than whites in the country and they will be the free race." Since that was intolerable, "I want to see them *got rid of soon*."[92]

Anxieties like hers were, in truth, not confined to women. Alabama's Benjamin H. Micou urged Benjamin and Davis to consider the collateral benefits of mobilizing the slave population for war, especially "the feeling of relief & security the people would feel & have by taking away all or nearly all the able bodied negroes and putting them in camps."[93] One recently discharged Confederate soldier expressed sentiments very similar to Mary Akin's. If the South deployed black troops and were then militarily defeated anyway, this man mused, many blacks would likely die in battle in the process. That result would make life in a reconstituted Union easier to bear. In that case "we will be rid of the bulk of them anyhow, which will be better than to let them live to be our masters."[94]

Indications that Union victory would mean the loss of planter property not only in people but also in land stoked the southern elite's anxieties even higher. Wherever masters fled before the approach of northern troops, the federal government temporarily became, willy-nilly, the landed proprietor. That fact alone was enough to fuel planter apprehensions about Northern intentions. Much more alarming was deliberate, calculated Union confiscation of such plantation lands. The most important case was that of General William T. Sherman's Special Field Orders No. 15.

The order in question was not the product of a religious epiphany, mature strategic plan, or spontaneous burst of sympathy on Sherman's part for the downtrodden blacks all around him. It was the result, instead, of a meeting in Savannah between the general and Union Secretary of War Henry M. Stanton, on one side, and twenty black ministers and church officers, fifteen of whom were themselves former slaves, on the other. Sherman was anxious to reduce and if possible remove the column of some ten thousand fugitives that was following in his army's wake. "The way we can best take care of ourselves," the black representatives responded, "is to have land, and turn in and till it by our own labor . . . and we can soon maintain ourselves and have something to spare . . .We want to be placed on land until we are able to buy it, and make it our own." Out of that discussion emerged Sherman's Special Field Orders No. 15. Issued in January 1865, it declared that coastal lands from Charleston, South Carolina, down to Jacksonville, Florida, "are reserved and set apart for the settlement of the negroes now made free by the acts of war and the proclamation of the President of the United States." As a result of this order, some forty thousand blacks came into possession of almost half a million acres of land.[95]

Southern newspapers reported this development in tones mixing alarm, indignation, and vindication in equal parts.[96] Sherman's decree, they declared, shows clearly what Yankee rule will mean for the South. "If we fail," the Confederate Congress warned in its last public address, "not only political degradation, but social humiliation must be our wretched lot. We would not only be political vassals, but social serfs . . . Not only would the property and estates of vanquished 'rebels' be confiscated, but they would be divided and distributed among our African bondsmen."[97] To Mississippi congressman Ethelbert Barksdale, northern plans "to seize the lands and other property of the Southern people and distribute them as a reward" to black southerners confirmed the need to take any steps necessary—including the enlistment of slaves—to avoid such conquest.[98]

So did the fact that southern slaves were proving of great military use to the Union in various ways. Escaped slaves who reached Yankee camps offered invaluable assistance. The quartermaster department put men to work at a wide range of tasks—building fortifications, driving wagons, digging graves, caring for the horses, and cultivating food crops. "Contraband" women cooked, washed clothes, and nursed the sick and wounded. Fugitives offered information to Union raiding parties.[99] A citizens' committee in one coastal Georgia county reported in August 1862 that "absconding negroes . . . go over to the enemy and afford him aid and comfort by revealing the condition of the districts and cities from which they come, and aiding him in erecting fortifications and raising provisions for his support." Blacks also served "as guides to expeditions on the land and as pilots to their vessels on the waters of our inlets and rivers. They have proved of great value thus far to the coast operations of the enemy."[100] "A negro brought the Yankees from Pineville," South Carolinian Susan R. Jervey confirmed grimly, "and piloted them to where our men were camped, taking them completely by surprise."[101] "They are traitors who may pilot an enemy into your *bedchamber!*" Charles Colcock Jones, Sr., warned his family. "They know every road and swamp and creek and plantation in the county, and are the worst of spies."[102]

The freedpeople's contribution to the Union war effort escalated sharply, of course, when Washington changed its mind about employing black troops.

In this wood engraving, Union prisoners of war, having escaped from Confederate captivity, receive aid from a family of slaves. *Harper's Weekly*, March 12, 1864.

Hostility toward blacks and a firm belief in their inferiority was strong, deep-seated, and widespread in the antebellum North, and the U.S. army had for decades refused to enlist African Americans. But the North's very different economy and social structure allowed it, under the pressure of necessity, to alter that policy far more easily than could the Confederacy. Thus, as the Union's need for manpower grew, Union policy evolved from excluding blacks to accepting them in support roles to welcoming their participation in combat. In July 1862 both the second Confiscation Act and the Militia Act authorized Lincoln to place blacks in the armed forces. And Lincoln's final Emancipation Proclamation reiterated his determination to see "such persons, of suitable condition, . . . received into the armed forces of the United States."[103]

By the end of the war, some 180,000 African Americans had served in the Union army, another 10,000 in the navy. More than three-quarters of these men had been recruited in the slave states, and many had had to overcome daunting perils in order to enlist.[104] A Kentucky bondsman named Elijah Marrs and a group of others escaped from their owner in September 1864. Marrs later recalled "the morning I made up my mind to join the United States Army. I started to Simpsonville, and walking along I met many of my old comrades on the Shelbyville Pike." Marrs "told them of my determination," and within twenty-four hours twenty-seven others had decided "to join my company." Conscious of crossing territory regularly subject to Confederate raids, Marrs and his comrades breathed a sigh of relief when they reached Louisville, where they joined the Union army.[105] Not all such attempts fared as well. Just a few months later a southern newspaper reported that "A negro man was recently hung by the citizens near Duck Hill, Carroll County, Mississippi. He was raising a company of negroes to go to Memphis," which was in Union hands. "When he was overtaken he resisted so defiantly that he had to be shot before surrendering. He was then tried and hung. Many other negroes were implicated in the move."[106]

Black Union troops performed crucial services, guarding vulnerable supply lines and performing many other essential support tasks. They also soon distinguished themselves in combat. As early as October 1862, black troops mustered in Kansas saw action in neighboring Missouri. "The men," a northern journalist reported, "fought like tigers, each and every one of them."[107] Black soldiers participated in their first major engagement in May 1863, displaying conspicuous valor in an unsuccessful early assault on Port Hudson, Louisiana. "You have no idea of how my prejudices with regard to negro troops have been dispelled by the battle the other day," a white northern officer present wrote afterward. "The brigade of negroes behaved magnificently and fought splendidly; could not have done better. They are far superior in discipline to the white troops, and just as brave."[108] Two weeks later, outnumbered black Union soldiers bravely bore the brunt of a Confederate attack at nearby Milliken's Bend. The southern commander that day acknowledged that his charge "was resisted by the negro portion of the enemy's force with considerable obstinacy." The Confederate officer thought that all the more remarkable because "the white or true Yankee portion ran like whipped curs almost as soon as the charge was ordered."[109]

By the war's end, black soldiers had taken part in some 450 military engagements, about 40 of which were major battles.[110] In the spring of 1865, Grant's forces besieging Richmond and Petersburg included 33 black regiments, which meant that blacks represented about one out of every eight Union soldiers there.[111] Col. Thomas Wentworth Higginson, commander of the First South Carolina Volunteers, summarized their most striking qualities as soldiers: "Instead of leaving their homes and families to fight, they are fighting for their homes and families; and they show the resolution and sagacity which a personal purpose gives," Higginson reported early in 1863. "It would have been madness to attempt with the bravest White troops what I have successfully accomplished with Black ones."[112] Gen. David Hunter, commander of the Union's Department of the South, informed Secretary of War Stanton in April that his black troops were "hardy, generous, temperate, strictly obedient, possessing remarkable aptitude for military training, and deeply imbued with that religious sentiment (call it fanaticism, such as like) which made the soldiers of Oliver Cromwell invincible."[113]

This engraving depicts black Union troops under General Edward A. Wild liberating slaves in North Carolina. It appeared in *Harper's Weekly*, January 23, 1864.

The black soldiers themselves made the same point in plainer and more immediate terms. "We are fighting for liberty and right," a black sergeant explained, "and we intend to follow the old flag while there is a man left to hold it up to the breeze of heaven. Slavery must and shall pass away."[114] "'Fore I would be a slave 'gain, I would fight till de last drop of blood was gone," a middle-aged black sergeant named Spencer told his comrades in Mississippi in the summer of 1863 as they gathered in a new freedman's school. "I has 'cluded to fight for my liberty, and for dis eddication what we is now to receive."[115] Christian Fleetwood, a free black resident of Baltimore who had joined the Union army, reflected in his journal a few months later on the fact that "this year has brought about many changes that at the beginning were or would have been thought impossible. The close of the year finds me a soldier for the cause of my race. May God bless the cause, and enable me in the coming year to forward it on."[116] Even more indelibly symbolizing the dramatic changes taking place and the exhilaration they brought to so many was the reaction of a black Union soldier who discovered that the Confederate prisoners he was guarding included his own his former owner. "Hello, massa," the soldier sang out. "Bottom rail top dis time!"[117]

Prewar spokesmen of the planters *knew* that none of these things would ever happen. "Our slaves could not be easily seduced," South Carolina's James Henry Hammond had predicted. And if some invader somehow managed to draw a few blacks into his own army, the great mass of loyal slaves would soon take their errant brethren in hand. Nothing, in fact, would "delight them more than to assist in stripping Cuffee of his regimentals to put him in the cotton-field."[118]

Especially at the war's start, but in many cases much later as well, white southerners derided reports of slaves aiding the North. Confederate loyalists assured one another that black Union soldiers had proven cowardly and buffoonish in combat. And that black soldiers served the Union not out of choice but under compulsion, or as the result of lies told and trickery practiced by Union officers. "Generally not of their own accord," the Charleston *Mercury* typically averred, "but by compulsion, those who have been captured have been forced to take up arms against us."[119] Or else, the Richmond *Sentinel* suggested, slaves had been lured into the Yankees' ranks "by dint of the frauds and falsehoods for which they are notorious." Union officers had "invite[d] them to a perpetual holiday, with nothing to do, plenty to eat and drink, and with music and dancing at all hours."[120] Mississippi congressman Henry C. Chambers also liked the idea that slaves had gone over to the enemy simply "to avoid work."[121] But once the black recruits grasped the true nature of their new masters (according to the Charleston *Courier*) they sought to escape from those deceivers and return to their old owners, thereby demonstrating anew "the great fidelity of Southern negroes, when they are allowed by the Yankees an opportunity of manifesting it."[122]

Among some such self-delusion seemed to know no bounds. Even as black fugitives flocked to and followed after Sherman's columns in Georgia, southern newspapers announced that "negroes in Sherman's rear are now arresting most of the straggling Yankees and delivering them up to our authorities."[123] A Texas cavalry colonel was still declaring in January 1865 that although his neighbors were "becoming more and more frightened every day about keeping slaves," *he* would "never give them up until I am obliged to, and that will be a long time." Indeed, he reassured a fellow southerner, both "you and your children" would "be waited upon by slaves as long as you all live."[124]

Eventually, however, more perceptive and frank southern whites came to recognize that the vast majority of slaves were *not* proving loyal to their masters, much less to the Confederate cause, *did* aspire fervently to be free, and were prepared to act—and fight—in pursuit of that aspiration. Therefore, one Virginian saw, "we see one-half of our entire population of no avail to us, but on the contrary ready at every opportunity to join the ranks of our enemies."[125] Thus, Gen. Joseph E. Johnston confided to Texas Sen. Louis T. Wigfall in January 1864 that "we never have been able to keep the impressed Negroes with an army near the enemy. They desert."[126]

Deserters like these, moreover, included not only field laborers but also some of the more privileged drivers and domestic servants. "[A]s to the idea of the faithful servant," Catherine Edmondston of North Carolina therefore concluded, "it is all a fiction. I have seen the favorite and most petted negroes the first to leave in every instance."[127] "Those we loved best, and who loved us best—as we thought," fretted one Virginian, "were the first to leave us."[128] "This war," Georgia planter Louis Manigault observed, "has taught us the perfect impossibility of placing the least confidence in any Negro," since "in too numerous instances those we esteemed the most have been the first to desert us."[129] "The recent trying scenes through which we have passed," planter John H. Ransdell wrote to his friend, Louisiana's governor Thomas O. Moore, show "that *no dependence is to be placed on the negro*—and that they are the greatest hypocrites and liars that God ever made."[130]

Surveying the ruins of the Confederacy in July 1865, War Bureau chief R. G. H. Kean listed "the causes of the failure of southern independence" in his private journal. Conspicuous among them was the slaves' "desertion to the enemy and joining their army as recruits."[131] Just a few days after Appomattox, South Carolina planter Augustin L. Taveau reflected with even greater candor on that experience. "Born and raised amid that Institution, like a great many others," Taveau wrote, he had believed "that these people were content, happy, and attached to their masters." But "the conduct of the

Negro in the late crisis of our affairs convinced me that we have all been labouring under a delusion." For "if they were content, happy, and attached to their masters, why did they desert him in the moment of his need and flock to an enemy, whom they knew *not*?" No, Taveau concluded, it is now apparent that "the Negro for forty years [has] been looking for the Man of Universal Freedom" and that finally "his eager ear caught the sounds of his voice thundering at the bars of his Prison door."[132]

More open acknowledgment of these painful truths had really begun with Patrick Cleburne's explosive memorandum of December 1863. "Slavery," the general had then boldly announced, "from being one of our chief sources of strength at the commencement of the war, has now become, in a military point of view, one of our chief sources of weakness." "All along the lines slavery is comparatively valueless to us for labor," he specified, "but of great and increasing worth to the enemy for information. It is an omnipresent spy system, pointing out our valuable men to the enemy, revealing our positions, purposes, and resources." The slaves' obvious pro-Union partisanship created "fear of insurrection in the rear" and "anxieties for the fate of loved ones when our armies have moved forward." And when federal troops advanced, the slaves became "recruits awaiting the enemy with open arms," with those who donned Union blue proving fully able "to face and fight bravely against their former masters."[133]

That memorandum did not circulate widely. But eventually sections of the Confederate press also began to grant that the Yankees "have met with some degree of success" in their "strenuous efforts to secure the special aid" of the slaves.[134] A North Carolinian conceded that "vast numbers of them . . . have voluntarily gone over to the enemy whenever a favorable opportunity presented itself to them, and, in many instances, joined their army of their own free choice."[135] The Lynchburg *Virginian* similarly admitted "the fact that wherever the enemy goes, our slaves follow him in droves."[136]

To many whites this conduct proved the blacks' inconstancy and ingratitude. "Instead of manifesting the loyalty for which some give them credit," an angry Georgian typically charged, "the men, women and children, prompted by abolition emissaries, rushed to the Yankees from every quarter."[137] But others drew more sober (and sobering) conclusions. The slaves' behavior, acknowledged editor Charles Button, "shows their estimate of Liberty."[138] The Davis administration's favorite newspaper changed its tune as well. Just a few months after attributing the slave's defection to Union lines to a childlike yearning for "perpetual holidays," the Richmond *Sentinel* conceded that "liberty . . . excites his interests and hopes."[139] "Proceeding up our rivers, on the banks of which the slaves are most numerous," northern vessels "had little more to do than display their colors," that paper complained. "The negroes at once threw down their hoes, axes and spades, and quitted their plows, and flocked to the Yankee steamers and other craft by tens of thousands."[140] "The negro," concluded the Richmond *Enquirer*, "wants his freedom."[141] "That large numbers of them do think it a desirable boon," the Richmond *Whig* conceded in mid-February 1865, "is proved by the fact that they run off to the Yankees in quest of it."[142]

Those finally forced to face facts like these found it hard not to feel bitter and to direct that bitterness toward the blacks who had "betrayed" them. But some blamed secession leaders for staking so much on a fundamentally false picture of reality. "When we look back now," Georgia editor Henry L. Flash observed in the war's last weeks, "we wonder at the amount of nonsense that passed for great truths, and the sage axioms which were retained as great philosophical principles" just a few years earlier. Indeed, he guessed, "no people were ever so badly instructed as our poor chivalrous children of the South." Secession advocates had promised them that "the Yankees wouldn't fight." Edmund Ruffin's *Anticipations of the Future* had retailed not only this but also "a thousand kindred fallacies," including the one serenely predicting "the faithfulness of the slaves." Painful experience had shown Southerners the bitter truth concealed behind these comforting fallacies; unfortunately, this was "knowledge bought indeed with blood."[143]

By the end of 1864, even Edmund Ruffin was conceding having entertained some profoundly flawed views about southern slavery. "I had before believed in the general prevalence of much attachment & affection of negro slaves for the families of their masters," he wrote in his diary, "& especially in the more usual circumstances of careful & kind treatment of the slaves." But the war had not borne out that assumption. "Though some few cases of great attachment & fidelity have been exhibited," he now confessed, "there have been many more of signal ingratitude & treachery of slaves to the most considerate & kind of masters—& the far greater number have merely shown indifference & entire disregard of all such supposed ties of attachment & loyalty."[144]

Eventually the understanding that Ruffin here voiced worked its way into the Confederate leadership's political calculations. On November 10, 1864, congressman Henry C. Chambers opposed the enlistment of slaves on the familiar grounds that "negroes . . . will not fight. All history shows this." Not true, South Carolina congressman William D. Simpson interjected under his breath: "the Yankees made them fight." A third congressman quickly denied that, but by now all such denials were wearing quite thin.[145] Growing numbers of Confederate stalwarts were being forced to recognize (in the words of one letter to the editor) "the fighting capacity of the negro as displayed by those in the Yankee army."[146] "We have learned from dear-bought experience that negroes can be taught to fight," Louisiana governor Henry Allen told James A. Seddon in late September 1864.[147] A well-informed Georgian similarly reminded Gen. Howell Cobb that black soldiers "have done some very good fighting for the Yanks."[148] The Lynchburg *Virginian* specified that engagements around Petersburg and Saltville, Virginia, "where negro soldiers were in the van and suffered most, show that they can be disciplined to take the post of danger and fight for the men who prepare them for it."[149] The Macon *Telegraph and Confederate* published the acknowledgment by an anonymous "distinguished Tennessean" that the Union's use of black troops "has weakened us very much, and added very manifestly to the effective strength of their army."[150] "Some people say the negroes will not fight," a Georgian wrote, but "I say they will fight. They fought at Ocean Pond, Honey Hill, and other places" under Yankee officers.[151]

Thus it was that Gen. Francis A. Shoup informed a Confederate senator in early January that "it is by no means certain that the negro is so deficient in courage as is generally believed." The Army of Tennessee's former chief of artillery and chief of staff added that "the experiences of this war are abundantly sufficient to show his adaptability as a soldier." "The enemy has taught a lesson to which we ought not to shut our eyes," Shoup advised. Lincoln had induced blacks "to fight as well if not better than have his white troops of the same length of service."[152] Writing to Jefferson Davis, a Louisiana-born infantryman attributed "the protracted duration of the war" to the part that former slaves were playing in the Union war effort. "Seward," this soldier noted, "has boldly laid down the proposition of an irresistible conflict between free and slave labour." In light of how the armed struggle itself had evolved, he imagined, the Union's secretary of state now "no doubt often recalls this, as the most sage remark of his life."[153] Georgia editor Henry L. Flash put it more succinctly. The black Union soldier, his *Telegraph and Confederate* granted, "fights willingly and fiendishly for his own freedom."[154]

As these realities sank in, the more perceptive Confederates drew the inescapable conclusion—that slavery was dying and would not be resurrected. At the end of 1863, even as Patrick Cleburne was composing his memorandum, a southern journalist in Atlanta "often hear[d] remarks such as that slavery is doomed; that though the South achieve her independence, she will lose slavery."[155] Simultaneously Margaret Daily of Georgia was confiding in her diary, "I tremble for the institution of slavery; it is well nigh done for."[156] The Tennessee planter John H. Bills was not so far behind, concluding in the summer of 1864 that "Negro slavery is about played out."[157] By the beginning of 1865, even such stalwart Confederates as Georgia's Mary Akin and South Carolina's Mary Jones could read the handwriting on the wall. "I think slavery is now gone," Akin wrote her husband on January 8.[158] "The foundations of society are broken up," Jones wrote in her journal the next day. "What hereafter is to be our social and civil status we cannot see."[159] "Slavery is certainly abolished," Lt. Col. Walter Clark wrote from camp in the spring, "and the only use of the Institution now is to aid us in gaining our Independence."[160]

The same kind of realism informed the thinking of those who pointed the way toward putting slaves in the Confederate army. By the war's third year, the frankest and most cold-blooded Confederate leaders were coming to recognize a series of key facts. Slaves had demonstrated that they were not content in bondage, that they were not loyal to those who kept them there, and that they were ready to act boldly and decisively in pursuit of freedom. It was time to acknowledge all this and to conclude from it that slavery was doomed, that it had become not a military advantage but a military weakness, and that (partly for this reason) the South was losing the war. Only by enlisting southern blacks into its own armies, as fully fledged soldiers, did the Confederacy stand any chance at all of surviving. Dithering now about whether it was advisable to draw slaves into the war was similarly pointless. That had already happened. The only question that remained was: on which side should they fight? If they did not fight for the Confederacy, they would most surely continue to fight—and in ever greater numbers—on behalf of the Union. "If we fail to call them out, and employ them," Judah P. Benjamin told a mass public meeting in Richmond in February 1865, "the Yankees will come and take them."[161] "It is now becoming daily more evident to all reflecting persons," Jefferson Davis averred, "that we are reduced to choosing whether the negroes shall fight for or against us."[162] Indeed, Davis confided to Virginia governor William Smith, he had fashioned his own proposal in order to "draw into our military service" precisely "that portion of the negroes which would be most apt to run away and join the army of the enemy."[163]

This raised another question, however: How *could* the Confederacy draw those slaves into its own military service? And how, if it managed to do so, could the Confederacy be sure of receiving loyal service from such black soldiers? Wartime experience suggested a solution to this puzzle, too. Since slaves indisputably wanted to be free, those anxious to place them in the army had better grant them that fervent wish. A candidate for the Virginia legislature was "convinced that we cannot induce them to fight to perpetuate their own slavery."[164] Only the hope of freedom, Jefferson Davis noted in November 1864, would give the slave a "motive for a zealous discharge of duty."[165]

To ignore that hope, to try to arm slaves *without* freeing (or at least promising to free) them, would be simply foolhardy. Judah P. Benjamin said so in his speech in Richmond in February 1865. If the Confederacy simply tried to force its slaves into the army, "they will go against us."[166] A letter published earlier in a Richmond newspaper (also possibly written by Benjamin) warned that it would be "a dangerous experiment to withhold from the negro soldier his personal freedom—a boon which *he* highly esteems—whilst that boon is freely offered to him in the neighboring hostile camp."[167] Robert E. Lee saw clearly that "unless their freedom is guaranteed to them," the Confederacy "shall get no volunteers."[168] He also advised that to try to compel blacks to serve while still enslaved "would be neither just *nor wise*."[169]

A letter appearing in a Georgia newspaper in April, signed "Woodson," made the same point more sharply. Woodson recalled that Confederate Brig. Gen. Francis Shoup had declared his wish to arm blacks while "let[ting] the slavery question remain where it is." Unfortunately, Woodson responded, the general's wish was not the only one that mattered. "Suppose that after the negro has learned the power that lies in fire-arms, has been taught how to wield that power, has exercised the right of using arms in his own defense, has become accustomed to killing white men, he the negro soldier, formerly the slave, should decline 'to let the slavery question remain where it is,' what then?"[170]

But it was Patrick Cleburne who had addressed this aspect of the subject, as so many others, with the greatest clarity and boldness. Coupling emancipation with enlistments was not only just and fair, Cleburne declared; "it is politic besides." The inescapable fact was that "the negro has been dreaming of freedom" for "many years," and "to attain it he will tempt dangers and difficulties not exceeded by the bravest soldier in the field." "The hope of freedom"—and the Union's promise to grant it—made the slaves in our midst "dangerous now" to the Confederacy. That danger would be multiplied "a thousand fold" if the same slaves were to be "armed, trained, and collected in an army" of our own. That was why "we must bind him to our cause by no doubtful bonds; we must leave no possible loophole for treachery to creep in." The only way to do that was to "make free men of them" and "thus enlist their sympathies."[171]

Nations commonly tell their stories in the form of biographies of their great men, and the United States is certainly no exception. In such narratives, celebrated and powerful individual leaders appear as history's authors, making the decisions that decide the fate of the country and shape the lives of the great mass of its anonymous common people. Often lost in such accounts is the fact that the actions of those same common people—including the most apparently powerless of them—can profoundly influence the thought and conduct of much more obviously influential and certainly better-known elites.

The wartime initiatives of American slaves represent a case in point. Taking advantage of opportunities created by the war, slaves helped induce Union political and military leaders to alter radically the assumptions, plans, and methods with which they had begun the conflict. That is how such unlikely individuals as Benjamin Butler and William T. Sherman had become liberators. Historians of the Civil War have come to recognize this fact. Less well known is the way in which the combination of slave initiative and altered

Union policy also compelled Confederate leaders to revise their plans. By deserting their masters, by aiding and joining Union armies, black southerners aggravated Confederate manpower problems while also suggesting a way to resolve them. Only by placing slaves in *gray* uniforms, it seemed increasingly clear by 1864, did the South have a prayer of fielding armies large enough to avoid defeat. But blacks' conduct during the war constrained Confederate planning even further than that. It forced Confederate realists to recognize that only by promising liberty to such slaves could they even hope to enlist such assistance.

Whether or not even that promise could enlist such aid was a question yet to be answered. In the meantime, critics of the proposal asked another and perhaps even more fundamental one: Why would slaveowners want to win the war if victory required surrendering their "peculiar institution"?

4

"WE CAN DEVISE THE MEANS"

The Long-Term Plan

T he wartime disintegration of bondage—and black southerners' active and effective aid to the Union armies—encouraged Confederate plans to avoid military defeat by placing slaves in gray uniforms and offering them freedom in exchange. But why would the planter elite and its political representatives consider *such* a victory worth winning? Wouldn't that kind of triumph prove Pyrrhic? For most southern leaders, the Confederate cause was inseparable from that of preserving slavery. Everything else—states' rights, southern self-government, southern honor, white supremacy, the "southern way of life" as a whole—served, grew out of, required, or derived its meaning from chattel slavery. What was the point of winning the war if victory required sacrificing the war effort's key aim and purpose?

Some well-informed Northerners, closely following the debate raging in the southern press, asked themselves these same questions. They could only conclude that the war had driven desperate southern leaders to idiocy, madness, or suicide. Horace Greeley's New York *Tribune* dismissed as simply "hare-brained" the idea of "arming the slaves to uphold a Rebellion whose sole purpose was the aggrandizement and perpetuation of Slavery."[1] In now deciding to dismantle "their 'divine institution' for which they commenced the war," Illinois Republican governor Richard Yates declared, Confederate leaders reveal that they have been "driven to madness and despair." They claim to be doing this in defense of self-government. But "of what use" will their own "government be to the rebels when their slaves are free," Yates quite reasonably wondered.[2] Confederate talk about arming and freeing slaves reminded the New York *Times* of a "scorpion gut[ted] with fire that turns and stings itself to death."[3] The New York *Herald* thought it yet another proof that "whom the gods would destroy they first make mad."[4]

Beneath all these similes and metaphors lay the assumption that for the Confederacy to free its slaves meant abandoning its core war program. Like most contemporaneous critics and subsequent commentators, these observers assumed that Confederate plans to arm and emancipate slaves demonstrated a weak (or, at least, a now weakened) commitment to the southern elite's most vital economic institutions and interests. Some denied that protecting slave-worked plantations had ever been central to the Confederate cause. Others acknowledged that it had been a priority at first but claimed that such concerns had declined in importance during the war, to be replaced eventually by a nationalistic commitment to southern independence for its own sake.[5] "The bill providing for the arming and freeing of the slaves," according to one modern scholar, "perfectly demonstrated the depth of southern nationalism and its new life independent of the slave culture that had originally given birth to the Confederacy."[6]

This reading of the proposal's meaning gained additional credibility from the way in which various contemporaries justified it. Some southerners did champion this measure in the name of patriotic duty, calling on slaveowners to sacrifice their own interests for the sake of the southern nation. Subsequent writers then accepted this way of framing both the alternatives posed and their authors' motives.

That is how Patrick Cleburne and his proposal have gone into most of the books and essays that discuss them. There Cleburne commonly appears as an immigrant non-slaveholder uninterested in preserving bondage but dedicated to the right of his neighbors to govern themselves. He had been living in the South for almost a dozen years by the time of the Civil War's outbreak. But, he told his brother in May of 1861, he had "never owned a Negro and care nothing for them." He was marching off to fight on behalf of his adoptive Arkansas to preserve neither its plantations, labor system, nor even its code of white supremacy. He rallied to the Stars and Bars because "these people," who "have been my friends and have stood up [for] me on all occasions," were resisting tyranny.[7] Two and a half years later, Cleburne seemed once again to elevate southern patriotism and independence above slavery when he declared that, given a choice between defeat and emancipation, "every patriot will. . . freely give up the negro slave rather than be a slave himself."[8] Soon thereafter, an angry Brig. Gen. Clement H. Stevens dismissed Cleburne's proposal as the work of a man who, because "foreign born and reared," was "opposed to slavery" and had no "proper conception of the Negro." Many others, then and later, viewed the subject in the same light.[9]

A number of modern accounts portray Jefferson Davis, too, as being narrowly preoccupied with attaining the goal of southern independence. "From the first days of the war," writes one very able historian, the "attainment of independence" (and no longer the preservation of slavery) had become Davis's "paramount goal."[10] And, as in the case of Cleburne, some go still further and assert that Davis had reconciled himself some years earlier to eventual emancipation.[11]

Of all Confederate leaders it is Robert E. Lee who still enjoys the strongest and most widespread reputation for being hostile to slavery.[12] Throughout his life, according to biographer Douglas Southall Freeman, Lee "had believed steadfastly in gradual emancipation."[13] Even a writer less enamored of Lee, Prof. T. Harry Williams, accepted this view of the Virginian. "He did not believe in slavery and he did not believe in secession," Williams wrote, "yet he elected to fight to defend both because his state seceded . . . The pull of his home state—its houses, its soil, its rivers, its people—overpowered his mental or rational nature."[14] Contemporary opponents of the Cleburne-Davis measures, as we have seen, reinforced that reputation by attributing the general's support for a black-soldier law to deeply ingrained antislavery opinions of his own.[15] Lee's postwar claim to have foreseen even in 1861 the need not only for "the use of negroes as soldiers" but also for "a proclamation of gradual emancipation" helped further strengthen the antislavery credentials of the Confederacy's erstwhile general in chief.[16] So did his postwar assertion that slavery's end had gladdened both him and the rest of the South's best men.[17]

These portraits of Cleburne, Davis, and Lee, by reinforcing their subjects' antislavery reputations, reciprocally strengthened the presumption that black-soldier proposals must have embodied just such heterodox opinions, must have represented a definite turn away from slaveowner interests and values. And so a basic misconception was born.

In fact, each of these men was a tested upholder of bondage. Both Patrick Cleburne and his longtime associate Thomas C. Hindman stood firmly in the proslavery camp. Before the war Hindman had been a lawyer and an aggressively proslavery Democratic party leader in (and congressman from) Helena, the seat of a cotton-growing Arkansas county where slaves outnumbered whites. Hindman supported the slave-state cause in "Bleeding Kansas" and later even endorsed the extreme measure of reopening the international slave trade that Congress had outlawed about a half-century earlier.[18] Cleburne did not hold public office, but during the 1850s he and Hindman were partners not only in the practice of law but also in political life; and both men continued steadfastly to support the most proslavery wing of the national Democratic party down through secession and war.[19]

As for Lee, it is true, as his admirers stress, that the general manumitted some 170 slaves at the end of December 1862. This, however, tells us little about Lee's personal views on the merits of the peculiar institution. Lee had inherited those bondspeople from his father-in-law, Washington Parke Custis. Custis had stipulated in his will that all those people be manumitted within five years of his own death, which occurred in 1857.[20] Robert E. Lee was thus merely executing the provisions of that will when he freed the slaves in question.

Lee's reputation as an opponent of slavery also rests in part on a letter he wrote to his wife, Mary, in 1856 that referred to bondage as "a moral and political evil."[21] But those words merely expressed an opinion long common among Upper South masters, an opinion that had prevented few from remaining masters. It was an evil, they held, but a necessary one.[22] Like so many of his neighbors, therefore, Lee was perfectly able to acknowledge slavery's shortcomings and anticipate its eventual extinction even as he continued to affirm slavery's essential role in his own time and even as he rejected all practical efforts to hasten bondage's demise. This outlook informed the letter to Mary Custis Lee. While slavery was indeed an evil, Lee argued there, it was "useless to expatiate on its disadvantages" because "the painful discipline" that the slaves "are undergoing, is necessary for their instruction as a race." Only such discipline and instruction, Lee explained, could "prepare and lead them to better things" some day. It was just as useless to speculate about when that day might arrive, moreover, because just "how long their subjugation may be necessary is known & ordered by a wise Merciful Providence." Lee expressed little sense of urgency about the pace of this providential process. "We must leave the progress as well as the result" of this process, he advised, "in his hands who sees the end; who Chooses to work by slow influences; & with whom two thousand years are but a Single day." In the interim slavery would remain the proper status for blacks in America.[23] Lee adhered to this view in deed as well as word. In 1859, a number of slaves on his Arlington estate tried to escape to Pennsylvania. Apprehended in Maryland, they were returned to Lee, who reportedly ordered them sent into southern Virginia, where (as Lee's admiring biographer, Douglas Southall Freeman, explained) "there would be less danger of their absconding."[24]

Six years later, Lee reaffirmed his belief in slavery's rightness, when he wrote to state senator Andrew Hunter about employing blacks as Confederate soldiers. "The relation of master and slave, controlled by humane laws and influenced by Christianity and enlightened public sentiment," he solemnly declared on that occasion, was "the best that can exist between the white and black races while intermingled as at present in this country."[25] Unfortunately, Lee continued, events beyond the masters' control had now made the survival of that ideal relationship impossible; the war had already doomed slavery as such. That fact and the military needs of a hard-pressed Confederacy, he emphasized—and no long-standing critique of bondage— lay behind his support for this emergency measure.

Jefferson Davis, a prominent defender of slavery and champion of the slaveholder's prerogatives, had reached the same conclusion in much the same way.[26] The notion that Davis had long accepted slavery's impermanence rests partly on a misunderstanding—in this case, on a misreading of a manuscript that Davis drafted sometime in the 1850s. Some read that manuscript as anticipating that the growth of population would ultimately lead to the replacement of black slaves by more efficient free white workers. Davis supposedly concluded from this expectation (in the words of one historian) that "the South could not preserve its world forever."[27]

A closer reading of that document, however, suggests a diametrically opposite interpretation. Davis was trying in that manuscript to discredit antebellum northern attempts to confine slavery to the states in which it already existed. To do that, he employed a line of argument that had by then already become rather commonplace in proslavery circles. At present, it held, blacks were valuable property, and for that reason masters carefully maintained them year-round in good health and tolerable comfort. But if restricted to the places where they already lived, slave populations there would eventually increase to the point where black labor became plentiful (and therefore cheap) enough there to be devalued. They would be discharged from year-round service and hired and fired (like any other wage-earner) according to the momentary needs of the employer. They would be poorly paid or not employed at all, would likely be replaced by wage-earners of the inherently superior white race, and finally left to starve in great numbers.[28] Davis's manuscript, in short, was intended to furnish a humane justification for slavery's unfettered geographical expansion—"to enable our people," as Davis put it in one 1851 speech, "to develop an outlet for the black population of the country."[29] Here was no recognition of slavery's ineluctably transient character; here was an attempt to prolong its life indefinitely.

The Confederate military and political figures who took the lead in pushing for the arming and emancipating of slaves were thus by no means hostile to slavery on principle. They certainly did not eagerly await its early demise. It is equally mistaken to believe that their purblind southern nationalism had led them to discard or devalue the interests of the planter class. Confederate nationalists they may have become, and haters of the Yankee-dominated Union they certainly were. But they had come to their iconoclastic proposals because they were able, sooner or later, to recognize unpleasant realities and to reformulate their plans in the light of those realities.

The combined efforts of Union armies and the slaves themselves, they saw, had driven the plantation system and the planters' government to the brink of destruction. If events continued to unfold in that way, the rest of the South's military-age male slaves would likely also be drawn into Union ranks. Thus reinforced, the enemy's forces would overwhelm their already outnumbered foes. Confederate military defeat would inevitably follow. The social and political consequences of such a defeat, Davis and his co-thinkers believed, would be disastrous for southern patriots generally but for slaveholders in particular. A militarily triumphant Republican government would surely make good its 1864 platform promise to complete the destruction of chattel slavery. "If we fail in the establishment of our independence," as one North Carolinian pointed out, "slavery is lost beyond the possibility of a doubt."[30]

Bleak as the prospect of imposed emancipation seemed, moreover, it would only constitute the first step in the Union's postwar program. As experience along the Atlantic coast and in the lower Mississippi valley seemed to prove, Republicans would also confiscate southern farms and plantations and turn them over to their own supporters, black and white. Complete Yankee victory would mean our utter "robbery and spoliation and ruin," explained the Richmond Sentinel.[31] If the Confederacy is conquered "all our property [will] be swept from us into the public coffers of the Yankees, or divided out in portions and rewards to a hireling soldiery."[32]

The organization of political life and the distribution of civic liberties in the South would also change dramatically for the worse. The conquerors would wrench legislative, executive, and judicial power from the grasp of the region's traditional leaders (the planters) and place it instead into the hands of northern interlopers, southern white traitors, and—worst of all—the South's black former laborers and servants.

To those willing to arm and free slaves on the Confederacy's behalf, this apocalyptic vision of defeat's consequences justified even the most extreme sacrifices. "If Lincoln succeeds in arming our slaves against us," the Jackson Mississippian had warned in August of 1863, "he will succeed in making them our masters. He will reverse the social order of things at the South."[33] Patrick Cleburne had begun his December 1863 memo by urging his fellow officers "to understand the meaning of subjugation before it is too late. We can give but a faint idea when we say it means the loss of all we now hold most sacred—slaves and all other personal property, lands, homesteads, liberty, justice, safety, pride, manhood" and acceptance of a world in which "our former slaves" will control us like a "secret police."[34] Lose this war, Louisiana Governor Henry W. Allen warned his state's legislature in mid-January, and "your negroes will be made your equals, your lands will be declared confiscate, and you will become the slaves of the very hirelings who are now waging war upon you."[35]

There was only one way to avoid this terrible fate, Cleburne, Davis, and company agreed. The Confederacy must deprive the Union of thousands of potential black soldiers and place them instead in the Confederate ranks. And—given the starkly displayed slave desire for freedom and the Union emancipation policy already in place—only a Confederate promise of manumission could conceivably induce slaves to risk death on the South's behalf.

But, claimed R. M. T. Hunter and many others, implementing such a policy was incompatible with the *status quo ante bellum*. Of course it is, calmly replied Benjamin, Davis, and Lee; but antebellum life no longer provided the proper yardstick with which to measure current policy options. Prewar southern society was already irrevocably lost. Davis and his allies flatly denied that arming and freeing slaves was to abandon—indeed, was to betray—the cause of the plantation South. They did grant that the course they advocated involved large costs and real risks. They nonetheless insisted that their plan—and their plan alone—offered a way to salvage at least something of slavery from the Old South's wreckage.

The Richmond *Whig* initially opposed the measure but eventually acquiesced in it. And the *Whig*'s editor, James McDonald, then bridled when die-hard opponents accused Robert E. Lee and other advocates of disloyalty to the Old South. Support for the proposal reflected no "unsoundness in this State, on the subject of slavery," the *Whig* indignantly declared. "People who think that the gift of emancipation would better enable us to utilize the resources presented by our supply of negroes, are not therefore abolitionists." Their proposal was instead "the natural development of the necessities of the crisis." As for slavery, McDonald explained, "we hope to preserve it. We believe we can preserve it."[36]

The Virginian who styled himself "Barbarrossa" (and who, as noted, may have been Judah P. Benjamin) had said as much in his December 1864 open letter. Some might fear, Barbarrossa noted, "that these bold and novel principles may unsettle the foundation of slavery," but the truth "is exactly the reverse." By making the slave more militarily useful to the southern nation, "you do not shake the institution, but, in reality, give it broader bottom." Those who *truly* threatened slavery's future were those would-be defenders who opposed this essential measure. "We must rescue the infant," Barbarrossa admonished, "from the fond, delusive, stifling caresses of those who claim to be its only friends."[37]

Especially at first, defenders of the proposal tended to measure its conservative nature quantitatively. Their plan would not emancipate and arm *all* of the South's slaves but only a relatively small proportion of them. These black soldiers would then, by salvaging the Confederate military effort, secure Confederate independence—and, in the bargain, secure the continuing enslavement of all the rest.

To some proslavery purists, this was an impossibility. "When a part is sacrificed," Texas cavalry colonel Clayton Gillespie proclaimed, "the whole is tarnished, worthless."[38] But to others it was just good, basic arithmetic. One planter thus wrote concerning his own slave property, "I prefer to give a part of mine to fight for the country" in order that "I may keep the remainder."[39] The proposal at hand, explained the Mobile *Register*, only "affects units of the race and not the whole institution."[40] The Richmond *Sentinel* chimed in a few weeks later. "If the emancipation of a part is the means of saving the rest, then this partial emancipation is eminently a proslavery measure. If the liberation of forty thousand adds such strength to the military service as to secure the defeat of the enemy, it will save the four millions who remain." Far from signaling capitulation concerning slavery's survival, thus, the plan was "the very means to gain it!"[41] Acting in this way, Lynchburg editor Charles W. Button explained, "is like a man giving up a portion of his property to secure undisturbed possession of the residue."[42]

The Richmond *Sentinel*'s Richard M. Smith sought to clarify the idea with a colorful analogy. "When pirates are pursuing," he explained, "it is better to sacrifice the cargo, if need be, in order to facilitate escape, rather than lose both ship and cargo."[43] Louisiana's Thomas J. Semmes liked the image well enough to repeat it on the floor of the Confederate Senate.[44] Rep. Ethelbert Barksdale of Mississippi amended it to emphasize the partial nature of the emancipation contemplated. We will sacrifice a part to save the whole, Barksdale explained, just "as a part of a cargo of a vessel in a storm at sea is thrown overboard in order to save the remainder." "If we triumph in the end," Barksdale concluded, "the institution itself will be preserved."[45]

Such words remind us that for those who uttered them, at least, military triumph and the Confederacy's survival were not nationalistic ends in themselves. They were the practical and necessary means with which to preserve the old regime and the forced-labor system on which it rested.[46] The only real choice facing the South, the Richmond *Sentinel* held, was between "submission and Emancipation complete, oppressive, ruinous" or "independence with Slavery complete, if possible, or as much of it as may be."[47] Those planters who villified the Davis administration for trying to take away their property were completely missing the point, ignoring the bigger picture. They reminded Judah P. Benjamin (as he told a mass meeting in February 1865) of "a man rushing forth from his burning house, and begging his neighbors, for Heaven's sake, not to throw water on his blazing roof, because it might spoil his furniture." The telling jibe earned Benjamin an appreciative round of applause.[48]

Ultimately, however, the hope of freeing some slaves while maintaining most in chains came to seem unrealistic to the most perceptive, far-sighted Confederates. The peculiar institution was simply disintegrating too swiftly for such a plan to succeed. Benjamin and Lee agreed with their critics on one point, at least—that even a limited manumission of slave-soldiers must eventually lead to universal emancipation.[49] Would blacks fight to keep their own family members, friends, and neighbors in chains? Especially when they knew that a Union victory *would* bring freedom to all? And if some did agree to fight in exchange only for their own liberty, what would prevent them subsequently from employing the experience, skills, organization, and arms that they thereby acquired to force the Confederacy to emancipate all the others as well?

These concerns did not induce proslavery advocates of the plan to abandon it. Even if all of the South's slaves had to be freed in order to preserve the Confederacy, they believed, it was still worth the price. Because even in that case southern whites would still retain not only their own personal freedom but all the rest of their considerable property as well. Even more important, as the Richmond *Sentinel* pointed out, we will retain political supremacy; we will retain control of our own government. If our plan leaves us "stripped of our property, but master of the government," then "our situation . . . would be infinitely better than if despoiled by the enemy, and wearing his bonds."[50] This was everything. As still "master of the government," southern planters would find that many other things would remain possible, too. Planter-controlled governments in Richmond and the various Confederate state capitals would shape an emancipation process that best fit planter needs.

The Jackson *Mississippian* had seen and said much of this in the summer of 1863. If by using black troops, its editor argued, we are able to fend off Lincoln's forces, then "our liberties will remain intact; the land will be ours, and the industrial system of the country [will be] still controlled by Southern men."[51] Southern men would exert that control in order (as the Richmond *Sentinel* phrased it) to preserve "as much of it [slavery] as may be" preserved. But this would mean limiting emancipation's scope not quantitatively but qualitatively. Salvaging as much as possible of slavery would not mean withholding the largest possible number of slaves from the emancipation process. Instead it would mean preserving as much as possible of the kernel, the core, the functional essence of the slave-labor system as a whole. It meant maintaining control of the black labor force not merely through northern-style market-based compulsion but through the physical coercion that southerners had always considered necessary in their economy. It was urgent to preserve a separate and independent Confederate regime, in fact, precisely so that it could dictate the pace, the terms, the nature and the degree of freedom that was to be conferred upon the former slaves.

The Mobile *Register* doubted it would come to "universal emancipation." But should the survival of the Confederacy require it, even such an outcome "would be better than to confront *both* our subjugation and emancipation."[52]

If the road to independence does lead through "the destruction of slavery in the South," the Lynchburg *Virginian* editorialized, surely "we should still be better off as masters of the situation than to have the slaves freed by our Yankee masters." In the former case, after all, "we should have the satisfaction of accomplishing it [emancipation] our own way," a way that would leave southern blacks more "useful to us" than if our sworn enemies controlled the process. In contrast, if southern whites retained that control, then at the very least "the fact that their [blacks'] freedom was due to our action would make them much more docile and obedient to our rule than if they should owe their liberty to the enemy." Perhaps more importantly, the survival of the Confederacy would allow the white South to dictate the status of the former slaves—to "regulate their conditions among us." If we lose the war, in contrast, editor Charles Button elaborated, "universal emancipation follows" anyway, but in that case "not we, but our villainous foes would fix the status of the freedmen."[53]

Just how might Confederate emancipation differ from a Union-imposed version? Perhaps in its pacing, the Wilmington *North Carolinian* suggested. The Confederate government could choose to slow the emancipation process, perhaps drastically. "If, to secure our independence, the abolition of slavery be necessary," the editor volunteered, he for one was "prepared to adopt a conservative, safe and practical course in the matter." One such would be "the extinguishment of the institution after a series of years" so that "a century hence, it would be extinct in these Confederate States."[54]

But ultimately, the key difference between Union and Confederate emancipation would be found in the nature of the legal status that would replace slavery. Judah P. Benjamin's old college friend, Prof. Frederick A. Porcher, elaborated.[55] Porcher was no less ardent a devotee of slavery than was Davis, Benjamin, or Lee. During the 1850s he had published a series of essays that movingly evoked the miseries and injustices borne by the Northern poor and the hypocritical justifications thereof favored by the Northern rich.[56] They also enthused that the South had been spared such shameful abominations because paternalistic slavery had inculcated into masters an "unselfish consideration of the claims of others." Indeed, Porcher contended further, this "considerateness pervades our whole civilization" precisely because "our whole fabric of society is based upon slave institutions." So it had been, and so it would continue to be. "The fact of slavery is here," he asserted, "and a fact it must remain," not only in the short run, indeed, but "until the end of time." Porcher's secessionism grew directly out of his regard for southern distinctiveness. For the South to remain bound to the philosophically and culturally alien free states would be, he concluded, "under any circumstances" a mistake.[57]

But his admiration for the peculiar institution did not prevent Porcher from deciphering the wartime writing on the wall. The slave system he had long championed was now doomed, he understood, and that fact must now become the point of departure in charting the South's future policy. In mid-December 1864 Porcher communicated that conviction to his old school-mate, now the Confederate secretary of state. If we do nothing or act with insufficient haste, he warned Benjamin, "we shall find ourselves in fact controlled by the inferior race, instead of being their masters." In contrast, the right kind of "plan of emancipation," if enacted in due time, "would keep our negroes under our control." It would do that by permitting white men to design and supervise "the change from slavery to freedom." In the process, they could specify "the conditions on which freedom shall be granted" and "make statutes for the regulation of labour."[58]

Judah P. Benjamin wholeheartedly concurred with his old friend. He had been reconsidering his views about this subject for about a year, he told Porcher. Perhaps reading a copy of Patrick Cleburne's memorandum back in January 1864 had initiated that reevaluation. Or perhaps the prodding of some other old acquaintances, Duncan Kenner and Benjamin H. Micou, had done so. A number of historians believe that it was Benjamin who inspired Jefferson Davis's about-face on the subject in the fall of 1864.[59] Identifying Benjamin's precise role in and thinking about this matter is greatly complicated by his cautious postwar decision to destroy much of his correspondence and whatever private journals he may have kept.[60] The little that survives, however, is sufficient to indicate how he anticipated reconciling emancipation with the needs of postwar southern planters.

Benjamin provided one clue when he proposed before a large public meeting in Richmond in early February that the Confederacy "yield what we believe to be the best system on earth under protest, and take the next best system which could be obtained."[61] By then Benjamin had already enlarged upon that idea in his private correspondence with Frederick Porcher. When the Richmond government proposed manumissions, Benjamin had confided in December 1864, it was looking ahead to neither interracial democracy nor the end of plantation society. On the contrary, "ultimate emancipation" would come to southern blacks only after they had passed through "an intermediate state of serfage or peonage" of unspecified duration. So that, "while vindicating our faith in the doctrine that the negro is an inferior race and unfitted for social or political equality with the white man," the South could still "modify and ameliorate the existing condition of that inferior race" by affording it "legal protection for the marital and parental relations" and "by providing for it *certain* rights of property" and "a *certain* degree of personal liberty."[62] But no more.

Jefferson Davis read an even fuller elaboration of this line of thinking in a letter he received a few months later. That missive's author, Dr. John Henry Stringfellow of Virginia, was certainly not a longtime doubter of slavery's

value or legitimacy nor even a single-minded southern nationalist who val-
ued slavery less than regional pride and independence. Stringfellow had played
a prominent role in the antebellum campaign to spread the peculiar institution westward. During the mid-1850s, he had helped to lead the proslavery
militia in the conflict-torn Kansas Territory. As speaker of that territory's
House of Representatives in 1855, he sponsored a resolution declaring it
"the duty of the pro-slavery party" to "know but one issue, Slavery" and to
regard anyone less dedicated and clearly focused "as an ally of Abolition."[63]
At Stringfellow's instigation, proslavery Kansas legislators that same year
formally barred antislavery individuals from public office, made it unlawful
to question slavery's legality, and resolved to execute anyone who aided a
fugitive slave.[64] Lest any ambiguity remain, Stringfellow warned (in his capacity as editor of the proslavery Atchison *Squatter Sovereign*) that "to enforce the laws" he and his allies would "make the blood flow as freely as do
the turbid waters of the Missouri." Indeed, he promised, we will "continue to
lynch and hang and to tar and feather, and drown every white-livered abolitionist who dares to pollute our soil."[65]

In short, Stringfellow was a passionate and violent paladin of slavery.
But he was also a realist, and by the end of 1857 the proslavery cause in
Kansas had been irretrievably lost.[66] In 1858 Stringfellow returned to his
native Virginia.[67] With the outbreak of war three years later, he raised a
company of Old Dominion volunteers and led it to the front; he later served
as an army surgeon. In February 1865 Stringfellow was living on a farm in
the town of Glen Allen, near the Confederate capital, when he shared his
thoughts about black troops and the South's future with the Confederacy's
president.[68]

Stringfellow told Davis that he
was "amazed to see that no one thus
far has conceived, or if conceived had
the boldness to present, in my judgment, the only solution of all these
perils and difficulties." But he did
grant that Davis had "already taken
a long stride in the right direction"
and guessed that the president's

Dr. John Henry Stringfellow had
helped to lead the proslavery forces in
Kansas during the 1850s. This
photograph was taken later in his life.
(The Kansas State Historical Society,
Topeka, Kansas)

"mind has already reached the true solution, but owing to peculiar circumstances has hesitated to enunciate it." Stringfellow then proceeded to lay out the case for proceeding down the road on which he presumed the administration had already embarked.

Before doing so, however, he wished to reiterate his firm belief in slavery's moral legitimacy and practical utility. I have "always believed, and still believe," he affirmed, "that slavery is an institution sanctioned, if not established, by the Almighty, and the most humane and beneficent relation that can exist between labor and capital." The fact remained, however, that "if the war continues" along its current lines "we shall in the end be subjugated, our negroes emancipated, our lands parceled out amongst them, and if any of it be left to us, only an equal portion with our own negroes, and ourselves given only equal (if any) social and political rights and privileges." It was therefore necessary to reverse the war's course. And that was possible only through "a change of policy in relation to the conduct of the war, and that a radical one." At the core of such a radical policy change, he continued, was the "prompt abolition of slavery."[69]

But that did not have to mean the plantation system's demise, Stringfellow hastened to explain. Indeed, he had concluded, only the measures he had in mind could save that system. The key, for Stringfellow as for others before him, lay in the identity of the emancipator. For "if *we* emancipate, our independence is secured, the white man only will have any and all political rights" and will "retain all his real and personal property" except for his slaves. He alone, therefore, will be in a position to "make laws to control the free negro."[70] The latter, meanwhile, "having no land, must labor for the landowner"—indeed, will have to do so "on terms about as economical as though owned by him."

Stringfellow hammered at that point over and over again. "[I]f we emancipate," Stringfellow reiterated, the slave-owner of today will still "have all his labour on his farm that he had before," because the ex-slave, "having no home & no property to buy one with," will have no choice but to "live with & work for his old owner for such wages as said owner may choose to give," those wages "to be regulated by law hereafter as may suit the change of relation." After suggesting how the Confederate government might finance the compensation of masters for their slaves, Stringfellow returned yet again to his more fundamental point: "In my judgment, the only question for us to decide is whether we shall gain our independence by freeing the negro, we retaining all the power to regulate them by law when so freed, or permit our enemies through our own slaves to compel us to submit to emancipation with equal or superior rights for our negroes, and partial or complete confiscation of our property for the benefit of the negro."

Stringfellow offered his letter as "food for thought" in hopes that it might "aid you in guiding our ship through the perils and darkness which surround her." Perhaps he thought Davis might find it useful to circulate it privately for the purposes of clarifying government policy. It apparently reached Davis on February 11, and after reading it, the president did pass it along to his new secretary of war, John C. Breckinridge, who had evidently supported the slave-soldier idea since his days with the Army of Tennessee.

John Henry Stringfellow considered himself Davis's friend, and the postwar Republican regime would treat him like a member of the Rebel leadership.[71] In 1865, however, he was evidently not privy to discussions within the Confederacy's upper echelons. His letter was all the more remarkable, therefore, for spelling out in detail and at length a line of long-term planning that key Confederate political and military leaders had (as Stringfellow surmised) already endorsed, although chiefly in private communications and conversations—no doubt because, as Stringfellow noted, "it might be imprudent to discuss this thing publicly."

In frankness, clarity, and completeness, this letter ranked with Patrick Cleburne's remarkable memorandum of December 1863. In its treatment of the policy's implications for the plantation system and its labor force, it was unmatched. (Perhaps Stringfellow's disappointment in Kansas had made him begin thinking earlier than most others about the choices left to masters when slavery was removed from the equation.) But although he had formulated the problem with exceptional clarity, the substance of Stringfrellow's message was not unique. Robert E. Lee had made many of the same points in more compressed form in his January 11 letter to Andrew Hunter. The question facing the Confederacy, Lee there explained, was "whether slavery shall be extinguished by our enemies and the slaves used against us," or whether we shall "use them ourselves at the risk of the effects which may be produced upon our social institutions." Those institutions would be damaged by the change, Lee acknowledged, but the war was fast eroding slavery anyway. Since it was no longer possible to prevent that, the practical questions had narrowed to the way in which bondage would end and what would take its place. The continuing penetration of Union forces into the Confederacy would eventually "destroy slavery in a *manner* most pernicious to the welfare of our people." And "whatever may be the effect of *our* employing negro troops, it cannot be as mischievous as this." Because even if the Confederacy's use of black troops "ends in subverting slavery," at least that "will be accomplished by ourselves, and we can devise the means of alleviating the evil consequences to both races."[72]

These more far-sighted Confederate leaders had thus already arrived at a general consensus about both how to avoid military defeat and how to preserve the plantation system and white supremacy generally. More than a year earlier, Patrick Cleburne had anticipated that consensus in framing his first approximation of the same plan. "It is said slaves will not work after they are freed," Cleburne had noted in December 1863, but "we think necessity and wise legislation will compel them to labor for a living."[73] Cleburne enlarged on that thought soon afterward, during a conversation in Atlanta with Arthur St. Clair Colyar, a Confederate congressman from Tennessee. Cleburne told Colyar that he "considered slavery at an end." But as the general saw it, slavery's demise was only the beginning, not the end, of wisdom. "[I]f the Yankees succeed in abolishing slavery," Cleburne reasoned, "equality and amalgamation will finally take place." But "if we take this step now, we can mould the relations, for all time to come, between the white and colored races." And in that case "we can control the negroes, and . . . they will still be our laborers as much as they now are; and, to all intents and purposes, will be our servants, at less cost than now."[74] Benjamin, Lee, Stringfellow, and others would all later elaborate on this prescription, but not much. In aggregate, their words reveal how a section of the southern elite and its representatives—in the face of powerful external assault and the active rebellion of the slave population within—sought to save what could be saved of its social relations and economic power.

Like the Civil War itself, much about this proposal was, of course, uniquely American. It was not, however, without parallel. For one thing, trans-Atlantic history was filled with forms of coerced labor beside chattel slavery. As southern writers such as George Fitzhugh and J. D. B. De Bow well knew, for example, the laws and practices of the ancient and medieval Mediterranean world offered precedents aplenty for granting people personal but not political rights.[75] Aggressive state action to provide a cheap and intimidated labor force to elites who needed it was also common down through the ages. Following the decline of serfdom in England, for example, monarchs had used political power both to dispossess small producers and to compel them and others to labor for proprietors in return for minimal compensation.[76] Fitzhugh would soon be calling on government to compel southern freedmen to labor just "as the emancipated white slaves of England were forced to labor."[77] In Ireland, "penal laws" that restricted the economic options of Catholics had helped to accomplish similar ends.[78] As the Irish Protestant Patrick Cleburne assured Arthur St. Clair Colyar in January 1864, "writing a man 'free' does not make him so, as the history of the Irish laborer shows."[79] More recent guidelines could be found closer to hand. In the slave states of North America, a network of laws had long strictly curtailed the social, political, and economic rights of free black minorities. So-called apprenticeship laws imposed a form of semi-slavery on free black youths, and various forms of debt peonage were used to maintain control over adults.[80] In contrast, the record of slave emancipation in the British West Indies during the 1830s joined the Saint Domingue (Haiti) experience as a negative object lesson for North

American masters. In Britain's Caribbean colonies, a post-emancipation program of "apprenticeship" intended to restrict the occupational options of former slaves had been quickly abandoned. The destruction of the plantation system, it was widely reported then and later, had been the inevitable result. What was needed, a convention of U.S. cotton planters would later argue, specifically invoking the West Indian experience, was "some well regulated system of labor, . . . devised by the white man."[81]

Without doubt, these and other trans-Atlantic experiments with diverse forms of compulsory labor helped Confederate planners plan for their own post-slavery future. But their attempts to fashion a pro-planter form of emancipation linked these Southerners not only to the past but also to other dramatic developments in their own era. The Confederate proposal to arm and emancipate slaves bore a strong family resemblance to a series of maneuvers attempted by various autocratic regimes threatened with destruction during the eighteenth and nineteenth centuries. The sharp but uneven acceleration of economic, political, and social change that then occurred threw conservative regimes throughout the world onto the defensive. Those unable or unwilling to adapt to the swiftly changing circumstances were swept away. Others sought to avoid destruction by modifying the way they held and exercised power—by bending, that is, in order not to break. Those maneuvers commonly required making some concessions to segments of the lower classes. Each regime attempted to do so, however, in ways that would strengthen itself politically while also safeguarding as much as possible the wealth and privileges of those elite social groups allied with it. Although members of those elites commonly resisted such transformations, the changes involved were considerably less radical than those likely to be imposed by popular revolution or foreign conquest.

One of the earliest of these dramas unfolded in France during the summer of 1789, early in that country's epochal revolution. As peasants in many parts of the country rose in revolt against the privileges, exactions, and representatives of the Old Regime, the newly established National Assembly sought to appease the rural rebels.[82] On the night of August 4, liberal-minded aristocrats encouraged that body to offer peasants the outright abolition of serfdom's vestiges, various compulsory labor services, and other forms of personal obligation. Those concessions would not have given peasants free and clear title to the land they worked, and some seigneurial burdens would also have survived. The National Assembly offered to allow peasants to retire some of those obligations, too, in return for undertaking a stipulated schedule of substantial cash payments to the lords.[83]

The decree embodying this offer proudly announced that it "destroys the feudal regime *entirely*." That was a considerable overstatement, however, since (as Georges Lefebvre pointed out) the peasants' payments to the lords would still have "assured that regime a long life."[84] The National Assembly's decree nevertheless promised a definite reduction in the elite's traditional power and exactions. The liberal nobles who proposed it considered it a prudent concession far preferable to full-fledged rural revolution and all that might entail. The maneuver failed, however. Neither Louis XVI and his inner circle nor the bulk of the French nobility was ready to accept even the limited concessions proposed on August 4.[85] The peasants, it turned out, were scarcely more enthusiastic. Unwilling to pay indefinitely to cancel obligations they considered illegitimate in the first place, they continued to press for more fundamental change. Hopes of arresting the revolutionary process therefore came to naught. Instead, escalating conflict would eventually bring more radical-minded regimes to power in Paris; in 1792–93, governments that stood on the shattered ruins of the monarchy and aristocracy decreed the immediate, uncompensated abolition of all the peasantry's remaining seigneurial burdens.[86]

In August 1789, thus, representatives of France's Old Regime had attempted to quell a menacing challenge from below by proposing to grant from above what they considered a timely set of reforms. Unfortunately for them, however, they had offered too little too late and with insufficient support from the aristocracy as a whole. The tardiness, hesitancy, and inadequacy of that gesture doomed hopes of quelling rural unrest and restricting the revolution's further development. The French nobility would before long pay dearly for that short-sightedness.

Some seven decades later and half a world away, another regime strove more successfully to cope with threats to vested power and privilege. In Japan during the early and mid-nineteenth century, a group of aristocrats, warriors, and merchants gathered around the Meiji emperor nervously eyed both growing domestic turmoil and especially the advancing European domination of India and China, fearing that the same fate awaited their own land.[87] Promising to "revere the emperor, drive out the barbarian," in the late 1860s this group destroyed the increasingly ineffectual military dictatorship that had for centuries governed in the monarchy's name.[88] The restored monarchy soon initiated policies that would eventually centralize and streamline the government, modernize and expand the armed forces, and stimulate industrial development. Pledging to seek knowledge "throughout the world," it thus adapted to change in order to protect itself against it.[89] As one historian observed, the Meiji emperor's policies added up to "the destruction of . . . feudalism *from above*" and the creation of a more modern state.[90] But, as another scholar aptly noted, the architects of this transformation "did not wish to see just *any* kind of modern state, but one that would preserve as much as possible of the advantages the ruling class had enjoyed under the *ancien regime*" while strengthening their hand against domestic and foreign threats to their power.[91] The Meiji government permitted members of the old seigneurial elite to participate in and profit handsomely from the society's transformation. Meanwhile political power remained firmly in the hands of an autocratic and repressive regime.[92]

But the closest and most illuminating parallels to the Confederate emancipation proposals occurred in central and eastern Europe, where rulers strove during the nineteenth century simultaneously to make government and the military more efficient, defuse peasant anger and resentment, and still keep a cheap labor force available to cultivate the aristocracy's landed estates. The violent, bloody, and very radical revolution that engulfed France after 1789 naturally made a tremendous impression on the beneficiaries and upholders of the Old Regime elsewhere on the continent. Some of France's German-speaking neighbors determined to draw and apply the cautionary lessons of that experience in order to spare themselves the French aristocracy's ordeal. They also sought to absorb the lessons of their own defeat in the Napoleonic wars, hoping to avoid future humiliations at the hands of foreign armies that were more numerous, more efficient, and more highly motivated than their own.[93]

After 1807, therefore, Prussian officials introduced a series of reforms aimed at streamlining and strengthening the administrative and military apparatus, drawing talented but not noble-born individuals into the government bureaucracy, encouraging commercial and industrial development, and ameliorating some of the most explosive sources of popular dissatisfaction. They hoped to accomplish all that, however, without significantly redistributing wealth or political power.[94] These measures have gone into history as the Stein-Hardenburg reforms after their architects, Baron Heinrich Karl von Stein and Karl August von Hardenburg. Hardenburg referred to them as the introduction of "democratic principles in a monarchical government"— or, more simply and memorably, as a "revolution from above."[95]

The nature and purpose of the Prussian reforms were perhaps clearest as they affected relations between peasants and landlords.[96] Prussian chancellor Heinrich von Goldbeck captured their purpose when he explained that "it is better to give up something voluntarily than to be forced to sacrifice everything."[97] In Prussia's western territories, peasants working on small farms were permitted to cancel their manorial dues outright in exchange for agreeing to pay the lord a fee equal to from twenty to twenty-five times the previous annual bill.[98] The payment of these fees allowed nobles to evolve into absentee coupon-clippers whose importance in the day-to-day life of the peasants declined apace.[99] But in eastern Prussia, where much larger and very profitable estates dominated, change took a distinct form. There peasants gained legal emancipation only by simultaneously surrendering claims to great blocks of land, which the upper nobility (the *Junkerdom*) absorbed into their own estates. *Junker* power over their laborers, their neighbors, and the Prussian state, meanwhile, was assured by the fact that their previous political supremacy remained unimpaired by other reforms introduced.[100]

The more efficient and strengthened German regimes that emerged from these transformations survived the attempted democratic revolutions that broke out in 1848–49. During the second half of the nineteenth century, under chancellor Otto von Bismarck, a modernized Prussia became the nucleus of a German empire that continued to modernize in the top-down manner that Stein and Hardenburg had pioneered. Indeed, Bismarck accelerated the pace of industrialization despite the resistance of nervous and tradition-minded *Junker* even as he preserved much aristocratic privilege and continued to restrict civil liberty and popular control over government. "If there is to be a revolution," he said, "we want to make it rather than suffer it."[101]

Another variation on this theme took shape in Russia. Beginning in the fourteenth century, the landed elite in Russia (as in most of eastern Europe) had steadily tightened its grip and increased its demands on those who tilled the soil, enserfing most of them by the late sixteenth and early seventeenth centuries.[102] Serfs still comprised about half of the population two hundred years later, at the start of the nineteenth century.[103] But during the next decades international wars and domestic social turmoil induced the Russian monarchy to reevaluate the peasants' condition and status. In the Crimean War (1853–56) Russia suffered a humiliating military defeat at the hands especially of England and France, a defeat that was widely attributed to the backward state of Russian society and especially the underdevelopment of industry, transportation, and communications. Agrarian reform seemed a necessary prerequisite—or, at least, accompaniment—to improvements in those sectors. Successive waves of peasant protest, both before and after the war, added to the sense that large-scale agrarian changes were overdue.[104] As Tsar Alexander II explained to his nobles in 1856, "It is better to abolish serfdom from above than to await the day when it will begin to abolish itself from below."[105]

The example of emancipating peasants while depriving them of the land, roughly on the model of eastern Prussia, appealed to some members of the Russian aristocracy.[106] And just such a plan was in fact implemented in the tsar's Baltic provinces in 1816–19. But the hostile reaction that this program provoked among the peasants there discouraged attempts to apply the same model elsewhere in the empire.[107] The plan finally enacted in 1861 abolished serfdom (that is, granted the peasants legal personal freedom) and provided a mechanism through which peasants might become property owners.[108]

That mechanism, however, favored the interests of the landlords more than those of the peasants. Under its terms, peasants would initially work the land as tenants while paying a regressive scale of rents. Later they might seek title to land. But nothing compelled the landlords to agree, and even when they did the purchase prices demanded were commonly pegged high above the land's actual value. Those peasants who were able to buy land in this way, therefore, often struggled under a heavy debt burden for the next half-century.

The Russian government did provide another means through which a peasant family could obtain some land. It could elect to accept a very small piece of land immediately and without assuming any further obligation in exchange. But because most such farms were too small to sustain families, many who lived on them would still need to supplement meager harvests by working as low-paid laborers on the landlords' estates. More generally, furthermore, all of the technically emancipated peasants remained (as in eastern Prussia) subject to the political domination of the landed nobility; their personal liberties were still sharply circumscribed.[109] Here, then, was another attempt to avoid radical change by making concessions that limited the damage to elite power and wealth.

The Confederate leaders who pointed the way toward a pro-master form of emancipation shared a good deal with these other eighteenth- and nineteenth-century revolutionaries-from-above. All of them confronted the prospect of losing everything to enemies from either within or without. All sought to avoid that fate by sacrificing part of their existing privileges in order to salvage the rest. The Prussian and Russian autocrats hoped to exchange the forms of domination with which rural workers had previously been controlled for other forms that were in one way or another more adaptable to current requirements. The Confederate government saw, with Louisiana governor Henry W. Allen, that "we will have to give up the institution of domestic slavery." But it believed that this concession would not require abandoning the plantation system or the degree of control over labor required to make it lucrative. "The civilized world is opposed to the name of slavery," Allen had acknowledged, but it was content to live with "bondage under some other name." Surely the South could find a way to accommodate itself to such a preference.[110]

Frederick Douglass followed developments within the Confederacy closely, and he understood quite well what Allen, Davis, and their allies were trying to accomplish. Just a few weeks after Appomattox, he reminded members of the American Anti-Slavery Society of the Confederacy's latter-day debate over arming and freeing slaves. That measure's supporters, Douglass noted, had not feared formal emancipation precisely because they expected to retain state power. Douglass paraphrased their reasoning as follows: "We may make these negroes fight for us; but while we retain political power in the South, we can keep them in a subordinate position." "That was their argument," Douglass now recalled, "and they were right. They might have employed the negro to fight for them, and while they retained in their hands the power to exclude him from political rights, they could have reduced him to a condition similar to slavery. They would not call it slavery, but some other name."[111]

The Confederate plan for emancipation was neither incomprehensible, pointless, nor self-defeating. It did not arise from the kind of naive underestimation of slavery's importance that is so often attributed to Cleburne, or from the kind of dislike of slavery credited especially to Lee, or from the nearly obsessive preoccupation with southern independence for its own sake and at any cost often associated with Jefferson Davis. Neither did it mean a fundamental reversal of traditional slaveowner priorities. It rested, instead, upon a cold-blooded appraisal of the slaveholders' desperate situation and dwindling options after about the middle of 1863.

Cleburne and those southern leaders who endorsed his idea then or later sought to harness the military power of the slaves on behalf of the Confederacy while preserving—indeed, *in order to preserve*—key aspects of the antebellum South's economic and social relations and institutions. Given the almost certain demise of slavery, one way or the other, Cleburne, and later Davis, Benjamin, Lee, and others, asked, What is the next-best state of affairs from the planters' point of view? And they answered, A minimal amount of personal liberty for black laborers whose real options would be severely limited by both the planters' monopoly of land and their control of the state apparatus.

This proposal's architects no doubt despised the Yankee foe. But preserving Confederate independence of a Yankee-dominated federal union was a goal dear not only to fervent southern-nationalist ideologues and inveterate haters of all things Yankee. It was also the very practical key to salvaging a South in which political power remained securely in the hands of white planters and farmers, political power that alone would allow them to shape social and economic relations as well, to "make laws to control the free negro" and "to regulate [their wages] by law," in the words of veteran proslavery palidan John Henry Stringfellow. To retain that supreme political power in friendly hands, and thereby ensure the best possible conditions for the survival of plantation society, many things were possible.

5

"ON THE FOOTING OF SOLDIERS"

Enacting and Implementing New Policy, 1864–1865

By freeing and arming slaves, Cleburne, Lee, Davis, and Benjamin sought simultaneously to win the war and to salvage as much as they could of the Old South, including the plantation system and the white-supremacist social order more generally. But to achieve these goals, they first had to clear other hurdles. Both houses of Congress had to endorse the plan. The army would then have to actually recruit black soldiers. That meant inducing masters to yield their expensive and highly prized human property. It also meant convincing large numbers of slaves that the shortest route to freedom led through aiding the southern war effort. Once recruited, such black soldiers would have to be trained, organized into units, and placed in the field. Once there, they would have to fight, and fight effectively. Finally, in order to constitute a net increase in southern military power, the new black troops would have to enter the army without thereby inducing other troops to leave it. The great mass of white Confederate soldiers, that is, officers and enlisted men alike, would have to accept the idea of serving alongside black troops.

None of these hurdles was insignificant.

One of the most daunting was the congress's longtime refusal to cooperate. The swift deterioration of the Confederacy's military situation after Atlanta's fall in September 1864 helped jolt some politicians out of their complacency and break the legislative impasse. First, Abraham Lincoln's convincing electoral triumph in November foreclosed one of the South's last hopes of achieving victory by political means—the hope of placing a Democrat in the

White House who would quickly sue for peace. "Lincoln has been re-elected President of the United States by overwhelming majorities," Confederate ordnance chief Josiah Gorgas recorded in his journal in mid-November. "There is no use in disguising the fact that our subjugation is popular at the North, & that the war must go on," he concluded—at least until some new Southern victories could force the North to sue for "peace at any cost."[1]

Such victories seemed unlikely prospects, however. Fewer and fewer Confederate partisans could ignore the seriousness of their country's military predicament by the end of 1864. In September and October, Union troops under the command of Philip H. Sheridan repeatedly routed and then all but destroyed Jubal A. Early's storied force in Virginia's Shenandoah Valley, previously a graveyard of Union hopes. Then, in November and December the battles of Franklin and Nashville decimated the Army of Tennessee. Meanwhile, Sherman's force took Savannah on the coast of Georgia in December, and by February it had entered South Carolina, slashing through that state even more thoroughly than it had just cut through Georgia. On February 17, Sherman's army captured South Carolina's capital, Columbia. The next day, Charleston, the Confederacy's spiritual capital, surrendered to Union forces that had been besieging it since 1863. A black regiment, some of whose members had only recently been slaves in that city, was the first to occupy it. Through all of this, Lee remained at bay in Petersburg.

Back-to-back diplomatic rebuffs confirmed the Confederacy's dwindling options. At the end of December 1864, Jefferson Davis decided to make a last bid to persuade Britain and France to come to his aid. Through the intermediary of Louisiana planter and congressman Duncan F. Kenner, Davis would at last offer gradual emancipation of the slaves in exchange for diplomatic recognition.[2] But France refused to act without Britain, and by the time that Kenner finally managed to reach London and present his case, Lord Palmerston, the sympathetic British prime minister, had written off the Confederate cause as hopeless; he regretfully rebuffed Davis's overture.[3] By then, as the Richmond *Dispatch* observed grimly, "No one would receive us as a gift."[4]

In the meantime, flickering prospects of rescuing southern independence through negotiation with the Union also winked out. This became apparent at Hampton Roads, Virginia, where representatives of the U.S. and Confederate governments met informally on February 3. Lincoln attended the conference in person along with his secretary of state, William H. Seward. Davis sent Vice President Alexander Stephens, Senate president pro tempore R. M. T. Hunter, and Assistant Secretary of War (and former U.S. Supreme Court justice) John A. Campbell. By prior agreement, no written records were kept of the Hampton Roads discussions. Subsequent accounts agree, however, that Lincoln adhered to the instructions he had earlier presented to

Seward, insisting that the war must end with "the restoration of the National authority throughout all the States" and thus ruling out any discussion predicated on the Confederacy's survival as an independent nation.[5]

Nor would Lincoln's advance guidelines have offered much encouragement to those southerners still hoping to reenter the old Union with slavery intact. Those guidelines emphasized, on the contrary, that any peace settlement must include implementation of all prior Union measures concerning "the Slavery question."[6] And Seward reported a few days after the conference that Lincoln had conducted himself in accord with his own strictures on this matter, too, telling Stephens and company that "he [Lincoln] must not be expected to depart from the positions he had heretofore assumed in his proclamation of emancipation and other documents." Lincoln and Seward also drew the Confederate representatives' attention to the prospective thirteenth constitutional amendment outlawing slavery immediately throughout the United States, which had just been endorsed by the House of Representatives and had then been sent to the states for ratification.[7]

The Hampton Roads conference therefore ended without producing any substantive agreements. Both Jefferson Davis and R. M. T. Hunter (who still opposed the black-troops idea) told large public gatherings that the Union delegation had demanded both the South's unconditional surrender and return to the Union and the complete and permanent abolition of chattel slavery. Lincoln demands that we "come back as a conquered people," Davis reported, "submitting to all the recent legislation of the Washington Government, including the abolition clause recently enacted in Congress."[8] "If we go back to the bonds of the Union," Hunter affirmed, we will have to do so with "three millions of slaves loosed in the midst of Southern society; we ourselves slaves, and our slaves freedmen."[9]

The final phase of the debate about arming and freeing slaves thus occurred against a backdrop of fading Confederate hopes and disappearing policy alternatives. Since the fall of 1864, the news reaching Richmond from southern battlefields, northern ballot boxes, and diplomatic conclaves had steadily eroded dreams that southern independence or slavery's survival could be purchased with some means other than armed force. By February 1865, as Col. Richard L. Maury therefore observed, nothing remained but "war to the knife, and the knife to the hilt."[10] "Peace & every prospect thereof has for the present vanished & nothing now [remains] but war war," soldier James B. Jones told his family.[11] There was "nothing to do," Louisiana artillery officer William Miller Owen informed his diary, "but fight it out."[12]

That conclusion, given the South's obviously dwindling armies, made the discovery of some new source of military manpower more urgent than ever. Support for arming slaves had therefore begun to grow anew at the end of 1864. "Our late adverses," as the Richmond *Sentinel* reported, "have done much towards preparing the minds of our people for the most extreme sacrifices if they shall be adjudged necessary for the success of our cause."[13] Walking through Macon, Georgia, the editor of the *Southern Confederacy* was distressed to "hear people talking on the street corners in favor of the measure. Put arms in the hands of the slaves, and make them fight for us, they say."[14] Congressman Warren Akin was in late December "surprised to find so many officers and men in favor of putting negroes in the army" and to discover that "this feeling is increasing very rapidly." It continued to grow in strength during the months that followed.[15] "A great change is going [on] in the public mind about putting negroes in the army," Akin informed his wife in late January. "I have heard from different portions of Georgia, and the People are for it."[16]

Georgians were not alone in this respect. Word reached Jefferson Davis from Alabama that "many now think that you were right in recommending the placing in the service the able-bodied negroes in the field."[17] At the end of January, South Carolina secession leader John A. Inglis detected the same sentiment in his state.[18] Virginian Edmund Ruffin, who initially had dismissed the measure as sheer suicide for the South, acknowledged in mid-February that "the suggestion is evidently growing in the public favor, or tolerance."[19] During February and March, public meetings in various locales endorsed the measure.[20] So did the governor of Mississippi.[21] This shift in public opinion could be traced in the pages even of some newspapers that had originally taken a firm stand against the black-troop proposal. In Richmond, for example, both the *Examiner* and the *Whig* grudgingly swallowed their objections to recruiting black soldiers (although not their objections to emancipating such recruits).[22] Undoubtedly encouraged by this trend (and influenced by the same alarming developments that had produced it), congressional supporters of arming slaves finally began to appear.

The Army of Northern Virginia also played a pivotal political role in reorienting popular opinion. On February 11, Judah P. Benjamin asked Robert E. Lee for a public expression of his army's support for recruiting "such negroes as for the boon of freedom will volunteer to go to the front."[23] Lee promptly complied, ordering his generals to poll their troops about a proposition framed in phrases lifted directly from Benjamin's note: "Are you in favor of putting the negroes who for the boon of freedom would volunteer as soldiers into the field"?[24]

Not surprisingly, the resulting army discussions crackled with tension, both in the ranks and in the upper echelons. Attempting to influence the outcome, officers sent conflicting signals down the chain of command. Lee's First Corps commander, James Longstreet, clearly telegraphed his doubts about the proposal's wisdom to his subordinates. He believed that "the adoption of such a measure will involve the necessity of abolishing slavery entirely in the future, and that, too, without materially aiding us in the present." One of Longstreet's division commanders, Gen. George Pickett of Gettysburg fame, just as forcefully communicated an opposing view to his own subordinates.[25]

When orders to poll the troops reached the regiments, they raised the curtain on a most unusual and dramatic scene. In meetings specifically called for that purpose, the officers and soldiers of the Confederacy's largest army, still struggling at Petersburg to hold off Grant's besieging forces, proceeded to discuss and formulate their views concerning the most extraordinary and momentous proposal of the war. During the third week of February, regiments raised in Virginia, Georgia, North and South Carolina, Alabama, and Texas duly reported the content of those discussions and the results of unit votes.

Opponents had long and credibly warned that white soldiers would vehemently reject the idea of placing slaves in Confederate gray and would desert in droves if that policy were adopted. And opposition in the ranks had seemed strong as late as the fall of 1864. But the passage of a few crucial, eventful, disappointment-laden months brought with it a change of view. By February, Mississippi congressman Ethelbert Barksdale was proclaiming the troops' "unexampled unanimity . . . in favor of the measure."[26]

In truth, Barksdale exaggerated, as did others. The Richmond *Enquirer* announced the voting results in the 56th Virginia Infantry Regiment, which (it said) was "composed of companies from the most populous slave districts in Virginia" and whose "members, perhaps, own in the aggregate as many slaves as any other regiment from Virginia." The *Enquirer* trumpeted that a resolution to endorse the government's proposal "passed with great spirit and entire unanimity" in that regiment.[27] Col. W. E. Greene more candidly reported to his superiors that two officers and forty enlisted men in the Virginia regiment had in fact opposed the motion.[28] Reports from many other units also noted uncertainty, hesitation, abstention, and outright opposition. Gen. John B. Gordon, who supported the proposal, claimed that "the opposition to it is now confined to a very few" throughout his whole Second Corps.[29] But Brig. Gen. George H. Steuart reported "much difference of opinion" among the men of his brigade.[30] In the South Carolinian Bratton's Brigade, a quarter of the troops opposed the idea.[31] So did a third of those voting in both the 8th and 38th Virginia regiments.[32] In the 53rd Virginia, about a fourth of the officers and very nearly half the enlisted men demurred.[33] Col. Thomas F. Toon added that only a bare majority of his regiment, the 20th North Carolina, endorsed the motion put to it.[34] The picture was the same in the 38th Georgia.[35] In the 9th and 57th Virginia, outright majorities of the enlisted men voted no.[36] About two-thirds of both the officers and men in the 60th Georgia took the same position.[37]

Among those who did approve the proposition, furthermore, the degree of enthusiasm on display varied widely. General Gordon claimed that his corps was "decidedly in favor."[38] The 31st Georgia was also "strongly in favor," and the 1st Virginia "would hail with acclamation the enrollment into our army of Negro troops."[39] The rather less enthused 18th Virginia was prepared to "cheerfully acquiesce," and Bratton's Brigade would "willingly submit to, and acquiesce in" the measure.[40] Brig. Gen. David A. Weisiger reported that the 16th Virginia "has no objection to the measure," but he added that "the men seem indisposed to taking any part in recommending it."[41]

But while soldier sentiment remained considerably more ambivalent than many wanted to acknowledge, the shift in its center of gravity was unmistakable. Most soldiers who expressed a firm opinion now did support arming slaves, and that support continued to grow from day to day.[42] General Weisiger reported that, despite lingering resistance in his command, "the sentiment is rapidly changing. . . and a few weeks will I think find the command almost unanimously for the Employment of negroes."[43] Col. W. E. Greene similarly noted that "the sentiment of the Regt is still undergoing a change" and that support for the proposal had increased "very much in the past few days."[44] The Richmond *Whig* conceded in late February that "so far from exciting the repugnance on the part of the army at first apprehended," the proposal "has gained favor rapidly of late."[45]

The thinking that drove forward the soldiers' change of opinion did not echo the sophisticated long-term societal planning taking place in the Confederacy's upper echelons and in some editorial offices. For officers and enlisted men on the front lines, more immediate considerations took precedence, including desperate hopes of staving off imminent conquest and, more basically still, of avoiding an early death. It was here in the trenches that the prioritizing of military victory over its socioeconomic costs—the factor that numerous modern writers have emphasized—probably played its biggest role. And as soldiers tried to calculate the military utility of the proposal before them, Robert E. Lee's well-publicized views may well have proven decisive. Many of his men were prepared to support virtually anything proposed by the commander who had led them to so many previous victories. "Gen Lee is in favor of it," Silas Chandler typically wrote his wife, and "I shall cast my vote for it. I am in favor of giving him any thing that he wants in the way of gaining our independence."[46] While "it is hard for us to bring ourselves to it," Col. Richard L. Maury wrote, and while he, for one, "would rather wait a little longer—before calling in their aid," still "General Lee says he wants them, and so give them to him I say—what ever that great and good Soldier wants give him in Heaven's name."[47] Gen. George H. Steuart reported that despite the disagreements in his brigade "almost all including myself are in favor of leaving the matter to the discretion of General Lee."[48] Lt. William

Miller Owen thought it "a bad move, and too late." "Still," he added immediately, "if Gen. Lee says it is all right, why, go ahead!"[49]

The soldiers' sense of dwindling options also reconciled many of them to the use of black troops. One North Carolina colonel's words captured a spreading mood of despair underlying much of the latter-day support for the measure. "We are forsaken by all the world & our friends deserting," grieved Samuel Hoey Walkup. "The enemy are exultant & numbers 5 or 6 to our one. An army against an unarmed, unorganized mob. The sea before us, the mountains on each side, behind us a mighty and desperate enemy. Where can we look for help but upwards[?]"[50] Or, in the more succinct verdict of the 1st Va. Infantry, "disaster and gloom now hover over us."[51] As defeat and death stared them in the face, southern soldiers abandoned the lines in swiftly mounting numbers.[52] "We have been decimated & more than decimated by desertion," Col. Walkup complained.[53] "We are having many desertions," confirmed Gen. John B. Gordon in late February, "caused I think by the despondency in our ranks."[54]

Of those who remained at their posts, some inevitably began to view black recruitment as the only way to save their own lives. Maj. Gen. Howell Cobb so advised the War Department. One source of "the favor with which the proposition is received in portions of the Army," he believed, "is the hope that when negroes go into the Army they [white soldiers] will be permitted to retire."[55] Cobb probably knew whereof he spoke. Some of the earliest advocates of black recruitment had argued that "the life of a white man is as worthy of preservation as that of a negro."[56] By the last six months of the war such calculations had acquired considerably greater weight. In December, Georgia congressman Warren Akin heard several soldiers call for "put[ting] the negroes in now" rather than waiting "until all the [white] soldiers were killed."[57] "In God's name," exclaimed an open letter published in Georgia, "do not sacrifice every white man in the Confederacy in preference to taking a few negroes from their fondling masters."[58] In February 1865, Pvt. Samuel McAbe of the 1st South Carolina infantry regiment still found the prospect of fighting alongside blacks repulsive, but he saw no reason to spare their lives while risking his own. And "if we don't get the help we are gone up for sure, they [Yankees] are coming in on every side and half of [our] men won't fight."[59]

This motive for endorsing the use of black soldiers, of course, hardly testified to a fundamental change in racial views. Support for emancipation seemed in similarly short supply. Few officers' summaries of regimental discussions and votes directly addressed that question at all. Some soldiers' letters specifically distinguished between the subjects of black enlistment and black freedom. Col. Clayton C. Gilespie of the 25th Texas Cavalry apparently spoke for many others when he insisted that "we of the army, while we approve of President Davis['s] proposition to avail ourselves of all the help our able-bodied negroes can give us in the struggle, are not yet ready to fight for a free negro Confederacy. Or to allow one to exist on this Southern land."[60] Col. Richard L. Maury, after finally endorsing the use of black troops, added immediately, "Don't free the negroes though."[61] The 3rd Virginia cavalry regiment incorporated the same sentiment into its formal resolutions. "Holding our independence as paramount to all other considerations," these Old Dominion cavaliers declared, we favor enlisting "as many negroes . . . as the Commander-in-chief may deem necessary," but "without changing their social status."[62] That this last proviso showed that some considerations were, in fact, "paramount" to independence seemed not to trouble the troopers.

The subject of emancipation proved a major—ultimately, an insurmountable—obstacle within the Congress as well. The resolution that Mississippi's Albert Gallatin Brown had brought into the Senate on February 7 would have empowered the president both to enroll (either voluntarily or by impressment) and ultimately to free as many as 200,000 slaves.[63] But only two of Brown's Senate colleagues (Missouri's George G. Vest and Tennessee's Gustavus A. Henry) were prepared to support so strong a measure, and it went down to overwhelming defeat.[64]

Meanwhile on February 10 Jefferson Davis's old friend Ethelbert Barksdale introduced a bill into the House of Representatives that would become the administration proposal. It did not empower the Confederate government either to conscript or emancipate a single slave. It proposed only to allow Jefferson Davis "to ask for and accept from the owners of slaves, the services of such number of able-bodied negro men as he may deem expedient." It would permit the president, that is, to invite masters to volunteer their slaves to the army. (In this respect, as General Thomas C. Hindman later observed unhappily, the Barksdale bill gave slaveowners "greater license" to demur than they had enjoyed when confronted by "the conscription of their sons."[65]) Barksdale's bill also specified that nothing in it "authorize[d] a change in the relation which said slaves shall bear towards their owners as property."[66] Masters who decided to offer their slaves for military duty would retain legal title to them.

The bill's supporters presumed that its "voluntary feature must obviate, in great part, if not, indeed, altogether, the principal objections which have been raised."[67] After all, as Barksdale himself put it on the House floor, the measure proposed to accomplish its purpose "not by wholesale conscription—not by compulsion—not by exercise of unauthorized power to interfere with the relation of the slave to his owner as property, but by leaving this question, where it properly belongs—to the owners of slaves, by the consent of the States and in pursuance of the laws thereof."[68] The House did, however, amend that bill. Concerned that a call for voluntary slaveholder assistance might fail to elicit an adequate response, it added language that would allow Richmond in such a case to call upon each state government to raise its own share of a total of 300,000 black troops, presumably employing whatever means it chose in order to do so.

Ten days later, on February 20, in a close vote (40–37), the House passed this bill, which then went to the Senate.[69] On February 21, the upper house voted to table (and thereby effectively kill) a similar bill that Sen. William S. Oldham of Texas had introduced on February 10, the same day that Barksdale had brought his measure into the House. And the Senate then delayed consideration of the House bill for another two weeks.[70] At that point, only the intervention of Virginia's state government prevented the Confederate Senate from rejecting the Confederate House bill as well.

Virginia's state legislators, like their counterparts in the Confederate congress, had for many months refused to take positive action on this matter. But by late February 1865, a combination of the deteriorating military situation, prodding by Gov. William Smith, and the publicized wishes of Virginian Robert E. Lee had brought about a change of heart.[71] By March 4, both houses of the state legislature had passed resolutions endorsing the key provisions of the Barksdale bill. Like that bill, the Virginia legislature's resolutions made no provision to emancipate any slave recruits. They did instruct Virginia's Confederate senators (R. M. T. Hunter and Allen T. Caperton) to cast their votes in favor of the Barksdale bill regardless of their own continuing personal opposition to it.[72] Virginia's Confederate senators unhappily complied with their new instructions, and as a result the Confederate Senate was able to pass an only slightly amended version of the Barksdale bill on March 8 by the knife-edge margin of nine to eight.[73] The Confederate House agreed to accept the Confederate Senate's version the next day. Davis signed it into law on March 13.[74]

Just what had been accomplished thereby? It has often been said, mistakenly, that Abraham Lincoln's 1863 Emancipation Proclamation failed to free a single slave. In truth, as the policy declaration of an advancing army, it promised to (and did indeed) free many thousands of slaves once they reached Union lines—or once those lines reached them. In contrast, the newly enacted Confederate law did not free a single slave, nor did it attempt to do so. During the legislative debate, Ethelbert Barksdale had flung just that fact into the teeth of his opponents, underscoring thereby just how little his bill would do. "Are gentlemen unwilling to let the people have the privilege of contributing their slaves as a free-will offering"? he challenged.[75]

Lee's headquarters urged quick implementation of the new law so that "some of this force should be put in the field as soon as possible."[76] From the Adju-

PROSPECTS OF THE SOUTHERN SAMBO.

Lee—*" Hold on there, Driver, we want Sambo now to fight for Liberty and Independence. You can thrash him as much as you like when he comes back."*

A Northern view of the Confederacy's black soldier policy. Here, Robert E. Lee calls out to a slave driver whipping a slave, "Hold on there, driver, we want Sambo now to fight for Liberty and Independence. You can thrash him as much as you like when he comes back." The cartoon appeared in *Frank Leslie's Illustrated Newspaper*, March 25, 1865. (The New York Public Library)

tant and Inspector General's Office came General Orders No. 14, intended to translate legislation into army policy. In these orders the Davis administration took a step often characterized as giving to black recruits by fiat the freedom that the Confederate Congress had withheld.[77]

In fact, Davis did considerably less than that. It was true that he, Lee, and others had by now agreed that arming blacks while keeping them enslaved would be foolhardy if not disastrous. But it was also true that Davis remained unwilling to impose manumission upon a single master. These contradictory considerations yielded a set of orders carrying the apparent promise but no guarantee of freedom for black soldiers. They stipulated that "no slave will be accepted as a recruit unless with his own consent and with the approbation of his master by a written instrument conferring, as far as he may, the rights of a freedman."[78] In other words, they announced that only those slaves whose masters had already (and voluntarily) freed them would enter the prospective black companies. The legal power to grant or refuse freedom remained, as ever, in the hands of individual slaveowners.[79] Just as important, General Orders No. 14 ignored and contained no mechanism for implementing the new law's fall-back provisions in case of slaveowner stonewalling.

The task of recruiting, training, and fielding the first black army units was as politically sensitive and delicate in its own way as the legislative struggle had been. The specific provisions of the black soldier law of 1865 had been shaped by concerns that often worked at cross-purposes with one another—the needs to win the confidence of both the hoped-for slave recruits and the farmers and planters who legally still owned them. Those who sought to implement the new law struggled against those same powerful but often whip-sawing pressures. General Orders No. 14 repeated the law's promise that each slave recruit would be enlisted only with both "his own consent" and "the approbation of his master."[80]

To oversee the project, Lee turned to Lt. Gen. Richard S. Ewell, who was already supervising Richmond's defenses. The general in chief evidently knew of Ewell's early and abiding support for the idea and counted upon the "energetic and intelligent effort by someone who fully appreciates the vital importance of the duty."[81] Major Isaac Carrington of Ewell's command would supervise the project in Virginia, assisted by Majs. James W. Pegram and Thomas P. Turner.[82]

The Davis regime's desire to obtain the voluntary compliance of both slaveowners and slaves influenced the selection of recruiters. Both Lee and his adjutant and inspector general believed that masters would more readily offer their human property to men they knew than to those they did not.[83] Black soldiers, too, Lee believed, would be more likely to serve well if their all-black companies were placed in regiments hailing from their home states.[84] As members of the 49th Georgia infantry regiment put it, such an arrangement would allow the army to benefit from paternalist relationships already in place. It would "create or rather cement, a reciprocal attachment between the men now in service, and the negroes."[85]

Many officers and enlisted men now offered to raise black Confederate units, more than a few of them volunteering to leave the Petersburg front and return to their home communities in order to carry out that work.[86] Gen. James Longstreet, Lee's veteran division commander, voiced strong doubts about such offers. To him they indicated only that "the desire for promotion" has "taken possession of our army," and that "nearly all the officers and men think that they could gain a grade or more if allowed to go home" and participate in the enterprise.[87] As if to confirm those suspicions, one Virginia enlisted man, seeking to obtain "command of a negro regiment," complained from Petersburg that "too much of the heart and brains of our country has been sacrificed in subordinate positions without adequate return."[88] Alabamian Joseph Stapp suggested how common such careerist talk had become in the ranks by lampooning it in a letter home. "I suppose we will soon have a force of 300,000 Negro troops in the field & it will take all the whites for officers (ha ha ha) I expect to be Brigadier General."[89]

Longstreet harbored still deeper misgivings about the motives of more than a few who volunteered to raise troops in their home states. How many of them, he asked skeptically, would ever return to the front? If previous experience was any guide, he warned, "many will furnish the necessary evidence" of their ability to enlist such troops and then "go home and there remain for eight and ten and twelve months."[90]

Lee brushed aside Longstreet's concerns.[91] Accordingly, Maj. John Tyler went to Petersburg in late March in search of black recruits before continuing on through surrounding counties.[92] Two Petersburg residents—Capt. W. E. Cameron, the adjutant of David A. Weisiger's Brigade, and Pvt. Stephen H. Britton, of the Washington Artillery—carried on there.[93] Col. Kirkwood Otey of the 11th Virginia Regiment went to his hometown of Lynchburg, and Lt. John L. Cowardin, the adjutant of the 19th Virginia Artillery Battalion, went to Halifax County.[94] The adjutant general's office dispatched Capt. Edward Bostick of the 26th South Carolina Volunteers to raise a battalion of four black companies in his native state.[95] Pvt. James B. Nelson of the 16th Georgia Battalion solicited recruits out of a storefront location in downtown Macon.[96] At Governor Thomas H. Watts's suggestion, Joseph E. Johnston dispatched Brig. Gen. John T. Morgan to supervise recruitment in Alabama, to be assisted by Alabama natives Capts. William B. Jones and George P. Ring.[97] Ten officers in Florida received authorization to raise black companies in that state at the end of April.[98]

Despite their local credentials, these recruiters confronted a complicated and daunting task. Attempting simultaneously to win the confidence of both slaves and masters would tax the skills of the most adroit diplomat, and even of today's cleverest advertising executives.

The Confederacy's desperate situation unavoidably altered its public stance toward those blacks upon whom its hopes for survival now depended. It had become necessary, as Lee's headquarters stressed, "to conciliate their good will." Official policy now implicitly repudiated early predictions that slaves would flock eagerly to the defense of the peculiar institution itself.

The southern high command, intimately acquainted through almost four years of wartime experience with black southerners' powerful desire for liberty, now recognized that the only chance of mobilizing blacks in its own military service lay in dissociating the prospective black recruits' soldierly future from their enslaved past. Even as they privately planned to curtail severely the scope of postwar black freedom, government and military leaders understood and stressed the importance of convincing slaves that the promises and intentions of the Confederacy could be trusted. "Everything should be done to impress them with the responsibility and character of their position" as soldiers, the adjutant and inspector general's office added. Indeed, the AIGO earnestly emphasized, these black recruits must "be made to forget as soon as possible" that they had so recently been "regarded as menials."[99]

Robert E. Lee thus understood that a promise of freedom was the *minimum* basis for attracting slaves into the Confederate army. "Strict orders should be given as to their treatment," he advised the secretary of war in mid-March, "placing them on the footing of soldiers, with their freedom secured."[100] The Richmond *Sentinel* assured black soldiers that "their service in the public defence" would become "a badge of merit and certificate of honor as long as they may live," demarcating them as "a sort of aristocracy in their own class." In the postwar Confederacy they would "enjoy a popular favor and respect from which they will reap large advantages."[101]

It was equally necessary that the rest of white Virginia make clear its good-will toward the new troops. "Let all unite to cheer on the colored soldiers," the *Sentinel* admonished, "by showing them the favor and giving them the praise so justly due to their conduct."[102] In that spirit, recruiters in Petersburg offered slaves "freedom and undisturbed residence at their old homes in the Confederacy after the war." And this, they added, would be "not the freedom of sufferance but honorable and self won by the gallantry and devotion which grateful countrymen will never cease to remember and reward."[103] The Macon *Telegraph* similarly enjoined Georgia masters to pledge not only to "emancipate such negroes as will volunteer in the Confederate service" but also to assure such volunteers that after the war "proper provisions will be made for them and their families and fair wages given."[104] It was crucial that southern blacks believe in the sincerity and dependability of all these promises. "Above all," the *Sentinel* emphasized, "let it be well and clearly understood that promises made" to black recruits about their new and future legal status "are to be redeemed with the most scrupulous fidelity, and at all hazards." The authorities must carefully avoid "the least appearance, the slightest semblance, of bad faith."[105]

In this spirit General Orders No. 14 instructed all recruiters and commanders to give "provident, considerate, and humane attention to whatever concerns the health, comfort, instruction, and discipline of those troops."

And it called upon such officers to practice "kindness, forbearance, and indulgence" toward their troops and especially to "protect them from injustice and oppression."[106] To that end, "harshness and contemptuous or offensive language or conduct to them must be forbidden." The government felt it necessary to underline, repeat, and detail such injunctions precisely because they represented so sharp a departure from past practice.

Once again, however, winning the confidence and support of the slaves alone would not be sufficient. The Davis regime's unwillingness or inability to force masters to surrender slaves to the army compelled it instead to plead for the owners' voluntary assistance.[107] It was "necessary that masters should heartily co-operate," explained the newspaper now most closely in tune with the Davis government, precisely because "it is *they* who practically are the *recruiting officers*. It is they who are to present the opportunity and supply the motive" to the people they owned. Like Davis, Lee, and their allies, therefore, the Richmond *Sentinel* could only hope that the masters "will bring this subject to the attention of those of their slaves who would be suitable to the object, and that they will deal very liberally with such as may have the inclination to assist in driving back the detested Yankee."[108] Surely, Majors Pegram and Turner exhorted, "the people of Virginia in this hour of peril and danger" would "promptly respond to the call of their loved General-in-Chief and the demands of the Confederate and State Governments." Or, the two officers wondered, "will those who have freely given their sons and brothers, their money and their property to the achievement of the liberties of their country, now hold back from the cause their servants"?[109]

The way in which masters responded would have profound and multifaceted consequences, Gen. John T. Morgan advised his fellow Alabamians. "This contribution to the strength of our armies, if made promptly," he promised, "will change our reverses into assured victory and ultimate independence." Refusals to cooperate, conversely, would carry unmistakable and weighty implications. "Should our slaveholders, in this hour of severe trial, refuse to answer this call upon their patriotism, or delay until compelled by law to respond to it," Morgan warned, "they will prove to the world that they count . . . their wealth as of greater value than their independence." That kind of selfish conduct, the general specified, would also arouse the intense and enduring contempt of the white South's slaveless majority. Not only the recalcitrant masters but also "their posterity" would "incur the just penalty of scorn from the larger class of our people, who, owning no slaves, have devoted every power of body and soul, all earthly comfort, and their blood to our common cause."[110]

But government officials expressed confidence that slaveowners were ready to do their bit. From the first, after all, advocates of enlisting slaves had claimed the backing of local masters. And as Robert E. Lee now reminded

Jefferson Davis, quite a few masters had previously promised "to select the most suitable among their slaves, as soon as Congress should give the authority." Lee therefore assumed that "a considerable number would be forthcoming for the purpose if called for."[111] Gov. William Smith, in turn, reassured Lee a few weeks later that "there is a very favorable disposition in the country to promote this policy."[112] Confederate War Department clerk John B. Jones hoped the army would gain "100,000 recruits from this source."[113]

There seemed to be grounds for such optimism. Word reached Richmond that "a number of prominent Slaveholders" were anxious to cooperate.[114] Twenty-three in Roanoke County publicly offered to manumit any military-aged male slaves who would volunteer for such service.[115] A candidate for the Virginia state legislature pledged to contribute "a portion of my able bodied colored men, with the promise of their freedom after the war, provided they stand and fight it out like true and loyal soldiers."[116] Some thirty of the Lynchburg area's largest slaveholders were reportedly ready to follow that lead.[117] Yet another wealthy Virginian, having taken refuge in Richmond from advancing Union troops, offered to purchase ten suitable slaves from local masters and place them in the army.[118] The owner of seven plantations near Staunton, in north central Virginia, offered "twenty able bodied young men for the war."[119] A former artillery colonel promised that he and "several owners of negroes" in the state would send as many as 1,200 black recruits to army training camps "at once."[120]

Encouraging noises came from other parts of the Confederacy, too. A group of Alabama masters in early April offered an unspecified number of slaves to department commander General Richard Taylor.[121] Meanwhile, P. G. T. Beauregard, falling back to Charlotte, North Carolina, was reportedly rounding up "all the negroes from the evacuated country" in order to place them in the Confederate army.[122] The Tar Heel state as a whole, according to another account, would soon place fifteen thousand black troops in the field.[123] Still another bulletin had twenty-five thousand black Confederate troops already enlisted in Kirby Smith's Trans-Mississippi Department.[124] Reports of even larger accessions of black troops to the Confederate armies worried northern soldiers and journalists. In Alabama, a Union cavalry officer heard in mid-February that "the rebel authorities are doing their utmost to . . . put in the field a large number of negro troops," that "the enrollment is nearly completed," and that "they expect to have 200,000 under arms in sixty days."[125] About two weeks later a northern reporter got word "that the Rebels have been for weeks, if not months, busily engaged in drilling an army of negroes, and that at this moment they are about to enter the field."[126] At the end of March, rumors circulating through Richmond (and then reaching the ears of besieging northern forces) told of at least twenty thousand black troops organized into twenty-two regiments already training outside Richmond at Camp Lee.[127]

The actual results of these Confederate recruitment efforts were far, far smaller. Only in Richmond is there solid evidence of any units of black Confederate soldiers ever forming. Those units were recruited from two sources. One was the staff of two local hospitals—Winder and Jackson. In mid-February, surgeon F. W. Hancock of Jackson Hospital assembled seventy-two slaves employed there as orderlies or nurses and asked if they were willing to take up arms in defense of Richmond. According to Dr. Hancock, sixty said they were.[128] Confederate officials anxious to raise public confidence and to encourage emulation promptly passed this account along to the press.[129] At least some of these black hospital workers were then mustered into a company or two attached to Major H. C. Scott's three-battalion-strong local defense corps, most of whose members were convalescing hospital patients.[130] Although not incorporated into the regular Confederate army, at least some of these soldiers were ordered into the trenches to bolster Richmond's defense against a Union raid in mid-March. General Longstreet had previously suggested doing just that because "their good behavior would do much to overcome a prejudice existing in the minds of many adverse to their employment as troops."[131] After the raid, Major Scott duly reported that his black soldiers "behaved in an extraordinary [*sic*] acceptable manner" in that encounter.[132] That their active role on that occasion was likely limited, however, was suggested by the cancellation a few days later of an anticipated public review of this unit. The black soldiers could not parade, it was explained, because they had still not received the requisite uniforms, equipment, or arms.[133]

A second source of black Confederate soldiers was the formal recruiting center that General Ewell had created and Majors Pegram and Turner directed. On March 11, the two majors designated a public meeting place for black volunteers at a former tobacco factory on 21st street between Cary and Main.[134] A local newspaper was "glad to report that the owners of slaves are coming up heartily" to Turner and Pegram's support, as a result of which "recruiting is going on rapidly."[135] Richmond residents were also told that "quite an enthusiasm" for the new program, a veritable "military fever," was "spreading among the negroes."[136] "Already," the Richmond *Sentinel* enthused on March 24, "quite a number of these colored soldiers have been enlisted, all of them, be it remembered, *volunteers*."[137]

The booster tone could hardly conceal the meager actual results. The state auditor's office calculated at the end of March that Confederate Virginia contained more than 4,700 free black males and more than 25,000 male slaves between eighteen and forty-five years of age who were fit for service under the new legislation.[138] Gov. William Smith thought this estimate accurate enough to deduce that the Old Dominion would muster about that number of free blacks and between four and five thousand slaves into the Confederate army, or about 9,000 black soldiers in all.[139] In the event, however, only a tiny fraction of those numbers was ever recruited in Virginia. Thomas P. Turner would have been happy to meet a far more modest goal. He hoped to bring his unit up to a strength of eighty to one hundred by mid-April. By late March, he was still struggling to reach even that goal, having apparently received somewhere between thirty and forty recruits. And a full month later, the Richmond *Whig* was still referring to "the forty or fifty colored soldiers, enlisted under the act of congress."[140]

Not 4,700 but just half a dozen free black males enlisted in Pegram and Turner's unit.[141] One, a boatman named John Scott, had appeared at the recruitment office bristling with hostility toward the Yankees. After enlisting, he seemed for all the world to be an enthusiastic soldier and an apt student of infantry drill. But then, early one Sunday morning, Scott gathered up some twenty-five full uniforms and (the *Examiner* reported drily) "putting in brilliant practice one of the military movements, the 'double quick,' decamped." Pursued, the erstwhile soldier, by "executing another dexterous movement, the 'right wheel,' eluded his pursuers and escaped."[142] That inauspicious development amused the *Examiner*. The Richmond *Whig* advised Major Turner against putting any more faith in the "patriotic" pretensions of "negro boatmen, all of whom are sharp fellows and can't be trusted."[143] Governor Smith, for his part, could hardly have been shocked by the incident; he had only recently warned the state legislature that "many" of "our free negroes" were "doubtless disloyal" and "sometimes are found co-operating with the enemy, and occasionally indulging in the utterances of treasonable sentiments and threats against our fellow-citizens."[144]

Recruitment of soldiers from among the slave population proceeded no more smoothly than among free blacks. A few weeks before the John Scott embarrassment, Governor Smith tried to lend Majors Pegram and Turner a helping hand. Two local slaves named Oliver and George had earlier been sentenced to hang for the crime of burglary. Smith now pardoned those men— on condition that they enlist in the black infantry unit being formed.[145] The condemned duo was said to be "delighted with this reversal of their fate"; Majors Pegram and Turner were not.[146] Striving to free their project from menial, penal, or servile associations, they moved hurriedly and publicly to reject these two newly proffered recruits.[147]

But Governor Smith might have been forgiven for assuming that condemned prisoners belonged in Pegram and Turner's command. Many aspects of the unit's life suggested the same thing. The *Examiner* reported, for example, that "the company of negroes are drilled daily for several hours by Lieutenant Virginius Bossieux, whose talent peculiarly adapts him to imparting instructions in the manual."[148] The special talent delicately referred to was evidently the one Bossieux had honed as commandant of the Confederacy's military prison at Belle Isle. Nor was he the only officer assigned to this project boasting such specialized training and experience. Bossieux's superior, Maj. Thomas P. Turner, superintended two Confederate military prisons in Richmond (Belle Isle and Libby).[149] The man to whom Major Turner reported, Maj. Isaac H. Carrington, was Richmond's provost marshal, its supervisor of military police, who was also charged with maintaining slave discipline in the city.[150] The place where Turner and Pegram's troops drilled and were quartered, the former Smith's tobacco factory, served during the war as a military prison; and the black soldiers' meals were prepared in Libby prison.[151]

Placing the new recruits in the hands of military police and jailers highlighted yet again the contradiction that plagued all plans to bring blacks and especially slaves into the Confederate army. African Americans had demonstrated that they despised bondage and were ready to assist the Union army in defeating the slaveholders' republic. Recognition of that fact had produced a two-sided reaction in the South. As noted, it helped persuade more clear-eyed Confederate leaders to offer freedom in return for military service and to try to convince potential black soldiers of the regime's respect and good will. But African Americans' wartime conduct (and the Union's increasingly friendly and successful overtures toward them) also heightened southern whites' distrust of blacks, their loyalties, and their intentions—a distrust already pronounced in the spring of 1861 when (for example) the Tennessee legislature passed a law to raise "a Home Guard of Minute Men" whose duties included the responsibility "to see that all the slaves are disarmed; to prevent the assemblage of slaves in unusual numbers; to keep the slave population in proper subjection; and to see that peace and order is observed."[152] Throughout the South, slavery's wartime breakdown and the promulgation of the Emancipation Proclamation stoked such concerns and multiplied efforts to tighten security measures. In Richmond, municipal authorities had already been tightening restrictions on slaves' movements and activities four years before the war's outbreak.[153] The minutes of Richmond's city council show that the determination to regulate slaves and free blacks had only grown during the war itself.[154] To have exercised any less vigilance or control over *armed* blacks in their midst must have seemed out of the question.

Authorities were not shy about enforcing such controls, either. Two members of Pegram and Turner's unit were walking in full uniform through Richmond's streets one day in late March when they found themselves stopped, accused of being runaways, and arrested on the spot.[155] A few weeks later, as Lee's army withdrew from Richmond toward Appomattox Court House, at least some of Pegram and Turner's troops went, too. On April 4, Confederate scout Moses Purnell Handy came upon some two dozen of those black soldiers laboring to fashion makeshift fortifications in a field. They were performing this task, the scout recalled, under the direction of several white officers and also "under the watchful eye of an overseer."[156]

These examples of white distrust and domination foreshadowed the type of freedom that awaited such black soldiers should they and the Confederacy survive the war. So did the hostility toward and ridicule of them that some of Richmond's citizens expressed with impunity. White boys pelted black soldiers with mud on city streets. Gen. Richard S. Ewell fumed that "some of the blk [*sic*] soldiers were whipped they were hooted at and treated generally in a way to nullify the law."[157]

Inevitably, that kind of treatment left its mark on the *esprit* of Turner's and Pegram's men. Watching black troops laboring under an overseer on the road to Appomattox, Confederate scout Moses P. Handy thought it "evident" that "the darkeys . . . regarded their present employment in no very favorable light."[158] Others had made similar observations earlier. Two Richmond newspapers encouragingly reported that black soldiers drilling at their barracks on March 21 "seemed certainly proud of the position they occupied"—were, indeed, "as happy as larks"—and loudly declared "their determination to fight the Yankees to the last."[159] But Thomas Hughes, a white youth who watched the same exercise, came away from it with a very different impression. Hughes's father was a member of the Virginia legislature and in that capacity had "warmly advocated the enlistment of negroes." The son was nonetheless taken with a "striking peculiarity" of the black troops whom he watched marching and countermarching that day. The soldiers showed little martial enthusiasm, he later recalled, and during drill "they appeared to regard themselves as isolated or out of place, as if engaged in a work not exactly in accord with their notions of self interest." To Thomas Hughes that dispirited air suggested that "their inclination must have been against engaging on the Southern side."[160] A prominent local journalist, Edward A. Pollard, detected a similar sentiment among the rest of the city's black population. "The mass of the colored brethren" in Richmond, he wrote, looked upon the black soldiers parading before them "with unenvious eyes."[161]

The Davis government's public optimism about the black-troops policy in the spring of 1865 could thus not silence doubts about the policy's viability nor conceal the policy's disappointing upshot. Were these disappointments inevitable ones, endemic to the project? Or did they result merely from the project's faulty implementation? Could the Confederacy have pursued the same policy in a more effective manner and thereby changed the outcome of the war? Attempting to answer these and related questions requires a still closer look at the way that various sectors of Confederate society—governmental, military, and civilian; black and white; free and slave—responded in practice to Richmond's attempt to muster black troops into its army.

6

"LIKE A DROWNING MAN CATCHING AT STRAWS"

Could It Have Worked?

A few companies of home guards and regulars, hastily organized on the eve of Appomattox, displaying dubious elan, and seeing no significant action—this achievement fell far short of the two to three hundred thousand eager black troops that architects of this policy had promised. Why had all the plans and appeals of Cleburne, Lee, Benjamin, and Davis ultimately yielded such meager, inconsequential results?

The fault, claimed some Confederate leaders, lay not in themselves but in their stars. The plan was sound, they held; it failed only because, unfortunately, too little time remained in the spring of 1865 in which to implement it. The war's speedy termination simply made it impossible to put a sound policy to a fair test. Jefferson Davis defended this view then and for the rest of his life. On March 13, 1865, he lashed out at Congress for failing to pass the bill "at an earlier date" and for thereby depriving the army of sufficient "time for their [black units'] organization and instruction."[1] Success could have crowned the enterprise, he implied, if the Congress had simply given him what he had asked for some four months earlier. Two decades later, Davis was still arguing that "there did not remain time enough to obtain any result" that fateful spring because "the passage of the act had been so long delayed."[2]

Many others endorsed that version of events. Their ranks included even Edward Pollard, one of Davis's sharpest critics, who asserted that by the spring of 1865 "there was no time to drill and perfect negro recruits before the resumption of the active and decisive campaign." By that time, moreover, "the country, in its exhausted state, could not half feed and clothe the few soldiers left in the ranks." A policy seeking to add 200,000 black troops had by then become "impracticable and absurd." But, Pollard granted, had the program gone into effect somewhat earlier, it "might have turned the scale in favour of the South."[3] Journalist J. D. B. De Bow said much the same thing a couple of years after Appomattox.[4] The editors of Raleigh's *Daily Confederate* had taken a similar stand if more truculently back in January of 1865. "If Congress and the States, had taken steps early last fall to have given Gen. Lee two hundred thousand negroes," they declared, "we should scarce to day [*sic*] have had a Yankee foot print on Southern soil."[5]

More recently some historians have endorsed a similar perspective. It "can not be doubted," declared Robert Selph Henry almost half a century later, that "large numbers of the slaves would have fought with their masters, if given the chance."[6] Robert F. Durden considers it an "important and startling fact" that "there were Negroes," and "possibly quite a few," who in exchange "for freedom and assurances about their postwar future were willing to become Confederates, not only at the beginning of the war but right up to the end of it."[7] Clarence L. Mohr thinks that Davis's policy offered slaves "a more direct" route to freedom than did the Union and concludes that "had the war lasted longer" a "considerable number" of blacks probably "would have exited slavery by [this] shortest and least hazardous thoroughfare," as a result of which "white Confederates might have fielded a black army in 1864–65."[8] Ervin L. Jordan, Jr., believes that the noncombatant labor that southern blacks had performed for the Confederate army shows that "under appropriate situations the South could have mobilized them into a potent fighting force for independence." "The potential existed," he specifies, to mobilize 100,000 in Virginia alone during the Confederacy's final spring, and that "might have tipped the scales in favor of the Confederacy."[9]

Common to most of these claims is the notion that in March of 1865 the only thing that the Confederacy lacked in order to implement this policy successfully was sufficient time in which to do so. In fact, however, the shortage that bedeviled this policy during the Confederacy's last six months of life was not so much one of calendar time as of strategic and political opportunity. By this stage in the war, too much had transpired, too many basic realities had been drastically transformed, for this plan to be practically viable. If the prerequisites for this plan's success had ever existed, they certainly did no longer.

As most of the plan's advocates—from Cleburne through Lee and Davis—understood, for one thing, its success required the slaves themselves to cooperate willingly, fully, even enthusiastically. To fight effectively for the South, slaves would have to believe that such military service offered the best—the safest, the quickest, the surest—route to freedom. That belief, in turn, required having confidence in a Confederate victory and confidence as well in the Confederacy's promise to repay their service with freedom. It would make little sense to throw in with the Confederacy if one expected the South to lose the war; defeat would, at the very least, leave Richmond unable to make good on any promise to anyone. And if one doubted that promise's sincerity, putting on a gray uniform would seem even more foolish.

Early in the war, at least some of the conditions existed to make such a policy viable. For one thing, the Union's poor showing at Bull Run and elsewhere, which was trumpeted and magnified throughout the South, could only have helped make betting on a Confederate victory seem prudent. For another thing, as already noted, the Union at first did little to endear itself to the South's black population. In 1861 it was still flatly refusing to champion emancipation of southern slaves, still insisting that it fought exclusively to restore the Union. Many Union officers were returning fugitives to their masters, a stance that further antagonized black southerners. Accompanying federal troops in northern Virginia, the northern black journalist George E. Stephens was already hearing predictions in November 1861 that "the Southern Confederacy will, as the last resort . . . declare their slaves free" and arm them against the North. And at that point Stephens thought that such a policy might indeed find favor in the slave quarters. Southern blacks might well say to themselves, Stephens judged, "I shall give my life to him who enfolds the scroll of emancipation, no matter who he may be, Northerner or Southerner."[10] Six months earlier, a prominent black minister in Boston, himself a former slave, had heard from a correspondent in Alabama that such sentiments were rife among slaves in that state. Union policy toward them, reported the minister's informant, had "made the slaves determined to fight for the South, in the hope that their masters may set them free after the war."[11]

Offers to exchange freedom for military service might have continued to find a receptive audience for some time afterward, perhaps down through January 1, 1863, when Lincoln finalized the emancipation proclamation. Benjamin S. Ewell (Gen. Richard Ewell's brother and Gen. Joseph E. Johnston's adjutant) thought so. "If this had been done in 1862," he later concluded, "the results might have proved important."[12] Former Confederate colonel William C. Oates thought the plan remained practical even later than that. Had enabling legislation been passed in the spring of 1863 and had it "made provision for emancipation," Oates subsequently contended, "the Confederacy could have raised up and kept in the field three hundred thousand negro soldiers," a force that might have spelled the difference between victory and defeat.[13]

But what was conceivable at one stage of the war would become impossible at a later one. The end of 1863 may have constituted a Rubicon here. After that point it became too clear too quickly which army defended slavery and which fought to end it. The Union army, penetrating ever more deeply into the southern black belt, was making good on its promise to emancipate slaves and was incorporating black men into its ranks. From then onward, as Edmund Ruffin and others anticipated, slaves would likely recognize that the planter regime was being driven to offer freedom only by the Union's prior (and far more generous) proclamation and by the South's rapidly deteriorating military situation. As Ruffin later noted, such bondspeople "would (truly) ascribe the benefit being proposed . . . to previous Yankee action," and—placing greater trust in the Yankees' motivations—would "be more disposed to take Yankee service, (by deserting from ours)."[14] And Ruffin was hardly alone in that estimation.[15]

Patrick Cleburne proposed his plan just at the turning point identified above. Had the Confederacy accepted Cleburne's recommendation in January 1864, Gen. Thomas C. Hindman subsequently opined, Sherman's march could not have occurred. And in that case "Georgia and the Carolinas could not have been overrun, Virginia and Tennessee might have been recovered, the unfortunate Missouri expedition successful, and the enemy driven to the east portion of Arkansas."[16] Gen. John Bell Hood, too, later held that if Cleburne's counsel had been taken "this stroke of policy and additional source of strength to our Armies, would, in my opinion, have given us our independence."[17]

Perhaps Cleburne, Hindman, and Hood were right; maybe there was still time to implement this idea successfully by the time of the meeting in Dalton, Georgia.[18] But that possibility was not put to the test, at least in part because Davis knew the hostile reaction it would provoke among the southern elite. The reaction to Davis's belated trial balloon eleven months later confirmed that hostility. Plantation mistress Catherine Edmondston's diary explains why. "Slaveholders on principle," she subsequently wrote, "& those who hope one day to become slaveholders in their time, will not tacitly yield their property & their hopes & allow a degraded race to be placed at one stroke on a level with them."[19] War Department clerk John B. Jones confirmed that "the rich men are generally indignant at the President and Gov. Smith for proposing to bring a portion of the negroes into the army."[20] At no point during the war—and least of all during the war's first years—did the idea of arming and freeing hundreds of thousands of slaves receive any significant degree of approval from the master class, individual letters to the contrary notwithstanding. And especially on a question as central to southern society and as important to their own interests as this one, the opinion of the masters counted for a great deal in Richmond.

The political power that slaveowners wielded comes through even in the most basic statistical analysis. Simply put, masters dominated government. Although less than a third of all free Confederate families owned slaves, more than 90 percent of all Confederate congressmen did so. Fully 40 percent of all those who served in Congress were full-fledged planters, men who owned at least twenty slaves each; in contrast, planters made up only 5 percent of the southern white population as a whole.[21] As Robert E. Lee's aide-de-camp, Col. Charles Marshall, recorded in his memoirs, slaveowners exercised a "controlling influence" in "the management of affairs in the Southern States," and that influence accounted for "the indulgence always conceded by the law . . . to the exercise of the authority of the master."[22]

The masters' domination of southern politics helps explain why the War Department had spurned suggestions about arming slaves throughout the first three and a half years of the conflict; why the Hindman-Cleburne proposal received such an icy reception in Davis's cabinet and why (as Hindman later recalled) it had found "not a friend in either House" of congress; why Lee and Davis began to advocate it only in the fall of 1864 and why Davis was so circumspect in doing so even then; why the legislation that finally emerged from Congress in March 1865 was so toothless; and why even that defanged bill had passed the Senate by only the narrowest possible majority—and a narrow majority achieved only through considerable arm-twisting.[23]

The effect of such direct and overwhelming slaveholder power—and, in Colonel Marshall's words, the "indulgence" it meant for the "authority of the master"—was clearly on display throughout these congressional discussions and votes. Endorsement of the use of black troops generally appeared first among congressmen representing districts immediately threatened or already occupied by the Union army, places in which slavery was therefore already palpably doomed, in which slaveholders consequently felt they had far less to lose from radical experimentation. Masters in such occupied areas who might still be inclined to demur, moreover, had by then usually lost contact with (and had certainly lost political control over) the men who claimed to speak and vote for them in Richmond. In districts where Confederate power yet prevailed, in contrast—in districts where slavery survived and where slaveowners could still impose their views on legislators—most congressmen continued adamantly to oppose the enlistment (and especially the emancipation) of slaves.

This fact revealed itself over time in shifting geopolitical patterns in Congress. In February of 1863, Col. William C. Oates went to Richmond to urge the use of black troops upon various congressmen. Most receptive, he discovered, were "the members from Missouri, Kentucky, and Border States, where the institution of slavery was practically doomed," while "the members from States in which the institution was still unshaken were opposed even to the slightest experiment in that direction."[24] More than a year and a half later, in November 1864, the chief of the War Bureau, R. G. H. Kean, again discovered that "in our Congress the suggestion of the employment of negroes as soldiers finds little favor except with that portion who represent imaginary constituencies"—that is, constituencies already in federal hands and that thus remained part of the Confederate polity only symbolically, only in imagination. The principal difference between Oates's and Kean's observations was that in the interim the war's military geography had changed. By November of 1864 not only the Upper South but also the Mississippi Valley and much of the adjoining terrain had fallen to Union armies brandishing the Emancipation Proclamation. But, as Kean observed, in those portions of the Confederacy still unoccupied, where slavery therefore remained less scathed, "the representatives of the planters are averse to it [Davis's proposal] strongly."[25]

By late February 1865, continuing setbacks in the field had finally led a slim majority in the House of Representatives to enact the diluted version of the Cleburne-Davis proposal already described. The bill's margin of victory, as noted, was even narrower in the Senate. The Richmond *Whig* saw nothing politically significant in the way in which senators had cast their votes on that measure. "If there is any line of separation on this question" in that body, the *Whig* observed, "it separates the trans-Alleghanian from the Atlantic States . . . A large majority of the Gulf State Senators voted for the bill. A large majority of the Atlantic State Senators voted against the bill."[26]

That description of the vote's geographical pattern was formally accurate. Most of those who favored the black-soldier bill came from Kentucky, Tennessee Mississippi, Alabama, and Louisiana. Die-hard opponents hailed from the Carolinas, Georgia, Florida, and Virginia (although Virginia's two senators had been instructed to cast votes in favor). But the *Whig* dismissal of this voting pattern as "purely accidental" politically was less than perceptive. In truth, the "line of separation" in the Senate vote roughly coincided with the one that distinguished states that by now had been long and firmly in Union hands from those that Union armies had not yet (or had only recently) penetrated deeply. In the latter states, many masters still remained unconvinced that slavery was dead. They also remained unwilling to try to save the Confederacy at slavery's expense. For every master prepared to cooperate with the law of March 1865, many more were grimly determined to resist. Even at the Confederacy's eleventh hour, thus, even when facing imminent defeat at the hands of an emancipationist army, "active" slaveowners were still obsessed with protecting their status and their investment in black labor. That obsession goes far in accounting for the paltry number of black troops mustered by Richmond in the spring of 1865.

The Confederacy had confronted this problem before—indeed, during most of the war—as it strove to make use of the black labor force about whose wartime utility antebellum secessionists had so often boasted. Initially, it is true, planters had been willing to lend their slaves to the army as laborers to help win a war they expected would be glorious, brief, and relatively free of cost. But as that illusion faded, most slave owners reacted by withholding their bondspeople with ever greater determination; the voluntary proffering of slave laborers to the army had effectively ceased before the end of 1863. As James A. Seddon informed Jefferson Davis in November of that year, "they could not be obtained by voluntary engagements of service or hire from their owners."[27] That is precisely what forced a reluctant Congress to legislate impressment.

But the same planter recalcitrance that had necessitated the impressment laws in the first place then frustrated those laws in practice, as men like Howell Cobb and R. M. T. Hunter reminded the Davis regime.[28] "Have you ever noticed the strange conduct of our people during this war?" Georgia congressman Warren Akin asked a correspondent at the end of October 1864. "They give up their sons, husbands, brothers & friends, and often without murmuring, to the army; but let one of their negroes be taken, and what a houl [*sic*] you will hear."[29] The pattern was the same throughout the Confederacy, as were the phrases used to decry it. The Galveston *Tri-Weekly News* caustically observed of slaveowners a few months later that "they make a greater lamentation over what they consider a dollar lost, than they do over a hecatomb of their countrymen slain in battle."[30] The outrage that such selfishness provoked among Confederate army officers grew exponentially toward the war's end. Something drastic must be done to discourage the owners' attempts to frustrate impressment, Gen. W. H. C. Whiting wrote from North Carolina in January 1865. "Some very severe example such as trial by c[ourt]. m[artial]. and shooting is necessary."[31]

Robert E. Lee had first-hand knowledge of these frustrating facts. In February 1864 the Confederate congress had decided to impress 20,000 slaves and free blacks to serve as teamsters and in other army-support jobs that white men had previously filled. Ten months later Lee informed the secretary of war that "not one has yet been received for laboring purposes, and to any inquiries on the subject I get no satisfactory reply."[32] At the end of 1864 Jefferson Davis tried again, calling on Virginians to supply five thousand slaves to help maintain and extend the embattled defensive works protecting the Confederate capital. Gov. William Smith duly issued requisitions to the state's several counties.[33] County courts responded with a hail of evasions and protests. Some sought exemption on the grounds that prior requisitions had exhausted their supply of eligible slaves. Others claimed that urgent agricultural requirements made compliance impossible.[34] Still others objected to the damage that labor on fortifications had already inflicted on local owners' human property. Greene County wanted to know how it could be expected to meet such demands when a quarter of its slaves had already fled to the Union army.[35] Attempting to comply with this new requisition, Caroline

County warned, "would produce a stampede of the slaves" to Union lines and thus "would result in a much larger acquisition of slaves to the enemy than to the Confederate Government."[36] Greensville County similarly predicted that "any present effort on the part of the owners to send them would result in driving them to the Enemy."[37]

Governor Smith, an erstwhile army general, struggled to control his anger. "I have to express my deep regret," he wrote to Lynchburg officials in late January, "at the manifest reluctance of the Counties, Cities & towns" to meet their obligations to "the public defence." Masters, he added, were engaging in deceit and subterfuge to frustrate the impressment system. "At a time when the slave Institution itself is in peril & our inability to hold Richmond would make our interests in slave property worthless," Smith wrote incredulously, slaveowners nonetheless responded to Lee's call for help with "such coldness and reluctance as to fill the hearts of those deeply anxious for our Liberty & Independence with anguish if not despondency."[38] On February 10, Governor Smith complained bitterly to his legislature about "the indisposition, which too generally prevails, to obey such requisitions." Such implacable resistance had compelled him to scale down the size of his original impressment order. But even that reduced requisition, he observed with exasperation, "is but feebly responded to."[39] A day earlier, Robert E. Lee had warned Smith about the likely consequences. "At the rate at which they [slave laborers] are coming in," Lee wrote, "I see no prospect of securing a sufficient force" to build and maintain the fortifications "needed . . . to resist assaults of the enemy that we daily look for." Of the 5,000 laborers requested for that purpose in December, Lee glumly added, "we have received but 502."[40] More than a month later, Governor Smith was still reporting that many counties had "wholly neglected to respond."[41]

Masters in other southern states displayed no greater spirit of sacrifice. An anguished Lt. Col. R. W. Frobel discovered as much in Georgia.[42] In North Carolina Gen. W. H. C. Whiting had "great difficulties to contend with in procuring labor in the first place, and in keeping it," since "desertions are constant & I have no doubt that their owners encourage it." Meanwhile, Mississippi's governor petitioned to exempt all of his state's masters from the requisition.[43] In Texas Maj. Gen. J. G. Walker complained about the shameful contrast between "the urgent wants of the Government and the small number of Slaves heretofore obtained by conscription or impressment."[44] An open letter published in a Galveston newspaper blamed "unpatriotic planters [who] have become very liberal and generous with their families," dividing their impressment-eligible slaves among various relatives in order to avoid having them requisitioned.[45] Army officers in the Lone Star state were soon denouncing the "many slave-owners who either induce their negroes to desert the [Confederate] service, or protect and retain them at home when they do desert." Captain H. McKay, the Acting Commandant of Negro Labor in Texas, criticized "the *growing* abuses practised by a class who will send their sons and brothers to the front, but withhold their negroes."[46] In sum, reported Assistant Secretary of War John A. Campbell about this requisition, it "has been obstructed and rendered nearly abortive."[47]

It hardly seems surprising, in retrospect, that masters unwilling to lend Lee their slaves to build fortifications would refuse to emancipate those slaves outright so they could serve him as soldiers. Emancipation, after all, would involve a much larger sacrifice for slaveowners than temporary impressment. And it was not as though the black-soldier plan's opponents had concealed their obstructionist intentions. In November 1864, Georgia's principal newspaper had not only dismissed as utterly "unreasonable and unjust" the expectation that masters would volunteer their slaves as soldiers. It had added bluntly that "it is very certain it would not be done."[48]

That prediction proved prescient. In mid-March of 1865, Sen. William A. Graham notified friends back in North Carolina of the black-troops bill's narrow passage in Richmond. He then added advisedly, "I trust no master in N.C. will volunteer or consent, to begin this process of abolition, as I feel very confident the Gen'l Assembly [the state legislature] will not."[49] Graham, in turn, had good reason for such trust. Just two weeks earlier, the General Assembly had denounced the black-soldier proposal as unconstitutional and formally "protest[ed] against the arming of slaves by the Confederate government, in any emergency that can possibly arise."[50] One of North Carolina's Confederate senators was heard to say that adoption of this policy would leave his state without any reason to prosecute the war effort any longer.[51] Jefferson Davis took such words seriously enough to urge friendlier Virginia to send a special deputation to both North Carolina and Georgia to urge those states to abide by the new law—and to remain in the Confederacy.[52]

Some Confederate masters opposed to the black-soldier policy continued to hope that they could retain their slave property—or, at the very least, receive restitution for it—through a negotiated peace leading to reunification. Such hopes were widespread before Hampton Roads.[53] In January 1865, for example, the Richmond *Enquirer* had singled out for criticism "certain members of Congress, representing large slaveholding constituencies" that had not yet been occupied by Union forces, who opposed freeing and arming slaves because they had long ago lost faith in the Confederacy's ability to protect slavery. Such men, editor Nathaniel Tyler charged, now thought to retain their property by seeking surrender terms that included a "Federal guaranty of slavery," either in perpetuity or at least for a while. Tyler believed that those masters reasoned as follows: "As the object of the war was the safety of slave title, we must seek that object by another course. We shall throw ourselves upon the protection of the enemy. They will grant us, at least, the temporary use of our own slaves.'"[54]

The Hampton Roads conference in early February 1865 seemed to foreclose that option. But more than a few southern masters continued even afterward to hope that peaceful reunification might offer them a better deal than protracted war could do. Perhaps, some speculated, general emancipation could yet be slowed, postponed, or even prevented altogether in a reconstituted Union.[55] Senator William A. Graham thus privately suggested to North Carolina governor Zebulon Vance that "reunion, by which ten States may defeat the proposed amendment to the Constitution, & retain slavery," might yet be "preferable to the triumph of his [Lincoln's] arms, and the subjection of everything to his power." Surely the risks that such negotiated reunion entailed, in any case, were smaller than those posed by "the fatal policy of appealing to our slaves for assistance against the enemy."[56] The hopes of other recalcitrant masters were less sanguine than Graham's, looking forward not to slavery's survival within a reconstructed Union but simply to a compensated form of emancipation.[57] Those who nursed such dreams would have to know that such compensation would likely accrue only to those masters who still owned slaves at the time of reunion, not to those who had already manumitted them.[58]

Even after Hampton Roads, thus, Davis and his allies pointed accusing fingers at southern masters who placed their hopes in surrender and reunion. On the very eve of Appomattox, Raleigh's *Daily Confederate* charged that "thousands of our citizens"—"selfish, narrow-minded, grasping"—had simply abandoned the Confederacy to its fate and were now content to pray that a triumphant Lincoln would "let us keep our property; keep our gold; keep our negroes."[59] Charles Button of the Lynchburg *Virginian* angrily condemned not only North Carolinians but also "some prominent gentlemen from Virginia . . . whose more secret opinions have been made known to us confidentially." They "have opposed with the most vehemence and bitterness the conscription of slaves" precisely because "they want to fall back into the arms of Lincoln, hoping to save their property."[60] The Richmond *Enquirer* also denounced the masters' foot-dragging response to the Confederacy's new black-soldier policy, a response "calculated, if not designed, to defeat its operation and render it fruitless." Nathaniel Tyler warned slaveowners of the consequences. While they "may defeat temporarily the laws of their own government," he reminded them, they could not prevent the enemy from placing such prospective Confederate soldiers in blue.[61]

Fury at such masters' obstructionism worked its way up the army chain of command. Within two weeks of being appointed to recruit black soldiers in and around Richmond, Maj. Thomas P. Turner was inveighing against Virginia masters' stubborn determination to "hold back their slaves" from the war effort. Although "their wives and daughters and the negroes are the only elements left us to recruit from," Turner fumed, "it does seem that our people would rather send the former even to face death and danger than give up the latter."[62] "They were willing to give their sons and brothers to the Army, saw their lives offered as sacrifice upon the Altar of their Country," another Confederate officer wrote a few months later. But, while "there were many exceptions," still "the majority would I am convinced rather have placed in the Army two sons than one negro."[63]

General Richard S. Ewell had been one of the first Confederate leaders to champion the use of black troops. He now became one of the harshest critics of such planter perfidy. In late March of 1865 he communicated his frustration to Robert E. Lee. The letter in which he did so has since been lost, but its thrust is apparent both from the response it elicited and from another letter Ewell wrote on the subject just a few months later. Sections of the Richmond elite, Ewell wrote, strove "to prevent the blacks enlisting and to keep those that did from being useful."[64]

Robert E. Lee's headquarters also acknowledged and regretted "the unwillingness of owners to permit their slaves to enter the service." Perhaps, the newly appointed general-in-chief suggested, it was time to ask state-level officials to compel the masters to cooperate.[65] Lee considered it "almost certain that if we do not get these men" into gray uniforms, their stubborn masters might quickly find the same men wearing blue and arrayed "in armies against us"—and soon afterward, indeed, "relieving white Federal soldiers from guard duty in Richmond."[66]

Lee had expressed the hope in early March that planters would readily place their slaves in his ranks.[67] But the masters' refusal to cooperate had quickly disabused him of those hopes. The general-in-chief remained convinced that any blacks who fought had better be volunteers. But by the last week of March he was ready to employ coercion against the slaveowners. On March 24 he urged Jefferson Davis to "call upon the governor of the State of Virginia for the whole number of negroes, slave and free, between the ages of eighteen and forty-five, for services as soldiers."[68] Davis, however, demurred. He acknowledged that he, too, had "been laboring without much progress to advance the raising of negro troops." But he was still not ready to see slaves confiscated from their masters by force; neither was Governor Smith.[69]

In Alabama, meanwhile, fears of slaveowners' resistance apparently prompted Gen. John T. Morgan to make even further concessions to them. In publicly explaining the proposed slave recruitment policy, Morgan faithfully summarized the new congressional law but simply ignored the amendment that the adjutant and inspector general's office's implementation orders had added specifying that only slaves already freed by their masters would be mustered into army ranks. "The enlistment of slaves in the army, under existing laws," Morgan promised Alabama masters on April 7, "will not affect the title of the owner." It would merely mean that for the war's duration "the right to the services of the slave, for military purposes, will enure to the Government of the Confederate States." Alabama masters, he thus intimated, would *not* have to emancipate prospective slave soldiers or even permanently surrender legal title to such slaves to the government. And after victory, those masters could presumably reclaim any black Confederate soldiers who had managed to survive and put them back to work in the fields.

If Morgan hoped that those extra assurances would enlist the cooperation of Alabama slaveowners, he must have been disappointed. William C. Oates, who knew Morgan well both before and after the war, recalled that the general's efforts had yielded nothing by the time Lee surrendered to Grant.[70] Nor could Morgan's interpretation of government policy have done much to sow enthusiasm for the project among the slaves. In that respect, the Alabama case once again threw into relief the conflicting needs and pressures that both shaped and doomed this ill-starred policy.

If any considerable number of slaves might still have been recruited into Confederate service when Cleburne proposed doing so in January 1864, then, that was certainly no longer possible eleven months later, when the Davis government finally reversed itself and lofted its own hesitant trial balloon on behalf of the idea. It was now too late to convince more than a handful of slaves that rallying to the Confederacy was a promising course of action for them. This, because the same sense of desperation that had at last induced Jefferson Davis to act had by then become pervasive and difficult to miss; only the most isolated or insensitive slaves could fail to perceive it.[71] In that setting, indeed, Davis's proposal must surely have seemed just further proof that the Confederacy was in dire straits. As Georgia plantation mistress Ella Thomas (and many others) sadly noted at the time, it "clearly betrays the weakness of our force."[72] By enacting such a law, soldier James Wingard believed, "Congress is now owning to the world that we are whiped [*sic*]."[73]

That much must now be obvious to the slave, argued the Charleston *Mercury*. "What have we to offer him [the slave recruit]," editor Robert Barnwell Rhett, Jr., asked, but "a lank belly, hard work, a plenty of [enemy] bullets, scant clothing, and a cause so hard pressed as to require his help."[74] "They [the slaves] are to understand," Rhett summarized, "that the Yankees are getting the upper hand of us," and on that basis we will ask them "to choose between fighting with us the weaker party, or with the stronger party, our enemy."[75] Such an overture would probably look to the bondspeople the same way that it did to Mississippi planter P. K. Montgomery. "This measure comes too late," Montgomery glumly confided to his governor, and "seems at this late date like a drowning man catching at straws."[76]

The Richmond *Whig*, despite having come around to support of the measure, nonetheless warned the government at the end of March that it was "useless to expect many slaves to volunteer." They would "not go into the army unless made to go." The editor chose to attribute that unwillingness to blacks' being "naturally timid and averse to danger."[77] Others faced the truth more squarely. Very few, if any, slaves felt loyalty toward the Confederacy, they acknowledged. The evident shift in the war's fortunes would therefore remove the last plausible inducement to serve that cause—the desire to win the favor of the likely victors. The vast majority would now therefore either refuse to serve in the ranks or, formally agreeing to serve, would then promptly desert to the enemy or simply turn their muskets on their Confederate officers. "Can any sane man doubt," Mobile's John J. Seibels wondered, "which party the negro would prefer to serve?"[78] They would of course "go over to the enemy with arms in their hands," editor William W. Holden declared, "probably leaving desolation in their track in every undefended neighborhood through which they might pass."[79] The Richmond *Dispatch*, too, had "little hesitation as to the choice" that slaves would make.[80] "It is too late to make Negroes available as soldiers," Georgia infantryman John A. Speer informed his mother in early April. "They are too much demoralized."[81] Gov. Joseph E. Brown had expressed the same viewpoint six weeks earlier. Abraham Lincoln, he predicted, would find it a simple matter to induce black Confederate troops to desert. Just a few words from the Union president, Brown thought, "would disband them by brigades."[82] The Charleston *Mercury* expected that between 75 and 90 percent of the weapons handed to whatever black soldiers the Confederacy might muster would soon find their way into Union hands.[83] Similar estimates circulated privately even within the Richmond government. The Confederate War Bureau chief guessed that implementing the new policy would place four times as many black soldiers into the Union army as into Confederate service.[84]

Oracles such as these seemed all the more credible in light of the rising desertion rate among the South's white troops.[85] How could those whom the South had so recently held as slaves be expected to show greater confidence in and loyalty to it than its own white troops did? "If a few tens of thousands of deserters of our colors are too many to be arrested and forcibly carried back to their commands," asked the editor of the *Southern Confederacy*, "where is the force to come from to arrest and put back into the ranks one or two hundred thousand of black deserters?"[86] One North Carolinian put it more vividly: "If it requires—as it does in some cases—ropes, handcuffs, and bloodhounds to return deserters and recusant white conscripts to the ranks, what would be necessary to put the negroes in service and keep them in? They would have to be caught, knocked down, tied, and hauled to camps of instruction in wagons; and then, the first chance they got, they would escape to the enemy."[87] Just let us give our slave weapons, another Tar Heel warned, and they will "every where [*sic*] infest our country as armed banditti."[88]

Fears about slaves' affinities and intentions had long reinforced opposition to arming (and especially freeing) them. But by the war's final spring, even some of that plan's long-time champions doubted it could find much favor in the slave quarters. Congress's refusal to promise freedom to slave volunteers, they concluded, had doomed the whole undertaking. Gen. Thomas C. Hindman, who had first urged this policy at the end of 1863, scoffed in 1865 at those who seriously expected "that any considerable number of slaves will volunteer, in good faith, to fight for our freedom without the stimulus of thereby winning their own freedom also."[89]

Charles Button, another of the plan's earliest advocates, was no more optimistic. "Candor compels us," his Lynchburg *Virginian* confessed in mid-March of 1865, "to say that we do not hope [for] much" from the new law because of "the fatal omission" of the promise of freedom from it. Button shared Hindman's contempt for expectations "that slaves, generally, would fight for the freedom of others with fetters on their wrists." The South had always claimed that it understood blacks better than did Yankees. But Button thought that familiar boast patently deflated now. So "if the Yankees laugh such a policy to scorn," the journalist sighed, "they will show a truer appreciation of human nature, and of the motives that govern men, than our legislators have shown in framing this bill." Nor would trying to overcome black reticence by dragooning them into service accomplish anything useful. "If the negroes who may be *pressed* into our service as soldiers, desert to the enemy . . . they will do no more than we anticipate."[90] Col. William C. Oates agreed with Hindman and Button. By refusing to promise freedom to black volunteers, he recognized, Congress had effectively "nullified" the law. Oates doubted that any slave who might yet be enticed by so empty an offer could prove very useful in action. After all, he reflected wryly, "a negro who did not have sense enough, under that law, to have deserted to the enemy at the first opportunity would have been too much of an idiot to have made a good soldier."[91] A similar estimation led Abraham Lincoln in March 1865 lightly to dismiss the worry that any significant number of slaves would now fight for the Confederacy.[92]

But even if Confederate legislation *had* granted freedom to slave volunteers, the South's offer would still have suffered badly in comparison to the Union's. No great insight was needed to recognize the difference. Confederate policy at best offered conditional freedom to some adult males. But it offered nothing at all to other members of their families. It would keep the parents, children, siblings, friends, and neighbors of black Confederate soldiers in chains. Abraham Lincoln, in contrast, had declared *all* slaves free within the Confederacy as of January 1, 1863. Surely, then, Gov. Joseph E.

Brown told the Georgia legislature, the South could not expect black soldiers "to perform deeds of heroic valor" on its behalf "when they are fighting to continue the enslavement of their wives and children."[93] Extend such an offer, predicted an editor in Brown's state, and the slaves "would soon perceive the incentives are unequal, for Yankee ingenuity would teach them very clearly the difference between a partial and a universal action on the subject of freedom." And then "who can doubt which side they will take?"[94]

The Charleston *Mercury* entertained no such doubts. Believing that a slave facing those alternatives would favor the Confederate appeal was simply "desperate in its absurdity."[95] Even the deeply racist Rhett could not take seriously so low an estimate of the black man's intelligence. "He may not be a creature particularly given to logic or to metaphysical reasoning," Rhett wrote, "but he is not altogether a monkey. There are some simple things that he is able to understand."[96] At the other end of the Confederate political spectrum, William W. Holden too dismissed as ludicrous any plan that told a prospective slave recruit that "his wife and children, though he may fight like a Trojan, and even save the life of his master a dozen times in battle, are still to be held in bondage."[97] One Virginian considered the plan's bankruptcy even more pronounced than that, since to obtain his freedom in this way the black soldier must fight not only *despite* his family's continuing enslavement but precisely to *strengthen* the regime that enforced that slavery. "Will the freed man fight to conquer for us, when, if successful, he makes more secure the bonds of those he leaves at home?"[98]

Raleigh's *Daily Confederate* thought they might, and it invoked Frederick Douglass's testimony in support of that opinion.[99] In a January 1865 speech in New York, Douglass had warned the North that slaves might fight for the Confederacy if Jefferson Davis made them a good enough offer. Southern blacks, Douglass had predicted, would fight for whichever side "will nearest approach the standard of justice and magnanimity toward the negro."[100] But of course, Douglass knew quite well which side that would be. He was using the specter of black Confederate soldiers to gain additional leverage with the Republicans, to frighten the Union into further strengthening its own commitment to black rights. As Douglass later made clear, he actually regarded Davis's plan as evidence of a kind of "madness" precisely because it "called upon the Negro for help to fight against the freedom which he so longed to find, for the bondage he would escape—against Lincoln the emancipator for Davis the enslaver." Confederate leaders could convince themselves slaves might accept such an absurd offer, Douglass noted, only because "the South was desperate," and "desperation discards logic."[101]

White Confederates' doubts that very many slaves would fight on their behalf were well-founded. Speculation about why slaves would refuse to cooperate accurately read both the mood and the calculations of the South's bondspeople. Word of Davis's initiative had spread among the black population through the slave grapevine and elicited an energetic discussion there, too. A freedman in Petersburg, Virginia, subsequently told a northern writer how he had first re-acted to the Confederate black-soldier plan. Like most prudent bondspeople, he had previously "never felt at liberty to speak my mind." But now, perhaps emboldened by the Confederacy's evident crisis, the man could contain him-self no longer. "They asked me if I would fight for my country," he remem-bered. "I said, 'I have no country.'" Then "they said I should fight for my freedom." To which the man had retorted that "to gain my freedom" on their terms "I must fight to keep my wife and children slaves."[102]

In early February 1865, Thomas Morris Chester, the African American correspondent for the Philadelphia *Press* who was traveling with Union troops in the Old Dominion, talked with Richmond-area blacks about the emerging Confederate policy. They had discussed the subject among themselves, Chester learned, and those deliberations had "rapidly spread throughout Virginia." In the process, tactical disagreements had emerged about how to respond to the expected offer. Only a loyalist handful would genuinely welcome the chance to serve their masters arms in hand. The "great majority" was thoroughly hostile to the Confederacy and was interested only in calculating how best to frustrate its plans. But therein lay the principal disagreement. Some thought it best to flee to Union lines rather than serve in gray uniforms. But "the more thought-ful" and "best informed bondmen and freemen," Chester reported, had settled upon a bolder and more ambitious strategy. They decided "that black men should promptly respond to the call of the Rebel chiefs, whenever it should be made, for them to take up arms." And then, when they found themselves in battle, black Confederate soldiers should "raise a shout for Abraham Lincoln and the Union" and, in alliance with Union troops on the field, "turn like uncaged tigers upon the rebel hordes."[103]

Other expressions of slave opinion revealed strikingly similar sentiments and calculations at work. In early December 1864, William T. Sherman's troops were in eastern Georgia on their way to Savannah. The Union gen-eral and his entourage spoke with a group of older black men who had only recently obtained their freedom, and an officer recorded in his diary the con-versation that ensued. Sherman told one of the freedmen that Jefferson Davis "was talking about arming the negroes." "Yes, Sir, we knows dat," the man replied. "Well," Sherman asked, "what'll you all do—will you fight against us?" "No, *Sir*," came the reply. "De day dey gives us arms, *dat day de war ends*!" The words, according to the soldier diarist, were "eagerly spoken—and the rest [of them] as eagerly assented."[104] About six weeks later, Union Gen. Alpheus S. Williams conversed with another group of freedmen out-side Savannah. Williams asked one of these black men if they, too, had heard about plans to raise black Confederate army units. This man had also heard of them but, he assured the general, "Massa, they can't make us fight de Yankees, I habe heard de colored folks talk of it. They know'd all about it; dey'll turn the guns on the Rebs."[105]

From South Carolina came similar reports. There an aide-de-camp of Sherman's "found the blacks generally aware that the Rebels intended to put them in the army." Maj. George W. Nichols summarized the views gleaned from hundreds of conversations with slaves on that subject over the course of Sherman's march: "While the masters still have faith that the slaves will fight for them, and offer the additional inducement of their freedom if they come safe out of battle, the slaves distrust them, and understand that their own bondage was one of the principal questions involved in the rebellion." "I wouldn't go!" one man had assured the major. "Suppose they offer you your freedom," Nichols pressed. "Oh, dey lies a heap!" the man reportedly replied. "I'se not belieb 'em; I wouldn't fight." "No, sir," an elderly black woman had told him on another occasion; "the slaves know too well what it means; they'd [the Confederacy] never put muskets in the slaves' hands if they were not afeared that their cause was gone up. They are going to be whipped; they are whipped now."[106]

In late 1864, Lt. Col. Thomas J. Leigh of the 71st New York regiment escaped from a Confederate military prison in Columbia, South Carolina, accompanied by a second Union officer. While making their way back to Union lines, the two fugitives received aid from a group of plantation slaves, who spoke with them about the Confederacy's black-soldier plans. "My master offers me my freedom if I will take up arms," one of the men told Colonel Leigh, "but I have a wife and five children, and he does not offer them their freedom." He had discussed the point with others, "and we have come to the conclusion that there is no use fighting for our masters and our freedom" when whatever "children we may want to have are to be made slaves." This consideration did not necessarily dictate refusing to enter the gray army. But it might well influence the nature of black conduct once in that army. "Only let them give us arms," said one, "and we will show them who we will fight for." "We have thought when we get arms and are allowed to be together in regiments," the man explained, "we can demand freedom for our wives and children, and take it."[107]

Of course, skeptics might doubt that refugees and freedmen such as those quoted above were likely to say anything very different to northern soldiers and writers. But many stalwart Confederate witnesses attested to the prevalence of such opinions among their slaves. Edmund Ruffin noted in mid-February 1865, for example, that "since the agitation of the question in R[ichmon]d & the general but imperfect reports reaching the negroes thereabout, the numbers going to the enemy's lines has [*sic*] been tripled or quadrupled."[108] Strolling through Macon the previous month, southern editor J. Henly Smith came upon some white boys taunting "a negro man of stalwart frame who stood near them. One of the boys said to the negro, 'Uncle, why don't you go and fight?' 'What I fight for?' asked the Ebon. 'For your country,' replied the boy. The negro man scowled and said instantly, 'I have no country to fight for.'"[109] Smith's *Southern Confederacy* also reported an exchange between a Georgia master and "a well disposed, faithful, and intelligent slave."[110] Slaves placed in the Confederate army, this loyal bondsman warned, would most likely desert to the enemy or simply flee into the swamps, where—now armed and trained in the use of arms— they would become bandits preying upon nearby farms and plantations. And should Confederate authorities then try to suppress them, the South would find itself embroiled in war on yet another front.[111]

Other southern loyalists also acknowledged that slaves understood both what the North and South really stood for and which of them enjoyed the military advantage when—and acknowledged as well that slaves were making choices in the light of that knowledge. In early April 1865, Mississippi's governor heard that "our negroes are again stampeding" for fear of being pressed into the Confederate army because they "know *too well* on which side to *fight*."[112] Some four year's earlier, South Carolina planter and Confederate official James Chesnut had queried some of his most trusted bondsmen about the matter and discovered (as his wife later recorded) that "they were keen to go in the army" if afterward they would receive their freedom and a bounty. But the readiness of 1861 had disappeared by November 1864, the Chesnuts discovered; "now they say coolly they don't want freedom if they have to fight for it." What accounted for this apparent change of heart? Simply the fact that they could now see a shorter and straighter route to freedom, could see that "they are pretty sure of having it anyway" when Union troops arrived. Why, then, take up arms precisely against those Union troops?[113] A Confederate officer told of a slave named Jack who cautiously tried to explain that reasoning to a southern white physician. Jack told the doctor that he didn't want to fight. "But," the doctor prompted him, "you surely won't allow the Yankees to come here and rob your master and carry you and all the boys away for Yankee soldiers." "Tell you, massa, I knows nothing 'bout politics," Jack replied. "Why," urged the doctor, "if you become a [Confederate] soldier you'll be free. Surely you'd like to be a free man." "Dat's berry well, massa," Jack countered. "We niggers dat fight will be free, course; but you see, massa, if some ob us *don't* fight, we *all* be free, massa Lincum says."[114]

In the spring of 1865, the sharp decline of Confederate military fortunes since Atlanta's fall at last permitted passage of a law authorizing the creation of black infantry units. Even then, however, fierce opposition to emancipation stripped the original plans of inducements that Cleburne, Lee, Davis, and Benjamin had forcefully advocated. By refusing to guarantee the freedom of black volunteers—much less of their family members, and *much* less of the slave population in general—the Confederate government demonstrated that it could not, even at the brink of defeat and destruction, bring itself to initiate an effective revolution from above. The impact of this default upon hopes of raising a "black army" for Jefferson Davis was dramatic. Confederate civilian and military officials, who had confidently predicted the swift recruitment of black soldiers by the hundreds of thousands, in the event managed to raise no more than two hundred and very likely considerably fewer. The elan and commitment of even that small force, moreover, left much to be desired.

The armed rebellion of black Confederate troops that white southerners feared and about which some slaves had dreamed did not occur—in part, perhaps, because so few such troops had ever been mustered. But the black aspirations and loyalties expressed in those dreams did reveal themselves in other ways. On April 2, the Confederate army and government officials pulled out of Richmond. The next morning Union soldiers marched in, thousands of black troops prominent among them, including the 5th Massachusetts cavalry regiment and Gen. Godfrey Weitzel's all-black 25th Army Corps.[115]

As these soldiers entered the city, well-to-do whites shuttered themselves in their houses and peered indignantly but fearfully through their windows.[116] Meanwhile, the city's black residents thronged the victorious soldiers in the streets, some cheering in exultation, others weeping with joy.[117] Black reporter Thomas Morris Chester noted the "pious old negroes, male and female, indulging in such expressions: 'You've come at last'; 'We've been looking for you these many days'; 'Jesus has opened the way'; 'God bless you'; 'I've not seen that old flag for four years'; 'It does my eyes good'; 'Have you come to stay'; 'Thank God', and similar expressions of exultation."[118] White Richmond resident Sallie Putnam was transfixed by the "long lines of negro cavalry" that surged past the Exchange Hotel, "brandishing their swords and uttering savage cheers, replied to by shouts of those of their own color," some of whom, "laughing and exulting," were "trudging along under loads of plunder" taken from shops and warehouses. "On passed the colored troops," she noted grimly, "singing, 'John Brown's body is mouldering in the grave.'"[119]

These scenes and others like them offered vivid reminders of many things—including that Richmond's black population could display great enthusiasm when the right kind of black soldiers passed before them serving the right kind of cause; that slaves could and would fight when doing so truly served their own and their people's emancipation; and that precisely such a combination of slave initiative and Union policy had forced the Confederacy into its own half-hearted, feeble, and ultimately fruitless attempt to mimic and co-opt it.

CONCLUSION

From Black Troops to Black Codes:
"Confederate Emancipation" in War and Peace

The political struggle in the Confederacy over whether to emancipate and arm its slaves revealed much about both the war and about the South more generally. It illuminated the conditions that gave birth to that proposal, the vision of a postwar South that informed it, and the bitter opposition and recrimination that it called forth. Equally instructive was the grim practical resistance that the new law provoked, for very different reasons, among both white and black southerners.

During the years and decades after the Civil War, the Confederacy's champions strove to depict that conflict not as a struggle born of slavery's existence and requirements but as a contest between rival geographical sections, cultures, and peoples in which slavery played only a marginal role, if any. That version of events found support in a number of corollary arguments that southern leaders had fashioned in earlier decades. One of those depicted southern slaveholders as generally kind, humane, lenient, and trusting of their human charges and already moving toward a policy of gradual emancipation, a movement interrupted only because of irresponsible abolitionist meddling and a war forced upon the South. A second corollary claimed that slaves were satisfied with their place in southern society, were therefore not attracted by Union promises of emancipation, generally saw the world through their masters' eyes, and therefore chose to stand loyally by those masters throughout the war.[1]

Nearly four decades after Appomattox, thus, a Tennessee infantry veteran was still fondly reminiscing about wartime slave fidelity to the masters.

"While our men were out in the field of battle," he wrote, "what kept the farm hands growing meat and bread to feed them? Was it fear of his master, who was away in the army? What enabled our refined women to remain at home for four years of the war, surrounded by a throng of blacks, without a thought of fear, but a feeling of protection?" The explanation lay in "the close relation and love that existed between master and slave! His contact with the Southern white man gave him a moral training that was the wonder of the world."[2] At the turn of the twentieth century, a ruined cotton planter turned author embroidered on the point. "The old-age pension, the employer's indemnity law, the foundling hospital . . . in effect, were legalized features of the southern plantation discipline, and the African was the sole real or prospective beneficiary."[3]

By the time those words were written, the same view of slavery and of how slaves had responded to the Civil War had become enshrined not only in popular opinion but also in the writings of professional historians. Central figures in this process were Columbia University's Professor William A. Dunning and his best-known student, Ulrich B. Phillips. The generations of scholars that they represented held (in Phillips's words) that slavery "was benevolent in intent and on the whole beneficial in effect"—"was in fact just what the bulk of the negroes most needed." The latter, in turn, "for the most part were by racial quality submissive rather than defiant," and their "very defects invited paternalism rather than repression."[4]

Other southern-born historians endorsed this portrayal of master benevolence and slave appreciation and applied it to the history of the war. Walter W. Fleming, another Dunning student, declared that slaves who labored in the service of the Confederate war effort "were as devoted Confederates as the whites, all in all, perhaps more so." "Many a bullet," Fleming added with evident satisfaction, "was sent into the northern lines by the slaves secretly using the white soldiers' guns," and "as a rule only the negroes of bad character or young boys deserted to the enemy or gave information to their armies."[5] In 1950, the University of Georgia's E. Merton Coulter endorsed a kindred version of events in his much-heralded history of the Confederacy. "The slaves soon heard of Lincoln's [Emancipation] Proclamation," Coulter wrote, "and all of the wild fears in the minds of some Confederates subsided, for the Negroes continued in their even course of life."[6]

Claims like these did not remain the exclusive property of southern writers. Over time, as increasingly conservative northern business, political, and intellectual elites soured on and retreated from the commitments of the Civil War era, they made peace with the Lost Cause version of that era.[7] At the beginning of the twentieth century, the Civil War era's leading northern historian was Ohio-born James Ford Rhodes. Rhodes's Pulitzer Prize–winning account of that conflict stressed "the peaceful labor of three and one-half million negro slaves" who "remained patiently submissive and faithful to their owners" even as their own "freedom was fought for after September, 1862, by Northern soldiers."[8] Even Prof. Charles H. Wesley, a pioneer in African American history, reaffirmed "the loyalty of the slave while the master was away," a loyalty that slaves manifested by "remaining at home and doing their duty."[9] In the most influential U.S. history text published between the world wars, Charles and Mary Beard repeated that "the overwhelming majority" of the slaves "were loyal to their masters who were fighting against their freedom—proof of their contentment, their affection for their owners, their inertia, or their helplessness—or all four combined."[10] In a prominent study published almost thirty years later, Prof. Stanley Elkins noted how many contemporaneous accounts described the typical slave as "docile but irresponsible, loyal but lazy, humble but chronically given to lying and stealing," how many asserted that the slave's "relationship with his master was one of utter dependance and childlike attachment." The sheer weight and consistency of that testimony convinced Elkins that "the widespread existence" of such slaves in the antebellum South should now be "taken for granted."[11]

After the Civil War, southern loyalists wasted little time in trying to incorporate the story of how the South nearly armed its legions of loyal black retainers into the nostalgic "Lost Cause" saga. In 1867, J. D. B. De Bow invoked that story to show that mutual affection and loyalty had always existed between black slaves and their white masters; the former served the latter willingly and cheerfully both on the front lines and behind them. Thus it was, De Bow claimed, that even "without dissolving the bond of slavery" the Confederacy had begun to recruit enough black soldiers to turn the tide of war "had the war continued."[12] During the following decade, the Philadelphia *Weekly Times* published a series of reminiscences about the war, some of which it soon repackaged as a popular book. One of these essays recounted the Confederate decision to arm southern slaves. The author, Maryland writer Edward Spencer, couched his account in emphatic assertions of the slave's wartime fidelity to their masters and of the slaveowners' confidence in that loyalty. "Treated kindly," having "few cares," and generally "happy," Spencer wrote, slaves were "attached to their masters, with whom they had been associated all their lives," just as they honored others whom "they were used to look up to." Contrary to northern hopes, therefore, when war came "the negroes . . . refused to disturb the Confederates with any fire in the rear." Instead "they behaved in the most exemplary manner everywhere." As Union armies advanced, "the best of the negroes" simply "stayed at home and worked along as usual . . . " Southern leaders—and "this was especially the case with the slave owners"—had "found by experience that the negroes, as a rule, were faithful and well behaved" and consequently "trusted them."[13]

Thereafter this version of the slave's response to the war only increased in currency and influence. By the time that Charles H. Wesley published his 1919 essay, "The Employment of Negroes as Soldiers in the Confederate Army," it had become embedded in conventional wisdom. Wesley's essay accepted the claims of postwar Confederate diehards, Dunningites, and James Ford Rhodes. The slaves had demonstrated their wartime loyalty to their masters, Wesley repeated, "in offering themselves for actual service in the Confederate army." "Believing their land invaded by hostile forces," he wrote, "they were more than willing . . . to offer themselves for the service of actual warfare."[14] Wesley was still agreeing almost twenty years later that "the loyalty of thousands of them [Negroes] had been thoroughly tested by the war," and that the plan to arm them reflected confidence in that fidelity.[15]

Buried under this accumulated sediment lay the very different truth about "Confederate emancipation." It was a truth less useful to ideologues and propagandists for the Confederacy's Lost Cause, but it was the truth nonetheless. W. E. B. DuBois had tried to excavate it during the 1930s with little evident effect on most of the history profession. It took the civil rights movement and its dramatic successes in the 1960s and 1970s to begin to reorient the historical profession as a whole.

African Americans had begun early in the war to show in action how they truly felt about bondage and where their real loyalties lay. Far from rescuing the Confederacy from defeat, they ultimately became indispensable instruments of its destruction. Slaves resisted their masters' commands, escaped from their masters' control, aided and entered the ranks of advancing Union armies. By the time that a handful of black southerners donned gray uniforms in Richmond in the spring of 1865, nearly 200,000 were already wearing Union blue and helping to force the Confederacy to its knees.

Soon after citing Richmond's black-recruitment policy as proof of slaves' wartime loyalty to the South, J. D. B. De Bow died. The new editors of *De Bow's Review*, R. G. Barnwell and Edwin Q. Bell, implicitly acknowledged that their illustrious predecessor and former associate had gotten that story wrong. The fact was, a July 1868 editorial conceded, that "under our system we had a population numbering one-third of our aggregate, that could not be trusted with a gun. They made provisions, it is true, and behaved with much fidelity, but nevertheless many of the men ran away . . . and at last, as teamsters, soldiers, and fatigue corps, they lent to the Federal army an aid of 200,000 men." Far from becoming the "element of military strength" that so many had boasted about, thus, slavery—by filling the south's black population with so much "disaffection and even . . . hostility"— had imposed a "great burden" on the Confederacy and proved an "obstacle to our success."[16]

De Bow's version of the war had misrepresented other parts of the record, too. The masters whom he depicted as enthusiastically offering their slaves to the army had in reality acted very differently. The Confederacy had come into the world to protect slavery. But as its leaders begged slaveowners to help them stave off military defeat and ruin, most masters coldly closed their ears and turned their backs. In doing so, they revealed much about their own core values and priorities. It would be hard to imagine, in fact, a starker demonstration of just how tenacious and single-minded was their attachment to their human property.

Equally instructive was the conduct of Jefferson Davis's government on this question. As southern journalist Edward Pollard later observed, if Davis and others had truly believed "that the prize was not slavery, but independence and liberty," they could "have sacrificed the former" much earlier and then "fought the war on the basis of the emancipation of the Negro" by the Confederacy itself. That, Pollard believed, would "have assured one of the most splendid successes of statesmanship that the world has ever seen."[17] Instead, however, Davis, his cabinet, and the congress firmly rejected all such ideas. Initiatives for change had therefore had to originate outside the government, and the government strove to discourage and suppress those initiatives. When adverse military and diplomatic developments at last compelled Congress to discuss arming and freeing slaves, it did so in secret session. The Senate consigned one such measure to oblivion as late as February 21; it finally passed another a few weeks later only under duress—and by only the narrowest possible margin and after drastically diluting its contents. After that bill become law masters still refused to yield their slaves to the Confederate army. But even when confronted by this naked slaveowner defiance, both the Confederate and Virginia state governments balked at adopting any stronger measures in response.

What accounted for this stunning leadership default in the Confederacy? Prof. David Donald once contended that the South lost the Civil War largely because of its citizens' refusal to be governed and because of its government's failure to enforce its will.[18] The vociferous anti-Davis opposition in Richmond and some southern state capitals, which regularly denounced Davis for seeking autocratic power, would have found that judgment ludicrous. But a solid case can be made that in this instance, at least, Richmond failed in good time to formulate, ratify, and impose a crucial policy on its populace—and, in that failure, contributed significantly to the Union's ultimate triumph.

Confederate statesmen had defaulted on their responsibilities, Edward Pollard believed, because they "had not nerve enough to make a practical and persistent effort" to force through and implement an audacious policy. Pollard traced that lack of nerve to the government's "sense of insecurity."[19] Even the Charleston *Mercury*, which opposed the whole notion of black soldiers, thought that "the grand crying deficiency in our affairs" was the government's "want of *nerve*" when faced with popular opposition.[20] A more specific diagnosis points to the government's refusal or inability to face down the slaveowners and their allies.

The masters' stubborn opposition and resistance, which depicted the use of black troops as social and cultural suicide for the white South, had not only prevented the proposal's enactment and implementation. It also obscured the debate's actual stakes and real meaning. Notwithstanding the charges of racial and cultural treason leveled against them, the plan's architects were inspired not by doubts concerning the merits or justice of slavery and white supremacy, nor by a late-in-the-day decision to prize southern independence more highly than the social and economic foundations of southern life. Political and military leaders came to champion the use of black troops not despite their antebellum values but because of them. In pushing to enact this measure, they were trying to preserve as much of the Old South as they could.

But unlike their critics, champions of recruiting black troops had come to recognize the developing logic of the wartime situation and the necessity of taking that reality into practical account. By the end of 1863, some of them recognized, slavery was swiftly becoming a dead letter; it was succumbing to the combined blows of northern armies and the slaves themselves. These farsighted defenders of the plantation system recognized the need to calculate pragmatically how best to cope with slavery's demise, how to minimize the damage that it would inflict upon them and their beloved social order.

The key to doing all this, they saw, was battlefield success, because such success was the necessary condition for the Confederacy's survival. But placing a premium on military victory and the South's continuing political independence did not mean neglecting, dismissing, or slighting the Old South's social and economic institutions. Rather, it signified the understanding that only continued southern separation from a northern-dominated Union could save what remained of those institutions. Political independence was not simply an end in itself, at least not for Davis and the other Confederate leaders who thought like him. It was the *sine qua non* of continued social and economic supremacy.

But just what did military success require at the end of 1863? How could southern independence be won at that point? The Confederacy was losing the war on the ground at least in part because of its inadequate supply of white manpower and because its slave population was becoming a potent source of strength to the enemy. Reversing the South's military decline patently necessitated, therefore, turning black southerners into a new source of Confederate military recruits.

But how could *that* be accomplished? Southern nationalists had boasted before the war that their slaves were pleased with their lot, were loyal to their masters, and would therefore sustain those masters in any armed conflict with external foes. The war's progress exposed the hollowness of that claim. It did so, at least, to the satisfaction of those willing to face evidence set squarely before them. The slaves' wartime conduct—forcing masters to grant concessions, escaping altogether from their masters, aiding Union soldiers, *becoming* Union soldiers by the tens of thousands in order to defeat the slaveholders' republic—demonstrated their determination to become free men and women.

This conduct powerfully influenced Union political and military policy. It also influenced policy in the Confederacy, simultaneously imposing limits on what Confederate leaders could do and forcing them to contemplate doing what had previously been unthinkable. To induce slaves bent on gaining freedom to fight for the Confederacy, the South would have to offer them freedom in return. All the principal architects of the proposals to arm slaves recognized this ineluctable fact. The more perceptive saw still farther, saw that even manumission of individual recruits would be insufficient. The soldiers' families would have to be set free as well. So, indeed, would the slave population as a whole. Only on such a basis, as both Cleburne and Lee explained, was there any hope that any significant numbers of southern blacks would respond to Richmond's overture. To recognize this simple fact was to acknowledge the black population's fierce hatred of bondage and its refusal thus far to identify with the interests and war effort of the masters. Far from showcasing slaves' contentment and loyalty, therefore, the proposal to arm and free them revealed that precisely the opposite was the case.

But—much like would-be revolutionists from above elsewhere, from France through Prussia and Russia and across to Japan—Cleburne, Benjamin, Lee, and Davis hoped to have their cake and eat it, too. They hoped to win black cooperation with an offer of freedom. But the freedom they expected actually to grant would be severely circumscribed. The former slaves would cease to be the personal property of individual masters. They would gain the legal rights to marry, to learn to read, to attend church, to own property, and to sign contracts. But they would receive no land at the point of emancipation. To survive, therefore, they would have to return to the white landowners and work for them. And to make certain that they did so and that they worked intensively, for long hours, and in return for only a bare subsistence, the Confederate government and the individual southern states and locales would (as Prof. Frederick A. Porcher put it) "make statutes for the regulation of labour."[21] And the former slaves would be unable to block or change those or any other statutes because they would also lack any important political rights, including the rights to vote and hold office.

In this revised Confederate vision of the South's future, blacks would no longer be slaves, but they would be free only in the narrowest possible sense of that word.

Some believe that slavery would likely have transformed itself gradually and peacefully into much the same kind of half-slave, half-free status had the Civil War never occurred. Various Confederate partisans claimed both then and subsequently that such a metamorphosis was already underway long before Lincoln's election. More than a few modern scholars with no Confederate sympathies whatever have also suggested that, absent the war's intervention, slavery would have evolved along such lines before too long. Antebellum and wartime attempts to reform chattel slavery (by strengthening the bondspeople's religious, educational, and familial rights) are offered as evidence of this probable course of events.[22]

But the wartime debate over arming and emancipating slaves, far from confirming this view, instead exposes its flaws. The claim that slavery would have evolved this way even without war radically underestimates the tenacity with which the antebellum South resisted such changes and what it would—and did—take to overcome that resistance. It also thereby minimizes at least some of the achievements of that terrible and bloody war.

While some slavery-reformers were doubtless driven by the demands of conscience, the movement derived its principal political strength from expectations that a less extreme form of bondage could better weather challenges from below (from among the slaves) and from its enemies outside the South.[23] Robert Toombs had thus cautioned in 1856 that the failure to give legal weight to slave marriages was "a fruitful source of agitation among the opponents of slavery."[24]

But prior to 1861, such concerns and such warnings never managed to induce the white South to concede the principal changes that reformers sought. For every legislative advance they could boast, consequently, reformers suffered an offsetting instance of frustration, defeat, and rollback.[25] Only the powerful blows that the war dealt to the master's self-assurance succeeded in substantially boosting reform's political support. The mobilized and manifest power of slavery's enemies allowed reform advocates convincingly to portray the changes they sought as essential to the Confederacy's survival. In 1863, Protestant minister and educator Calvin H. Wiley published a reform tract tellingly subtitled *The True Road to the Independence and Peace of the Confederate States of America.* Reverend Wiley warned the South that "it is extremely probable that God is now chastising the country for its sins in connection with the subject of slavery." Bondage itself was no sin, Wiley hastened to add, but the failure to respect the bonds between enslaved spouses and between parents and children was.[26] Rev. James A. Lyon made the case for reform in even more utilitarian terms. If the South would only correct "the evils and abuses connected with slavery," he claimed during the war's second year, "we can defend the institution against the wily assaults of the world." Strengthening the slave's family ties would especially increase the institution's solidity, since in that case "the slave will not be so likely to make his escape" or "to engage in insubordinate schemes and insurrectionary enterprises." The slave family would then "serve as hostage for the good behavior of its several members, and will act with more potency than all 'fugitive slave laws,' in bringing the fugitive back to his home."[27]

The wartime crisis of slavery did elicit unprecedented interest in reforms of this and other kinds. Even with their backs to the wall, however— even in the face of such life-or-death arguments—neither the masters nor their political allies could bring themselves to take more than the most hesitant, tentative steps toward even modest changes in the slave code.[28] That they would have moved more quickly and resolutely under *less* pressure— without the spur of war—seems unlikely in the extreme. The negligible results that the Davis government's black-troops initiative yielded even *with* that spur should remind us just how obdurate the politically powerful southern masters truly were.

Was the Cleburne-Davis policy's failure inevitable? Was there no way for Richmond to free itself from the political control of stubborn slaveowners, to free itself at least sufficiently to emancipate and arm a large enough number of slaves to save the Confederacy from destruction? Some southern partisans believed that such a way did exist. It was first of all necessary, they held, for the Richmond government to shake off constitutional and congressional restraints. "Are we to sit down quietly and be destroyed because a constitutional scruple stands in the way of our solutions," Frederick A. Porcher had asked the secretary of state at the end of 1864. "In times of war and invasion the constitution is dead. The safety of the people is the supreme law of the land, superior even to the constitution . . . Now is the time for our government to act."[29] Nathaniel Tyler of the Richmond *Enquirer* spelled it out further and publicly some six weeks before Lee's surrender. "The public safety is above law and constitutions," he insisted. "If a mistaken respect for the laws and the Constitution permits the public safety to be compromised," then the executive branch will confront "an awful responsibility." It will have to recognize that "these States and this cause stand to-day in need of a Dictator," a man who "would, with strong hand, seize power and exercise it for the public safety."[30] Some southern Napoleon would have to compel the slaveowners to do what they had neither the foresight nor the insight to do voluntarily.

But bonapartist dictatorship, too, has its prerequisites. To rule effectively, to implement such urgent but radical policies that powerful slaveowners opposed, a Confederate dictator would have needed to identify and consolidate an alternative political constituency, an alternative base of mass civic support upon which to stand while battling stubborn masters.

Various reform-minded governments elsewhere in the nineteenth-century world did find such alternative popular constituencies as they grappled with their opponents within those nations' propertied elites.

In the American South, however, such potential allies were in short supply. White families who owned no slaves might conceivably have provided Richmond with such a base of support. But the great mass of that population consistently proved unable to play that role. Yes, quite a few of them harbored long-standing grievances against masters, and especially against the big planters, and they especially resented making such costly sacrifices for the sake of a "rich man's war." Some advocates of the black-soldier plan had offered it as a way to soothe those grievances and resentments. The problem was that many of these same disgruntled non-slaveholders also swore fierce and eternal allegiance to white supremacy and believed that white supremacy needed to be anchored in black slavery. Those racial preoccupations left them repelled at the thought of mass emancipation and of serving in arms alongside black soldiers, at least until the war was all but lost. During the conflict just as before it, therefore, its crippling racial fears and antipathies seriously limited the slaveless white majority's ability to play the role of political counterweight to the masters.[31]

Archimedes had promised that, given a lever and a place to stand, he could move the earth. But southern society seemed to offer neither of those things to Jefferson Davis or any other imaginable Confederate dictator who might try to budge the slaveholding class. And so it was, as William C. Oates put it, that even "after slavery was practically dead the Confederacy clung to its putrid body and expired with it."[32]

The meaning of the Confederacy's internal struggle over slavery and its future transcends the Civil War proper; it sheds light on the postwar decades as well. Much of the American South's past has been shaped by the struggle between white proprietors and black laborers concerning their respective rights and status and their mutual relations. The history of neither group, as the historian C. Vann Woodward noted long ago, is intelligible without reference to the intentions and actions of the other.[33] The "Confederate emancipation" episode represents no mere isolated oddity or anomaly; it formed, instead, a phase of that longer struggle. The Davis government's proposal grew out of and was a response to the masters' failure to preserve chattel slavery intact against the challenge posed by the wartime alliance of slaves, Republicans, and Union soldiers. It was a desperate, last-minute attempt to save what could still be saved from the wreckage of the Old South. It failed, as noted, because of opposition by both blinkered masters and clear-eyed slaves—slaves who had their eyes on a much bigger prize than the one that Jefferson Davis was belatedly and grudgingly offering.

But the war's conclusion and the Confederacy's destruction by no means put an end to the larger, longer-term struggle between black and white. It did alter the terrain on which that struggle would proceed. The postwar setting would prove far less favorable to southern landowners and their allies than the one to which they were accustomed. After Appomattox, they had to accept the bitter reality that neither slavery nor a politically independent South could be revived or restored. Along with the staunch wartime foe of Confederate emancipation Howell Cobb, they had finally to "recognize as a fixed fact the abolition of slavery" and begin to adapt to it pragmatically. Only then could slaveowners like Georgia's Wiley T. Burge resignedly acknowledge that "it is all over, and we must make the best of it."[34] Carl Schurz ably summarized matters well in a letter he sent to Andrew Johnson in late July 1865 during a tour of the postwar South: "I believe . . . that the more intelligent recognize the impossibility of restoring slavery in its old form at some future time." Not that the old masters "did not desire it," Schurz knew; they did. But they had also concluded that black resistance (which southern whites preferred to call "demoralization") simply "renders it impossible."[35]

Both Patrick Cleburne and Jefferson Davis had looked to a salvaged Confederacy to enforce strict limits on prospective postwar black freedom, to deal with just such "demoralization." The Union's military victory removed the factor of an independent, self-governing South from the equation. Schurz noted how that change influenced the plans of white southerners. Resigned to live within the constitutional framework of the restored Union, they now expressed a keen "anxiety to have their State governments restored *at once*, to have the troops withdrawn, and the Freedmen's Bureau abolished"— that is, to have power over southern social, economic, and political life vested solely in the states and to once again place control over state governments in friendly hands.[36] The South Carolina planter Samuel McGowan, lately a Confederate general and in September 1865 a delegate to a convention charged with drawing up a new constitution for the Palmetto State, was prepared to ratify slavery's abolition "with one condition in return,—that we are hereafter to be left political masters in the State. We must be left free to legislate for all the people here, white or black."[37] It quickly became clear how McGowan and others intended to use that political power.

The connection between the Confederacy's black-soldier perspectives and the white South's postwar goals and actions is instructive. Some scholars believe that wartime emancipation talk signaled a turn toward more enlightened racial views. That same turn, they add, could and should also have inspired a more cooperative attitude toward the project of Reconstruction. Robert F. Durden found it tragic that, instead, the white South so quickly "forgot all about" the "uncharacteristic flirtation with unorthodoxy" that had occurred during wartime.[38] Another historian goes considerably further than that. Confederate leaders who planned to emancipate slaves during the war, Raimondo Luraghi believes, would surely have designed a postwar policy for the South that was "more humane" and "less demagogic and more solicitous . . . of the fate of the blacks" than the one actually implemented by the victorious Republicans.[39]

Some nineteenth-century observers saw very different long-term implications in the Davis government's black-soldier plans. After Appomattox, Frederick Douglass pointed to the real content of the Confederacy's wartime emancipation plans in order to foreshadow later attempts to restrict radically the postwar rights of the freedpeople. The Confederacy's defeat and dissolution, Douglass warned, had not eliminated the intention to keep blacks in a condition of subordination and servitude. If the planter elite and its allies managed to retain or regain control over southern state governments, he said, they would certainly use that power to pursue that same agenda. (When published, appropriately, Douglass's words appeared under the title, "In What New Skin Will the Old Snake Come Forth?"[40]) Alabama's William C. Oates, who would become a Jim Crow governor decades later, also recognized the connection between Confederate-emancipation plans and long-term hopes of keeping blacks under white thumbs. If only Jefferson Davis had been able to put his policy into effect, Oates reflected wistfully, he would thereby not only have preserved southern independence. He would also have prepared the ground for a postwar southern Confederacy whose version of black emancipation could have spared the South any "great shock or violent change in the labor system."[41]

Both the former slave and the former Confederate officer saw matters clearly. As each recognized, albeit from very different angles, the idea of qualifying nominal emancipation by means of aggressive state action to keep the freedpeople propertyless and forced to work for white landowners was in 1864–65 already in the minds of people like Cleburne, Porcher, Benjamin, Davis, Lee—as well as the editors of the Jackson *Mississippian*, the Montgomery *Mail*, the Mobile *Register*, the Lynchburg *Virginian*, and the Richmond *Enquirer*. The long and heated public discussion of those years served for at least part of the planter elite and its champions as a programmatic bridge to and an intellectual "rehearsal for reconstruction."[42] The white South, as Georgia's Capt. James Appleton Blackshear put it in January 1865, would simply replace slavery with "a system of serfdom."[43] In Union-occupied Savannah just a few months earlier, planter William B. Hodgson had envisioned a similar future. If the South were defeated, Hodgson conceded, "slavery as it has existed may be modified." But "the European race" would have to remain able to "contract the labor of the African under some forms." To enforce such service, "a state of serfage, or ascription to the soil" would prove "a necessity from which there is no escape."[44]

During the months after the Confederate surrender, northern reporter Sidney Andrews discovered during a tour of the South that "the labor question" remained "the main question among intelligent thinking men" there.[45] Planters and politicians of various political backgrounds echoed Blackshear's and Hodgson's words as well as those spoken earlier by Patrick Cleburne, Judah P. Benjamin, Robert E. Lee, and Jefferson Davis. Southern blacks, even if now legally free, they agreed, must still be made to serve, as obediently and as cheaply as possible, and guaranteeing such an arrangement would require the use of legal coercion. Reporter Whitelaw Reid wrote of southern landowners that "they do not comprehend any law for controlling laborers save the law of force. When they speak of a policy of managing free negro laborers, they mean a policy by which they can *compel* them to work."[46] "Many of the people hope some system of peonage or apprenticeship will be established as soon as the State gets full control of her affairs," Sidney Andrews discovered.[47] Carl Schurz, too, had encountered a consensus among southern whites that while "slavery in the old form *cannot* be maintained," it was necessary "to introduce into the new system that element of physical compulsion which would make the negro work" for them—that is, "to make free labor compulsory by permanent regulations."[48]

The broad-based agreement that these observers described soon gave birth to the "black codes" of 1865–66. These laws passed in the states of the former Confederacy attempted to define the status and control the conduct of the freedpeople.[49] Once again, continuities were striking between these codes and the restricted conception of black freedom that Cleburne, Davis, Lee, and Benjamin had entertained during the war.

The transition from wartime to postwar thinking was easiest for those, like sugar cane planter Duncan F. Kenner, who actively pushed for both Confederate emancipation and then the black codes. As a leader of Louisiana's postwar state senate, Kenner was soon calling for laws to guarantee "the protection and security of the personal property of the Freedmen," govern "their social relations toward each other," and "make their labor available to the agricultural interest of the State" while "protect[ing] the State from the support of the minors, vagrants, and paupers."[50] The black-owned New Orleans *Tribune* charged that controlling the freedpeople's labor was the legislature's principal concern. As if to prove the point, a newly enacted state law required Louisiana blacks to obtain "a comfortable home and a visible means of support within twenty days after the passage of this act." Those who failed to meet that deadline would "be immediately arrested . . . and hired out" to "the highest bidder, for the remainder of the year in which hired." Should said freedman leave his employer's service before the year's end, he would be apprehended and made "to labor on some public work without compensation until his employer reclaimed him." Louisiana lawmakers also provided that a freedman's children be assigned to the same employer and that if a freedman died during his term of employment, his children would remain in the employer's "service until they are twenty-one years of age, under the same conditions as the father."[51]

Louisiana was one of the first ex-Confederate states to adopt laws like these in 1865. Jefferson Davis's home state of Mississippi acted quickly, too.[52] On November 20, 1865, Gov. Benjamin G. Humphreys, a planter and former Confederate brigadier general, urged Mississippi's state legislators to "meet the question as it is, and not as we would like to have it." War and southern surrender had destroyed the slave system as they had known it. "The Negro is free, whether we like it or not," Humphreys admonished. That, however, was not the end of the matter. Sounding very much like Patrick Cleburne, Humphreys explained that "to be free . . . does not make him a citizen, or entitle him to political or social equality with the white man." The freedman, Humphreys held, was now due "protection in his person and property." But the state had the right and responsibility to guard against "the evils that may arise from their sudden emancipation." Chief among these evils were "idleness and vagrancy," the doleful effects of which were already sorely felt, since "our rich and productive fields have been deserted."[53]

The solution, Humphreys concluded, was equally plain. We must "with an iron will and the strong hand of power take hold of the idler and the vagrant and force him to some profitable employment."[54] Mississippi's legislature responded promptly to the governor's call, drafting stern codes that the governor signed into law before November's end.[55] Other states acted in similar fashion. South Carolina's Black Code Commission set about drafting laws that permitted former slaves to "acquire, own, and dispose of property; to make contracts; to enjoy the fruits of their labor; to sue and be sued; and to receive protection under the law in their persons and property."[56] But freedpeople would also be compelled by law to labor for others on terms and under conditions set by governments controlled by others.

Unlike Duncan Kenner, many of those who now wrote or endorsed these laws had opposed Confederate military recruitment and emancipation of slaves. Most had resisted those steps in hopes of preserving the peculiar institution intact, whether in an independent postwar South or in a reconstructed Union. The war's outcome had eliminated that option, and by the fall of 1865 no important segment of the white population any longer expected to restore slavery per se.[57] The half-free status for blacks that Confederate emancipation's proponents had projected in 1864–65 had by 1865–66 therefore become the best that masters thought they could hope for.

In wartime South Carolina, thus, both antebellum unionists like James L. Orr and antebellum secessionists like William Henry Trescot had rejected the use of black troops. (Orr voted against the measure in the Confederate

Senate; Trescot chaired the state legislative committee that protested against it.) In December 1865 the same two men, finally compelled to acknowledge slavery's passing, joined forces once again, but this time to enshrine in law very much the same kind of status for the freedpeople that Cleburne, Davis, Benjamin and Lee had envisioned while the Confederacy yet lived.[58] Like some other states, Georgia sought to accomplish these ends with laws that were ostensibly colorblind but that empowered race-conscious officials to exercise strict controls over those deemed to be vagrants. The Georgia law received the blessing of such steadfast opponents of Confederate emancipation as Alexander Stephens, Herschel V. Johnson, Joseph E. Brown, and the editors of the Macon *Telegraph*.[59]

This early attempt to dictate the shape of the postwar South, and especially its racial order, failed. In trying to impose the Black Codes, southern leaders once more overreached; they again underestimated their opponents and exaggerated the real power at their own disposal.

African Americans, the Republican party, and the United States army blocked and then repealed the Black Codes.[60] The same forces, armed with a newly amended federal constitution, then proceeded to build new state governments in the South that not only consecrated the end of slavery but also extended to former slaves the personal and political rights previously reserved for whites. Meanwhile, freedpeople reconstituted families, created schools and community institutions both religious and secular, and instructed and mobilized themselves politically. Reconstruction did not, contrary to the fears of the Confederate Cassandras, break up the plantations and give the lands to the freedpeople; private property in land remained far too sacred to Republicans to permit that. But the federal Freedman's Bureau and Republican office-holders in the South did try to protect the legal and contractual rights of black field workers.[61]

The former masters clearly understood the dolorous effect of all this on their own interests. They could not do as they wished with "negro labor," a Mississippi editor complained, "especially as the negro is now a politician and office holder." The campaign of terror and intimidation with which they and other whites responded to this situation aimed first of all at placing local and state-level political power back in their own hands. When they managed to achieve that, a Georgia politician expected, "we may hold inviolate every law of the United States, and still so legislate upon our labor system as to retain our old plantation system."[62] When we "have a white man's civil government again," South Carolina planter William Heyward expected, the landowners will once more impose their will on black laborers, and the latter "will be more slaves than they ever were."[63]

During the 1870s this terrorist campaign scored major successes. As southern Republican parties buckled and northern Republicans retreated, Reconstruction collapsed. The southern white elite then set out to reimpose labor discipline, social inferiority, and political impotence upon African Americans. With the active support or acquiescence of other whites, they accomplished much of this in the era of Jim Crow.

Energizing and consecrating this campaign was a resurgence of Lost Cause spirit and propaganda that idealized the Old South and especially the strict subordination of African Americans that slavery had sought to achieve and that the Confederacy had made into its "cornerstone." Eventual northern acquiescence in Jim Crow's triumph expressed itself practically in the Supreme Court's 1896 *Plessy v. Ferguson* verdict. It took the symbolic form of a sentimental nostalgia for the kinder, gentler world of mint juleps, columned mansions, and cheerfully obedient servants—and a tacit acceptance of the Lost Cause version of the Civil War.[64]

In the same year as the Plessy decision, the city of Richmond turned Jefferson Davis's executive mansion into a Confederate Museum. During the dedication ceremony, a former Confederate general characteristically denied that the South had fought for slavery's preservation even as he lamented slavery's abolition and branded it "the great crime of the century." In destroying "the apprenticeship by which savage races had been educated and trained into civilization by their superiors," Bradley T. Johnson declared, Union-imposed emancipation had doomed "the negro" to unequal competition "with the strongest race that ever lived"—and had done all that to the negro "against his will, without his assistance."[65] As a wave of lynchings sought to help blacks once again find their proper place in society, the renewed and now nationally observed cult of the Lost Cause piously celebrated the grateful slaves of yesteryear who had served their masters faithfully in both peace and war. It all served (as the recently-launched journal *Confederate Veteran* summarized) to teach "young negroes" that "their aspirations for social equality will ever be their calamity." They must instead "accept the situation, treat the whites with deference, and they will soon realize the best they need ever hope to exist between the races."[66]

But the postwar southern elite never succeeded in turning the clock back all the way, neither to the year 1860 nor even to 1864–65. It could not restore slavery, nor could it regain the degree of control over black southerners that slavery had once given them. In the event, it failed even to reintroduce the full complement of labor-coercion measures contained in the Black Codes of 1865–66. It could not eliminate altogether the greater freedom of action that southern blacks had won with emancipation.[67] In this respect, the wartime white opponents of Confederate Emancipation had been right; even a truncated type of abolition proved very damaging to the plantation system. As R. G. H. Kean had predicted, it had brought about "a dislocation of the foundations of society." After Reconstruction ended, black field hands successfully continued to refuse to work with the intensity of slaves, resisted the return of gang labor, and retained for themselves and their families far more of the fruits of their own efforts than they had ever been able to do in bondage.[68]

Just as important, as W. E. B. Du Bois observed, the same "mighty spirit" of rebellion that had earlier enabled southern blacks to help destroy slavery and bring down the Confederacy now "kept a vast number struggling for its rights, for self-expression, and for social uplift."[69] In that struggle, too, the rights already won during and retained after the 1860s proved crucial. Freedom from outright ownership, strengthened family and community ties, education and political experience, the ability to leave southern farms for towns and cities when such opportunities appeared—all these things and others helped the descendants of slaves not only to survive Jim Crow but eventually to triumph over it.[70]

Inseparable from this conflict over the future status of black Americans was the struggle over how to remember the South's (and the nation's) past. During the Jim Crow era, many published accounts of the Confederacy's black-troops policy reflected and reinforced the dominant spirit of reactionary nostalgia. Those accounts helped to depict that wartime policy as further proof of slavery's mildness, slaves' loyalty to their masters, and the masters' eagerness to abandon slavery for the sake of securing states' rights and southern self-government.

Conversely, the struggle against slavery and its grim legacy—the fight to complete the process of emancipation begun in the 1860s—drew strength from a determination to remember both the Old South and the Civil War as they had actually been, rather than as the Confederacy's heirs and mourners preferred to recall them. "The colored people of this country," Frederick Douglass admonished in 1888, "are bound to keep a fresh memory of the past till justice shall be done them in the present."[71] The truth about "Confederate emancipation"—its origins, the motives of its architects, the resistance it encountered for very different reasons among both whites and blacks, its striking failure, and its links to postwar southern history—must be remembered accurately, too, and for the same reason.

ACKNOWLEDGMENTS

This book has a long prehistory. Its seed was planted twenty years ago when I first encountered the mystery of Confederate emancipation. I formulated my solution to that mystery in a lecture that I have regularly presented in my Civil War courses ever since then. I've been happy to discover, year after year, that my students have joined enthusiastically in the task of making sense of this puzzling tale. At the University of California, Santa Cruz, Jorge Henkamer and Gail Hershatter invited me to share my interpretation of the subject first in the UCSC Humanities Dean's speaker series and then before a UCSC Center for Cultural Studies colloquium. Susan-Mary Grant and Brian Holden-Reid invited me to contribute an essay on the same subject to a festschrift honoring the late and much-missed Civil War scholar Peter J. Parish. Shortly afterward, Susan Ferber of Oxford University Press encouraged me to pursue the project in book form. The travel funds to support much of the research necessary to do that came in the form of a summer stipend from the National Endowment for the Humanities and a number of grants from the UCSC faculty senate's Committee on Research. UCSC's Institute for Humanities Research generously contributed one term of research leave, a stipend, and a small grant. A term spent at the University of California's center in Washington, D.C. gave me access to libraries and archives in both the capital district and Richmond. Seeking research support is a time-consuming and, especially these days, often frustrating undertaking. Terri Ediger's able assistance was invaluable. So was the aid of Ira Berlin, David Blight, Eric Foner, Elliott Gorn, William

Freehling, Rick Halpern, Jim Horton, and Joanne Meyerowitz. Former UCSC history department head Buchanan Sharp's support for this project is also gratefully acknowledged.

This book would, of course, have been impossible without the collaboration of many librarians and archivists ("assistance" seems far too pale a description of what they do). At the top of my list (like the lists of a whole generation of Civil War scholars) is Michael P. Musick, recently retired from the National Archives and Records Administration, for knowledgeably and patiently shepherding me through the Archives' labyrinths and for leading me to materials, both there and elsewhere, that I surely would not have found on my own. John Coski, the librarian of the Museum of the Confederacy and an accomplished historian, performed similar service in the Museum's collections and has remained a source of inestimable assistance and encouragement since we met. At the Library of Congress, Jeffrey M. Flannery and John R. Sellers have been particularly generous with their time and assistance. The Library of Virginia's assistant director, Brent Tarter, was also very helpful. So were Nancy Sherbert and Susan Forbes of the Kansas State Historical Society; Elaine Smyth at the Louisiana State University libraries; Susan A. Riggs of William and Mary's Swem Library; Frances Kern at the University of North Carolina, Chapel Hill, libraries; Anne Salsich of the Western Reserve Historical Society Library and Archives; Brenda Gunn of the Center for American History at the University of Texas, Austin; Jennie Rathbun and Tom Ford at Harvard's Houghton Library; James J. Holmberg and Jennifer Cole of the Filson Historical Society's Special Collections; and Siva M. Blake at the Historic New Orleans Collection. Countless additional long-distance research trips became unnecessary because of the intelligent and tireless work of the interlibrary loan staff at UCSC, including Lisa Landsberg, Kim Levy, Denice Sawatzky, Jennifer Walker, Kelly Gardner, and Laura McClanathan. Stefania Galante and David Tzall provided much-appreciated research assistance at various points along the way.

This book has benefitted from the substantive input of numerous colleagues. Buck Sharp shared his expertise in early modern English history. Michael O'Brien shared his encyclopedic knowledge of antebellum southern intellectual life. Dan Carter, Michael Fellman, and Chris Phillips were equally forthcoming concerning aspects of the antebellum and Reconstruction eras. Edmund (Terry) Burke helped me think about the book's subject in world-historical context. Lynda Crist, the director of the Jefferson Davis Papers project, generously provided me with copies of many documents in her possession. Leslie Rowland, a founder and now director of the estimable Freedmen and Southern Society Project, hosted me for a day, helped me to explore the Project's collections, and offered much additional research counsel. James M. McPherson even lent me the original research notes he had taken while preparing his own illuminating studies of soldiers' letters and diaries—thereby displaying a really remarkable degree of both generosity and trust.

An author's biggest creditors are those erudite and patient people whom we ask to read and evaluate our drafts and help keep our most embarrassing errors from ever reaching print. Ira Berlin, Alan Christy, Jonathan Beecher, Mark Traugott, and Dave Bowman graciously did this for individual sections of the manuscript. Joshua Brown, John Coski, Eric Foner, Steve Hahn, Ruth Hoffman, Peter Kolchin, James M. McPherson, Michael O'Brien, Bruce Thompson, and, of course, my editor Susan Ferber read it cover to cover. All criticized gently and praised extravagantly, no doubt conscious of the thin skin they were dealing with. Each deserves a share of the credit for whatever is valuable in the finished product. None is responsible for the errors and flaws that remain or my failure to adhere more closely to their suggestions. My friend Joshua Brown of the American Social History Project, an artist and historian, offered early, continuous, and enthusiastic support, advice, and expert assistance. In addition to closely reading and commenting on the manuscript, Josh helped me to track down and acquire copies of many of the illustrations reproduced here. The only thing more valuable than his help with this book has been his intellectual comradeship over the years.

Production editor Helen Mules and copyeditor Jen Simington performed yeoman service, and Kathleen Lynch graced the book with its elegant cover.

Ruth Hoffman has responded with tolerance, good cheer, and encouragement to my endless perorations about the manuscript, its central arguments, and the sundry problems encountered in preparing it. While teaching her own over-full complement of university classes, she has shouldered many responsibilities rightfully mine in order to let me get on with the endless writing and rewriting. Just by being who she is, meanwhile, she has made my life infinitely richer. Margaret, Annie, and Joey repeatedly broke my train of thought, made me laugh when I wanted to growl, and generally stopped me from taking myself too seriously.

I gratefully acknowledge the following institutions for permission to quote from materials in their collections: the University of Arkansas libraries; the Duke University libraries; the Filson Historical Society; the University of Georgia libraries; the Huntington Library; the Kansas State Historical Society; the Louisiana State University libraries; the Mississippi Department of Archives and History; the Missouri Historical Society; the Museum of the Confederacy; the North Carolina Office of Archives and History; the University of North Carolina, Chapel Hill, libraries; the University of Texas, Austin, libraries; the Library of Virginia; the Virginia Historical Society; and the library of the College of William and Mary.

A number of illustrations appear here courtesy of the General Research Division as well as the Milstein Division of United States History, Local

History and Genealogy of the New York Public Library, Astor, Lenox and Tilden Foundations; the Library of Congress; the University of Arkansas Libraries; and the Kansas State Historical Society.

I have dedicated this book to my sister, Nancy, as a small token of thanks for being a pillar of our family during very difficult times.

NOTES

Abbreviations

AIGO—Adjutant and Inspector General's Office
DU—Duke University
EBL/MOC—Eleanor S. Brockenbrough Library, the Museum of the Confederacy
HL—Huntington Library
HU—Harvard University
KHS—Kansas State Historical Society
LC—Library of Congress
LR—Letters Received
LS—Letters Sent
LSU—Louisiana State University
LV—Library of Virginia
MDAH—Mississippi Department of Archives and History
NA—National Archives Building, Washington, D.C.
OR—Official Records
RG—Record Group
SHSP—Southern Historical Society Papers
SW—Secretary of War
UGa—University of Georgia
UNC-CH—University of North Carolina, Chapel Hill
UTA—University of Texas, Austin
VHS—Virginia Historical Society

Introduction

1. James H. McNeilly, "In Winter Quarters at Dalton, Ga.," *Confederate Veteran* 28 (Apr. 1920), pp. 130–1; James Cooper Nisbet, *Four Years on the Firing Line* (Jackson, Tenn.: McCowat-Mercer Press, 1963), p. 171.

2. Irving A. Buck, *Cleburne and His Command*, ed. Thomas Robson Hay (1908; reprint, Jackson, Tenn.: McCowat-Mercer Press, 1959), p. 39; Atlanta *Southern Confederacy*, Feb. 3, 1865.

3. William J. Hardee, "Biographical Sketch of Major-General P. R. Cleburne," appendix to John Francis Maguire, *The Irish in America* (1868; reprint, New York: Arno Press, 1969), p. 651.

4. Cleburne's memo can be found in *The War of the Rebellion: A Compilation of the Official Records of the Union and Confederate Armies*, 128 vols. (Washington, D.C.: Government Printing Office, 1880–1901), ser. 1, vol. 52, pt. 2, pp. 586, 589–90. (This work will hereafter be cited as OR.)

5. By some accounts, both Hardee and Johnston agreed with Cleburne's proposal, as did Gen. John C. Breckinridge (who was not present at the meeting). See Buck, *Cleburne and His Command*, p. 189; William C. Davis, *Breckinridge: Statesman, Soldier, Symbol* (Baton Rouge: Louisiana State University Press, 1974), p. 403.

6. Craig L. Symonds, *Stonewall of the West: Patrick Cleburne and the Civil War* (Lawrence: University Press of Kansas, 1997), pp. 188–9.

7. William B. Bate to William H. T. Walker, Jan. 9, 1864, CW 17, Civil War Collection, Huntington Library (hereafter HL); OR, ser. 1, vol. 52, pt. 2, pp. 598–9.

8. Symonds, *Stonewall of the West*, p. 186.

9. Dunbar F. Rowland, ed., *Jefferson Davis, Constitutionalist: His Letters, Papers and Speeches*, 10 vols. (Jackson, Ms.: Mississippi Department of Archives and History, 1923), vol. 5, pp. 72–3.

10. Speech of Mar. 21, 1861, in Henry Cleveland, *Alexander H. Stephens in Public and Private. With Letters and Speeches, Before, During, and Since the War* (Philadelphia: National Publishing Co., 1866), p. 721.

11. Buck, *Cleburne and His Command*, pp. 188, 190; Symonds, *Stonewall of the West*, p. 292n25.

12. Benjamin spoke these words at a mass public meeting in Richmond. The Lynchburg *Virginian*, Feb. 13, 1865.

13. Hon. C. C. Langdon, *The Question of Employing the Negro as a Soldier! The Impolicy and Impracticability of the Proposed Measure Discussed* (Mobile, Ala.: Advertiser and Register Steam Job Press, 1864), p. 3.

14. Wilmington, N.C., *Journal*, Nov. 10, 1864.

15. William Kaufman Scarborough, ed., *The Diary of Edmund Ruffin* (Baton Rouge: Louisiana State University Press, 1989), vol. 3, p. 749.

16. Andrew Hunter to Robert E. Lee, Jan. 7, 1865, in OR, ser. 4, vol. 3, p. 1008.

17. Joseph F. Shaner to his sister, Feb. 15, 1865, Civil War Letters of Pvt. Joseph F. Shaner (C.S.A.), typescript, comp. James C. Bramham, Jr., and Margaret Tucker Scott, Manuscript Division, Virginia Historical Society (hereafter VHS).

18. Langdon, *The Question of Employing the Negro as a Soldier*, p. 3.

19. Douglas J. Cater to Cousin Fannie, Feb. 11, 1865, Douglas J. and Rufus W. Cater Papers, Manuscript Division, Library of Congress (hereafter LC).

20. Atlanta *Southern Confederacy*, Jan. 20, 1865; Beth G. Crabtree and James W. Patton, eds., *"Journal of a Secesh Lady": The Diary of Catherine Ann Devereux Edmondston* (Raleigh: North Carolina Division of Archives and History, 1979), pp. 552–3.

21. Frank Vandiver, ed., "Proceedings of the Second Confederate Congress," *Southern Historical Society Papers* (henceforth *SHSP*) 52, p. 289.

22. Mary F. Akin to her husband, Jan. 8, 1865, in Bell Irvin Wiley, ed., *Letters of Warren Akin, Confederate Congressman* (Athens: University of Georgia Press, 1959), p. 117.

23. Macon *Telegraph and Confederate*, Nov. 3, 1864.

24. Richard L. Maury Diary, entry of Feb. 1, 1865, Manuscript Division, VHS.

25. *Speech of Hon. Thomas S. Gholson of Virginia on the Policy of Employing Negro Troops and the Duty of All Classes to Aid in the Prosecution of the War* (Richmond, Va.: Geo. P. Evans and Co., 1865), p. 3.

26. Macon *Telegraph and Confederate*, Oct. 18, 1864.

27. Wirt Armistead Cate, ed., *Two Soldiers: The Campaign Diaries of Thomas J. Key, C.S.A., and Robert J. Campbell, U.S.A.* (Chapel Hill: University of North Carolina Press, 1938), pp. 17–8.

28. Richmond *Examiner*, Feb. 25, 1865.

29. Shelby Foote, *The Civil War: A Narrative* (New York: Random House, 1974), vol. 3, p. 766.

30. Rep. Robert P. Dick's speech of Dec. 20, 1864, published in the Raleigh *North Carolina Standard*, Jan. 18, 1865.

31. Charleston *Mercury*, Nov. 3, 1864.

32. Frank E. Vandiver, "Proceedings of the Second Confederate Congress," *SHSP* 51, p. 276.

33. Robert E. Lee to Ethelbert Barksdale, Feb. 18, 1865. The Richmond *Sentinel* published this letter on Feb. 23. The Richmond *Enquirer* carried the text on Feb. 25.

34. Gary W. Gallagher, *The Confederate War: How Popular Will, Nationalism, and Military Strategy Could Not Stave Off Defeat* (Cambridge, Mass.: Harvard University Press, 1997), p. 81; Jay Winik, *April 1865: The Month that Saved America* (New York: HarperCollins, 2001), p. 56; Eli N. Evans, *Judah P. Benjamin: The Jewish Confederate* (New York: Free Press, 1988), p. 249.

35. Out of print for years, Durden's volume was recently reissued without revision or emendation but with a new author's preface that generously encouraged further exploration of its subject. Those anxious to make sense of these puzzling developments, Durden quite rightly noted, "have some challenging work yet to do." Robert F. Durden, "Preface to the paperback edition," *The Gray and the Black: The Confederate Debate on Emancipation* (1972; reprint, Baton Rouge: Louisiana State University Press, 2000), p. x. A still unpublished addition to the literature is Philip D. Dillard, "Independence or Slavery: The Confederate Debate over Arming the Slaves" (Ph. D. dissertation, Rice University, 1999).

36. In researching this study, I have combed through seventeen newspapers published in seven Confederate states. That search by no means exhausts the record,

of course. Further sampling convinced me, however, that these papers did offer an accurate picture of southern journalistic opinion.

37. Reprinted in Ulrich Bonnell Phillips, *The Life of Robert Toombs* (New York: Macmillan, 1913), p. 158 (quotation).

38. Atlanta *Southern Confederacy*, Jan. 20, 1865.

39. Ruffin, *Anticipations of the Future, to Serve as Lessons for the Present Time. In the Form of Extracts of Letters from an English Resident in the United States, to the London Times, from 1864 to 1870* (Richmond, Va.: J. W. Randolph, 1860), p. 70.

40. James A. Seddon to Jefferson Davis, Nov. 3, 1864, in OR, ser. 4, vol. 3, p. 756.

41. Charleston *Mercury*, Dec. 27, 1864.

42. Jubal Anderson Early, *Jubal Early's Memoirs: Autobiographical Sketch and Narrative of the War between the States* (1912; reprint, Baltimore: Nautical and Aviation Publishing Company of America, 1989), pp. xxxv–xxxvi.

43. J. L. Reynolds, "Fidelity of Slaves," *De Bow's Review* 29, no. 5 (Nov. 1860), pp. 577, 582.

44. The Memphis *Avalanche*, Apr. 29, 1861, quoted in John Cimprich, *Slavery's End in Tennessee, 1861–1865* (University: University of Alabama Press, 1985), pp. 13–4.

45. Macon *Telegraph and Confederate*, Jan. 10, 1865, reprinting a letter originally published in the *St. Louis Republican*.

46. Lynchburg *Virginian*, Oct. 20, 1864.

47. Robert E. Lee to Andrew Hunter, Jan. 11, 1865, in OR, ser. 4, vol. 3, p. 1013.

48. A. T. Bledsoe to W. S. Turner, Aug. 2, 1861, ch. 9, vol. 1, Letter Book, pp. 732–3, Secretary of War (hereafter SW), Letters Sent (hereafter LS), War Department Collection of Confederate Records, Record Group (hereafter RG) 109, National Archives Building, Washington, D.C. (hereafter NA).

49. OR, ser. 4, vol. 3, p. 762.

50. Richmond *Dispatch*, Mar. 20, 1865; Montgomery *Daily Mail*, Apr. 8, 1865.

51. Richard Taylor, *Destruction and Reconstruction: Personal Experiences in the Late War* (1877; reprint, New York: Longmans, Green and Co., 1955), p. 257.

52. Benjamin told a public meeting that "My own negroes have been to me and said, 'Master, set us free, and we will fight for you; we had rather fight for you than for the Yankees.'" Lynchburg *Virginian*, Feb. 13, 1865.

53. The Editor [J. D. B. De Bow], "Memories of the War," *De Bow's Review* 3 (Mar. 1867), pp. 225–33 (quotation on pp. 226–7).

54. The quoted words were those of historian Ulrich B. Phillips, *Life and Labor in the Old South* (1929; reprint, Boston: Little, Brown, 1963), p. 366.

55. Macon *Telegraph and Confederate*, Apr. 17, 1865, letter signed Woodson.

56. Richmond *Enquirer*, Jan. 26, 1865.

57. Richmond *Enquirer*, Jan. 12, 1865.

58. Richmond *Enquirer*, Nov. 14, 1864.

59. Spearheaded by such secular figures as T. R. R. Cobb, Henry Hughes, and Robert Toombs, these initiatives found their most numerous and consistent advocates among Protestant ministers like Calvin H. Wiley, James Henley Thornwell, George Foster Pierce, and James A. Lyon. The slavery-reform movement has been treated in many studies, including Bell I. Wiley, "Movement to Humanize the Insti-

tution of Slavery during the Confederacy," *Emory University Quarterly* 5 (Dec. 1949): 207–20; Donald G. Mathews, "Charles Colcock Jones and the Southern Evangelical Crusade to Form a Biracial Community," *Journal of Southern History* 41 (Aug. 1975): 299–320; Bertram Wyatt-Brown, "Modernizing Southern Slavery: The Proslavery Argument Reinterpreted," in *Region, Race and Reconstruction: Essays in Honor of C. Vann Woodward* (Baton Rouge: Louisiana State University Press, 1981), pp. 27–50; Clarence L. Mohr, *On the Threshold of Freedom: Masters and Slaves in Civil War Georgia* (Athens and London: University of Georgia Press, 1986), pp. 235–71; Drew Gilpin Faust, *The Creation of Confederate Nationalism* (Baton Rouge: Louisiana State University Press, 1988), pp. 72–81; Eugene D. Genovese, *The Slaveholders' Dilemma: Freedom and Progress in Southern Conservative Thought, 1820–1860* (Columbia: University of South Carolina Press, 1992), pp. 58–64; Genovese, *A Consuming Fire: The Fall of the Confederacy in the Mind of the White Christian South* (Athens: University of Georgia Press, 1998), pp. 101–21; William W. Freehling, *The Reintegration of American History: Slavery and the Civil War* (New York: Oxford University Press, 1994), pp. 59–81.

60. Raleigh *Daily Confederate*, Jan. 25, 1865.

61. Galveston *Tri-Weekly News*, Feb. 22, 1865, letter signed Caleb Cutwell.

62. Robert Manson Myers, ed., *The Children of Pride: A True Story of Georgia and the Civil War* (New Haven, Conn.: Yale University Press, 1972), p. 1244.

63. Edward A. Pollard, *Life of Jefferson Davis with a Secret History of the Southern Confederacy* (Atlanta: National Publishing Co., 1869), p. 453.

64. John Leyburn, "An Interview with Gen. Robert E. Lee," *Century Magazine* 30 (May 1885), pp. 166–7.

65. Alan T. Nolan, *Lee Considered: General Robert E. Lee and Civil War History* (Chapel Hill: University of North Carolina Press, 1991) pp. 24–5; and Myrta Lockett Avary, *Dixie after the War: An Exposition of Social Conditions Existing in the South, During the Twelve Years Succeeding the Fall of Richmond* (New York: Doubleday, Page and Co., 1906), p. 72 (quotation).

66. Myrta Lockett Avary, ed., *Recollections of Alexander H. Stephens: His Diary Kept When a Prisoner at Fort Warren, Boston Harbour, 1865* (New York: Doubleday, Page and Co., 1910), pp. 172–4 (quotation on p. 172); Richard Malcolm Johnston and William Hand Browne, *Life of Alexander H. Stephens* (Philadelphia: J. B. Lippincott, 1878), p. 394 (quotation).

67. Alexander H. Stephens, *A Constitutional View of the Late War Between the States; Its Causes, Character, Conduct and Results*, 2 vols. (Philadelphia: National Publishing Co., 1868), vol. 1, p. 11.

68. Jefferson Davis, *The Rise and Fall of the Confederate Government*, 2 vols. (1881; reprint, New York: Da Capo, 1990), vol. 1, pp. 66–7.

69. See, for example, J. William Jones, *The Davis Memorial Volume: Or, Our Dead President, Jefferson Davis and the World's Tribute to His Memory* (Richmond: B. F. Johnson and Co., 1890), pp. 283–4. More recently, see H. C. Blackerby, *Blacks in Blue and Gray: Afro-American Service in the Civil War* (Tuscaloosa, Ala.: Portals Press, 1979), p. 6.

70. William M. Polk, *Leonidas Polk, Bishop and General*, 2 vols. (New York and London: Longmans, Green, and Co., 1915), vol. 2, p. 340. Former Confederate

Gen. Bradley T. Johnson had said much the same thing almost twenty years earlier: Had war and war-imposed abolition not occurred, Johnson declared, "the negro would have been trained and educated into habits of industry, of self-restraint, of self-denial, of moral self-government, until in due course he would have gone into the world to make his struggle for survivorship on fair terms." *In Memoriam Sempiternam* (Richmond, Va.: Confederate Museum, 1896), p. 51. Thanks to John Coski for furnishing a copy of this document.

71. Thomas Robson Hay, "The South and the Arming of the Slaves," *Mississippi Valley Historical Review* 6 (June 1919), pp. 34–73.

72. Allan Nevins, *The Statesmanship of the Civil War* (New York: Macmillan, 1953), pp. 51–2. Slavery's relationship to the Civil War is presented equivocally and ambiguously in Nevins's multivolume work, *Ordeal of the Union*, 8 vols. (New York: Charles Scribner's Sons, 1947–1971).

73. That consensus, the product of generations of historians, informs such influential works as James M. McPherson, *Battle Cry of Freedom: The Civil War Era* (New York: Oxford University Press, 1988) and *Ordeal by Fire: The Civil War and Reconstruction*, 2d ed. (New York: McGraw-Hill, 1992); Eric Foner, *Politics and Ideology in the Age of the Civil War* (New York: Oxford University Press, 1980) and *Reconstruction: America's Unfinished Revolution* (New York: Harper and Row, 1988); and William W. Freehling, *The Road to Disunion: Secessionists at Bay, 1776–1854* (New York: Oxford University Press, 1990) and *The Reintegration of American History*. See also Bruce Levine, *Half Slave and Half Free: The Roots of Civil War*, rev. ed. (New York: Hill and Wang, 2005).

74. Charles H. Wesley, *The Collapse of the Confederacy* (1937; reprint, Columbia: University of South Carolina Press, 2001), p. 166.

75. Bill G. Reid, "Confederate Opponents of Arming the Slaves, 1861–1865," *Journal of Mississippi History*, 22 (Oct. 1960), p. 264; Emory M. Thomas, *The Confederate Nation, 1861–1865* (New York: Harper and Row, 1979), p. 299 (quotation). See also Paul D. Escott, *After Secession: Jefferson Davis and the Failure of Confederate Nationalism* (Baton Rouge: Louisiana State University Press, 1978), pp. 254–5; Laurence Shore, *Southern Capitalists: The Ideological Leadership of an Elite* (Chapel Hill: University of North Carolina Press, 1986), p. 93; Richard E. Beringer, Herman Hattaway, Archer Jones, and William N. Still, Jr., *Why the South Lost the Civil War* (Athens: University of Georgia Press, 1986), p. 391; Evans, *Judah P. Benjamin*, p. 287; Symonds, *Stonewall of the West*, p. 182; Winik, *April 1865*, p. 61. Clarence L. Mohr notes anomalous cases but agrees that the debate generally ranged "traditionalists," for whom secession was "merely a tactic to defend chattel bondage," against "Rebel patriots who reversed the priorities and saw political independence itself as the transcendent war aim." Mohr, *On the Threshold of Freedom*, pp. 275, 277. Contrast the suggestive comments in *Freedom: A Documentary History of Emancipation, 1861–1867*, ser. 2, *The Black Military Experience*, ed. Ira Berlin, Joseph P. Reidy, and Leslie S. Rowland (Cambridge, Eng.: Cambridge University Press, 1982), p. 281.

76. Emory M. Thomas, *The Confederacy as a Revolutionary Experience* (1971; reprint, Columbia: University of South Carolina Press, 1991), p. 119 (quotation). Philip D. Dillard's "Independence or Slavery" reaffirms this conclusion.

77. Winik, *April 1865*, pp. 62–3.

78. Ervin L. Jordan, *Black Confederates and Afro-Yankees in Civil War Virginia* (Charlottesville: University Press of Virginia, 1995), p. 250.

79. Durden, *The Gray and the Black*, pp. viii, 253. In the 2000 edition's preface, Durden qualified that characterization, limiting it to white attitudes toward blacks.

80. James Ronald Kennedy and Walter Donald Kennedy, *Was Jefferson Davis Right?* (Gretna, La.: Pelican, 1998), p. 140.

81. See, for example, Charles W. Harper, "Black Loyalty under the Confederacy," *Black Confederates*, ed. Charles Kelley Barrow, J. H. Segars, and R. B. Rosenburg (Gretna, La.: Pelican, 2001), p. 26; Wayne R. Austerman, "The Black Confederates," *Black Confederates*, p. 48.

82. J. H. Segars, *In Search of Confederate Ancestors: The Guide* (Murfreesboro, Tenn.: Southern Heritage Press, 1993), p. 97.

83. The quoted phrase comes from "Black History Month, Black Confederate Heritage," issued by the Sons of Confederate Veterans Education Committee. See http://www.scv.org/education/edpapers/blackhst.htm. Aimed at "professors, teachers, librarians, principals, ethnic leaders, members of the press, and others interested in promoting an understanding of Black contributions to United States history," this "fact sheet" claims to prove both that Confederate leaders cared little about slavery and that slaves stood loyally by their masters.

Chapter 1

1. John A. Inglis to Carrie, Jan. 29, 1865, John Auchincloss Inglis Collection, Miscellaneous Manuscript Collection, Manuscript Division, LC.

2. John B. Jones, *A Rebel War Clerk's Diary at the Confederate States Capital* (Philadelphia: J. B. Lippincott, 1866), vol. 2, p. 451.

3. This account of Ewell's 1861 conversation with Davis comes from a friend and relative of Ewell's, to whom the general recounted the exchange in 1866. See Tasker Gantt to Henry Hunt, May 19, 1886, Henry Jackson Hunt Papers, LC. Ewell expressed the same opinion in favor of arming slaves in a letter to his niece in the summer of 1862. See Richard S. Ewell to Lizzie Ewell, July 20, 1862, Richard S. Ewell Papers, LC. See also Donald C. Pfanz, *Richard S. Ewell: A Soldier's Life* (Chapel Hill and London: University of North Carolina Press, 1998), p. 139. All of this, in turn, squares with William C. Oates's memory of getting a favorable hearing from Ewell for the same idea relatively early in the war. William C. Oates, *The War between the Union and the Confederacy and Its Lost Opportunities* . . . (New York: The Neale Publishing Co., 1905), pp. 496–7.

4. Herman Hattaway and Archer Jones, *How the North Won: A Military History of the Civil War* (Urbana: University of Illinois Press, 1983), p. 114; McPherson, *Ordeal by Fire*, p. 184; E. B. Long with Barbara Long, *The Civil War Day by Day: An Almanac, 1861–1865* (Garden City, N.Y.: Doubleday, 1971), p. 706.

5. See Freehling, *Reintegration of American History*, p. 5; William W. Freehling, *The South vs. the South: How Anti-Confederate Southerners Shaped the Course of the Civil War* (New York: Oxford University Press, 2001), pp. xii–xiii.

6. J. E. Leigh, J. F. Hodges, and James B. Walton to J. J. Pettus, Memorial to

the Governor from Sunflower County, Apr. 1862, RG 27, Mississippi Department of Archives and History, Jackson (hereafter MDAH).

7. C. B. New to Gov. John J. Pettus, Nov. 14, 1861, RG 27, MDAH.

8. Wm. H. Lee to J. P. Walker, May 4, 1861, SW, Letters Received (hereafter LR), #957 1861, RG 109, NA; John J. Cheatham to L P. Walker, May 4, 1861, SW/ LR, #605 1861, NA; C. Vann Woodward, ed., *Mary Chesnut's Civil War* (New Haven, Conn.: Yale University Press, 1981), pp. 255, 313.

9. W. S. Turner to J. P. Walker, July 17, 1861, in OR, ser. 4, vol. 1, p. 482.

10. Richard M. McMurry, *Two Great Rebel Armies: An Essay in Confederate Military History* (Chapel Hill: University of North Carolina Press, 1989), pp. 14–9.

11. Leigh, Hodges, and Walton to J. J. Pettus, Memorial to the Governor from Sunflower County, Apr. 1862, RG 27, MDAH.

12. Howard Jones, *Union in Peril: The Crisis over British Intervention in the Civil War* (Chapel Hill: University of North Carolina Press, 1992), pp. 2–6. Some kind of British and French support for the Confederacy evidently remained a distinct possibility down through the Confederate defeat at Antietam in the fall of 1862 and the issuance of the preliminary Emancipation Proclamation soon afterward. See James M. McPherson, *Crossroads of Freedom: Antietam* (New York: Oxford University Press, 2002), pp. 56–61, 93–5, 141–6.

13. Thomas Donaldson, Notes of a Conversation with Duncan Farrar Kenner, New York City, Oct. 19, 1882, Duncan Farrar Kenner Collection, Manuscript Division, LC; Craig A. Bauer, *A Leader among Peers: The Life and Times of Duncan Farrar Kenner* (Fayetteville: University of Southwestern Louisiana, 1993), pp. 194–7, 204–5, 214–5; John Bigelow, "The Confederate Diplomatists and their Shirt of Nessus," *Century Magazine* 42 (Mar. 1891), pp. 113–26; Robert Douthat Meade, *Judah P. Benjamin: Confederate Statesman* (1943; reprint, Baton Rouge: Louisiana State University Press, 2001), pp. 191, 264, 309–10.

14. OR, ser. 4, vol. 2, pp. 664–5.

15. On this, see Bell Irvin Wiley, *The Road to Appomattox* (1956; reprint, Baton Rouge: Louisiana State University Press, 1994), pp. 43–7.

16. Albert Burton Moore, *Conscription and Conflict in the Confederacy* (1924; reprint, Columbia: University of South Carolina Press, 1996), pp. 13–6; OR, ser. 4, vol. 3, pp. 469–72, 897–8, vol. 4, pp. 207–9. The conscription law made every able-bodied white male citizen between the ages of eighteen and thirty-five (later raised to forty-five) years subject to call-up for three-year terms of service, unless they were otherwise exempted. Those already serving in the army would have their tours of duty equivalently lengthened.

17. Six southern states provided for impressing black labor, too. Benjamin Quarles, *The Negro in the Civil War* (1953; reprint, New York: Da Capo, 1988), p. 47.

18. A. T. Bledsoe to W. S. Turner, Aug. 2, 1861, Letter Book, ch. 9, vol. 1, pp. 732–3, SW/LS, RG 109, NA.

19. This second-hand account comes, once again, from a friend and relative of Ewell's to whom the general had related the story in 1866. Although Davis himself could not in later years recall this exchange, he acknowledged that he would have regarded any such proposal at the war's inception as "preposterous." Tasker Gantt

to Henry Hunt, May 19, 1886, Hunt Jackson Papers, Manuscript Division, LC; Jefferson Davis to Campbell Brown, June 14, 1886, George Washington Campbell Brown Papers, Manuscript Division, LC.

20. OR, ser. 4, vol. 1, p. 1020; Arthur W. Bergeron, *Confederate Mobile* (Baton Rouge: Louisiana State University Press, 1991), p. 105.

21. OR, ser. 4, vol. 1, pp. 1087–8, 1111.

22. James A. Seddon to Hon. E. S. Dargan, Dec. 18, 1863, ch. 9, vol. 14, p. 289, SW/LS, RG 109, NA; OR, ser. 4, vol. 2, p. 941; Bergeron, *Confederate Mobile*, pp. 104–6.

23. James A. Seddon to Hon. E. S. Dargan, Dec. 18, 1863, ch. 9, vol. 14, p. 289, SW/LS, RG 109, NA; OR, ser. 4, vol. 2, p. 941.

24. Benjamin Quarles, *The Negro in the American Revolution* (1961; reprint, New York: Norton, 1973); Woody Holton, *Forced Founders: Indians, Debtors, Slaves, and the Making of the American Revolution in Virginia* (Chapel Hill: University of North Carolina Press, 1999), pp. 133–63.

25. Clyde N. Wilson, ed., *The Papers of John C. Calhoun*, 28 vols. (Columbia, S.C., 1959–2003), vol. 13, p. 394.

26. George Fredrickson, *The Black Image in the White Mind: The Debate on Afro-American Character and Destiny, 1817–1914* (New York: Harper and Row, 1971), pp. 43–96.

27. Eric Foner, *Free Soil, Free Labor, Free Men: The Ideology of the Republican Party before the Civil War* (New York: Oxford University Press, 1970); Leonard L. Richards, *The Slave Power: The Free North and Southern Domination, 1780–1860* (Baton Rouge: Louisiana State University Press, 2000).

28. Charles B. Dew, *Apostles of Disunion: Southern Secession Commissioners and the Causes of the Civil War* (Charlottesville and London: University Press of Virginia, 2002), pp. 10–2, 30, 33, 53, 63–5.

29. James A. Seddon to E. S. Dargan, Dec. 18, 1863, ch. 9, vol. 14, p. 289, SW/LS, RG 109, NA; OR, ser. 4, vol. 2, p. 941.

30. Andrew Hunter to Robert E. Lee, Nov. 7, 1865, in OR, ser. 4, vol. 3, p. 1008.

31. When European sympathizers urged the Confederacy to conciliate antislavery sentiment on the continent, Davis's government in January 1863 "unequivocally and absolutely denie[d] its possession of any power whatever over the subject [of slavery in the several states] and can not entertain any propositions in relation to it." The words appeared in a circular dated January 15, 1863, that Secretary of State Benjamin sent to all diplomatic agents. Cited in Frank Lawrence Owsley, *King Cotton Diplomacy: Foreign Relations of the Confederate States of America*, 2d ed. (Chicago: University of Chicago Press, 1959), p. 531.

32. A. T. Bledsoe to W. S. Turner, Aug. 2, 1861, ch. 9, vol. 1, Letter Book, pp. 732–3, SW/LS, RG 109, NA.

33. OR, ser. 4, vol. 3, pp. 693–4. Seddon recorded that opinion on the letter from "Native Georgian" itself.

34. McPherson, *Battle Cry of Freedom*, p. 664; Stephen W. Sears, *Gettysburg* (Boston: Houghton Mifflin, 2003), pp. 6–17.

35. John H. Reagan, *Memoirs, with Special Reference to Secession and the Civil War* (New York and Washington: Neale Publishing Co., 1906), p. 147.

36. Edward Younger, ed. *Inside the Confederate Government: The Diary of Robert Garlick Hill Kean* (Baton Rouge: Louisiana State University Press, 1957), pp. 86, 119, 122 (hereafter *Kean Diary*).

37. Sarah Woolfolk Wiggins, ed., *The Journals of Josiah Gorgas, 1857–1878* (Tuscaloosa and London: University of Alabama Press, 1995), pp. 74–5 (hereafter *Gorgas Journals*).

38. Richard Taylor, *Destruction and Reconstruction: Personal Experiences of the Late War* (1879; reprint, New York: Longmans, Green, 1955), p. 281.

39. Jefferson Davis to Lt. Gen. T. H. Holmes, July 15, 1863, and Davis to Hon. R. W. Johnson, July 14, 1863, in Linda Lasswell Crist, et al., eds., *The Papers of Jefferson Davis*, 11 vols. to date (Baton Rouge: Louisiana State University Press, 1971–1977), vol. 9, pp. 276, 281.

40. *Kean Diary*, p. 86; *Gorgas Journals*, p. 136.

41. Jones, *Rebel War Clerk's Diary*, vol. 1, pp. 374, 378 (quotations); see also *Kean Diary*, p. 119.

42. Leonidas N. Walthall to Jefferson Davis, Aug. 11, 1863, in Crist, et al., eds., *Papers of Jefferson Davis*, vol . 9, p. 339.

43. E. S. Dargan to James Seddon, July 24, 1863, in OR, ser. 4, vol. 2, pp. 664–5.

44. O. G. Eiland to Jefferson Davis, July 20, 1863, SW/LR B-581 1863, RG 109, NA.

45. E. Kirby Smith to James A. Seddon, Sep. 11, 1863, in OR, ser. 1, vol. 22, pt. 2, p. 1011. See also Jefferson Davis to J. M. Howry, Aug. 27, 1863, in Rowland, ed., *Jefferson Davis: Constitutionalist*, vol. 6, pp. 17–8.

46. Atlanta *Southern Confederacy*, Oct. 30, 1862; Moore, *Conscription and Conflict*, pp. 64–7; Sally E. Hadden, *Slave Patrols: Law and Violence in Virginia and the Carolinas* (Cambridge, Mass.: Harvard University Press, 2003), pp. 175–7; Charles W. Ramsdell, *Behind the Lines in the Southern Confederacy* (1944; reprint, Baton Rouge: Louisiana State University Press, 1977), pp. 31–4.

47. Kenneth Rayner to Thomas Ruffin, Dec. 25, 1860, in J. G. De Roulhac Hamilton, ed., *The Papers of Thomas Ruffin*, 4 vols. (Raleigh: Edwards and Broughton, 1918–1920), vol. 3, pp. 108–9.

48. Hugh C. Bailey, "Disloyalty in Confederate Alabama," *Journal of Southern History* 23 (Nov. 1957), p. 525.

49. Gary W. Gallagher, *The Confederate War: How Popular Will, Nationalism, and Military Strategy Could Not Stave Off Defeat* (Cambridge, Mass.: Harvard University Press, 1997), p. 44. This evidence testified, as James M. McPherson has pointed out, less to a "lack of will" at the outset than a "loss of will" over time, a loss occasioned by the course and burdens of the war itself. James M. McPherson, "American Victory, American Defeat," in *Why the Confederacy Lost*, ed. Gabor S. Boritt (New York: Oxford University Press, 1992), pp. 15–42.

50. Frederick Maurice, ed., *Lee's Aide-de-Camp, Being the Papers of Colonel Charles Marshall Sometime Aide-de-Camp, Military Secretary, and Assistant Adjutant General of*

Robert E. Lee, 1862–1865 (1927; reprint, Lincoln and London: University of Nebraska Press, 2000), p. 42.

51. William McNeely to James A. Seddon, Oct. 25, 1864, in Berlin, et al., eds., *The Black Military Experience*, p. 290.

52. O. Goddin to Zebulon B. Vance, Feb. 27, 1863, in W. Buck Yearns and John G. Barrett, eds., *North Carolina Civil War Documentary* (Chapel Hill: University of North Carolina Press, 1980), p. 98.

53. Anonymous [Many Soldiers] to Jefferson Davis, Sept. 16, 1864, A-198 1864, SW/LR, RG 109, NA. See also Anonymous to Secretary of War, Nov. 17, 1865, A-7 1865, SW/LR, RG 109, NA. Recognizing and hoping to calm this mood, Congress repeatedly modified both the draft system and the exemption process without, however, noticeably reducing the ill will it had generated. Thomas, *Confederate Nation*, pp. 260–1; Moore, *Conscription and Conflict*, pp. 72–6, 83–5; OR, ser. 4, vol. 2, p. 553–4, and vol. 3, pp. 178–83.

54. Ella Lonn, *Desertion during the Civil War* (1928; reprint, Lincoln: University of Nebraska Press, 1998), p. 32.

55. OR, ser. 4, vol. 2, p. 674.

56. Norman D. Brown, ed., *One of Cleburne's Command: The Civil War Reminiscences and Diary of Capt. Samuel T. Foster, Granbury's Texas Brigade, CSA* (Austin and London: University of Texas Press, 1980), p. 49.

57. O. G. Eiland to Jefferson Davis, July 20, 1863, B-581 1863, SW/LR, RG 109, NA.

58. J. H. M. Barton to Jefferson Davis, July 29, 1863, B-588 1863, SW/LR, RG 109, NA.

59. Benjamin F. Bolling to Jefferson Davis, July 24, 1863, B-581 1863, SW/LR, RG 109, NA.

60. B. H. Micou to Judah P. Benjamin, Aug. 10, 1863, Confederate States of America records, Manuscript Division, LC; Robert Douthat Meade, *Judah P. Benjamin*, pp. 66, 289. For a survey of disaffection's growth during the summer and fall of 1863 and its reflection in Confederate politics, see James M. McPherson, *Battle Cry of Freedom: The Civil War Era* (New York: Oxford University Press, 1988), pp. 689–98.

61. J. H. M. Barton to Jefferson Davis, July 29, 1863, B-588 1863, SW/LR, RG 109, NA.

62. Bell Irvin Wiley, *Southern Negroes, 1861–1865* (Baton Rouge: Louisiana, 1938), p. 149; *Kean Diary*, p. 96; OR, ser. 4, vol. 2, p. 767.

63. G. Ward Hubbs, *Guarding Greensboro: A Confederate Company in the Making of a Southern Community* (Athens: University of Georgia Press, 2003), p. 164.

64. Durden, *The Gray and the Black*, pp. 30–2.

65. *Lynchburg Virginian*, Oct. 13, 1863; Mobile *Register and Advertiser*, Nov. 26, 1863; Durden, *The Gray and the Black*, pp. 32–4.

66. Memphis *Appeal*, Dec. 3, 1863.

67. Memphis *Appeal*, Dec. 3, 1863.

68. For Hindman's authorship of this letter, see his private correspondence dated April 10, 1865, published in the *Texas State Gazette*, May 3, 1865, and Diane Neal

and Thomas W. Kremm, *Lion of the South: General Thomas C. Hindman* (Macon, Ga.: Mercer University Press, 1993), pp. 183–6.

69. Thomas Lawrence Connelly, *Autumn of Glory: The Army of Tennessee, 1862–1865* (Baton Rouge: Louisiana State University Press, 1971), p. 274; McPherson, *Ordeal by Fire*, p. 337.

70. U. S. Grant, *Personal Memoirs of U.S. Grant*, two volumes in one (1885; reprint, New York: Konecky and Konecky, n.d.), pp. 383–4; Nisbet, *Four Years on the Firing Line*, pp. 158–9.

71. Mobile *Advertiser and Register*, Dec. 1, 1863.

72. *Gorgas Journals*, p. 86; Nisbet, *Four Years on the Firing Line*, p. 167 (quotation).

73. Connelly, *Autumn of Glory*, pp. 276–7; Larry J. Daniel, *Soldiering in the Army of Tennessee: A Portrait of Life in a Confederate Army* (Chapel Hill: University of North Carolina Press, 1991), pp. 137–8, 155–6; Neal and Kremm, *Lion of the South*, p. 184.

74. OR, ser. 1, vol.52, pt. 2, pp 586–92.

75. Buck, *Cleburne and His Command*, p. 187; OR, ser. 1, vol. 52, pt. 2, pp. 586, 589–90 (quotations).

76. Cleburne memo in OR, ser. 1, vol. 52, pt. 2, p. 589.

77. William B. Bate to Maj. Gen. W. H. T. Walker, Jan. 9, 1964, CW 17, Civil War Collection, HL.

78. Connelly, *Autumn of Glory*, p. 320; OR, ser. 1, vol. 52, pt. 2, pp. 595, 598 (Anderson quote).

79. Symonds, *Stonewall of the West*, p. 189.

80. W. H. T. Walker to Jefferson Davis, Nov. 12, 1864, in OR, ser. 1, vol. 52, pt. 2, p. 595; Symonds, *Stonewall of the West*, pp. 186–191.

81. The lone exception was postmaster general Reagan. Reagan, *Memoirs*, p. 148.

82. James A. Seddon to Joseph E. Johnston, Nov. 24, 1864, Joseph E. Johnston Papers, Earl Gregg Swem Library, College of William and Mary. Although Walker had gone outside the chain of command, the government expressed its appreciation of the general's "motives of zeal and patriotism" in doing so.

83. OR, ser. 1, vol. 52, pt. 2, pp. 593–9, 606–9; Connelly, *Autumn of Glory*, pp. 318–20; Buck, *Cleburne and His Command*, pp. 188, 190; Symonds, *Stonewall of the West*, p. 292n25. The *Official Records*'s version of the memo is based on a typescript copy held in the NA that bears the following notation in red ink: "Obtained May 1st '88 from Major L. H. Mangum, formerly of the C.S.A.—now 1st Comptroller's Office, Treasury Dept. H.M.L." Mangum was Learned H. Mangum, one of Cleburne's aides de camp. (Thanks to Michael Musick for this information.)

84. According to Hindman's April 10, 1865, letter published in the *Texas State Gazette*, May 3, 1865.

85. Macon *Telegraph and Confederate*, Oct. 15, 1864.

86. Cate, *Two Soldiers*, p. 32; A. S. Colyar to A.S. Marks, Feb. 5, 1864, in *The Annals of the Army of Tennessee and Early Western History*, vol. 1 (May 1878), p. 52; Macon *Telegraph and Confederate*, Oct. 15, 1864. Meanwhile, Gen. Patton Anderson, for example, informed Gen. Leonidas Polk of the debate. Tennessee governor Isham G. Harris also learned of this affair. Some of Cleburne's associates may have relayed the information to Gen. John C. Breckinridge. Breckinridge, in turn, may have in-

formed South Carolina's Mary Boykin Chesnut. See Patton Anderson to L. Polk, Nov. 14, 1864, in OR, ser. 1, vol. 52, pt. 2, pp. 598–9; Isham G. Harris to Jefferson Davis, Jan. 16, 1864, in Crist, et al., eds., *Papers of Jefferson Davis*, vol. 10, pp. 177–8; William C. Davis, *Breckinridge: Statesman, Soldier, Symbol* (Baton Rouge: Louisiana State University Press, 1974), pp. 402–3; and Woodward, ed., *Mary Chesnut's Civil War*, p. 545.

87. Patton Anderson to L. Polk, Nov. 14, 1864, in OR, ser. 1, vol. 52, pt. 2, pp. 598–9.

88. Judah P. Benjamin to Frederick A. Porcher, Dec. 21, 1864, in OR, ser. 4, vol. 3, pp. 959–60.

89. Gallagher, *The Confederate War*, pp. 36–40.

90. *Kean Diary*, p. 177.

91. Anonymous (Private) to Jefferson Davis, Sep. 28, 1864, Jefferson Davis Papers, 1861–1865, RG 109, NA.

92. D. B. Hurley to Jefferson Davis, Sept. 15, 1864, H-503 1864, SW/LR, RG 109, NA.

93. F. Kendall to Jefferson Davis, Sept. 16, 1864, K-73 1864, SW/LR, RG 109, NA, original emphasis.

94. Samuel Clayton to Jefferson Davis, Nov. 10, 1865, in OR, ser. 4, vol. 3, p. 1011.

95. Robert S. Hudson to Jefferson Davis, Nov. 25, 1864, in OR, ser. 1, vol. 45, pt. 1, p. 1248 (quotation); James Phelan to Jefferson Davis, Oct. 2, 1864, in OR, ser. 4, vol. 3, p. 710 (quotation).

96. Lonn, *Desertion during the Civil War*, pp. 22, 27; Long and Long, *The Civil War Day by Day*, p. 706.

97. Rowland, ed., *Jefferson Davis: Constitutionalist*, vol. 6, p. 343.

98. OR, ser. 4, vol. 3, pp. 707, 710.

99. Gallagher, *The Confederate War*, chapter 1.

100. Long and Long, *The Civil War Day by Day*, p. 706; *Kean Diary*, pp. 172, 181 (quotations).

101. John A. Campbell, *Reminiscences and Documents Relating to the Civil War during the Year 1865* (Baltimore: John Murphy and Co., 1887), p. 20.

102. OR, ser. 4, vol. 3, p. 354.

103. J. Tracy Power, *Lee's Miserables: Life in the Army of Northern Virginia from the Wilderness to Appomattox* (Chapel Hill: University of North Carolina Press, 1998), pp. 243–4.

104. Alexander W. Cooper to Jefferson Davis, Dec. 25, 1864, in the Jefferson Davis Papers, Rare Book, Manuscript, and Special Collections Library, Duke University (hereafter DU).

105. *Gorgas Journals*, p. 135.

106. F. Kendall to Jefferson Davis, Sep. 16, 1864, K-73 1864, SW/LR, RG 109, NA; "A Native Georgian" to James. A. Seddon, July 29, 1864, A-204 1864, SW/LR, RG 109, NA.

107. J. H. Stringfellow to Jefferson Davis, Feb. 8, 1865, S-57 1865, Documents Printed in *The War of the Rebellion*, RG 109, NA.

108. C. B. Leitner to Jefferson Davis, Dec. 31, 1864, L-40 1865, SW/LR, RG 109, NA.

109. F. Kendall to Jefferson Davis, Sep. 16, 1864, RG 109,SW/LR K-73 1864, RG 109, NA. See also M. E. Mills to Jefferson Davis, Sep. 19, 1864, SW/LR, RG 109, NA, copy courtesy of Lynda Crist.

110. OR, ser. 1, vol. 41, pt. 3, p. 774.

111. Raleigh *North Carolina Standard*, Oct. 26, 1864; Charleston *Mercury*, Nov. 3, 1864.

112. Raleigh *North Carolina Standard*, Nov. 2, 1864; Charleston *Mercury*, Nov. 14, 1864; Moore, *Conscription and Conflict*, p. 344n.

113. Richmond *Enquirer*, Oct. 6, 1864.

114. Raleigh *North Carolina Standard*, Oct. 26, 1864, quoting the Charlotte *Democrat*.

115. Lynchburg *Virginian*, Oct. 8, 12, 18, 20, Nov. 3, 1864; Mobile *Advertiser*, Oct. 12, 1863.

116. OR, ser. 4, vol. 3, p. 798.

117. OR, ser. 4, vol. 3, p. 798.

118. OR, ser. 4, vol. 3, pp. 797–9.

119. Langdon, *The Question of Employing the Negro as a Soldier!*, p. 9.

120. Archie Livingston to his sisters, Nov. 13, 1864, Archie Livingston Letters, Soldier Letters Collections, Eleanor S. Brockenbrough Library, the Museum of the Confederacy (hereafter EBL/MOC).

121. Richmond *Enquirer*, Dec. 20, 1864. Emphasis added.

122. R. Hawes [misfiled under the name "Harris"] to Jefferson Davis, Nov. 11, 1865, Frederick M. Dearborn Collection, Houghton Library, Harvard University (hereafter HU).

123. OR, ser. 4, vol. 3, pp. 915–6.

124. Judah P. Benjamin's subsequent letter to Frederick A. Porcher suggests as much. Judah P. Benjamin to Frederick A. Porcher, Dec. 21, 1864, in OR, ser. 4, vol. 3, pp. 959–60.

125. Frederick A. Porcher to Judah P. Benjamin, Dec. 16, 1864, Confederate States of America papers, Manuscript Division, LC.

126. OR, ser. 4, vol. 3, p. 959. At the end of January, Col. John B. Sale of the president's inner military circle reported on his own efforts to prepare the public mind for emancipation measures. See Sale to Jefferson Davis, Nov. 26, 1865, the Frederick M. Dearborn collection, Houghton Library, HU.

127. Lynchburg *Virginian*, Feb. 13, 1865.

128. Richmond *Enquirer*, Feb. 10, 1865.

129. J. P. Benjamin to R. E. Lee, Feb. 11, 1865, in OR, ser. 1, vol. 46, part 2, p. 1229.

130. The quotation comes from William Allan's summary of his interview with Lee on March 10, 1868. Lee soon told William Preston Johnston, too, that he had foreseen even in 1861 "the necessity of . . . a proclamation of gradual emancipation and the use of negroes as soldiers." See Gary W. Gallagher, ed., *Lee, The Soldier* (Lincoln and London: University of Nebraska Press, 1996), p. 12 (quotation); and

W. G. Bean, ed., "Memoranda of Conversation between General Robert E. Lee and William Preston Johnston, May 7, 1868, and March 18, 1870," *Virginia Magazine of History and Biography* 73 (Oct. 1965), p. 479.

131. Lee's letter to Porcher Miles is now lost, but see the two letters from Porcher Miles to Lee dated Oct. 24 and Nov. 3, 1864, both in the William Porcher Miles Papers, Southern Historical Collection, University of North Carolina, Chapel Hill Library (hereafter UNC-CH). Familiarity with the substance of Lee's letter to Miles can also be seen in Judah P. Benjamin's Dec. 21, 1864, letter to Frederick Porcher; and in Edmund Ruffin's diary entry of Dec. 30, 1864. Howell Cobb had evidently heard of Lee's views by early January, as had Missouri's congressman Thomas Snead and North Carolina plantation mistress Catherine Edmondston. On Cobb, see OR, ser. 4, vol. 3, p. 1009. See Snead's Jan. 10, 1865, letter to Gen. Sterling Price in OR, ser. 1, vol. 48, pt. 1, p. 1321; and Crabtree and Patton, eds., *"Journal of a Secesh Lady,"* pp. 552, 650–1.

132. Andrew Hunter to R. E. Lee, Nov. 7, 1865, and R. E. Lee to Andrew Hunter, Nov. 11, 1865, in OR, ser. 4, vol. 3, pp. 1007–9, 1012–3 (quotations on p. 1013), emphasis added.

133. It was apparently first published in 1888; see "General Lee's Views on Enlisting the Negroes," *The Century Magazine* 36, no. 4 (Aug. 1888), pp. 599–601.

134. *Kean Diary*, p. 192.

135. Lee to Barksdale, Feb. 18, 1865. The Richmond *Sentinel* published this letter on Feb. 23.

136. Raleigh *Daily Confederate*, Nov. 11, 1865.

137. Cleburne in OR, ser. 1, vol. 52, pt. 2, p. 590.

138. Montgomery *Mail*, Jan. 3, 1865.

139. Richmond *Enquirer*, Jan. 12, 1865.

140. Mobile *Advertiser and Register*, Dec. 17, 1863.

141. David Williams, Teresa Crisp Williams, and David Carlson, *Plain Folk in a Rich Man's War* (Gainsville: University Press of Florida, 2002), p. 73.

142. Macon *Telegraph and Confederate*, Nov. 19, 1864.

143. Whitelaw Reid, *After the War: A Tour of the Southern States, 1865–1866*, ed. C. Vann Woodward (1866; reprint, New York: Harper and Row, 1965), p. 319; and Rembert W. Patrick, *Jefferson Davis and His Cabinet* (Baton Rouge: Louisiana State University Press, 1944), pp. 193, 199.

144. Richmond *Enquirer*, Dec. 5, 1864, original emphasis.

145. Galveston *Tri-Weekly News*, Dec. 23, 1864.

146. OR, ser. 4, vol. 3, p. 915.

147. Adjutant General's Office, "The Negro in the Military Service of the United States, 1639–1886: A Compilation of Official Records, State Papers, Historical Extracts, etc., Relating to his Military Status and Service, from the date of his introduction into the British North American Colonies," [1885–1888], RG 94, NA, microfilm M-858, roll 4, frame 392.

148. Vandiver, ed., "Proceedings of the Second Confederate Congress," SHSP 52, p. 309; "The Negro in the Military Service of the United States," frame 395.

149. Richmond *Whig*, Nov. 26, 1864.

Chapter 2

1. William B. Bate to W. H. T. Walker, Jan. 9, 1864, CW 17, Civil War Collection, HL.

2. Leach, proposed "Joint Resolution Condemning the Use of Negroes in the Confederate Army," Jan. 25, 1865, in "The Negro in the Military Service of the United States," frame 0352.

3. Vandiver, ed., "Proceedings of the Second Confederate Congress," *SHSP* 52, p. 241.

4. Charleston *Mercury*, Feb. 3, 1865.

5. Richmond *Examiner*, Feb. 25, 1865.

6. Raleigh *North Carolina Standard*, Nov. 23, 1864. Charleston's other pro-secession paper, the *Courier*, admiringly reprinted congressman Turner's attack on Davis. Charleston *Courier*, Feb. 7, 1865.

7. William B. Bate to W. H. T. Walker, Jan. 9, 1864, CW 17, Civil War Collection, HL.

8. Mr. Rogers' Minority Report [on the House bill to arm slaves], House of Representatives, Feb. 15, 1865. Printed copy in VHS.

9. Vandiver, ed., "Proceedings of the Second Confederate Congress," *SHSP* 51, p. 268.

10. Richmond *Dispatch*, Nov. 9, 1864, emphasis added.

11. Richmond *Examiner*, Jan. 28, 1865.

12. P. K. Montgomery to Governor Clark, Apr. 4, 1865, Series 768, RG 27, MDAH.

13. Macon *Telegraph and Confederate*, Apr. 17, 1865, letter signed Woodson.

14. Vandiver, ed., "Proceedings of the Second Confederate Congress," *SHSP* 51, p. 293.

15. Galveston *Tri-Weekly News*, Feb. 13, 1865, letter signed H., dated Feb. 4.

16. Galveston *Tri-Weekly News*, Feb. 13, 1865, letter signed H.; Feb. 19, 1865, letter signed Clayton C. Gilespie; Feb. 24, 1865, letter signed A. S. Broaddus.

17. *Speech of Hon. Thomas S. Gholson of Virginia on the Policy of Employing Negro Troops and the Duty of All Classes to Aid in the Prosecution of the War* (Richmond: Geo. P. Evans and Co., 1865), p. 9.

18. [Varina Davis,] *Jefferson Davis, Ex-President of the Confederate States of America: A Memoir by his Wife*, 2 vols. (New York: Belford, 1890), vol. 1, pp. 373–6; Emory Thomas, *The Confederate State of Richmond: A Biography of the Capital* (1971; reprint, Baton Rouge: Louisiana State University Press, 1998), pp. 119–20; Thomas, *Confederate Nation*, pp. 203–5.

19. Wilmington *Journal*, Nov. 10, 1864.

20. Vandiver, ed., "Proceedings of the Second Confederate Congress," *SHSP* 52, p. 454.

21. Richmond *Whig*, Nov. 26, 1864.

22. Raleigh *North Carolina Standard*, Jan. 18, 1865.

23. Richmond *Enquirer*, Nov. 12, 1864, letter signed Virginius.

24. Macon *Telegraph and Confederate*, Nov. 2, 1864.

25. Charleston *Mercury*, Jan. 13, 1865.

26. See, for example, R. Blair, et al., to Maj. P. H. Nelson, n.d. [May 1862], EBL/ MOC—a petition from officers of Nelson's Battalion, South Carolina Volunteers, seeking the transfer of named "mulattoes" from their unit. The petition was granted.

27. Charley Baughman to his father, Oct. 23, 1864, Charley Baughman Letters, Soldier Letters Collections, EBL/MOC.

28. Jedediah Hotchkiss to Sara A. Hotchkiss, Nov. 8, 1864, Jedediah Hotchkiss Collection, LC.

29. M. E. Sparks to K. J. Warren, Feb. 12, 1865, reprinted in the Macon *Telegraph and Confederate*, Mar. 8, 1865.

30. Quoted Langdon, *The Question of Employing the Negro as a Soldier*, p. 11.

31. "Agreement made by Boys opposed to Negro Equality," signed by B. F. Wright, et al., Unfiled Slips and Papers, "Wright, B. F.," RG 109, NA.

32. Montgomery (Ala.) *Mail*, Dec. 3, 1864, letter reprinted from the Mobile *Advertiser* from "Soldat." An accompanying note described Soldat as "an officer of the Confederate service, distinguished for valor, patriotism, and some practical views."

33. Theodore Nunn to Jefferson Davis, Oct. 25, 1864, N-79 1864, SW/LR, RG 109, NA.

34. Vandiver, ed., "Proceedings of the Second Confederate Congress," *SHSP* 52, p. 294.

35. J. W. Ellis to Jefferson Davis, Jan. 29, 1865, in OR, ser. 4, vol. 3, pp. 1041–2; Raleigh *Daily Confederate*, Feb. 1, 1865.

36. Michael P. Johnson, *Toward a Patriarchal Republic: The Secession of Georgia* (Baton Rouge: Louisiana State University Press, 1977), pp. 127–30; Drew Gilpin Faust, *The Creation of Confederate Nationalism: Ideology and Identity in the Civil War South* (Baton Rouge: Louisiana State University Press, 1988), pp. 74–5.

37. T. M. Muldrow to Jefferson Davis, Nov. 4, 1864, M-579 1864, SW/LR, RG 109, NA, emphasis added.

38. Richmond *Examiner*, Dec. 30, 1864.

39. Macon *Telegraph and Confederate*, Feb. 18, 1865.

40. Governor Brown's Message to the legislature, in *Journal of the Senate of the Extra Session of the General Assembly, of the State of Georgia, Convened by Proclamation of the Governor, at Macon, February 15th, 1865* (Milledgeville, Ga.: Boughton, Nisbet, Barnes and Moore, 1865), pp. 15–6.

41. Richmond *Whig*, Nov. 9, 1864; Vandiver, ed., "Proceedings of the Second Confederate Congress," *SHSP* 52, p. 454 (quotation).

42. Governor Brown's Message to the legislature, pp. 15–6.

43. Raleigh *North Carolina Standard*, Nov. 23, 1864.

44. North Carolina General Assembly, *Resolutions against the Policy of Arming the Slaves* (Richmond, 1865).

45. Richmond *Dispatch*, Nov. 9, 1864.

46. In Thomas, *Confederate Nation*, p. 313.

47. David Yulee to Jefferson Davis, Oct. 27, 1864, Pritchard von David collection, Center for American History, University of Texas at Austin (hereafter UTA).

48. The words appeared in Federalist No. 54, signed with Madison's pen name, Publius. See James Madison, Alexander Hamilton, and John Jay, *The Federalist Papers*, ed. Isaac Kramnick (1788; reprint, New York: Penguin Books, 1987), p. 332.

49. Richmond *Enquirer*, Nov. 12, 1864, letter signed Barbarossa.

50. Macon *Telegraph and Confederate*, Nov. 3, 1864.

51. Richmond *Sentinel*, Mar. 6, 1865.

52. Montgomery *Daily Mail*, Mar. 1, 1865, letter signed J. J. Seibels.

53. Charleston *Courier*, Feb. 7, 1865.

54. Raleigh *North Carolina Standard*, Oct. 19, 1864.

55. Chambers's speech published in the Richmond *Whig*, Nov. 26, 1864.

56. Richmond *Examiner*, Jan. 14, 1865.

57. Memphis *Appeal*, reprinted in the *Macon Telegraph and Confederate*, Oct. 31, 1864.

58. Richmond *Enquirer*, Nov. 12, 1864, letter signed Virginius.

59. Charley Baughman to Pa, Oct. 23, 1864, Charley Baughman Letters, Soldier Letters Collections, EBL/MOC.

60. Raleigh *North Carolina Standard*, Oct. 19, 1864.

61. Charleston *Courier*, Feb. 7, 1865.

62. Judah P. Benjamin to Benjamin H. Micou, Aug. 18, 1863, Letterbook, Confederate States of America records, Manuscript Division, LC.

63. Louis Cruger to Jefferson Davis, Feb. 10, 1864, Jefferson Davis Papers, 1861–1865, RG 109, NA.

64. Macon *Telegraph and Confederate*, Oct. 31, 1864, apparently reprinted from the Memphis *Appeal*.

65. Raleigh *North Carolina Standard*, Nov. 4, 1864.

66. Charleston *Courier*, Feb. 7, 1865. Another North Carolinian agreed that if the plan were implemented "we should undoubtedly have re-enacted among us all the horrid scenes of the massacre of St. Domingo." Letter signed Veritas, originally published in the *Progress* and reprinted in the Raleigh *North Carolina Standard*, Nov. 16, 1864.

67. Richmond *Whig*, Nov. 26, 1864.

68. George M. Fredrickson, *The Black Image in the White Mind: The Debate on Afro-American Character and Destiny, 1817–1914* (New York: Harper and Row, 1971), pp. 43–70; George M. Fredrickson, *White Supremacy: A Comparative Study in American and South African History* (New York: Oxford University Press, 1981), pp. 154–6; James Oakes, *Slavery and Freedom: An Interpretation of the Old South* (New York: Knopf, 1990), pp. 130–3.

69. Clyde N. Wilson and W. Edwin Hemphill, eds., *The Papers of John C. Calhoun*, 28 vols. (Columbia, S.C., 1959–2003), vol. 13, p. 371.

70. Galveston *Tri-Weekly News*, Feb. 15, 1865, letter signed Southern.

71. Robert Toombs's speech at Emory College in Oxford, Ga., July 20, 1853, as quoted in Ulrich Bonnell Phillips, *The Life of Robert Toombs* (New York: Macmillan, 1913), p. 156.

72. Richmond *Examiner*, Feb. 16, 1865.

73. Macon *Telegraph and Confederate*, Oct. 27, 1864.

74. Richmond *Whig*, Nov. 9, 1864.

75. Richmond *Examiner*, Feb. 16, 1865.

76. Langdon, *Question of Employing the Negro as a Soldier*, p. 14. To treat "free-

dom as the highest hope and reward which can be offered to the slave," a resolution before the South Carolina legislature similarly objected, implied "that slavery is an inferior condition from which he has the capacity and ought to have the desire to secure." Lynchburg *Virginian*, Jan. 3, 1865.

77. Richmond *Enquirer*, Nov. 11, 1864.

78. Richmond *Examiner*, Feb. 16, 1865.

79. Langdon, *The Question of Employing the Negro as a Soldier*, p. 13.

80. Macon *Telegraph and Confederate*, Oct. 28, 1864, reprinted from the Lynchburg *Republican*.

81. Memphis *Appeal*, Dec. 23, 1863.

82. Rowland, ed., *Jefferson Davis: Constitutionalist*, vol. 5, pp. 49–53.

83. Charles B. Dew, *Apostles of Disunion: Southern Secession Commissioners and the Causes of the Civil War* (Baton Rouge: Louisiana State University Press, 2001), p. 15.

84. Jones, *Rebel War Clerk's Diary*, vol. 2, p. 353.

85. Buck, *Cleburne and His Command*, p. 188.

86. James Henry Hammond, *Letter to an English Abolitionist*, reprinted in Drew Gilpin Faust, ed., *The Ideology of Slavery: Proslavery Thought in the Antebellum South, 1830–1860* (Baton Rouge: Louisiana State University Press, 1981), pp. 184–5. Georgia planter J. Hamilton Cowper (or Couper) made the same point a decade later. See Sarah Forbes Hughes, ed., *Letters and Recollections of John Murray Forbes*, 2 vols. (Boston: Houghton, Mifflin and Co., 1899), vol. 2, pp. 148–51.

87. *Kean Diary*, p. 184.

88. Richmond *Whig*, Nov. 26, 1864.

89. Macon *Telegraph and Confederate*, Nov. 3, 1864, original emphasis.

90. Charleston *Courier*, Jan. 24, 1865; Galveston *Tri-Weekly News*, Feb. 22, 1865, letter signed Caleb Cutwell.

91. Crabtree and Patton, eds., "*Journal of a Secesh Lady*," p. 651.

92. Charleston *Mercury*, Nov. 19, 1864.

93. Speech of Jefferson Davis at Aberdeen, Miss., May 26, 1851 in Rowland, ed., *Jefferson Davis: Constitutionalist*, vol. 2, pp. 73–4 (quotations).

94. Charleston *Mercury*, Jan. 26, 1865.

95. William B. Bate to W. H. T. Walker, Jan. 9, 1864, Civil War Collection, CW 17, HL.

96. David Yulee to Jefferson Davis, Oct. 27, 1864, Pritchard von David collection, Center for American History, UTA.

97. Macon *Telegraph and Confederate*, Oct. 18, 1864.

98. Macon *Telegraph and Confederate*, Oct. 28, 1864, reprinted from the Lynchburg *Republican* (n.d.)

99. Macon *Telegraph and Confederate*, Jan. 6, 1865, letter signed "Q."

100. "Agreement made by Boys opposed to Negro Equality," Unfiled Slips and Papers, "Wright, B. F.," RG 109, NA.

101. Macon *Telegraph and Confederate*, Apr. 17, 1865, letter signed Woodson.

102. Raleigh *North Carolina Standard*, Nov. 4, 1864.

103. Galveston *Tri-Weekly News*, Feb. 22, 1865, letter signed Caleb Cutwell.

104. Langdon, *The Question of Employing the Negro as a Soldier*, p. 15.

105. Richmond *Enquirer*, Nov. 12, 1864, letter signed Virginius.

106. Charleston *Mercury*, Jan. 26, 1865.

107. On this general subject, see Jacqueline Dowd Hall, "'The Mind that Burns in Each Body': Women, Rape, and Racial Violence," in Anne Snitow, Chrisine Stansell, and Sharon Thompson, eds., *The Powers of Desire: The Politics of Sexuality* (New York: Monthly Review Press, 1983); Catherine Clinton, "'Southern Dishonor': Flesh, Blood, Race, and Bondage," in Carol Bleser, ed., *In Joy and Sorrow: Women, Family, and Marriage in the Victorian South, 1830–1900 (New York: Oxford University Press, 1991)*, pp. 52–68.

108. Macon *Telegraph and Confederate*, Mar. 30, 1865.

109. Quoted in the *Macon Telegraph and Confederate*, Oct. 31, 1864.

110. Charleston *Mercury*, Nov. 3, 1864.

111. Raleigh *North Carolina Standard*, Feb. 3, 1865.

112. Macon *Telegraph and Confederate*, Jan. 6, 1865, letter signed "Q."

113. Shelby Foote, *The Civil War, A Narrative*, 3 vols. (1974; reprint, New York: Vintage, 1986), vol. 3, p. 766. Foote did not supply the original source of this quotation, which has been cited widely since he quoted it. Perhaps it derives from Charles H. Wesley's summary of a speech that Hunter delivered in the Confederate Senate on March 7, 1865: "Said Senator Hunter, in substance: 'What did we secede for if it was not to save our slaves?'" See Charles H. Wesley, *The Collapse of the Confederacy*, ed. John David Smith (1937; reprint, Columbia: University of South Carolina Press, 2001), p. 159. A report of that speech, which did say this in substance, if less concisely, appears in Vandiver, ed., "Proceedings of the Second Confederate Congress," *SHSP* 52, pp. 453–6.

114. William B. Bate to Wm. H. T. Walker, Jan. 9, 1864, CW 17, Civil War Collection, HL; James Wingard to Simon Wingard, Jan. 4, 1865, Wingard Papers, DU.

115. Eathan A. Pinnell Civil War Journals, entry of Apr. 8, 1865, Missouri Historical Society.

116. Quoted in Reid, "Confederate Opponents of Arming the Slaves, 1861–1865," *Journal of Mississippi History* 22 (Oct. 1960), p. 267.

117. Charleston *Courier*, Feb. 8, 1865.

118. Galveston *Tri-Weekly News*, Mar. 3, 1865.

119. Macon *Telegraph and Confederate*, Jan. 6, 1865, letter signed "Q."

120. Montgomery *Mail*, Mar. 1, 1865, letter signed J. J. Seibels.

121. Mobile *Register and Advertiser*, Nov. 26, 1863.

122. Richmond *Sentinel*, Nov. 24, 1864.

123. Richmond *Enquirer*, Nov. 11, 1864.

124. Richmond *Enquirer*, Nov. 14, 1864.

125. Richmond *Enquirer*, Nov. 11, 1864.

126. Richmond *Enquirer*, Jan. 12, 1865.

127. Macon *Telegraph and Confederate*, Jan. 6, 1865, letter signed "Q."

128. Charleston *Courier*, Jan. 24, 1865.

129. Charleston *Mercury*, Jan. 13, 1865.

130. Raleigh *North Carolina Standard*, Nov. 4, 1864.

131. Vance quoted in the Raleigh *North Carolina Standard*, Feb. 15, 1865.

132. Galveston *Tri-Weekly News*, Feb. 22, 1865, letter signed Caleb Cutwell.

133. Galveston *Tri-Weekly News*, Feb. 13, 1865, letter signed "H."

134. Macon *Telegraph and Confederate*, Oct. 28, 1864, reprinted from the Lynchburg *Republican*.

135. Charleston *Mercury*, Jan. 13, 1865.

136. Nisbet, *Four Years on the Firing Line*, p. 173.

137. Charleston *Mercury*, Jan. 31, Feb. 1, 1865.

138. Freehling, *The Reintegration of American History*, pp. 176–219.

139. Lt. R. Howard Browne to his wife, n.d. [Nov. 1864?], R. H. Browne Papers, #95, Southern Historical Collection, UNC-CH.

140. Raleigh *North Carolina Standard*, Jan. 18, 1865.

141. Raleigh *North Carolina Standard*, Nov. 4, 1864.

142. Raleigh *North Carolina Standard*, Feb. 3, 1865. Tellingly, even members of Jefferson Davis's inner circle were ruminating along such lines. War Bureau chief R. G. H. Kean noted on New Year's Day, 1865, "that the public mind is rapidly familiarizing itself to the idea of general emancipation" and that some "look to it as smoothing the way to reconstruction" of the Union. Kean was probably thinking of Assistant Secretary of War John A. Campbell. Campbell told Kean at the end of December 1864 "that the only question now is the *manner*" in which the Union would be "reconstructed"—i.e., "whether the South shall be destroyed and subjugated" or whether it would "go back with honor and rights," even if "shorn of many advantages of power, influence, or political supremacy." *Kean Diary*, p. 183.

Chapter 3

1. Ruffin, *Anticipations of the Future*, p. ix.

2. Ruffin, *Anticipations of the Future*, quotations on pp. 220, 149–50, 130, 234–5, 130, 242, 130.

3. William Harper, "Memoir on Slavery," and James Henry Hammond, "Letter to an English Abolitionist" (1845), both reprinted in Faust, ed., *The Ideology of Slavery*, pp. 123–4 (quotation), 179 (quotation). *De Bow's Review* reprinted Chancellor Harper's essay in 1851. See "Chancellor Harper's Memoir on Slavery," *De Bow's Review* 10 (Jan. 1851), pp. 47–65.

4. "The Future of Our Confederation," *De Bow's Review* 31 (July 1861), pp. 35–40 (quotation on p. 36).

5. Montgomery *Advertiser*, Nov. 6, 1861, reprinted in William Gienapp, ed., *The Civil War and Reconstruction: A Documentary Collection* (New York: W. W. Norton, 2001), p. 197.

6. Samuel W. Melton to James A. Seddon, Nov. 11, 1863, in OR, ser. 4, vol. 2, p. 946.

7. Harper, "Memoir on Slavery," p. 124 (quotation).

8. Bell Irvin Wiley, *Southern Negroes, 1861–1865* (Baton Rouge: Louisiana, 1938), pp. 130–3; James H. Brewer, *The Confederate Negro: Virginia's Craftsmen and Military Laborers, 1861–1865* (Durham: Duke University Press, 1969); Clarence

L. Mohr, *On the Threshold of Freedom*; Joseph T. Wilson, *The Black Phalanx: A History of the Negro Soldiers of the United States* (Hartford: American Publishing Co., 1890), chapter 14.

9. *Journal of the Senate at an Extra Session of the General Assembly of the State of Georgia, Convened under the Proclamation of the Governor, March 25th, 1863* (Milledgeville, Ga.: Boughton, Nisbet and Barnes, 1863), p. 6.

10. Macon *Telegraph and Confederate*, Jan. 10, 1865, reprinting a letter originally published in the St. Louis *Republican.*

11. Atlanta *Southern Confederacy*, Jan. 24, 1865.

12. George Baylor, "The Army Negro," *SHSP* 31 (1903), pp. 365–9. Baylor's memoir originally appeared in the New Orleans *Picayune* of Sept. 6, 1903. The biblical reference is to 2 Samuel 1:23, 27.

13. Galveston *Tri-Weekly News*, Feb. 17, 1865, letter signed Caleb Cutwell.

14. Raleigh *North Carolina Standard*, Nov. 2, 1864.

15. Raleigh *Daily Confederate*, Jan. 25, 1865.

16. Macon *Telegraph and Confederate*, Jan. 10, 1865, reprinting a letter originally published in the St. Louis *Republican.*

17. Raleigh *Daily Confederate*, Jan. 13, 1865, letter signed H. K. B.

18. Macon *Telegraph and Confederate*, Jan. 10, 1865.

19. J. E. Leigh, J. F. Hodges, and James B. Walton to J. J. Pettus, Memorial to the Governor from Sunflower County, Apr. 1862, John J. Pettus Papers, RG 27, MDAH.

20. Raleigh *Daily Confederate*, Jan. 25, 1865.

21. Lynchburg *Virginian*, Oct. 20, 1864.

22. Quoted in the Lynchburg *Virginian* of Jan. 3, 1865.

23. Raleigh *Daily Confederate*, Jan. 13, 1865, letter signed H. K. B.

24. Galveston *Tri-Weekly News*, Mar. 31, 1865, letter signed Scipio Africanus, original emphasis.

25. Richmond *Whig*, Feb. 17, 1865.

26. Message of Mississippi Governor Charles Clark to the Mississippi Senate and House of Representatives, Feb. 20, 1865, *Journal of the House of Representatives of the State of Mississippi, Called Session at Columbus, February and March, 1865.* (Meridian, Miss.: J. J. Shannon and Co., State Printers, 1865), p. 13.

27. Richard L. Maury Diary, entry of Feb. 1, 1865, Manuscript Division, VHS; George W. Guess to Mrs. Sarah H. Cockrell, Jan. 5, 1865, George W. Guess Letters, Mss. 793, Louisiana and Lower Mississippi Valley Collection, Special Collections, Louisiana State University Libraries (hereafter LSU).

28. Macon *Telegraph and Confederate*, Apr. 5, 1865.

29. Thomas Wentworth Higginson, *Army Life in a Black Regiment*, ed. John Hope Franklin (1869; reprint, Boston: Beacon, 1962), p. 248.

30. Macon *Telegraph and Confederate*, Jan. 6, 1865, letter signed "Q."

31. Southern white reaction to those developments flared into a massive slave-revolt panic that year. See Harvey Wish, "The Slave Insurrection Panic of 1856," *Journal of Southern History* 5 (1939), pp. 213–20.

32. A useful survey of historians' treatment of the wartime breakdown of slavery may be found in Peter Kolchin, "Slavery and Freedom in the Civil War South," in

James M. McPherson and William J. Cooper, eds., *Writing the Civil War: The Quest to Understand* (Columbia: University of South Carolina Press, 1998), pp. 241–60.

33. Stephens was a free black Northerner who worked as a cook and personal servant for an officer in the Union's Army of the Potomac early in the war. While performing those duties, he sent reports about what he saw and heard to the New York *Weekly Anglo-African*. Donald Yacavone, ed., *A Voice of Thunder: The Civil War Letters of George E. Stephens* (Urbana and Chicago: University of Illinois Press, 1997), pp. 15, 138, 151.

34. Booker T. Washington, *Up from Slavery: An Autobiography* (1901; reprint, New York: Modern Library, 1999), p. 7.

35. Susie King Taylor, *Reminiscences of My Life in Camp with the 33d United States Colored Troops, Late 1st S. C. Volunteers* (Boston: The author, 1902), pp. 7–8; Higginson, *Army Life in a Black Regiment*, p. 34.

36. Yacavone, ed., *A Voice of Thunder*, pp. 146–7, 138; James M. McPherson, *The Negro's Civil War: How American Negroes Felt and Acted during the War for the Union* (New York: Knopf, 1965), pp. 57–8; Leon F. Litwack, *Been in the Storm So Long: The Aftermath of Slavery* (New York: Knopf, 1979), pp. 61, 127.

37. Charlotte Forten, "Life on the Sea Islands," *Atlantic Monthly* 13 (May 1864), p. 593.

38. Elizabeth Hyde Botume, *First Days amongst the Contrabands* (Boston: Lee and Shepard, 1893), p. 13. See also Higginson, *Army Life in a Black Regiment*, p. 173.

39. OR, series 2, vol. 1, p. 750.

40. Litwack, *Been in the Storm So Long*, p. 54.

41. Benjamin F. Butler, *Butler's Book: Autobiography and Personal Reminiscences . . .* , 2 vols. (Boston: A. M. Thayer, 1892), vol. 1, pp. 256–8.

42. McPherson, *The Negro's Civil War*, p. 28.

43. Edward McPherson, *The Political History of the United States during the Great Rebellion*, 2d ed. (Washington, D.C.: Philp and Solomons, 1865), pp. 211–2, 254, 239, 196.

44. Roy P. Basler, ed., *The Collected Works of Abraham Lincoln*, 9 vols. (New Brunswick, N.J.: Rutgers University Press, 1953), vol. 5, p. 434.

45. McPherson, *The Negro's Civil War*, p. 65; Litwack, *Been in the Storm So Long*, p. 21.

46. Joseph T. Glatthaar, "Black Glory: The African-American Role in Union Victory," in Boritt, ed., *Why the Confederacy Lost*, p. 142.

47. Clarence L. Mohr, *On the Threshold of Freedom*, p. 78.

48. Quoted in Grady McWhiney, *Braxton Bragg and Confederate Defeat* (New York: Columbia University Press, 1969), vol. 1, pp. 142–3. See also William Howard Russell, *My Diary North and South*, ed. Eugene H. Berwanger (New York: Alfred A. Knopf, 1988), p. 150.

49. This truth is brilliantly captured in Drew Gilpin Faust, *James Henry Hammond: A Design for Mastery* (Baton Rouge: Louisiana State University Press, 1982).

50. Armstead Louis Robinson, "Day of Jubilo: Civil War and the Demise of Slavery in the Mississippi Valley, 1861–1865" (Ph.D. dissertation, University of Rochester, 1976), p. 227.

51. Berlin, Ira, Thavolia Glymph, Steven F. Miller, Joseph P. Reidy, Leslie S. Rowland, and Julie Saville, eds., *Freedom: A Documentary History of Emancipation, 1861–1867*, ser. 1, vol. 3, *The Wartime Genesis of Free Labor: The Lower South* (New York: Cambridge University Press, 1990), 247–327. This analysis of slavery's wartime breakdown draws heavily upon W. E. B. Du Bois, *Black Reconstruction in America* (1935; reprint, New York: Atheneum, 1983), and Ira Berlin, Barbara J. Fields, Steven Miler, Joseph P. Reidy, and Leslie S. Rowland, *Slaves No More: Three Essays on Emancipation and the Civil War* (Cambridge: Cambridge University Press, 1992).

52. A. K. Farrar to Gov. Pettus, July 17, 1862, quoted in Herbert Aptheker, "Notes on Slave Conspiracies in Confederate Mississippi," *Journal of Negro History* 29 (Jan. 1944), p. 76.

53. John Eaton, *Grant, Lincoln, and the Freedmen: Reminiscences of the Civil War* (1907; reprint, New York: Greenwood, 1969), pp. 1–2.

54. Davis, *Rise and Fall*, vol. 2, pp. 161–2.

55. Janet Sharp Hermann, *The Pursuit of a Dream* (New York: Oxford University Press, 1981), pp. 3–34.

56. Hermann, *Pursuit of a Dream*, pp. 38–9; William C. Davis, *Jefferson Davis, The Man and his Hour* (Baton Rouge: Louisiana State University Press, 1991), pp. 409, 505; William J. Cooper, Jr., *Jefferson Davis, American* (New York: Random House, 2000), pp. 243–56.

57. C. Vann Woodward, ed., *Mary Chesnut's Civil War* (New Haven, Conn.: Yale University Press, 1981), p. 535; Thomas, *The Confederate State of Richmond*, p. 155.

58. Berlin, et al., eds., *Black Military Experience*, p. 259; OR, ser. 1, vol. 13, pp. 524–5 (quotation); Carl H. Moneyhon, *The Impact of the Civil War and Reconstruction on Arkansas: Persistence in the Midst of Ruin* (Baton Rouge: Louisiana State University Press, 1994), p. 138.

59. Stephen V. Ash, *Middle Tennessee Society Transformed, 1860–1870: War and Peace in the Upper South* (Baton Rouge: Louisiana State University Press, 1988), pp. 106–22.

60. Allan Nevins, *The War for the Union*, vol. 3, *The Organized War, 1863–1864* (New York: Charles Scribner's Sons, 1971), p. 430.

61. Cimprich, *Slavery's End in Tennessee*, p. 16.

62. McPherson, *The Negro's Civil War*, p. 205.

63. Bobby L. Lovett, "The Negro's Civil War in Tennessee, 1861–1865," *Journal of Negro History*, 61 (Jan. 1976), pp. 39–41; Ash, *Middle Tennessee*, pp. 113.

64. Joseph P. Reidy, *From Slavery to Agrarian Capitalism in the Cotton Plantation South: Central Georgia, 1800–1880* (Chapel Hill: University of North Carolina Press, 1992), pp. 128–35.

65. Henry W. Slocum, "Sherman's March from Savannah to Bentonville," *Battles and Leaders of the Civil War*, 4 vols. (1887–1888; reprint, Edison, N.J.: Castle, n.d.), vol. 4, pp. 688–9.

66. William T. Sherman, *Memoirs*, 2 vols. (New York: Appleton, 1875), vol. 2, pp. 180–1.

67. Nevins, *The Organized War, 1863–1864*, pp. 376–7.

68. J. H. Easterby, ed., *The South Carolina Rice Plantation as Revealed in the Papers of Robert F. W. Allston* (Chicago: University of Chicago Press, 1945), p. 328.

69. Berlin, et al., *The Destruction of Slavery*, pp. 193–4; and *idem*., *The Wartime Genesis of Free Labor*, pp. 356–7.

70. G. P. Whittington, "Concerning the Loyalty of Slaves in North Louisiana in 1863," *Louisiana Historical Quarterly* 14 (Oct. 1931), 491–2 (quotations), original emphasis.

71. Quoted in J. Carlyle Sitterson, "The William J. Minor Plantations: A Study in Ante-Bellum Absentee Ownership," *Journal of Southern History* 9 (Feb. 1943): 61.

72. William J. Minor, Plantation Diary 35, entry for Jan. 3, 1863, William J. Minor and Family Papers, Mss. 519, Louisiana and Lower Mississippi Valley Collection, Special Collections, LSU.

73. Minor, Plantation Diary 35, entry for Jan. 20, 1863, William J. Minor and Family Papers.

74. Minor, Plantation Diary 35, entry for Feb. 26, 1863, William J. Minor and Family Papers.

75. Minor, Plantation Diary 35, entry for June 8, 1863, William J. Minor and Family Papers. There were innumerable stories like this one. See, for example, Bell Irvin Wiley, *The Plain People of the Confederacy* (1943; reprint, Columbia: University of South Carolina Press, 2000), pp. 74–82.

76. Letter signed "An Old Planter" originally published in the New Orleans *Times* and reprinted in the Galveston *Tri-Weekly News*, Dec. 30, 1864.

77. Macon *Telegraph and Confederate*, Dec. 23, 1864. See also Dan T. Carter, *When the War Was Over: The Failure of Self-Reconstruction in the South, 1865–1867* (Baton Rouge: Louisiana State University Press, 1985), p. 150.

78. Richmond *Sentinel*, Feb. 10, 1865.

79. Robert Manson Myers, ed., *The Children of Pride: A True Story of Georgia and the Civil War* (New Haven, Conn.: Yale University Press, 1972), p. 1247.

80. Katherine M. Jones, *Heroines of Dixie: Confederate Women Tell Their Story of the War* (Indianapolis and New York: Bobbs-Merrill, 1955), pp. 118–9.

81. Litwack, *Been in the Storm So Long*, p. 147.

82. Aptheker, "Notes on Slave Conspiracies," p. 75.

83. Hadden, *Slave Patrols*, pp. 167–202; Gregg D. Kimball, *American City, Southern Place: A Cultural History of Antebellum Richmond* (Athens: University of Georgia Press, 2000), p. 248; Bernard H. Nelson, "Legislative Control of the Southern Free Negro, 1861–1865," *Catholic Historical Review* 32 (Apr. 1946), pp. 28–46; J. H. Unthank and Geo. S. Hebb, *A Digest of the Militia Laws of Tennessee Now in Force* (Memphis: Hutton and Freligh, 1861), p. 49 (quotation).

84. Russell, *My Diary North and South*, p. 98.

85. W. N. R. Beall, telegram, to Gen. Van Dorn, July 31, 1862, Earl Van Dorn Papers, Miscellaneous Manuscript Collection, Manuscript Division, LC.

86. John J. Cheatham to L. P. Walker, May 4, 1861, C-605 1861, SW/LR, RG 109, NA.

87. Jas. D. Lennard to James A. Seddon, 14 July 1864, L-237 1864, SW/LR, RG 109, NA.

88. Lynchburg *Virginian*, Dec. 24, 1864.

89. Benjamin F. Bolling to Jefferson Davis, July 24, 1863, SW/LR, B-581 1863, RG 109, NA.

90. Drew Gilpin Faust, *Mothers of Invention: Women of the Slaveholding South in the American Civil War* (New York: Random House, 1996), pp. 56–61.

91. Mrs. L. Cassels to Jefferson Davis, Oct. 29, 1864, SW/LR, RG 109, NA. Thanks to Lynda Crist for providing a copy of this letter.

92. Mary F. Akin to Warren Akin, Jan. 8, 1865, in Bell Irvin Wiley, ed., *Letters of Warren Akin, Confederate Congressman* (Athens: University of Georgia Press, 1959), p. 122.

93. B. H. Micou to Judah P. Benjamin, Aug. 10, 1863, Confederate States of America Records, Manuscript Division, LC.

94. William C. Davis, *Look Away! A History of the Confederate States of America* (New York: Free Press, 2002), p. 161.

95. OR, ser. 1, vol. 47, pt. 2, pp. 37–41 (quote on pp. 39–40); McPherson, *Battle Cry of Freedom*, pp. 841–2.

96. For example, the *Lynchburg Virginian*, Jan. 28, 1865; Macon *Telegraph and Confederate*, Mar. 23, 1865.

97. "Address of [the Confederate] Congress to the People of the Confederate States," in the Richmond *Dispatch*, Mar. 21, 1865.

98. Richmond *Sentinel*, Mar. 6, 1865.

99. Oscar Osburn Winther, ed., *With Sherman to the Sea: The Civil War Letters, Diaries and Reminiscences of Theodore F. Upson* (Bloomington: Indiana University Press, 1958), p. 73; Nevins, *The Organized War, 1863–1864*, p. 415; John W. Blassingame, ed., *Slave Testimony: Two Centuries of Letters, Speeches, Interviews, and Autobiographies* (Baton Rouge: Louisiana State University Press, 1977), pp. 358–9; Litwack, *Been in the Storm So Long*, pp. 51, 53.

100. OR, ser. 4, vol. 2, pp. 36–8.

101. *Two Diaries: From Middle St. John's, Berkeley, South Carolina, February–May, 1865* ([Pinopolis, S.C.]: St. John's Hunting Club, 1921), p. 7.

102. Myers, ed., *Children of Pride*, p. 930.

103. McPherson, *Political History*, pp. 197, 274; Litwack, *Been in the Storm So Long*, p. 73; Basler, ed., *Collected Works of Abraham Lincoln*, vol. 6, p. 30.

104. Joseph P. Glatthaar, "Black Glory: The African-American Role in Union Victory," in Boritt, ed., *Why the Confederacy Lost*, p. 159.

105. Elijah P. Marrs, *Life and History of the Rev. Elijah P. Marrs* (Louisville: Bradley and Gilbert Co, 1885), pp. 17–8 (quotation), 21.

106. Macon *Telegraph and Confederate*, Nov. 11, 1864.

107. Joseph P. Glatthaar, *Forged in Battle: The Civil War Alliance of Black Soldiers and White Officers* (New York: Penguin, 1991), p. 122.

108. McPherson, *The Negro's Civil War*, p. 185.

109. Glatthaar, *Forged in Battle*, pp. 131–3 (quote on 133).

110. Dudley Taylor Cornish, *The Sable Arm: Black Troops in the Union Army, 1861–1865* (1956; reprint, Lawrence: University Press of Kansas, 1987), pp. 265, 288.

111. Cornish, *The Sable Arm*, pp. 265, 288; Glatthaar, *Forged in Battle*, p. 167.

112. OR, ser. 1, vol. 14, p. 198.

113. OR, ser. 3, vol. 3, p. 177.

114. Glatthaar, *Forged in Battle*, p. 79.

115. William Wells Brown, *The Negro in the American Rebellion: His Heroism and His Fidelity*, ed. John David Smith (1867; reprint, Athens: Ohio University Press, 2003), pp. 280–1.

116. McPherson, *The Negro's Civil War*, p. 192.

117. Litwack, *Been in the Storm So Long*, p. 111.

118. Hammond, "Letter to an English Abolitionist," in Faust, *Ideology of Slavery*, p. 178.

119. Charleston *Mercury*, Nov. 19, 1864. See also the letter signed H. K. B. in the Raleigh *Daily Confederate*, Jan. 13, 1865. Union recruiters callously employed brute force often enough to lend credence to such exaggerated Confederate claims.

120. Richmond *Sentinel*, Nov. 24, 1864.

121. Richmond *Whig*, Nov. 26, 1864.

122. Charleston *Courier*, Jan. 24, 1865

123. Macon *Telegraph and Confederate*, Dec. 12, 1864, paraphrasing the *Augusta Constitutionalist*.

124. Col. Geo. W. Guess, to Mrs. Sarah H. Cockrell, Jan. 5, 1865, George W. Guess Letters, Mss. 793, Louisiana and Lower Mississippi Valley Collection, Special Collections, LSU.

125. J. H. Stringfellow to Jefferson Davis, Feb. 8, 1865, S-WD-57, Documents Printed in The War of the Rebellion, RG 109, NA.

126. Benjamin Quarles, *The Negro in the Civil War* (1953; reprint, New York: Da Capo, 1989), p. 275.

127. James L. Roark, *Masters without Slaves: Southern Planters in the Civil War and Reconstruction* (New York: W. W. Norton and Co., 1977), p. 82.

128. Wiley, *Plain People of the Confederacy*, p. 83.

129. Litwack, *Been in the Storm So Long*, p. 114.

130. Whittington, "Concerning the Loyalty of Slaves," p. 495; emphasis added.

131. *Kean Diary*, p. 215.

132. Augustin L. Taveau to William Aiken, Apr. 24, 1865, in Augustin Louis Taveau Papers, DU.

133. OR, ser. 1, vol. 52, pt. 2, pp. 588–91.

134. Richmond *Sentinel*, Feb. 16, 1865.

135. Raleigh *North Carolina Standard*, Nov. 16, 1864, letter reprinted from the Raleigh *Progress*.

136. Lynchburg *Virginian*, Mar. 16, 1865.

137. Macon *Telegraph and Confederate*, Oct. 29, 1864.

138. Lynchburg *Virginian*, Mar. 16, 1865.

139. Richmond *Sentinel*, Feb. 16, 1865.

140. Richmond *Sentinel*, Nov. 24, 1864.

141. Richmond *Enquirer*, Nov. 11, 1864.

142. Richmond *Whig*, Feb. 17, 1865.

143. Macon *Telegraph and Confederate*, Mar. 22, 1865.

144. William Kauffman Scarborough, ed., *The Diary of Edmund Ruffin*, 3 vols. (Baton Rouge: Louisiana State University Press, 1972–1989), vol. 3, p. 692.

145. Vandiver, ed., "Proceedings of the Second Confederate Congress," *SHSP* 51, p. 295. Senator Albert Gallatin Brown of Mississippi repeated that "the enemy employed negroes, and made them fight well," in early February, in order to argue that "we might do the same." Ibid., p. 309.

146. Raleigh *Daily Confederate*, Jan. 12, 1865, letter signed Tank.

147. OR, ser. 1, vol. 41, pt. 3, p. 774.

148. Anonymous to Howell Cobb, Jan. 3, 1865, in Ulrich Bonnell Phillips, ed., *The Correspondence of Robert Toombs, Alexander H. Stephens, and Howell Cobb* (1911; reprint, New York: Da Capo, 1970), p. 657.

149. Lynchburg *Virginian*, Oct. 8, 1864.

150. Macon *Telegraph and Confederate*, Oct. 21, 1864.

151. OR, ser. 4, vol. 3, p. 1010.

152. Brig. Gen. F. A. Shoup's memorandum reprinted in the Macon *Telegraph and Confederate*, Apr. 5, 1865.

153. Edward Pollard to Jefferson Davis, Jan. 13, 1865, P-16 1865, SW/LR, RG 109, NA.

154. Macon *Telegraph and Confederate*, Oct. 12, 1864.

155. Memphis *Appeal*, Dec. 23, 1863.

156. Bell Irvin Wiley, *Confederate Women* (Westport, Conn.: Greenwood, 1975), p. 154.

157. Litwack, *Been in the Storm So Long*, p. 126.

158. Mary F. Akin to Warren Akin, Jan. 8, 1865, in Wiley, ed., *Letters of Warren Akin*, p. 117.

159. Myers, ed., *Children of Pride*, p. 1244.

160. Aubrey Lee Brooks and Hugh Talmage Lefler, eds., *The Papers of Walter Clark*, 2 vols. (Chapel Hill: University of North Carolina Press, 1948), vol. 1, 138.

161. Richmond *Sentinel*, Feb. 11, 1865.

162. Jefferson Davis to John Forsyth, Feb. 21, 1865, Crist, et al., eds., *Papers of Jefferson Davis*, vol. 11, pp. 412–3.

163. Jefferson Davis to Gov. William Smith, Mar. 25, 1865, in OR, ser. 1, vol. 46, pt. 3, pp. 1348–9.

164. Lynchburg *Virginian*, Mar. 21, 1865.

165. OR, ser. 4, vol. 3, p. 798.

166. Lynchburg *Virginian*, Feb. 13, 1865.

167. Richmond *Enquirer*, Nov. 12, 1864.

168. R. E. Lee to John C. Breckinridge, Mar. 14, 1865, Army of Northern Virginia Headquarters Papers, R. E. Lee Papers, VHS.

169. Lee to Barksdale, Feb. 18, 1865, as published in the Richmond *Sentinel*, Feb. 23, 1865, emphasis added.

170. Macon *Telegraph and Confederate*, Apr. 17, 1865, letter signed Woodson.

171. OR, ser. 1, vol. 52, pt. 2, pp. 590–1.

Chapter 4

1. New York *Daily Tribune*, Feb. 14, 1865.

2. Gov. Richard Yates to the Illinois General Assembly in "The Negro in the Military Service of the United States," frame 0498.

3. Quoted in the Lynchburg *Virginian*, Mar. 2, 1865.

4. New York *Herald*, Nov. 7, 1864.

5. Still others, declining to depict the Confederacy's economic and political leadership as a whole in such terms, have nonetheless presented the proposal's chief architects in this light.

6. Richard Franklin Bensel, *Yankee Leviathan: The Origins of Central State Authority in America, 1859–1877* (New York: Cambridge University Press, 1990), p. 153.

7. Patrick R. Cleburne to Robert Cleburne, May 7, 1861, Patrick Ronayne Cleburne Papers, Special Collections, University of Arkansas Libraries.

8. OR, ser. 1, vol. 52, part 2, pp. 586–92.

9. Symonds, *Stonewall of the West*, p. 182; Nisbet, *Four Years on the Firing Line*, p. 172 (quotation). Prof. Thomas Robson Hay subsequently went still further, claiming that "in common with many Irish immigrants" Cleburne "believed that slavery, in itself, was wrong and that steps should be taken looking towards its gradual abolition." Thomas Robson Hay, "The South and the Arming of the Slaves," *Mississippi Valley Historical Review* 6 (June 1919), p. 49.

10. Escott, *After Secession*, pp. 254–5.

11. "Much like Lincoln and Thomas Jefferson," one recent account declares, Jefferson Davis "did not believe slavery was the blacks' permanent condition." Winick, *April 1865*, p. 326 (quotation). See also Escott, *After Secession*, p. 244.

12. On historians' treatment of Lee and slavery, see Alan T. Nolan, *Lee Considered: General Robert E. Lee and Civil War History* (Chapel Hill: University of North Carolina Press, 1991), pp. 9–10.

13. Douglas Southall Freeman, *R. E. Lee: A Biography* (New York and London: Charles Scribner's Sons, 1934), vol. 1, p. 371.

14. T. Harry Williams, "Freeman, Historian of the Civil War: An Appraisal," *Journal of Southern History* 21 (Feb. 1955), p. 99.

15. See chapter 2 in this book.

16. W. G. Bean, ed., "Memoranda of Conversation between General Robert E. Lee and William Preston Johnston, May 7, 1868, and Mar. 18, 1870," *Virginia Magazine of History and Biography* 73 (Oct. 1965), p. 479.

17. See the introduction to this book, p. 11.

18. Neal and Kremm, *Lion of the South*, pp. 15–22, 64–85; Jack B. Scroggs, "Arkansas and the Secession Crisis," *Arkansas Historical Quarterly* 12 (autumn 1953), pp. 190, 193, 200.

19. Symonds, *Stonewall of the West*, pp. 32–44 (quotation on p. 36).

20. Nolan, *Lee Considered*, p. 16; Emory M. Thomas, *Robert E. Lee: A Biography* (New York: W. W. Norton, 1995), p. 273.

21. In Freeman, *R. E. Lee*, vol. 1, pp. 371–3.

22. The survival of such "necessary evil" views of slavery in the Upper South is a theme running through William W. Freehling's fine *Road to Disunion*.

23. In Freeman, *R. E. Lee*, vol. 1, pp. 371–3.

24. Freeman, *R. E. Lee*, vol. 1, p. 390. Freeman thought only two slaves had fled Arlington and insisted that there was "no evidence, direct or indirect, that Lee ever had them or any other Negroes flogged." But in 1866, the *National Antislavery Standard* published a convincing account of the whole episode by a man who identified himself as one of three slaves involved, an account that described the punishments that Lee had inflicted on the captured fugitives in grisly detail. John W. Blassingame, ed., *Slave Testimony: Two Centuries of Letters, Speeches, Interviews, and Autobiographies* (Baton Rouge: Louisiana State University Press, 1977), pp. 467–8; and Bertram Wyatt-Brown, *Southern Honor: Ethics and Behavior in the Old South* (New York: Oxford University Press, 1982), pp. 371–2.

25. Robert E. Lee to Andrew Hunter, Jan. 11, 1865, in OR, ser. 4, vol. 3, pp. 1012–3.

26. On Davis's role in the debates of the 1850s, see, for example, Freehling, *Road to Disunion*, pp. 498–500.

27. Escott, *After Secession*, p. 244 (quotation).

28. [Jefferson Davis,] "Notes on the Proposition to Restrict the Institution of African Slavery as it Exists in the United States to Its Present Limits," n.d., 1860 general correspondence file, Jefferson Davis Papers, LC.

29. Rowland, ed., *Jefferson Davis: Constitutionalist*, vol. 2, p. 73.

30. Raleigh *Daily Confederate*, Jan. 12, 1865, letter signed Tank.

31. Richmond *Sentinel*, Feb. 28, 1865.

32. Richmond *Sentinel*, Jan. 20, 1865.

33. Jackson *Mississippian*, in Durden, *The Gray and the Black*, pp. 30–1.

34. OR, ser. 1, vol. 52, pt. 2, p. 587.

35. *Annual Message of Governor Henry Watkins Allen, to the Legislature of the State of Louisiana* (Shreveport: Caddo Gazette, Jan. 1865), p. 18.

36. Richmond *Whig*, Feb. 17, 1865.

37. Richmond *Enquirer*, Dec. 5, 1864, letter signed Barbarrossa.

38. Galveston *Tri-Weekly News*, Feb. 19, 1865, letter signed Clayton C. Gilespie.

39. Anonymous [Scipio] to James Campbell, n.d. [1863], B-588 1863, SW/LR, RG 109, NA

40. Lynchburg *Virginian*, Nov. 3, 1864.

41. Richmond *Sentinel*, Nov. 24, 1864. See also the Lynchburg *Virginian*, Mar. 24, 1865.

42. Lynchburg *Virginian*, Mar. 16, 1865.

43. Richmond *Sentinel*, Nov. 24, 1864.

44. Vandiver, ed., "Proceedings of the Second Confederate Congress," *SHSP* 52, p. 454.

45. Barksdale speech as published in the Richmond *Sentinel*, Mar. 6, 1865.

46. The point of the plan, Barksdale explained, was to make the slave "available as a soldier, in order to secure the independence of these States, and to preserve their social, political and industrial systems, including the institution of African slavery." A North Carolina farmer grasped that idea firmly. The only proper question, he believed, was whether "the employment of one or two hundred thousand of our blacks

give [*sic*] us material aid in obtaining our independence and enabling us to keep the remainder of our negroes as our property." "That, and that only," he stressed, "ought to be the question." For if independence could not be maintained, as the Raleigh *Daily Confederate* explained, if political power were wrested from the hands of the slaveowners and their representatives, then *all* of the masters' wealth and power would be lost as well. "What were all the wealth of this stricken land," the *Confederate* asked, "if we should fail to achieve our independence? Confiscation would sweep it away as a gossamer, in less time than it takes to write this paragraph." Richmond *Sentinel*, Mar, 6, 1865; Raleigh *Daily Confederate*, Jan. 13, 1865 (letter), and Apr. 6, 1865 (editorial).

47. Richmond *Sentinel*, Nov. 24, 1864.

48. Lynchburg *Virginian*, Feb. 13, 1865.

49. See chapter 2 of this book, pp. 51–2.

50. Richmond *Sentinel*, Dec. 28, 1864.

51. Jackson *Mississippian*, late August or early September, 1863, reprinted in Durden, *The Gray and the Black*, pp. 30–1.

52. Mobile *Register*, quoted in the Macon *Telegraph and Confederate*, Jan. 5, 1865, emphasis added.

53. Lynchburg *Virginian*, Feb. 18, Mar. 24, 1865.

54. Quoted in the Richmond *Enquirer*, Jan. 12, 1865.

55. Porcher and Benjamin attended Yale College, as did many young southern men of their social class. "The Memoirs of Frederick Adolphus Porcher," *South Carolina Historical and Genealogical Magazine* 45, no. 4 (Oct. 1944), p. 207.

56. Frederick A. Porcher, "Conflict of Capital and Labour," *Russell's Magazine* 3 (July 1858), pp. 289–98.

57. Frederick A. Porcher, "Southern and Northern Civilization Contrasted," *Russell's Magazine* 1, no. 2 (May 1857), pp. 97–107, esp. pp. 98, 101–2, 105–6. Porcher remained convinced of slavery's virtues years after the Civil War ended. His memoirs, written in the late 1860s, reaffirmed that slavery was "the basis on which Republican institutions are most securely constructed." See "Memoirs of Frederick Adolphus Porcher," *South Carolina Historical and Genealogical Magazine* 46, no. 4 (Oct. 1945), p. 200.

58. Frederick A. Porcher to Judah P. Benjamin, Dec. 16, 1864, Confederate States of America papers, LC.

59. Pierce Butler, *Judah P. Benjamin* (1907; reprint, New York: Chelsea House, 1980), pp. 348–9; Robert Douthat Meade, *Judah P. Benjamin, Confederate Statesman* (New York: Oxford University Press, 1943), pp. 305–6; Eli N. Evans, *Judah P. Benjamin: The Jewish Confederate* (New York: Free Press, 1988), pp. 5, 233–6, 249–50, 259–75; Benjamin to Frederick A. Porcher, Dec. 21, 1864, in OR, ser. 4, vol. 3, pp. 959–60.

60. J. Morton Callahan, "The Confederate Diplomatic Archives—The 'Pickett Papers,'" *South Atlantic Quarterly* 2 (Jan. 1903), p. 7n.

61. Lynchburg *Virginian*, Feb. 13, 1865.

62. Benjamin to Frederick A. Porcher, Dec. 21, 1864, in OR, ser. 4, vol. 3, pp. 959–60; emphasis added.

63. [W. E. Stringfellow,] "Biographical Sketch of Dr. J. H. Stringfellow, Speaker of the First Kansas Legislature," typescript, 1902; clippings from *The Kansas Chief*,

Jan. 23, 1879, and the *Atchison Daily Globe*, July 16, 1894 and May 13, 1905; all in the Benjamin and John Stringfellow Collection, Kansas State Historical Society (hereafter KHS). Stringfellow's legislative resolution is quoted in F. B. Sanborn, ed., *The Life and Letters of John Brown* (1885; reprint, New York: New American Library, 1969), p. 176.

64. David M. Potter, *The Impending Crisis: 1848–1861* (New York: Harper and Row, 1976), p. 204.

65. Thomas Goodrich, *War to the Knife: Bleeding Kansas, 1854–1861* (Mechanicsburg, PA: Stackpole Books, 1998), pp. 77 (quotation), 46 (quotation).

66. Kenneth M. Stampp, *America in 1857* (New York: Oxford University Press, 1990), p. 148.

67. Although he continued to spend time in Atchison. In 1858, he had co-founded the Atchison and St. Joseph Railroad Co., and he continued to act as a booster for that city. Christian Ludwig Rutt, *History of Buchanan County and the City of St. Joseph and Representative Citizens* (Chicago: Biographical Publishing Co., 1904), chapter 9.

68. Stringfellow, "Biographical Sketch of Dr. J. H. Stringfellow," KHS; Col. Daniel Leasure, "Personal Observations and Experiences in the Pope Campaign in Virginia," *Glimpses of the Nation's Struggle: A Series of Papers Read before the Minnesota Commandery of the Military Order of the Loyal Legion of the United States* (St. Paul: St. Paul Book and Stationery Co., 1887), pp. 135–66.

69. J. H. Stringfellow to Jefferson Davis, Feb. 8, 1865, S-WD-57, Documents Printed in The War of the Rebellion, RG 109, NA

70. Emphasis added.

71. The U.S. Congress lifted Stringfellow's Reconstruction-era "political disabilities" only in 1870. See *Statutes at Large and Proclamations of the United States of America from December 1869 to March 1871* (Boston: Little, Brown, and Co., 1871), vol. 16, p. 626.

72. Lee to Andrew Hunter, Jan. 11, 1865, in OR, ser. 4, vol. 3, pp. 1012–3, emphases added; Andrew Hunter, "Memoranda on the Civil War," *Century Magazine* 36 (Aug. 1888), pp. 599–601.

73. OR, ser. 1, vol. 52, pt. 2, p. 591.

74. A. S. Colyar to Col. A. S. Marks, Jan. 30, 1864, in *The Annals of the Army of Tennessee and Early Western History* 1 (May 1978), pp. 50–2.

75. George Fitzhugh, "What's to Be Done with the Negroes?" *De Bow's Review*, new series, 1 (June 1866), p. 579; Carter, *When the War Was Over*, p. 186; M. I. Finley, *Ancient Slavery and Modern Ideology* (Harmondsworth, Eng.: Penguin, 1980), pp. 142–7; Marc Bloch, *Feudal Society*, trans. L. A. Manyon (Chicago: University of Chicago Press, 1964), vol. 1, pp. 256–60.

76. Karl Polanyi, *The Great Transformation: The Political and Economic Origins of Our Time* (Boston: Beacon Press, 1957), pp. 86–8; Christopher Hill, *Reformation to Industrial Revolution*, vol. 2 of the *Pelican Economic History of Britain* (Baltimore: Penguin, 1969), pp. 268–74; Buchanan Sharp, "Common Rights, Charities and the Disorderly Poor," *Reviving the English Revolution*, ed. Geoff Eley and William Hunt (London: Verso, 1988), pp. 107–38.

77. Fitzhugh, "What's to Be Done with the Negroes?" p. 580 (quotation).

78. Those eighteenth-century laws made it illegal for Catholics to purchase or bequeath land or to lease it for more than thirty-one years; they also mandated that land rents be set high enough to absorb most of a Catholic tenant's income. By the time that this legal onslaught began to ease toward the end of the century, it had already done its work. In 1750, the Catholic majority retained ownership of just 5 percent of all the land in the country. J. C. Beckett, *Making of Modern Ireland, 1603–23* (New York: Knopf, 1966), pp. 158–9, 172–6; J. G. Simms, "The Establishment of Protestant Ascendancy, 1691–1714," in *Eighteenth-Century Ireland, 1691–1800*, ed. T. W. Moody and W. E. Vaughan (Oxford: Oxford University Press, 1986), pp. 19–20; J. L. McCracken, "The Social Structure and Social Life, 1714–60," in ibid., p. 34–9; L. M. Cullen, "Economic Development, 1750–1800," in ibid., pp. 163–80; R. F. Foster, *Modern Ireland, 1600–1972* (London: Penguin, 1988), pp. 154–5, 205–11; S. J. Connolly, "Eighteenth-Century Ireland: Colony or *Ancien Regime*?" in *The Making of Modern Irish History: Revisionism and the Revisionist Controversy*, ed. D. George Boyce and Alan O'Day (London: Routledge, 1996), pp. 15–33.

79. Colyar to Marks, Jan. 30, 1864, in "General Cleburne's Views on Slavery," *The Annals of the Army of Tennessee and Early Western History*, vol. 1 (May 1978), p. 52. Cleburne's best and most recent biographer describes Cleburne's place in Irish society well: He was "part of a tiny but dominant class of well-to-do Protestants in a land peopled largely by poor Catholics." Symonds, *Stonewall of the West*, p. 9.

80. See especially Ira Berlin, *Slaves without Masters: The Free Negro in the Antebellum South* (New York: Random House, 1974), pp. 225–6, 381–2; and Barbara Jeanne Fields, *Slavery and Freedom on the Middle Ground: Maryland during the Nineteenth Century* (New Haven, Conn.: Yale University Press, 1985), pp. 35–8, 79–80.

81. Thomas C. Holt, "'An Empire Over the Mind': Emancipation, Race, and Ideology in the British West Indies and the American South," from *Region, Race, and Reconstruction: Essays in Honor of C. Vann Woodward*, ed. J. Morgan Kousser and James M. McPherson (New York: Oxford University Press, 1982), pp. 283–313; O. Nigel Bolland, "Systems of Domination after Slavery: The Control of Land and Labor in the British West Indies after 1838," *Comparative Studies in Society and History* 23 (Oct. 1981), pp. 591–619; Joe B. Wilkins, "Window on Freedom: The South's Response to the Emancipation of the Slaves in the British West Indies, 1833–1861" (Ph.D. dissertation, University of South Carolina, 1977); Eric Foner, *Nothing but Freedom: Emancipation and Its Legacy* (Baton Rouge and London: Louisiana State University Press, 1983), pp. 41–3.

82. Georges Lefebvre, *The Coming of the French Revolution* (New York: Random House, 1947), chaps. 10 and 11, and especially pp. 136–8.

83. Lefebvre, *Coming of the French Revolution*, pp. 141–2. This is an aspect of the Revolution not disputed during recent controversies. See, thus, Francois Furet and Mona Ozouf, eds., *A Critical Dictionary of the French Revolution* (Cambridge, Mass.: Harvard University Press, 1989), pp. 110–1; and Francois Furet, *Revolutionary France, 1770–1880* (Oxford, Eng.: Blackwell, 1992), pp. 70–2.

84. Lefebvre, *Coming of the French Revolution*, p. 143.

85. Lefebvre, *Coming of the French Revolution*, p. 142.

86. Lefebvre, *Coming of the French Revolution*, p. 180; Georges Lefebvre, *The*

French Revolution, 2 vols. (New York: Columbia University Press, 1964), vol. 2, pp. 55–6, 261–2.

87. Matthew B. Jensen, "Introduction," *The Cambridge History of Japan*, vol. 5, *The Nineteenth Century*, ed. Jensen (Cambridge: Cambridge University Press, 1989), pp. 8, 13–5, 21; and Harold Bolitho, "The Tempo Crisis," *Cambridge History of Japan*, vol. 5, pp. 117–33.

88. Marius B. Jensen, "The Meiji Restoration," in *Cambridge History of Japan*, vol. 5, *The Nineteenth Century*, p. 313 (quotation).

89. John W. Dower, ed., *Origins of the Modern Japanese State: Selected Writings of E. H. Norman* (New York: Pantheon, 1975), pp. 114–5, 119, 127, 206, 247; Jensen, "The Meiji Restoration," p. 359 (quotation); Barrington Moore, Jr., *Social Origins of Dictatorship and Democracy: Lord and Peasant in the Making of the Modern World* (Boston: Beacon, 1966), p 156.

90. Jensen, "Introduction," *Cambridge History of Japan*, pp. 20–5; Dower, ed., *Origins of the Modern Japanese State*, p. 115 (quotation).

91. Moore, *Social Origins*, p. 246.

92. Jensen, "Introduction," pp. 28–31; Stephen Vlastos, "Opposition Movements in early Meiji, 1868–1885," in *Cambridge History of Japan*, vol. 5, pp. 367–431; Dower, ed., *Origins of the Modern Japanese State*, p. 254; Moore, *Social Origins*, p. 258.

93. Hans Rosenberg, *Bureaucracy, Aristocracy and Autocracy: The Prussian Experience, 1660–1815* (1958; reprint, Boston: Beacon Press, 1966), chapter 9; David Blackbourn, *The Long Nineteenth Century: A History of Germany, 1780–1918* (New York: Oxford University Press, 1998), pp. 81–8. See also Steven Hahn, "Class and State in Postemancipation Societies: Southern Planters in Comparative Perspective," *American Historical Review* 95 (1990), pp. 75–98.

94. Rosenburg, *Bureaucracy, Aristocracy, and Autocracy*, pp. 203, 226.

95. Rosenburg, *Bureaucracy, Aristocracy, and Autocracy*, pp. 202–3 (quotations), 219–20; and Blackbourn, *The Long Nineteenth Century*, p. 70–86.

96. Theodore S. Hamerow, *Restoration, Revolution, Reaction: Economics and Politics in Germany, 1815–1871* (Princeton, N.J.: Princeton University Press, 1958), chapter 3; Werner Conze, "The Effects of Nineteenth-Century Liberal Agrarian Reforms on Social Structure in Central Europe," in *Essays in European Economic History, 1789–1914*, ed. F. Crouzet, W. H. Chaloner, and W. M. Stern (New York: St. Martin's Press, 1969), pp. 53–81.

97. Jerome Blum, *The End of the Old Order in Rural Europe* (Princeton, N.J.: Princeton University Press, 1978), p. 361 (quotation).

98. Hamerow, *Restoration, Revolution, Reaction*, p. 45.

99. Hamerow, *Restoration, Revolution, Reaction*, p. 50.

100. Hamerow, *Restoration, Revolution, Reaction*, pp. 46, 49, 50–4; Blackbourn, *The Long Nineteenth Century*, pp. 85–6. An interesting, extended commentary on this subject appears in Shearer Davis Bowman, *Masters and Lords: Mid-19th Century U.S. Planters and Prussian Junkers* (New York: Oxford University Press, 1993).

101. Hans-Ulrich Wehler, *Das Deutsche Kaiserreich* (Goettingen: Vandenhoeck and Ruprecht, 1973), esp. pp. 33–40, 60–8; Blackbourn, *The Long Nineteenth Century*, pp. 256–7 (quotation on p. 256).

102. Jerome Blum, "The Rise of Serfdom in Eastern Europe," *American Historical Review* 62 (July 1957), pp. 819–21; Jerome Blum, *Lord and Peasant in Russia from the Ninth to the Nineteenth Century* (Princeton, N.J.: Princeton University Press, 1961), chapters 25 and 26.

103. Blum, *Lord and Peasant*, p. 420.

104. Blum, *Lord and Peasant*, pp. 552, 575; Terence Emmons, *The Russian Landed Gentry and the Peasant Emancipation of 1861* (Cambridge: Cambridge University Press, 1968), p. 49.

105. Blum, *Lord and Peasant*, pp. 536–600; Emmons, *Russian Landed Gentry*, p. 51 (quotation); Alfred J. Rieber, "Alexander II: A Revisionist View," *Journal of Modern History* 43 (1971), 42–58.

106. Blum, *Lord and Peasant*, p. 571.

107. Blum, *Lord and Peasant*, pp. 543–4; Emmons, *Russian Landed Gentry*, pp. 55–6.

108. Blum, *Lord and Peasant*, p. 589.

109. Blum, *Lord and Peasant*, p. 593; Peter Kolchin, "Some Controversial Questions Concerning Nineteenth-century Emancipation from Slavery and Serfdom," *Serfdom and Slavery: Studies in Legal Bondage*, ed. M. L. Bush (London and New York: Longman, 1996), pp. 55–8; and Kolchin, "After Serfdom: Russian Emancipation in Comparative Perspective," in *Terms of Labor: Slavery, Serfdom, and Free Labor*, ed. Stanley L. Engerman (Stanford, Calif.: Stanford University Press, 1999), pp. 88–95.

110. *Message of Gov. Allen*, p. 18.

111. John W. Blassingame and John R. McKivigan eds., *The Frederick Douglass Papers*, ser. 1, vol. 4 (New Haven, Conn. and London: Yale University Press, 1991), p. 85.

Chapter 5

1. *Gorgas Journals*, p. 139 (entry for Nov. 17, 1864); Power, *Lee's Miserables*, pp. 218–9.

2. Thomas Donaldson, Notes of a Conversation with Duncan Farrar Kenner, New York City, Oct. 19, 1882, Duncan Farrar Kenner Collection, Manuscript Division, LC; Craig A. Bauer, *A Leader among Peers: The Life and Times of Duncan Farrar Kenner* (Lafayette: University of Southwestern Louisiana, 1993), pp. 216–35; Owsley, *King Cotton Diplomacy*, pp. 532–4. If Paris and London wished "to exact terms or conditions" before granting the Confederacy diplomatic recognition, then Secretary of State Judah P. Benjamin was anxious to tell them that "the sole object, for which we would ever have consented to commit our all to the hazards of this war, is the vindication of our rights to self-government and independence" and that "for that end no sacrifice is too great, save that of honor." Quoted in Robert Selph Henry, *The Story of the Confederacy*, rev. ed. (New York: Bobbs-Merrill, 1936), p. 441.

3. Bauer, *A Leader among Peers*, pp. 233–7; Owsley, *King Cotton Diplomacy*, pp. 536–41.

4. Richmond *Dispatch*, Feb. 6, 1865.

5. Lincoln, *Collected Works*, vol. 8, p. 279 (quotation).

6. Cooper, *Jefferson Davis, American*, pp. 550–1; McPherson, *Battle Cry of Freedom*, pp. 822–3; Lincoln, *Collected Works*, vol. 8, p. 279 (quotation); U.S. Grant, *Personal Memoirs*, vol. 2, p. 591.

7. William H. Seward to Charles F. Adams, Feb. 7, 1865, in OR, ser. 1, vol. 46, pt. 2, p. 473 (quotation); William C. Harris, "The Hampton Roads Peace Conference: A Final Test of Lincoln's Presidential Leadership," *Journal of the Abraham Lincoln Association* 21 (2000): 31–61; James M. McPherson, "No Peace without Victory, 1861 1865," *American Historical Review* 109 (Feb. 2004), esp. p. 17n.; *Kean Diary*, pp. 194–8.

8. Richmond *Enquirer*, Feb. 9, 1865.

9. Richmond *Examiner*, Feb. 10, 1865.

10. Richard L. Maury Diary, entry of Feb. 6, 1865, Manuscript Division, VHS.

11. James B. Jones to his brother and sister, Feb. 19, 1865, misdated 1864, in the Jones Family Papers, #2884, Southern Historical Collection, UNC-CH.

12. William Miller Owen, *In Camp and Battle with the Washington Artillery of New Orleans* (Boston: Ticknor, 1885), entry for Mar. 10, 1865, p. 366 (quotation); Power, *Lee's Miserables*, pp. 240–2, 250.

13. Richmond *Sentinel*, Dec. 28, 1864.

14. *Southern Confederacy*, Jan. 20, 1865.

15. Warren Akin to his wife, Dec. 26, 1864, in Wiley, ed., *Letters of Warren Akin*, p. 54.

16. Warren Akin to his wife, Jan. 23, 1865, in Wiley, ed., *Letters of Warren Akin*, p. 94.

17. Edmund Harrison to Jefferson Davis, Jan. 14, 1865, in OR, ser. 1, vol. 45, pt. 2, p. 784.

18. John A. Inglis to Carrie, Jan. 29, 1865, John Auchincloss Inglis Collection, Miscellaneous Manuscript Collection, Manuscript Division, LC.

19. Scarborough, ed., *The Diary of Edmund Ruffin*, vol. 3, p. 749.

20. Lynchburg *Virginian*, Feb. 25, 1865, Mar. 2, 1865; Richmond *Sentinel*, Mar. 4, 1865; Richmond *Whig*, Feb. 28, 1865.

21. *Journal of the House of Representatives of the State of Mississippi, Called Session at Columbus, February and March, 1865*. (Meridian, Miss.: J. J. Shannon, 1865), p. 13.

22. Richmond *Examiner*, Feb. 16, 1865; Richmond *Whig*, Jan. 30, 1865, Feb. 20, 1865.

23. OR, ser. 1, vol. 46, part 2, p. 1229.

24. OR, series 1, vol. 46, part 2, p. 1236; J. C. Timberlake to Captain [J. D. Darden], Feb. 20, 1865, P-206 1865, Adjutant and Inspector General's Office (hereafter AIGO)/LR, RG 109, NA.

25. O. Latrobe to J. B. Kershaw, Feb. 16, 1865, in OR, ser. 1, vol. 46, pt. 2, p. 1236 (quote); Maj. Gen. George Pickett to division commanders, Feb. 16, 1865, P-206 1865, AIGO/LR, RG 109, NA. Pickett specifically quoted Longstreet's opinion (as summarized by Longstreet's adjutant Osmun Latrobe) in order to reject it.

26. Richmond *Sentinel*, Mar. 6, 1865.

27. Richmond *Enquirer*, Feb. 18, 1865.

28. W. E. Greene to E. C. Fitzhugh, Feb. 19, 1865, P-206 1865, AIGO/LR, RG 109, NA.

29. OR, ser. 1, vol. 51, pt. 2, p. 1063.

30. Brig. Gen. George H. Steuart to Major, Feb. 21, 1865, P-206 1865, AIGO/LR, RG 109, NA.

31. Capt. F. G. Latham, O. A. Wylie, S. B. Clowney, and others to Brig. Gen'l, Feb. 23, 1865, G-207 1865. AIGO/LR, RG 109, NA.

32. Col. N. Berkeley to Capt. E. C. Fitzhugh, Feb. 20, 1865, P-206 1865, AIGO/LR, RG 109, NA; E. B. Mentefiore to Capt. J. D. Darden, Feb. 20, 1865, P-206 1865, AIGO/LR, RG 109, NA.

33. J. C. Timberlake to Captain J. D. Darden, Feb. 20, 1865, P-206 1865, AIGO/LR, RG 109, NA.

34. Col. T[homas] F[entress] Toon to Maj. H. K. Douglass, Feb. 16, 1865; G-181 1865, AIGO/LR, RG 109.

35. P. E. Daers to Lt. Walker, Feb. 15, 1865, 1865, G-181 1865, AIGO/LR, RG 109, NA.

36. Col. Jas. J. Phillips to Capt. J. D. Darden, Feb. 20, 1865, P-206 1865, AIGO/LR, RG 109, NA; C. R. Fontaine to Capt. J. D. Darden, Feb. 20, 1865, P-206 1865, AIGO/LR, RG 109, NA.

37. Undated, unaddressed message from W. B. Jincy, G-181 1865, AIGO/LR, RG 109, NA. See also James M. McPherson, *What They Fought For, 1861–1865* (New York: Doubleday, 1995), pp. 55–6.

38. OR, ser. 1, vol. 51, pt. 2, p. 1063.

39. G. H. Lowe to Lt. O. K. Walker, Feb. 15, 1865, G-181 1865, AIGO/LR, RG 109, NA; F. H. Langley, Chairman [of the meeting], no addressee, n.d., P-206 1865 AIGO/LR, RG 109, NA.

40. F. H. Langley to no addressee, n.d., P-206 1865, AIGO/LR, RG 109, NA; I. S. Carrington to no addressee, Feb. 20, 1865, P-206 1865, AIGO/LR, RG 109, NA; Capt. F. G. Latham, O. A. Wylie, S. B. Clowney, and others to Brig. Gen'l, Feb. 23, 1865, G-207 1865, AIGO/LR, RG 109, NA.

41. D. A. Weisiger to Col. W. H. Taylor, Feb. 17, 1865, V-47 1865, AIGO/LR, RG 109, NA.

42. See also "Resolutions passed at a meeting of Kentucky soldiers . . . near the city of Richmond," Feb. 25, 1865, introduced into the Confederate Senate and ordered to be printed. Copy in the LV.

43. D. A. Weisiger to Col. W. H. Taylor, Feb. 17, 1865, V-47 1865, AIGO/LR, RG 109, NA.

44. Col. W. E. Greene to Capt. E. C. Fitzhugh, Feb. 19, 1865, P-206 1865, AIGO/LR, RG 109, NA.

45. Richmond *Whig*, Feb. 20, 1865.

46. Silas Chandler to his wife, Feb. 21, 1865, Silas Chandler Letters, Accession no. 23984a, Personal Papers Collection, Archives and Manuscripts Department, LV.

47. Richard L. Maury Diary, Entry of Feb. 1, 1865, Manuscript Division, VHS.

48. George H. Steuart, to Major, Feb. 21, 1865, P-206 1865, AIGO/LR, RG 109, NA.

49. Owen, *In Camp and Battle with the Washington Artillery*, p. 366.

50. Col. Samuel Hoey Walkup, Diary, entry of Mar. 3, 1865, Samuel H. Walkup Papers, #1401, Southern Historical Collection, UNC-CH.

51. (Signed) F. H. Langley, Chairman [of the meeting], no addressee, n.d., P-206 1865, AIGO/LR, RG 109, NA.

52. Power, *Lee's Miserables*, pp. 228, 234–7, 264. See, for example, the Maury diary, entry of Mar. 3, 1865, Manuscript Division, VHS; Silas Chandler to Ann Elizabeth, Feb. 21, 1865, Feb. 25, 1865, Silas Chandler Letters, Personal Papers Collection, Archives and Manuscripts Department, LV; Sam Watson to Harriet C. Lewis, Feb. 2, 1865, Harriet C. Lewis Papers, DU.

53. Col. Samuel Hoey Walkup, Diary, entry of Mar. 3, 1865, Samuel H. Walkup Papers, #1401, Southern Historical Collection, UNC-CH.

54. J. B. Gordon to Major, Feb. 26, 1865, Gordon Family Papers, Hargrett Library, University of Georgia (hereafter UGa).

55. OR, ser. 4, vol. 3, pp. 1009–10.

56. C. M. Hubbard to Gov. Letcher, Apr. 26, 1861, in OR, ser. 1, vol. 51, pt 2, p. 47.

57. Warren Akin to his wife, Dec. 26, 1864, in Wiley, ed., *Letters of Warren Akin*, p. 54.

58. Macon *Telegraph and Confederate*, Nov. 19, 1864. See also Samuel to Harriet C. Lewis, Feb. 2, 1865, Harriet C. Lewis Papers, DU.

59. Wiley Sword, *Southern Invincibility: A History of the Confederate Heart* (New York: St. Martin's, 1999), pp. 319–20 (quotation).

60. Galveston *Tri-Weekly News*, Feb. 19, 1865, letter from Clayton C. Gilespie.

61. Maury Diary, entry of Feb. 1, 1865, Manuscript Division, VHS.

62. Richmond *Examiner*, Feb. 25, 1865.

63. Vandiver, ed., "Proceedings of the Second Confederate Congress," *SHSP* 52, p. 309.

64. See N. W. Stephenson, "The Question of Arming the Slaves," *American Historical Review* 18 (Jan. 1913): p. 298; Vandiver, "Proceedings of the Second Confederate Congress," *SHSP* 52, p. 309; "The Negro in the Military Service of the United States," frame 395.

65. T. C. Hindman to William S. Davis, Apr. 10, 1865, reprinted in the *Texas State Gazette*, May 3, 1865.

66. Vandiver, ed., "Proceedings of the Second Confederate Congress," *SHSP* 52, p. 329. A copy of the original bill is also folded into the Subject Index of RG 109 in the NA under the heading, "Slaves."

67. Richmond *Sentinel*, Feb. 14, 1865.

68. Vandiver, ed., "Proceedings of the Second Confederate Congress," SHSP 52, p. 330.

69. *Journal of the Congress of the Confederate States of America, 1861–1865*, 7 vols. (Washington: Government Printing Office, 1904–1905), vol. 7, pp. 612–3.

70. Vandiver, ed., "Proceedings of the Second Confederate Congress," *SHSP* 52, pp. 338–9; "The Negro in the Military Service of the United States," frames 411–2.

71. Thomas M. Preisser, "The Virginia Decision to Use Negro Soldiers in the Civil War, 1864–1865," *The Virginia Magazine of History and Biography* 83 (Jan. 1975), pp. 103–4, 108–11.

72. On March 6, Virginia's legislature followed up this decision by enabling any such black enlistee to bear arms (thus superceding existing state law forbidding blacks to do that). The Virginia resolutions may be found in G-44 1865, SW/LR, RG 109, NA; and OR, ser. 1, vol. 51, pt. 2, p. 1068. See also Preisser, "Virginia Decision," pp. 110–2.

73. The amendment generalized throughout the Confederacy Virginia's proviso that no more than 25 percent of military-age male slaves could be called into military service. Vandiver, ed., "Proceedings of the Second Confederate Congress," *SHSP* 52, p. 464–5.

74. Vandiver, ed., "Proceedings of the Second Confederate Congress," *SHSP* 52, p. 470; Crist, et al., eds., *Papers of Jefferson Davis*, vol. 11, p. 460.

75. Vandiver, ed., "Proceedings of the Second Confederate Congress," *SHSP* 52, p. 330.

76. Col. Charles Marshall to Lt. Gen. R. S. Ewell, Mar. 30, 1865, Richard Stoddert Ewell Papers, Manuscript Division, LC.

77. Robert F. Durden wrote that "although both the Confederate Congress and the Virginia legislature had steered clear of any legal promise of emancipation, Jefferson Davis and the War Department bootlegged freedom into the plan. . . " Thomas M. Preisser held that while the new Confederate law had not "provided for the emancipation of slave soldiers, the Confederate Army general order for implementing the measure did." Emory M. Thomas thought that these orders "transformed an ambiguous public law into a radical public policy." Durden, *The Gray and the Black*, p. 268; Preisser, "The Virginia Decision to Use Negro Soldiers," p. 112; Thomas, *Confederate Nation*, p. 296.

78. OR, ser. 4, vol. 3, pp. 1161–2.

79. *Journal of the Confederate Congress*, vol. 4, pp. 585, 670–1; Wilfred Buck Yearns, *The Confederate Congress* (Athens: University of Georgia Press, 1960), p. 98; OR, ser. 4, vol. 3, pp. 1161–2. The new law was thus a far cry from Raimondo Luraghi's depiction: "The Southern plan . . . not only freed slave-soldiers, but also granted them southern citizenship and a homestead." Luraghi, *The Rise and Fall of the Plantation South* (New York: Franklin Watts, 1978), p. 143.

80. OR, ser. 4, vol. 3, p. 1161.

81. Charles Marshall to Lt. Gen. R. S. Ewell, Mar. 30, 1865, Richard Stoddert Ewell Papers, Manuscript Division, LC.

82. OR, ser. 4, vol. 3, pp. 1193–4, 1144; Lynchburg *Virginian*, Mar. 18, 1865.

83. S. Cooper to Robert E. Lee, Mar. 28, 1865, in "The Negro in Military Service," frame 0476; Robert E. Lee to James Longstreet, Mar. 28, 1865, Mss2 L515 a 42, Manuscript Division, VHS; Charles Marshall to R. S. Ewell, Mar. 30, 1865, Richard Stoddert Ewell Papers, Manuscript Division, LC.

84. Lee to Longstreet, Mar. 28, 1865, Nss1 F1613a4, Manuscript Division, VHS; Robert E. Lee to John C. Breckinridge, Mar. 14, 1865, Army of Northern Virginia Headquarters Papers, Robert E. Lee Papers, VHS.

85. Col. J. T. Jordan, Major J. B. Duggan, and ten other officers, to Col. W. H. Taylor, Mar. 15, 1865, W-86 1865, Letters and Telegrams Received by Robert E. Lee 1861–1865, Papers of Various Confederate Notables, Collection of Officers Papers, Records of the Military Commands, RG 109, NA.

86. Jones, *Rebel War Clerk's Diary*, vol. 2, pp. 451, 461–2. See, for example, J. E. Shuman to Thomas S. Hayward, Mar. 20, 1865, J. E. Shuman Letter, 1865, Manuscript Division, VHS; J. A. Caldwell to Secretary of War, Feb. 17, 1865 [erroneously dated 1864], C-51 1864, SW/LR, RG 109; Wm. S. Southall, to the Secretary of War, Mar. 20, 1865, S-98 1865, SW/LR, RG 109; R. C. Donnan to J. C. Breckinridge, Mar. 21, 1865, SW/LR, D-43 1865, RG 109, NA; O. S. Acee to Lt. Gen. S. D. Lee, Jan. 1865, AIGO/LR, A-225 1865, RG 109, NA; James Buchanan to J. C. Breckinridge, n.d., (received Feb. 29, 1865), B-110 1865, SW/LR, RG 109, NA; J. P. Wilcox to Maj. G. A. Henry, Mar. 30, 1865, in "The Negro in the Military Service of the United States," frames 0486–0487; Col. William M. Inge to Jefferson Davis, Mar. 17, 1865, Compiled Service Records, RG 109, NA; Capt. L. W. Brandon to Jefferson Davis, Mar. 29, 1865, B-121 1865, SW/LR, RG 109, NA; G. W. Custis Lee to John William Carter, Mar. 14, 1865, Manuscript Division, VHS.

87. James Longstreet, *From Manassas to Appomattox: Memoirs of the Civil War in America* (Philadelphia: J. B. Lippincott, 1896), p. 651.

88. Edward Pollard to Jefferson Davis, Jan. 13, 1865, P-16 1865, SW/LR, RG 109, NA.

89. J. D. Stapp to his mother, Mar. 4, 1865, Joseph D. Stapp Letters, Manuscript Division, VHS. See also James H. McWhorter to David C. Barrow, Mar. 29, 1865, Accession 69, David Crenshaw Barrow Papers, Hargrett Rare Book and Manuscript Library, UGa.

90. Longstreet, *From Manassas to Appomattox*, p. 653.

91. Lee to Longstreet, Mar. 28, 1865, Manuscript Division, VHS; Robert E. Lee to John C. Breckinridge, Mar. 14, 1865, Army of Northern Virginia Headquarters Papers, Robert E. Lee Papers, VHS.

92. "The Negro in the Military Service of the United States, 1639–1886," frame 0479.

93. Reprinted in the *New York Times*, Apr. 8, 1865; Robert E. Lee to John C. Breckinridge, Mar. 27, 1865, in OR, ser. 1, vol. 46, pt. 3, pp. 1356–7.

94. Col. Charles Marshall, to Lt. Gen. R. S. Ewell, Mar. 30, 1865, Richard Stoddert Ewell Papers, Manuscript Division, LC; OR, ser. 4, vol. 3, p. 1194; Special Orders No. 78, AIGO, Special Orders, 1865, p. 232, Old Records Division, Confederate Records Section, Records of the Adjutant General's Office, 1780s–1917, RG 94, NA; OR, ser. 4, vol. 3, p. 1194.

95. OR, ser. 4, vol. 3, p. 1193.

96. Macon *Telegraph and Confederate*, Apr. 15, 1865.

97. OR, series 1, vol. 47, pt. 3, p. 737, ser. 1, vol. 49, part 2, p. 1175, ser 4, vol. 3, p. 1193; Oates, *The War between the Union and the Confederacy*, pp. 502–3.

98. OR, ser. 4, vol. 3, p. 1194.

99. Charles Marshall to R. S. Ewell, Mar. 27, 1865, Richard Stoddert Ewell Papers, Manuscript Division, LC.

100. Robert E. Lee to John C. Breckinridge, Mar. 14, 1865, Army of Northern Virginia Headquarters Papers, R. E. Lee Papers, VHS.

101. Richmond *Sentinel*, Mar. 24, 1865.

102. Richmond *Sentinel*, Mar. 24, 1865.

103. "The Negro in Military Service of the United States," frame 0473.

104. Macon *Telegraph and Confederate*, Apr. 17, 1865.

105. Richmond *Sentinel*, Mar. 24, 1865. Promises of "fair wages" and residence in their "old homes," however, might signal to attentive readers that some early loose talk about giving black soldiers homesteads of their own had been quietly forgotten.

106. OR, ser. 4, vol. 3, p. 1162.

107. Lynchburg *Virginian*, Mar. 17, 1865.

108. Richmond *Sentinel*, Mar. 24, 1865, original emphasis.

109. Lynchburg *Virginian*, Mar. 18, 1865. Georgia farmers, too, must "come forward at once and tender your able-bodied and most intelligent negroes to the Government." Macon *Telegraph and Confederate*, Apr. 4, 17, 1865.

110. Montgomery *Daily Mail*, Apr. 8, 1865.

111. Lee to Jefferson Davis, Mar. 10, 1865, in *The Wartime Papers of Robert E. Lee*, ed. Clifford Dowdey and Louis H. Manarin (1961; reprint, New York: Da Capo, 1987), p. 914.

112. William Smith to Gen. R. E. Lee, Mar. 25, 1865, Virginia Governor's Office, William Smith Executive Papers, RG 3, State Records Collection, LV.

113. Jones, *Rebel War Clerk's Diary*, vol. 2, p. 461.

114. A. F. Robertson to J. C. Breckinridge, Mar. 26, 1865, SW/LR, R-60 1865, RG 109, NA.

115. Richmond *Dispatch*, Mar. 27, 1865, clipping in EBL/MOC.

116. Lynchburg *Virginian*, Mar. 21, 1865.

117. Raleigh *Daily Confederate*, Mar. 31, 1865.

118. Richmond *Examiner*, Mar. 21, 1865.

119. M. G. Harman to Jefferson Davis, Jan. 12, 1865, H-38 1865, SW/LR, RG 109, NA. The offer, Harman explained, was "induced by the impending crisis"—and perhaps by the fact that Harman had "already lost nearly half" of his slaves to the war.

120. C. E. Thorburn to John C. Breckinridge, Mar. 12, 1865, in "The Negro in the Military Service of the U.S.," frame 0444.

121. Taylor commanded the Confederacy's department of Alabama, Mississippi, and East Louisiana. E[ustace] Surget to William Lyon, Apr. 4, 1865, Records of Military Commands, Dept. of Ala, Ms., and E. La., ch. II, v. 14, LS 1865, p. 429, RG 109, NA.

122. Richard L. Maury Diary, entry of Feb. 18, 1865, Manuscript Division, VHS.

123. Raleigh *Daily Confederate*, Mar. 29, 1865.

124. Raleigh *Daily Confederate*, Mar. 22, 1865.

125. OR, ser. 1, vol. 49, pt. 1, p. 711.

126. New York *Daily Tribune*, Feb. 27, 1865.

127. R. J. M. Blackett, ed., *Thomas Morris Chester, Black Civil War Correspondent* (New York: Da Capo, 1991), p. 282.

128. F. W. Hancock to Richard S. Ewell, Feb. 14, 1865, in OR, ser. 4, vol. 3, p. 1193. A physician who was at that time working in another Richmond hospital (Howard's Grove) later recalled hearing a young black man employed there exhort his comrades with "the most eloquent and earnest plea for every man to enlist in our glorious cause and help drive the ruthless invader from the sacred soil of Virginia." The doctor did not specify whether the speaker was a slave or free man. In any case, however, no evidence has come to light that any blacks employed at Howard's Grove hospital responded to that speech by volunteering to serve. Joseph A. Mudd, "The Confederate Negro," *Confederate Veteran* (Sept. 1915), p. 411.

129. Richmond *Examiner*, Feb. 15, 1865.

130. Richmond *Examiner*, Mar. 9, 1865.

131. O. Latrobe to R. S. Ewell, Feb. 17, 1865, in OR, ser. 1, vol. 46, pt. 2, pp. 1237–8.

132. H. C. Scott to Sir, Mar. 16, 1865, Subject Index (folded into envelope marked "Slaves" . . . "Negroes, enlistment of"), RG 109, NA; Lynchburg *Virginian*, Mar. 23, 1865.

133. Richmond *Examiner*, Mar. 21, 1865; Richmond *Dispatch*, Mar. 24, 1865; Richmond *Dispatch*, Mar. 22, 1865; Lynchburg *Virginian*, Mar. 23, 1865.

134. Richmond *Dispatch*, July 1, 1862; Richmond *Enquirer*, Mar. 23, 1865; Special Orders No. 63, AIGO, Mar. 17, 1865, Records of the Adjutant General's Office, 1780s–1917, Old Records Division, Confederate Records Section, Special Orders, 1865, AIGO, p. 191, RG 94, NA.

135. Richmond *Examiner*, Mar. 22, 1865; the Richmond *Whig*, reprinted in the Lynchburg *Virginian*, Mar. 24, 1865.

136. Richmond *Examiner*, Feb. 15, Mar. 21, 1865.

137. Richmond *Sentinel*, Mar. 24, 1865, original emphasis.

138. Statement of the Auditor of the Numbers of Slaves Fit for Service, Mar. 25, 1865, William Smith Executive Papers, Virginia Governor's Office, RG 3, State Records Collection, LV.

139. Smith's projection reflected the law's provision that no more than a fourth of military-age slaves would be recruited into the army. William Smith to R. E. Lee, Mar. 25, 1865, William Smith Executive Papers, Virginia Governor's Office, RG 3, State Records Collection, LV; William Smith to Jefferson Davis, Mar. 27, 1865, Jefferson Davis Papers, DU.

140. The Richmond *Examiner*, Mar. 27, 1865; Richmond *Whig*, Apr. 29, 1865. Thomas Hughes recalled sixty such troops. See Thomas Hughes, *A Boy's Experience in the Civil War, 1860–1865* (Baltimore: Daily Record, 1904), p. 13.

141. Richmond *Examiner*, Mar. 27, 1865.

142. Richmond *Dispatch*, Mar. 25, 1865, clipping in EBL/MOC; Richmond *Examiner*, Mar. 29, 1865.

143. Richmond *Whig*, Mar. 30, 1865, clipping in the EBL/MOC.

144. Message of the Governor of Virginia, and Accompanying Documents, Dec. 7, 1864, (p. 10), William Smith Executive Papers, Virginia Governor's Office, RG 3, State Records Collection, LV.

145. Extract from the Executive Journal of the State of Virginia for Mar. 16, 1865, in "The Negro in the Military Service of the United States," frame 0455; Ernest Taylor Walthall, *Hidden Things Brought to Light* (Richmond: Dietz, 1933), p. 34. Walthall wrote the manuscript in 1908.

146. Richmond *Examiner*, Mar. 18, 1865.

147. Richmond *Examiner*, Mar. 20, 1865, letter dated Mar. 18, 1865.

148. Richmond *Examiner*, Mar. 27, 1865.

149. From Bossieux's obituary notice in the Richmond *Times-Dispatch*, Apr. 30, 1910.

150. Hadden, *Slave Patrols*, p. 186.

151. OR, ser. 2, vol. 6, pp. 852–3; Richmond *Examiner*, Mar. 27, 1865, in EBL/MOC.

152. Hadden, *Slave Patrols*, pp. 167–96; Kimball, *American City, Southern Place*, p. 248; Bernard H. Nelson, "Legislative Control of the Southern Free Negro, 1861–1865," *Catholic Historical Review* 32 (Apr. 1946), pp. 28–46; J. H. Unthank and Geo. S. Hebb, *A Digest of the Militia Laws of Tennessee Now in Force* (Memphis: Hutton and Freligh, 1861), p. 49 (quotation).

153. Thomas, *Confederate State of Richmond*, pp. 27–9.

154. Louis H. Manarin, ed., *Richmond at War: The Minutes of the City Council, 1861 1865* (Chapel Hill: University of North Carolina Press, 1966), pp. 346, 349, 519.

155. Richmond *Whig*, Mar. 31, 1865, reprinted in Durden, *The Gray and the Black*, p. 276; Jordan, *Black Confederates*, pp. 247–8.

156. Moses Purnell Handy, "A Courier's Experience during the Great Retreat," *The Watchman*, Feb. 3, 1866, pasted in scrapbook, Handy Family Papers, William L. Clements Library, University of Michigan.

157. Richard L. Maury Diary, entry for Mar. 23, 1865, Manuscript Division, VHS; Nelson Lankford, *Richmond Burning: The Last Days of the Confederate Capital* (New York: Penguin, 2002), p. 34; Pollard, *Life of Jefferson Davis*, p. 456; Richard S. Ewell to L. C. [Lizinka Campbell Brown] Ewell, May 12, 1865, Brown-Ewell Family Papers, Filson Historical Society (quotation).

158. Handy, "A Courier's Experience."

159. Richmond *Dispatch*, Mar. 22, 1865.

160. Hughes, *A Boy's Experience*, pp. 12–3.

161. Pollard, *Life of Jefferson Davis*, p. 456.

Chapter 6

1. OR, ser. 4, vol. 3, p. 1133.

2. Davis, *The Rise and Fall of the Confederate Government*, vol. 1, p. 443. See also Jefferson Davis to Maj. Campbell Brown, Jan. 14, 1886, letter no. 208–9, George Washington Campbell Papers, Manuscript Division, LC.

3. E. A. Pollard, *The Lost Cause* (1866; reprint, New York: Gramercy Books, 1994), p. 660.

4. The Editor [J. D. B. De Bow], "Memories of the War," *De Bow's Review, Agricultural, Commercial, Industrial Progress and Resources* 3, no. 3 (Mar. 1867), pp. 225–33 (quotation on pp. 226–7).

5. Raleigh *Daily Confederate*, Jan. 25, 1865.

6. Robert Selph Henry, *The Story of the Confederacy*, rev. ed. (New York: Bobbs-Merrill, 1931, 1936), p. 440.

7. Durden, *The Gray and the Black*, p. 296.

8. Mohr, *On the Threshhold of Freedom*, p. 291.

9. Jordan, *Black Confederates and Afro-Yankees*, pp. 251, 247.

10. Yacavone, ed., *A Voice of Thunder*, p. 134.

11. McPherson, *The Negro's Civil War*, p. 23.

12. Benjamin S. Ewell wrote these words below the text of a letter in which James A. Seddon had years earlier instructed Johnston to suppress the discussion of Cleburne's proposal in the Army of Tennessee. See James A. Seddon to Joseph E. Johnston, Jan. 24, 1864, Joseph E. Johnston Papers, Manuscripts and Rare Books Department, Earl Gregg Swem Library, College of William and Mary.

13. Oates, *The War between the Union and the Confederacy*, p. 503.

14. Scarborough, ed., *The Diary of Edmund Ruffin*, vol. 3, p. 748.

15. See, for example, a letter to the Raleigh *Progress* signed "Veritas," reprinted in the *North Carolina Standard*, Nov. 16, 1864; and the Feb. 4, 1865, letter from "Friend" to "Judge" in the EBL/MOC.

16. T. C. Hindman to William S. Davis, Apr. 10, 1865, published in Austin's *Texas State Gazette* of May 3, 1865.

17. J. B. Hood, *Advance and Retreat: Personal Experiences in the United States and Confederate States Armies* (New Orleans: G. T. Beauregard, 1880), p. 296.

18. William W. Freehling thinks so. See Freehling, *The South vs. The South*, p. 195.

19. Crabtree and Patton, eds., *"Journal of a Secesh Lady,"* p. 653.

20. Jones, *Rebel War Clerk's Diary*, vol. 2, p. 353.

21. Figures on congressional slaveholding are derived from the tabular data in Thomas B. Alexander and Richard E. Beringer, *The Anatomy of the Confederate Congress: A Study of the Influence of Member Characteristics on Legislative Voting Behavior, 1861–1865* (Nashville: Vanderbilt University Press, 1972), pp. 354–89. The percentage of white Confederate families holding slaves was calculated from the report of the 1860 census. See also McPherson, *Battle Cry of Freedom*, pp. 611–2; and James Oakes, *The Ruling Race: A History of American Slaveholders* (New York: Random House, 1982), p. 52.

22. Frederick Maurice, ed., *Lee's Aide-de-Camp, Being the Papers of Colonel Charles Marshall Sometime Aide-de-Camp, Military Secretary, and Assistant Adjutant General of Robert E. Lee, 1862–1865* (1927; reprint, Lincoln and London: University of Nebraska Press, 2000), p. 41.

23. Thomas C. Hindman to William S. Davis, Apr. 10, 1865, in the *Texas State Gazette*, May 3, 1865. Even as Jefferson Davis drafted plans to modify that policy, his secretary of war was reaffirming the government's refusal to use slaves as soldiers. Davis proposed the change publicly on November 7. Five days later, a Georgia militia major offered to raise a black regiment for the Confederate army. James A. Seddon doggedly informed the major on November 24 that "the Department is not prepared to consider such applications" and added that it was "not probable that any such policy will be prescribed by Congress." OR, ser. 4, vol. 3, pp. 761–2; E. B. Briggs to James A.

Seddon, Nov. 12, 1864, B-673 1864, SW/LR, RG 109, NA; James A. Seddon to Major E. B. Briggs, Nov. 24, 1864, chap. 9, vol. 18, p. 323, SW/LS, RG 109, NA.

24. Oates, *War between the Union and the Confederacy*, pp. 496–7.

25. *Kean Diary*, p. 177.

26. Raleigh *Daily Confederate*, Mar. 9, 1865, reprinted from the Richmond *Whig*.

27. See, for example, the complaint that then Secretary of War Randolph lodged with Alabama governor John G. Shorter in Oct. 1862, in OR, ser. 4, vol. 2, p. 106; James A. Seddon to Jefferson Davis, Nov. 26, 1863, in OR, ser. 4, vol. 2, p. 998 (quotation); John A. Campbell to John C. Breckinridge, Mar. 5, 1865, in Campbell, *Reminiscences and Documents*, p. 28; Bell Irvin Wiley, *The Life of Johnny Reb: The Common Soldier of the Confederacy* (1943; reprint, Baton Rouge: Louisiana State University Press), p. 329.

28. OR, ser. 4, vol. 3, p. 1010; Vandiver, ed., "Proceedings of the Second Confederate Congress," *SHSP* 52, p. 455.

29. Warren Akin to Nathan Land, Oct. 31, 1864, in Wiley, ed., *Letters of Warren Akin*, p. 33.

30. Galveston *Tri-Weekly News*, Dec. 23, 1864.

31. W. H. C. Whiting to Maj. Gen. Gilmer, Jan. 9, 1865, Letter Book (not paginated), ch. II, vol. 338, Gen. W. H. Whiting's Command, Aug. 4, 1864–Jan. 1865, Records of Military Departments, LS, RG 109, NA.

32. R. E. Lee to James A. Seddon, Dec. 11, 1864, in OR, ser. 1, vol. 42, part 3, p. 1267.

33. William Smith, "Message to the General Assembly," Feb. 10, 1865, William Smith Executive Papers, 1864–1865, Governor's Executive Papers, Virginia Governor's Office, RG 3, State Records Collection, LV.

34. Jno. D. Alexander to Col. Munford, Mar. 23, 1865; R. B. Shaw, Jr., to William Smith, Mar. 24, 1865; J. Wade to William Smith, Jan. 12, 1865; Robert A. Scott [to William Smith], Jan. 11, 1865; William Smith, Message to the General Assembly, draft dated Feb. 10, 1865; all in William Smith Executive Papers, 1864–1865, Governor's Executive Papers, Virginia Governor's Office, RG 3, State Records Collection, LV.

35. Application from S. Beezley to William Smith, Jan. 24, 1865, William Smith Executive Papers, 1864–1865, Governor's Executive Papers, Virginia Governor's Office, RG 3, State Records Collection, LV.

36. Geo. K. Taylor, attesting to it as a fair copy, n.d., Governor's Executive Papers, William Smith Executive Papers, 1864–1865, Governor's Executive Papers, Virginia Governor's Office, RG 3, State Records Collection, LV.

37. Jno. W. Potts to William Smith, n.d. [filed Jan. 27, 1865], William Smith Executive Papers, 1864–1865, Governor's Executive Papers, Virginia Governor's Office, RG 3, State Records Collection, LV.

38. Many masters, Smith charged, had deliberately hired their slaves out to residents of other counties as a way of evading the impressment order. William Smith to the Clerk of the Hustings Court of the City of Lynchburg, Jan. 23, 1865, William Smith Executive Papers, 1864–1865, Governor's Executive Papers, Virginia Governor's Office, RG 3, State Records Collection, LV. Commonwealth Secretary George Munford similarly deplored the "technical objections" raised to

evade masters' obligations to "the very salvation of the capital city of the State and the Confederacy." George W. Munford to the Hon. County Court of Greene County, Jan. 28, 1865; reply from Geo. K. Taylor, n.d.; both in William Smith Executive Papers, 1864–1865, Governor's Executive Papers, Virginia Governor's Office, RG 3, State Records Collection, LV.

39. Draft message to the General Assembly, Feb. 10, 1865, William Smith Executive Papers, 1864–1865, Governor's Executive Papers, Virginia Governor's Office, RG 3, State Records Collection, LV.

40. R. E. Lee to William Smith, Feb. 9, 1865, William Smith Executive Papers, 1864–1865, Governor's Executive Papers, Virginia Governor's Office, RG 3, State Records Collection, LV.

41. William Smith to the Honorable the Counties, Cities, &c. named in the annexed Schedule, Mar. 14, 1865, filed under heading "Slaves" in the Subject Index of RG 109, NA.

42. Macon *Telegraph and Confederate*, Apr. 19, 1865.

43. John A. Campbell to John C. Breckinridge, Mar. 5, 1865, in Campbell, *Reminiscences and Documents*, p. 28.

44. Galveston *Tri-Weekly News*, Oct. 28, 1864.

45. Galveston *Tri-Weekly News*, Dec. 30, 1864, letter signed Xenophon.

46. Galveston *Tri-Weekly News*, Feb. 12, 1865, emphasis added.

47. John A. Campbell to John C. Breckinridge, Mar. 5, 1865, in Campbell, *Reminiscences and Documents*, p. 28.

48. Macon *Telegraph and Confederate*, Nov. 2, 1864.

49. William A. Graham to David L. Swain, Mar. 12, 1865, William Alexander Graham Papers (P.C. 61), North Carolina Office of Archives and History.

50. North Carolina General Assembly, *Resolutions against the Policy of Arming Slaves* (Richmond, 1865), copy in the LV. On March 4, 1865, J. M. Leach brought the resolutions before the Confederate House of Representatives, which ordered them to be printed.

51. William Smith to Wyndham Robertson and F. B. Dean, Mar. 6, 1865, William Smith Executive Papers, 1864–1865, Governor's Executive Papers, Virginia Governor's Office, RG 3, State Records Collection, LV.

52. Governor William Smith to the General Assembly, Mar. 6, 1865; William Smith to Wyndham Robertson and F. B. Dean, Mar. 6, 1865, both in William Smith Executive Papers, 1864–1865, Governor's Executive Papers, Virginia Governor's Office, RG 3, State Records Collection, LV. The intransigent public position of Tar Heel planters, however, may explain why so little evidence has turned up of organized efforts to recruit slave soldiers in that state.

53. *Kean Diary*, pp. 183, 188; William C. Harris, *William Woods Holden: Firebrand of North Carolina Politics* (Baton Rouge and London: Louisiana State University Press, 1987), pp. 132, 142–3; Jones, *Rebel War Clerk's Diary*, vol. 2, p. 403.

54. Richmond *Enquirer*, Jan. 28, 1865.

55. Sidney Andrews, *The South since the War* (1866; reprint, Boston: Houghton Mifflin, 1971), p. 155.

56. William A. Graham to Zebulon B. Vance, Feb. 12, 1865, in Max R. Williams, ed., *The Papers of William Alexander Graham*, 8 vols. (Raleigh: North Carolina

Department of Cultural Resources, 1957–1992), vol. 6, p. 232 (quotation). One of Graham's allies, Thomas Settle, was still complaining six months later that slavery "might have been partially retained if the Davis government had not been obstinate" regarding peace negotiation and that slavery had "received its death-thrust when the Confederate government adopted the policy of taking negroes into the army." Quoted in Andrews, *The South since the War*, p. 155.

57. Journalist Sidney Andrews found such hopes surviving among some even into the fall of 1865. Andrews, *The South since the War*, pp. 57, 60. See also Carter, *When the War Was Over*, p. 83; William C. Davis, *An Honorable Defeat: The Last Days of the Confederate Government* (New York: Harcourt, Inc., 2001), pp. 163–4.

58. By some accounts, Lincoln and Seward had dropped just enough enticing hints at Hampton Roads to nourish one or another of these hopes. John A. Campbell to William A. Graham, Feb. 24, 1865, in *Papers of William Alexander Graham*, vol. 6, pp. 254–6; Campbell, *Reminiscences and Documents*, pp. 7–8, 14, 17, 22; Thomas E. Schott, *Alexander H. Stephens of Georgia: A Biography* (Baton Rouge: Louisiana State University Press, 1988), pp. 446–7; David Herbert Donald, *Lincoln* (New York: Simon and Schuster, 1995), pp. 558–9; William J. Cooper, *Jefferson Davis, American* (New York: Random House, 2000), p. 550; William C. Harris, "The Hampton Roads Peace Conference: A Final Test of Lincoln's Presidential Leadership," *Journal of the Abraham Lincoln Association* 21 (2000), esp. pp. 50–5.

59. Raleigh *Daily Confederate*, Apr. 6, 1865.

60. Lynchburg *Virginian*, Mar. 16, 1865.

61. Richmond *Enquirer*, Mar. 23, 1865.

62. OR, ser. 4, vol. 3, p. 1194.

63. Francis W. Dawson to his father, June 13, 1865, Francis Warrington Dawson Papers, DU.

64. Richard S, Ewell to L. C. Ewell [Lizinka Campbell Brown Ewell], May 12, 1865, Brown-Ewell Family Papers, Filson Historical Society.

65. Charles Marshall to R. S. Ewell, Mar. 27, 1865, Richard Stoddert Ewell Papers, Manuscript Division, LC.

66. Charles Marshall to R. S. Ewell, Mar. 30, 1865, Richard Stoddert Ewell Papers, Manuscript Division, LC.

67. Lee to Jefferson Davis, Mar. 10, 1865, in Clifford Dowdey and Louis Manarin, eds., *The Wartime Papers of Robert E. Lee* (1961; reprint, New York: Da Capo, 1987), p. 914.

68. Robert E. Lee to John C. Breckinridge, Mar. 14, 1865, Army of Northern Virginia Papers, R. E. Lee Papers, VHS; Robert E. Lee to Jefferson Davis, Mar. 24, 1865, in OR, ser. 1, vol. 46, pt. 3, p. 1339.

69. Jefferson Davis to William Smith, Mar. 25, 1865, in OR, ser. 1, vol. 46, pt. 3, pp. 1348–9; William Smith to Jefferson Davis, Mar. 27, 1865, Jefferson Davis Papers, Perkins Library, DU; Crist, et al., eds., *Papers of Jefferson Davis*, vol. 11, pp. 476, 486–92.

70. Oates, *The War between the Union and the Confederacy*, pp. 502–3.

71. Carter, *When the War Was Over*, pp. 7–9; Wiley, *The Life of Johnny Reb*, p. 134.

72. Virginia Ingraham Burr, ed., *The Secret Eye: The Journal of Ella Getrude Clanton Thomas, 1848–1889* (Chapel Hill and London: University of North Carolina Press, 1990), p. 243.

73. James Wingard to Simon Wingard, Jan. 4, 1865, Wingard Papers, Perkins Library, DU.

74. Charleston *Mercury*, Jan. 26, 1865.

75. Charleston *Mercury*, Jan. 3, 1865.

76. P. K. Montgomery to Governor Clark, Apr. 4, 1865, RG 27, MDAH. The same sense informs an exchange that Mary Chesnut recorded. Woodward, ed., *Mary Chesnut's Civil War*, p. 696.

77. The Richmond *Whig*, Mar. 28, 1865, clipping in the EBL/MOC.

78. Montgomery *Mail*, Mar. 1, 1865.

79. Raleigh *North Carolina Standard*, Oct. 26, 1864.

80. Richmond *Dispatch*, Nov. 9, 1864.

81. John A Speer to his mother, Apr. 2, 1865, EBL/MOC.

82. *Journal of the Senate of the Extra Session of the General Assembly, of the State of Georgia* (Milledgeville, Ga.: Boughton, Nisbet, Barnes and Moore, State Printers, 1865), pp. 15–6.

83. Charleston *Mercury*, Jan. 26, 1865.

84. *Kean Diary*, p. 204.

85. Powers, *Lee's Miserables*; J. B. Gordon to Major, Feb. 26, 1865, Gordon Family Papers, Hargrett Rare Book and Manuscript Library, UGa

86. Atlanta *Southern Confederacy*, Jan. 20, 1865.

87. Raleigh *North Carolina Standard*, Feb. 15, 1865.

88. Raleigh *North Carolina Standard*, Nov. 16, 1864, reprinting a letter first published in the Raleigh *Progress*.

89. T. C. Hindman to William S. Davis, Apr. 10, 1865, published in Austin's *Texas State Gazette*, May 3, 1865.

90. Lynchburg *Virginian*, Mar. 16, 1865, emphasis added.

91. William C. Oates, *The War between the Union and the Confederacy*, pp. 501–2.

92. Roy F. Basler, ed., *The Collected Works of Abraham Lincoln*, 8 vols. (New Brunswick, N.J.: Rutgers University Press, 1953), vol. 8, pp. 360–2.

93. Governor Brown's Feb. 15 message to the legislature, in Macon *Telegraph and Confederate*, Feb. 18, 1865.

94. Macon *Telegraph and Confederate*, Oct. 29, 1864. See also a letter from "Friend" to "Judge," written from Keachi, La., Feb. 4, 1865, EBL/MOC.

95. Charleston *Mercury*, Jan. 3, 1865.

96. Charleston *Mercury*, Jan. 26, 1865.

97. Raleigh *North Carolina Standard*, Nov. 4, 1864.

98. Richmond *Enquirer*, Nov. 12, 1864, letter signed Virginius.

99. Raleigh *Daily Confederate*, Jan. 25, 1865.

100. Blassingame and McKivigan, eds., *The Frederick Douglass Papers*, ser. 1, vol. 4, p. 52 (quotation).

101. Frederick Douglass, *Life and Times of Frederick Douglass* (rev. ed., 1892; reprint, London: Collier-Macmillan, 1962), p. 362 (quotation).

102. J[ohn] T[ownsend] Trowbridge, *The South: A Tour of Its Battle-fields and Ruined Cities, A Journey through the Desolated States, and Talks with the People* (Hartford, Conn.: L. Stebbins, 1866), pp. 208–9.

103. R. J. M. Blackett, ed., *Thomas Morris Chester, Black Civil War Correspondent: His Dispatches from the Virginia Front* (New York: Da Capo, 1991), pp. 249–50, 263–4. The free-black-owned New Orleans *Tribune* reprinted Chester's report three weeks later. See Du Bois, *Black Reconstruction in America*, pp. 119–20.

104. M. A. DeWolfe Howe, ed., *Marching with Sherman: Passages from the Letters and Campaign Diaries of Henry Hitchcock, Major and Assistant Adjutant General of Volunteers, November 1864–May 1865* (New Haven, Conn.: Yale University Press, 1927), p. 128.

105. The quotation comes from Williams's Jan. 23, 1865, letter to his daughter. Milo M. Quaife, ed., *From the Cannon's Mouth: The Civil War Letters of General Alpheus S. Williams* (Lincoln and London: University of Nebraska Press, 1995), p. 371. A group of black community leaders in Savannah told Sherman and Secretary of War Stanton that slaves enlisted into the Confederate armies would desert as soon as possible. OR, ser. 1, vol. 47, pt. 2, p. 40.

106. George Ward Nichols, *The Story of the Great March from the Diary of a Staff Officer* (New York: Harper and Brothers, 1865), pp. 134, 237–8.

107. New York *Daily Times*, Jan. 1, 1865; James Lindsay Smith, *Autobiography of James L. Smith, Including, Also, Reminiscences of Slave Life, Recollections of the War, Education of Freedmen, Causes of the Exodus, Etc.* (Norwich, Conn.: Bulletin Company, 1881), p. 115.

108. Scarborough, ed., *The Diary of Edmund Ruffin*, vol. 3, p. 754. The same intelligence appears in the "Minority Report" of the Select Committee of the Confederate House of Representatives formed to consider the black-troops bill, signed by Wm. Porcher Miles, Thos. S. Gholson, W. N. H. Smith, Julian Hartridge, and Stephen H. Darden, n.d., p. 2. Copy folded in the Subject Index, Box 5, RG 109, NA.

109. *Atlanta Southern Confederacy*, Jan. 20, 1865.

110. Letter in the Raleigh *Progress*, reprinted in the Raleigh *North Carolina Standard*, Nov. 16, 1864.

111. Atlanta *Southern Confederacy*, Jan. 20, 1865.

112. P. K. Montgomery to Governor Charles Clark, Apr. 4, 1865, RG 27, MDAH.

113. Woodward, ed., *Mary Chesnut's Civil War*, pp. 678–9.

114. New York *Daily Tribune*, Apr. 4, 1865, emphasis added. A *Tribune* reporter overheard a Confederate lieutenant named Lanier tell this story as "a good joke" in a public tavern in Montreal at the end of March. Lt. Lanier had evidently been sent to that city as a messenger. Confederate agents operating behind Union lines in the North used Montreal as a staging area, and southern couriers regularly moved back and forth between that city and the South. Oscar A. Kinchen, *Confederate Operations in Canada and the North* (North Quincy, Mass.: The Christopher Publishing House, 1970). Lanier may have been involved in other efforts to mobilize black manpower. See the certificate that a Lieut. R. S. Lanier issued on March 23, 1865, on behalf of Maj. A[?] Rowland, commandant

at Macon's Camp Cooper, for one Stephen Humphries, a free black resident of Bibb county exempted from "further service" because of that man's advanced age. Folded into Subject Index, heading "Negroes," entry 453, for RG 109, NA.

115. Cornish, *Sable Arm*, p. 266, 281–2.

116. Blackett, ed., *Thomas Morris Chester*, p. 289.

117. Jones, *Rebel War Clerk's Diary*, vol. 2, p. 468; New York *Daily Tribune*, Apr. 5, 1865.

118. Blackett, *Thomas Morris Chester*, p. 290.

119. [Sallie Putnam,] *Richmond during the War: Four Years of Personal Observation by a Richmond Lady* (New York: G. W. Carleton and Co., 1867), p. 367.

Conclusion

1. Alan T. Nolan, "The Anatomy of the Myth," *The Myth of the Lost Cause and Civil War History*, ed. Gary W. Gallagher and Alan T. Nolan (Bloomington: Indiana University Press, 2000), pp. 11–34; Thomas L. Connelly, *The Marble Man: Robert E. Lee and His Image in American Society* (Baton Rouge: Louisiana State University Press, 1977); Gaines M. Foster, *Ghosts of the Confederacy: Defeat, the Lost Cause, and the Emergence of the New South* (New York: Oxford University Press, 1987); David W. Blight, *Race and Reunion: The Civil War in American Memory* (Cambridge, Mass.: Harvard, 2001).

2. C. S. O. Rice (of the 9th Tennessee Infantry), "Incidents of the Vicksburg Siege," *Confederate Veteran* 12, no. 2 (Feb. 1904), pp. 77–8.

3. John Witherspoon DuBose, *General Joseph Wheeler and the Army of Tennessee* (New York: The Neale Publishing Co., 1912), p. 25. On DuBose's career, see William Stanley Hoole, *John Witherspoon DuBose: A Neglected Southern Historian with a Selection of His Uncollected Essays* (University, Ala.: Confederate Publishing Co., 1983), esp. pp. 26–34.

4. Thomas J. Pressly, *Americans Interpret Their Civil War* (1954; reprint, New York: Free Press, 1965), pp. 266–72; Peter Novick, *That Noble Dream: The 'Objectivity Question' and the American Historical Profession* (Cambridge: Cambridge University Press, 1988), pp. 72–80, 229; Ulrich B. Phillips, *American Negro Slavery: A Survey of the Supply, Employment and Control of Negro Labor as Determined by the Plantation Regime* (1918; reprint, Baton Rouge: Louisiana State University Press, 1966), pp. 328, 341–2 (quotations).

5. Walter L. Fleming, *Civil War and Reconstruction in Alabama* (New York: Columbia University Press, 1905), p. 207.

6. E. Merton Coulter, *The Confederate States of America, 1861–1865*, vol. 7 of *A History of the South* (Baton Rouge: Louisiana State University Press, 1950), p. 266.

7. C. Vann Woodward, *Reunion and Reaction: The Compromise of 1877 and the End of Reconstruction* (Boston: Little, Brown, 1951); Eric Foner, *Reconstruction: America's Unfinished Revolution* (New York: Harper and Row, 1988), chapter 11; Nina Silber, *The Romance of Reunion: Northerners and the South, 1865–1900* (Chapel Hill: University of North Carolina Press, 1993); Blight, *Race and Reunion*, p. 286; Heather Cox Richardson, *The Death of Reconstruction: Race, Labor, and Politics in the Post–Civil War North, 1865–1901* (Cambridge, Mass.: Harvard University Press, 2001).

8. Perhaps, after all, Rhodes mused, this record of peaceful, faithful passivity reflected well on slaves and masters alike, illuminating both "virtues in the Southern negroes" and the "merit in the civilization under which they had been trained." James Ford Rhodes, *History of the Civil War, 1861–1865*, ed. E. B. Long (1917; reprint, New York: Frederick Ungar, 1961), p. 381.

9. Charles H. Wesley, "The Employment of Negroes as Soldiers in the Confederate Army," *Journal of Negro History* 4 (July 1919), p. 241.

10. Charles Beard and Mary Beard, *The Rise of American Civilization* (New York: Macmillan, 1930), vol. 2, p. 116.

11. Stanley M. Elkins, *Slavery: A Problem in American Institutional and Intellectual Life* (1959; reprint, New York: Grosset and Dunlap, 1963), pp. 82, 89.

12. The Editor [J. D. B. De Bow], "Memories of the War," *De Bow's Review, Agricultural, Commercial, Industrial Progress and Resources* 3, no. 3 (Mar. 1867), pp. 225–33 (quotation on pp. 226–7).

13. Edward Spencer, "Confederate Negro Enlistments," in *Annals of the War, Written by Leading Participants North and South* (1879; reprint, Edison, N.J.: Blue and Grey Press, 1996), pp. 537–52.

14. Wesley, "The Employment of Negroes as Soldiers in the Confederate Army," p. 241.

15. Charles H. Wesley, *The Collapse of the Confederacy*, ed. John David Smith (1937; reprint, Columbia: University of South Carolina Press, 2001), p. 134.

16. Editorial, *De Bow's Review* 5, no. 7 (July 1868), pp. 665–6.

17. Edward Alfred Pollard, *The Lost Cause Regained* (New York: G. W. Carleton and Co., 1868), p. 20.

18. David Herbert Donald, "Died of Democracy," in David Herbert Donald, ed., *Why the North Won the Civil War* (1960; expanded edition, New York: Touchstone, 1996), pp. 81–92.

19. Pollard, *The Lost Cause*, p. 660.

20. Charleston *Mercury*, Jan. 11, 1865.

21. Frederick A. Porcher to Judah P. Benjamin, Dec. 16, 1864, Confederate States of America papers, LC.

22. Bell Irvin Wiley, "Movement to Humanize the Institution of Slavery during the Confederacy," *Emory University Quarterly* 5 (Dec. 1949), p. 220; Bertram Wyatt-Brown, "Modernizing Southern Slavery: The Proslavery Argument Reinterpreted," *Region, Race and Reconstruction: Essays in Honor of C. Vann Woodward*, ed. J. Morgan Kousser and James M. McPherson (Baton Rouge: Louisiana State University Press, 1981) pp. 32, 37, 40; Drew Gilpin Faust, *The Creation of Confederate Nationalism: Ideology and Identity in the Civil War South* (Baton Rouge: Louisiana State University Press, 1988), p. 80. In fact, Faust seems somewhat ambivalent on this subject.

23. James Oakes, *Slavery and Freedom: An Interpretation of the Old South* (New York: Knopf, 1990), p. 165; Robinson, "Day of Jubilo," pp. 522–71.

24. Macon *Telegraph and Confederate*, Mar. 17, 1865, letter signed Atticus G. Haywood. Haywood was a Methodist minister in Georgia who later became a bishop.

25. Anne C. Loveland, *Southern Evangelicals and the Social Order, 1800–1860* (Baton Rouge: Louisiana State University Press, 1980), pp. 187, 202–4, 209–11, 214–6.

William W. Freehling details such setbacks in the case of James Henley Thornwell, a founder of the journal in which Rev. Lyon's words appeared. See Freehling, *Reintegration of American History*, pp. 73–5, 78–9. Donald G. Matthews earlier made the same point concerning Charles Colcock Jones, probably the leading antebellum religious advocate of slavery reform. See Mathews, "Charles Colcock Jones and the Southern Evangelical Crusade," pp. 317–8; Genovese, *The Slaveholders' Dilemma*, pp. 58–64.

26. Calvin Henderson Wiley, *Scriptural Views of National Trials or, The True Road to the Independence and Peace of the Confederate States of America* (Greensboro, N.C.: Sterling, Campbell and Albright, 1863), pp. 187–9.

27. James A. Lyon, "Slavery, and the Duties Growing Out of the Relation," *The Southern Presbyterian Review* 16 (July 1863), pp. 14, 31. Bondspeople were not blind to the motives behind wartime improvements in some of their conditions. One slave thus told Union Lt. Col. Thomas J. Leigh that "their masters did not dare to whip them now; that they were fed a little better than before the war," but added that slaves "believed this was only to humor them and keep them still." Quoted in the New York *Daily Times*, Jan. 1, 1865.

28. Dan T. Carter, *When the War Was Over: The Failure of Self-Reconstruction in the South, 1865–1867* (Baton Rouge: Louisiana State University Press, 1985), p. 91.

29. Frederick A. Porcher to Judah P. Benjamin, Dec. 16, 1864, Confederate States of America Papers, LC.

30. Richmond *Enquirer*, Feb. 25, 1865.

31. William W. Freehling, *Reinterpretation of American History*, pp. 176–219. On the role of racial ideology in binding southern non-slaveholders to the masters politically, see especially George M. Fredrickson, *The Black Image in the White Mind: The Debate on Afro-American Character and Destiny, 1817–1914* (New York: Harper and Row, 1971), pp. 43–70; Harry L. Watson, "Conflict and Collaboration: Yeomen, Slaveholders, and Politics in the Antebellum South," *Social History* 20 (1985), pp. 273–98; and Bill Cecil-Fronsman, *Common Whites: Class and Culture in Antebellum North Carolina* (Lexington: University Press of Kentucky, 1992). In this case, however, the doctrine of white supremacy—which had evolved in part as a justification for New World slavery—actually compromised the defense of slavery's interests. To the degree that poorer whites *had* been able to express their class resentments, moreover, they had tended to do so by resisting, not championing, the power of the central Confederate government. See, for example, Marc W. Kruman, *Parties and Politics in North Carolina, 1836–1865* (Baton Rouge: Louisiana State University Press, 1983), pp. 243–9.

32. Oates, *The War Between the Union and the Confederacy*, p. 506.

33. C. Vann Woodward, *American Counterpoint: Slavery and Racism in the North-South Dialogue* (Boston: Little, Brown [1971]).

34. Roark, *Masters Without Slaves*, pp. 104, 105, 134.

35. Carl Schurz to Andrew Johnson, July 28, 1865, in Leroy P. Graf, ed., *Advice After Appomattox: Letters to Andrew Johnson, 1865–1866* (Knoxville: University of Tennessee Press, 1987), p. 80.

36. Carl Schurz, "Report on the Condition of the South," in *Speeches, Correspondence and Political Papers of Carl Schurz*, ed. Frederic Bancroft, 6 vols. (1913; reprint, New York: Greenwood, 1969), vol. 1, p. 359.

37. Andrews, *The South since the War*, p. 64; Carter, *When the War Was Over*, p. 62.

38. Durden, *The Gray and the Black*, p. xii.

39. Luraghi, *The Rise and Fall of the Plantation South*, p. 144.

40. John W. Blassingame and John R. McKivigan eds., *The Frederick Douglass Papers*, ser. 1, vol. 4 (New Haven, Conn. and London: Yale University Press, 1991), p. 85.

41. Oates, *The War Between the Union and the Confederacy*, p. 504.

42. The reference is to Willie Lee Rose's classic *Rehearsal for Reconstruction: The Port Royal Experiment* (New York: Oxford University Press, 1964).

43. Carter, *When the War Was Over*, pp. 82–3.

44. Hodgson Diary, p. 22, Charles Colcock Jones, Jr., Collection, Hargrett Library, UGa; Mohr, *On the Threshold of Freedom*, p. 292.

45. Andrews, *The South since the War*, p. 101 (quotation).

46. Whitelaw Reid, *After the War: A Tour of the Southern States, 1865–1866*, ed. C. Vann Woodward (1866; reprint, New York: Harper and Row, 1965), p. 343.

47. Andrews, *The South since the War*, p. 178.

48. "Report on the Condition of the South," in *Speeches, Correspondence and Political Papers*, vol. 1, pp. 316, 311, 321 (quotations). Corroborating testimony appears in the *Report of the Joint Committee on Reconstruction at the First Session, Thirty-Ninth Congress* (1866; reprint, New York: Greenwood, 1969), part 2, pp. 123–4, 126, 177; part 3, pp. 5–7, 15, 24–5, 36, 175, 184.

49. Carter, *When the War Was Over*, p. 216; Foner, *Reconstruction*, pp. 198–209; Theodore Brantner Wilson, *The Black Codes of the South* (University: University of Alabama Press, 1965), pp. 61–80.

50. Bauer, *A Leader among Peers*, pp. 263–4; Roland P. Constantin, "The Louisiana 'Black Code' Legislation of 1865" (M.A. thesis, Louisiana State University, 1956), pp. 53–4 (quotation), 69, 84; Roger W. Shugg, *Origins of Class Struggle in Louisiana: A Social History of White Farmers and Laborers during Slavery and After, 1840–1875* (1939; reprint, Baton Rouge: Louisiana State University Press, 1968), p. 213.

51. Constantin, "Black Code," pp. 64–7, 71 (quotation), 74 (quotation), 73 (quotation).

52. Michael Perman, *Reunion Without Compromise: The South and Reconstruction, 1865–1868* (Cambridge: Cambridge University Press, 1973), p. 81.

53. Vernon Lane Wharton, *The Negro in Mississippi, 1865–1890* (1947; reprint, New York: Harper and Row, 1965), p. 84; William C. Harris, *Presidential Reconstruction in Mississippi* (Baton Rouge: Louisiana State University Press, 1967), pp. 121–40.

54. "Message of the Governor of Mississippi," Nov. 20, 1865, in the *Report of the Joint Committee on Reconstruction*, part 3, p. 183.

55. Wharton, *The Negro in Mississippi*, p. 84; Harris, *Presidential Reconstruction in Mississippi*, pp. 121–40.

56. *Report of the South Carolina Commission on the Code*, p. 3, quoted in Carter,

When the War Was Over, p. 216.

57. Carter, *When the War Was Over*, pp. 216–9.

58. Foner, *Reconstruction*, p. 198.

59. Reidy, *From Slavery to Agrarian Capitalism*, p. 162; Alan Conway, *The Reconstruction of Georgia* (Minneapolis: University of Minnesota Press, 1966), pp. 55–7; C. Mildred Thompson, *Reconstruction in Georgia: Economic, Social, Political, 1865–1872* (1915; reprint, Gloucester, Mass.: Peter Smith, 1964), pp. 46, 66–7, 157–9; Joseph E. Parks, *Joseph E. Brown of Georgia* (Baton Rouge: Louisiana State University Press, 1977), pp. 346–9; Wilson, *Black Codes of the South*, pp. 102–5.

60. Steven Hahn, *A Nation under Our Feet: Black Political Struggle in the Rural South from Slavery to the Great Migration* (Cambridge, Mass.: Harvard University Press, 2003), pp. 236–8.

61. Foner, *Reconstruction*, chapter 8.

62. Eric Foner, *Nothing but Freedom: Emancipation and Its Legacy* (Baton Rouge: Louisiana State University Press, 1983), p. 53 (quotations).

63. William Heyward to James Gregorie, June 4, 1868, Gregorie and Elliott Family Papers, Southern Historical Collection, UNC-CH.

64. W. E. B. Du Bois drew this truth out in *Black Reconstruction in America*, especially in its final chapter, aptly entitled "The Propaganda of History." David Blight has brilliantly documented it in *Race and Reunion: The Civil War in American Memory* (Cambridge, Mass.: Harvard University Press, 2001).

65. *In Memoriam Sempiternam* (Richmond, Va.: Confederate Museum, 1896), pp. 50–1 (quotation). The Confederate Museum was subsequently renamed the Museum of the Confederacy.

66. Blight, *Race and Reunion*, pp. 255–84, quotation on p. 284.

67. Hahn, *Nation under Our Feet*, pp. 312–3, 443, 464.

68. Robert William Fogel, *Without Consent or Contract: The Rise and Fall of American Slavery* (New York: W. W. Norton, 1989), p. 100; Roger L. Ransom and Richard Sutch, *One Kind of Freedom: The Economic Consequences of Emancipation* (Cambridge, Eng.: Cambridge University Press, 1977), pp. 4–5; Carter, *When the War Was Over*, pp. 207–10; Foner, *Nothing but Freedom*, pp. 72–3; Hahn *Nation under Our Feet*, p. 441–2.

69. Du Bois, *Black Reconstruction*, p. 702.

70. Hahn, *Nation under Our Feet*, pp. 312–3, 443, 464.

71. Douglass's speech of April 17, 1888, on the twenty-sixth anniversary of emancipation in the District of Columbia, is reprinted in *The Voice of Black America: Major Speeches by Negroes in the United States, 1797–1971*, ed. Philip S. Foner (New York: Simon and Schuster, 1972), pp. 520–36 (quotation on p. 525).

SOURCES CITED

Manuscript Collections

University of Arkansas Libraries, Fayetteville, Ark.

    Patrick Ronayne Cleburne Papers, MC 398, Special Collections

Duke University, Rare Book, Manuscript, and Special Collections Library, Durham, N.C.

    Jefferson Davis Papers
    Francis Warrington Dawson Papers
    Harriet C. Lewis Papers
    Augustin Louis Taveau Papers
    Simon P. Wingard Papers

Filson Historical Society, Louisville, Ky.

    Brown-Ewell Family Papers

University of Georgia Libraries, Hargrett Rare Book and Manuscript Library, Athens, Ga.

    David Crenshaw Barrow Papers
    Gordon Family Papers
    Charles Colcock Jones, Jr., Collection

Harvard University, Houghton Library, Cambridge, Mass.

    Frederick M. Dearborn Collection

The Huntington Library, San Marino, Calif.

Civil War Collection

Kansas State Historical Society, Topeka, Kans.

Benjamin and John Stringfellow Collection

Library of Congress, Manuscript Division, Washington, D.C.

George Washington Campbell Papers
Douglas J. and Rufus W. Cater Papers
Confederate States of America Records
Jefferson Davis Papers
Richard Stoddert Ewell Papers
Jedediah Hotchkiss Collection
Henry Jackson Hunt Papers
John Auchincloss Inglis Collection
Duncan Farrar Kenner Collection
Earl Van Dorn Papers

Louisiana State University and Agricultural and Mechanical College,
Baton Rouge, La.

George W. Guess Papers, Mss. 793, Louisiana and Lower Mississippi Valley
   Collections.
William J. Minor Family Papers, Mss. 519, Louisiana and Lower Mississippi
   Valley Collection.

University of Michigan, William L. Clements Library, Ann Arbor, Mich.

Handy Family Papers

Mississippi Department of Archives and History, Jackson, Miss.

John J. Pettus Papers, Record Group 27

Missouri Historical Society, St. Louis, Mo.

Eathan A. Pinnell Civil War Journals

The Museum of the Confederacy, Eleanor S. Brockenbrough Library,
Richmond, Va.

Charley Baughman Letters, Soldier Letters Collections
R. Blair, et al., to Maj. P. H. Nelson, n.d. [May 1862]
Letter from Friend to Judge, Feb. 4, 1865
John A. Speer to his mother, Apr. 2, 1865

National Archives and Records Administration, Washington, D.C.

Records of the Adjutant General's Office, 1780–1917, Record Group 94
War Department Collection of Confederate Records, Record Group 109

North Carolina Office of Archives and History, Raleigh, N.C.

William Alexander Graham Papers

University of North Carolina, Chapel Hill, Southern Historical Collection, Chapel Hill, N.C.

R. H. Browne Papers, #95
Jones Family Papers, #2884
Samuel H. Walkup Papers, #1401

University of Texas at Austin, Center for American History

Pritchard von David Collection

Library of Virginia, Archives and Manuscripts Department, Richmond, Va.

Silas Chandler Letters, 1862–1865, #23984a, Personal Papers Collection
William Smith Executive Papers, 1864–1865, Governor's Executive Papers,
    Virginia Governor's Office, Record Group 3, State Records Collection

Virginia Historical Society, Richmond, Va.

G. W. Custis Lee to John William Carter, 14 Mar. 1865, Mss1 C2468 b 106
Robert Edward Lee Headquarters Papers, Mss3 L515 a
Robert E. Lee to James Longstreet, 28 Mar. 1865, Mss2 L515 a 42
Richard L. Maury Diary, Mss5:1 M4486:1–2
Civil War letters of Pvt. Joseph F. Shaner, C.S.A., Mss1 Sh183 a
J. E. Shuman Letter to T[homas] S. Hayward, 20 Mar. 1865, Mss2 Sh926 a 1
Joseph D. Stapp Letters, 1864–1865, Mss2 ST275b

College of William and Mary, Manuscripts and Rare Books Department, Earl Gregg Swem Library, Williamsburg, Va.

Joseph E. Johnston Papers

Newspapers

Atlanta *Southern Confederacy*
Charleston *Courier*
Charleston *Mercury*
Galveston *Tri-Weekly News*
Lynchburg *Virginian*
Macon *Telegraph and Confederate*
Memphis *Appeal*
Mobile *Register and Advertiser*
Montgomery *Daily Mail*
New York *Herald*
New York *Daily Times*
New York *Daily Tribune*
Raleigh *Daily Confederate*

Raleigh *North Carolina Standard*
Richmond *Dispatch*
Richmond *Enquirer*
Richmond *Examiner*
Richmond *Sentinel*
Richmond *Whig*
Wilmington *Journal*

Government Documents and Publications

Adjutant General's Office, "The Negro in the Military Service of the United States, 1639–1886: A Compilation of Official Records, State Papers, Historical Extracts, etc., Relating to his Military Status and Service, from the date of his introduction into the British North American Colonies," [1885–1888], Record Group 94. National Archives microfilm #M-858, roll 4.

Annual Message of Governor Henry Watkins Allen, to the Legislature of the State of Louisiana. Shreveport, La.: Caddo Gazette, Jan. 1865.

Journal of the Congress of the Confederate States of America, 1861–1865. 7 vols. Washington: Government Printing Office, 1904–1905.

Journal of the House of Representatives of the State of Mississippi, Called Session at Columbus, February and March, 1865. Meridian, Miss.: J. J. Shannon, 1865.

Journal of the Senate of the Extra Session of the General Assembly, of the State of Georgia, Convened by Proclamation of the Governor, at Macon, February 15th, 1865. Milledgeville, Ga.: Boughton, Nisbet, Barnes and Moore, State Printers, 1865.

Journal of the Senate at an Extra Session of the General Assembly of the State of Georgia, Convened under the Proclamation of the Governor, March 25th, 1863. Milledgeville, Ga.: Boughton, Nisbet & Barnes, 1863.

Manarin, Louis H., ed., *Richmond at War: The Minutes of the City Council, 1861–1865.* Chapel Hill: University of North Carolina Press, 1966.

North Carolina General Assembly, *Resolutions against the Policy of Arming Slaves.* Richmond, Va., 1865.

Report of the Joint Committee on Reconstruction at the First Session, Thirty-Ninth Congress. 1866. Reprint. New York: Greenwood, 1969.

Resolutions passed at a meeting of Kentucky soldiers . . . . near the city of Richmond, no date. Printed by the Confederate Senate.

Statutes at Large and Proclamations of the United States of America from Dec. 1869 to March 1871. Boston: Little, Brown, 1871.

Unthank J. H., and Geo. S. Hebb, *A Digest of the Militia Laws of Tennessee Now in Force.* Memphis, Tenn.: Hutton and Freligh, 1861.

Vandiver, Frank, ed., "Proceedings of the Second Confederate Congress," *Southern Historical Society Papers* (new series), vols. 51–2. Richmond, Va.: Virginia Historical Society, 1958–1959.

The War of the Rebellion: A Compilation of the Official Records of the Union and Confederate Armies. 128 vols. Washington, D.C.: Government Printing Office, 1880–1901.

Contemporary Publications, Letters, Diaries, Memoirs, and Documentary Collections

Andrews, Sidney, *The South since the War*. 1866. Reprint. Boston: Houghton Mifflin, 1971.

Avary, Myrta Lockett, ed., *Recollections of Alexander H. Stephens: His Diary Kept when a Prisoner at Fort Warren, Boston Harbour, 1865* New York: Doubleday, Page, 1910.

Bancroft, Frederic, ed., *Speeches, Correspondence and Political Papers of Carl Schurz*. 6 vols. 1913. Reprint. New York: Greenwood, 1969.

Barrett, John G., ed., *North Carolina Civil War Documentary*. Chapel Hill: University of North Carolina Press, 1980.

Barrow, Charles Kelley, J. H. Segars, and R. B. Rosenburg, eds., *Black Confederates*. Gretna, La.: Pelican, 2001.

Basler, Roy P., ed., *The Collected Works of Abraham Lincoln*, 9 vols. New Brunswick, N.J.: Rutgers University Press, 1953.

Baylor, George, "The Army Negro," *Southern Historical Society Papers* 31 (1903): 365–9.

Bean, W. G., ed., "Memoranda of Conversation between General Robert E. Lee and William Preston Johnston, May 7, 1868, and March 18, 1870," *Virginia Magazine of History and Biography* 73 (Oct. 1965): 474–84.

Berlin, Ira, Barbara J. Fields, Thavolia Glymph, Joseph P. Reidy, and Leslie S. Rowland, *Freedom: A Documentary History of Emancipation, 1861–1867*, ser. 1, vol. 1, *The Destruction of Slavery*. Cambridge, Eng.: Cambridge University Press, 1985.

Berlin, Ira, Joseph P. Reidy, and Leslie S. Rowland, eds., *Freedom: A Documentary History of Emancipation, 1861–1867*, ser. 2, *The Black Military Experience*. Cambridge, Eng.: Cambridge University Press, 1982.

Berlin, Ira, Thavolia Glymph, Steven F. Miller, Joseph P. Reidy, Leslie S. Rowland, and Julie Saville, eds., *Freedom: A Documentary History of Emancipation, 1861–1867*, ser. 1, vol. 3, *The Wartime Genesis of Free Labor: The Lower South*. Cambridge, Eng.: Cambridge University Press, 1990.

Blackett, R. J. M., ed., *Thomas Morris Chester, Black Civil War Correspondent: His Dispatches from the Virginia Front*. New York: Da Capo, 1991.

Blassingame, John W., ed., *Slave Testimony: Two Centuries of Letters, Speeches, Interviews, and Autobiographies*. Baton Rouge: Louisiana State University Press, 1977.

Blassingame, John W., and John R. McKivigan, eds., *The Frederick Douglass Papers*, ser. 1, *Speeches, Debates, and Interviews*. 5 vols. New Haven, Conn.: Yale University Press, 1979–1992.

Botume, Elizabeth Hyde, *First Days amongst the Contrabands*. Boston: Lee and Shepard, 1893.

Brown, Norman D., ed., *One of Cleburne's Command: The Civil War Reminiscences and Diary of Capt. Samuel T. Foster, Granbury's Texas Brigade, CSA*. Austin: University of Texas Press, 1980.

Buck, Irving A., *Cleburne and His Command*, ed. Thomas Robson Hay. 1908. Reprint. Jackson, Tenn.: McCowat-Mercer Press, 1959.

Burr, Virginia Ingraham, ed., *The Secret Eye: The Journal of Ella Getrude Clanton Thomas, 1848–1889*. Chapel Hill: University of North Carolina Press, 1990.

Butler, Benjamin F., *Butler's Book: Autobiography and Personal Reminiscences . . .* Boston: A. M. Thayer, 1892.

Campbell, John A., *Reminiscences and Documents Relating to the Civil War during the Year 1865*. Baltimore: John Murphy, 1887.

Cate, Wirt Armistead, ed., *Two Soldiers: The Campaign Diaries of Thomas J. Key, C.S.A., and Robert J. Campbell, U.S.A.* Chapel Hill: University of North Carolina Press, 1938.

Cleveland, Henry, *Alexander H. Stephens in Public and Private. With Letters and Speeches, Before, During, and Since the War*. Philadelphia: National, 1866.

Crabtree, Beth G. and James W. Patton, eds., *"Journal of a Secesh Lady": The Diary of Catherine Ann Devereux Edmondston*. Raleigh: North Carolina Division of Archives and History, 1979.

Crist, Linda Lasswell, et al., eds., *The Papers of Jefferson Davis*. 11 vols. to date. Baton Rouge: Louisiana State University Press, 1971–.

Davis, Jefferson, *The Rise and Fall of the Confederate Government*, 2 vols. 1881. Reprint. New York: Da Capo, 1990.

[Davis, Varina] *Jefferson Davis, Ex-President of the Confederate States of America: A Memoir by his Wife*. 2 vols. New York: Belford, 1890.

De Bow, J. D. B., "Memories of the War," *De Bow's Review* 3 (Mar. 1867): 225–8.

De Bow, J. D. B., "The Future of Our Confederation," *De Bow's Review* 31 (July 1861): 35–40.

Douglass, Frederick, *Life and Times of Frederick Douglass*. Rev. ed. 1892. Reprint. London: Collier-Macmillan, 1962.

Dowdey Clifford, and Louis H. Manarin, eds., *The Wartime Papers of Robert E. Lee*. 1961. Reprint. New York: Da Capo, 1987.

Durden, Robert F., *The Gray and the Black: The Confederate Debate on Emancipation*. 1972. Reprint. Baton Rouge: Louisiana State University Press, 2000.

Early, Jubal Anderson, *Jubal Early's Memoirs: Autobiographical Sketch and Narrative of the War between the States*. 1912. Reprint. Baltimore: Nautical and Aviation Publishing, 1989.

Eaton, John, *Grant, Lincoln, and the Freedmen: Reminiscences of the Civil War*. 1907. Reprint. New York: Greenwood, 1969.

Faust, Drew Gilpin, ed., *The Ideology of Slavery: Proslavery Thought in the Antebellum South, 1830–1860*. Baton Rouge: Louisiana State University Press, 1981.

Fitzhugh, George, "What's to Be Done with the Negroes?" *De Bow's Review*. New series, 1 (June 1866): 577–81.

Forten, Charlotte, "Life on the Sea Islands," *Atlantic Monthly* 13 (May 1864): 587–96.

"General Cleburne's Views on Slavery," *Annals of the Army of Tennessee and Early Western History* 1 (May 1878): 50–2.

Gholson, Thomas S., *Speech of Hon. Thomas S. Gholson of Virginia on the Policy of Employing Negro Troops and the Duty of All Classes to Aid in the Prosecution of the War*. Richmond, Va.: Geo. P. Evans, 1865.

Gienapp, William, ed., *The Civil War and Reconstruction: A Documentary Collection*. New York: W. W. Norton, 2001.

Graf, Leroy P., ed., *Advice After Appomattox: Letters to Andrew Johnson, 1865–1866*. Knoxville: University of Tennessee Press, 1987.

Grant, U. S., *Personal Memoirs of U.S. Grant*. 1885. Reprint. 2 vols. in 1. New York: Konecky and Konecky, n.d.

Hamilton, J. G. De Roulhac, ed., *The Papers of Thomas Ruffin*. 4 vols. Raleigh, N.C.: Edwards and Broughton, 1918–1920.

Hardee, William J., "Biographical Sketch of Major-General P. R. Cleburne," appendix to John Francis Maguire, *The Irish in America*. 1868. Reprint. New York: Arno Press, 1969.

Harper, William, "Chancellor Harper's Memoir on Slavery," *De Bow's Review* 10 (Jan. 1851): 47–65.

Higginson, Thomas Wentworth, *Army Life in a Black Regiment*, ed. John Hope Franklin. 1869. Reprint. Boston: Beacon, 1962.

Hood, J[ohn]. B[ell]., *Advance and Retreat: Personal Experiences in the United States and Confederate States Armies*. New Orleans: G. T. Beauregard, 1880.

Howe, M. A. DeWolfe, ed., *Marching with Sherman: Passages from the Letters and Campaign Diaries of Henry Hitchcock, Major and Assistant Adjutant General of Volunteers, Nov. 1864–May 1865*. New Haven, Conn.: Yale University Press, 1927.

Hughes, Sarah Forbes, ed., *Letters and Recollections of John Murray Forbes*. 2 vols. Boston: Houghton, Mifflin and Co., 1899.

Hughes, Thomas, *A Boy's Experience in the Civil War, 1860–1865*. Baltimore: Daily Record, 1904.

Hunter, Andrew, "Memoranda on the Civil War," *Century Magazine* 36 (Aug. 1988): 599–601.

In Memoriam Sempiternam. Richmond, Va.: Confederate Museum, 1896.

Jones, J. William, *The Davis Memorial Volume: Or, Our Dead President, Jefferson Davis and the World's Tribute to His Memory*. Richmond, Va.: B. F. Johnson, 1890.

Jones, Katherine M., *Heroines of Dixie: Confederate Women Tell Their Story of the War*. Indianapolis: Bobbs-Merrill, 1955.

Langdon, C. C., *The Question of Employing the Negro as a Soldier! The Impolicy and Impracticability of the Proposed Measure Discussed*. Mobile, Ala.: Advertiser and Register Steam Job Press, 1864.

Leasure, Daniel, "Personal Observations and Experiences in the Pope Campaign in Virginia," *Glimpses of the Nation's Struggle: A Series of Papers Read before the Minnesota Commandery of the Military Order of the Loyal Legion of the United States*. St. Paul, Minn.: St. Paul Book and Stationery, 1887.

Lee, Brooks Aubrey, and Hugh Talmage Lefler, eds., *The Papers of Walter Clark*, 2 vols. Chapel Hill: University of North Carolina Press, 1948.

Leyburn, John, "An Interview with Gen. Robert E. Lee," *Century Magazine* 30 (May 1885): 166–7.

Longstreet, James, *From Manassas to Appomattox: Memoirs of the Civil War in America*. Philadelphia: J. B. Lippincott, 1896.

Lyon, James A., "Slavery, and the Duties Growing Out of the Relation," *The Southern Presbyterian Review* 16 (July 1863): 1–37.

Marrs, Elijah P., *Life and History of the Rev. Elijah P. Marrs*. Louisville, Ky.: Bradley and Gilbert Co, 1885

Maurice, Frederick, ed., *Lee's Aide-de-Camp, Being the Papers of Colonel Charles Marshall Sometime Aide-de-Camp, Military Secretary, and Assistant Adjutant General of Robert E. Lee, 1862–1865*. 1927. Reprint. Lincoln: University of Nebraska Press, 2000.

McNeilly, James H., "In Winter Quarters at Dalton, Da.," *Confederate Veteran* 28 (Apr. 1920): 130–2, 157.

McPherson, Edward, *The Political History of the United States during the Great Rebellion*. 2d. ed. Washington: Philp and Solomons, 1865.

McPherson, James M., *The Negro's Civil War: How American Negroes Felt and Acted during the War for the Union*. New York: Knopf, 1965.

Mudd, Joseph A., "The Confederate Negro," *Confederate Veteran* (Sept. 1915): 411.

Myers, Robert Manson, ed., *The Children of Pride: A True Story of Georgia and the Civil War*. New Haven, Conn.: Yale University Press, 1972.

Nichols, George Ward, *The Story of the Great March from the Diary of a Staff Officer*. New York: Harper and Brothers, 1865.

Nisbet, James Cooper, *Four Years on the Firing Line*. Jackson, Tenn.: McCowat-Mercer Press, 1963.

Oates, William C., *The War Between the Union and the Confederacy and Its Lost Opportunities . . .* New York: Neale Publishing, 1905.

Owen, William Miller, *In Camp and Battle with the Washington Artillery of New Orleans*. Boston: Ticknor, 1885.

Phillips, Ulrich Bonnell, ed., *The Correspondence of Robert Toombs, Alexander H. Stephens, and Howell Cobb*. 1911. Reprint. New York: Da Capo, 1970.

Pollard, Edward Alfred, *Life of Jefferson Davis with a Secret History of the Southern Confederacy*. Atlanta: National Publishing, 1869.

Pollard, Edward Alfred, *The Lost Cause*. 1866. Reprint. New York: Gramercy Books, 1994.

Pollard, Edward Alfred, *The Lost Cause Regained*. New York: G. W. Carleton, 1868.

Porcher, Frederick Adolphus, "Conflict of Capital and Labour," *Russell's Magazine* 3 (July 1858): 289–98.

Porcher Frederick Adolphus, "The Memoirs of Frederick Adolphus Porcher," ed. Samuel Gaillard Stoney. *South Carolina Historical and Genealogical Magazine* 45 (Oct. 1944): 210–16, 46; (Oct. 1945): 198–208.

Porcher, Frederick Adolphus, "Southern and Northern Civilization Contrasted," *Russell's Magazine* 1(May 1857): 97–107.

[Putnam, Sallie,] *Richmond during the War: Four Years of Personal Observation by a Richmond Lady*. New York: G. W. Carleton, 1867.

Quaife, Milo M., ed., *From the Cannon's Mouth: The Civil War Letters of General Alpheus S. Williams*. Lincoln, Neb.: University of Nebraska Press, 1995.

Reagan, John H., *Memoirs, with Special Reference to Secession and the Civil War*. New York: Neale Publishing, 1906.

Reid, Whitelaw, *After the War: A Tour of the Southern States, 1865–1866*, ed. C. Vann Woodward. 1866. Reprint. New York: Harper and Row, 1965.

Reynolds, J. L., "Fidelity of Slaves," *De Bow's Review* 29 (Nov. 1860): 569–583.

Rice, C. S. O., "Incidents of the Vicksburg Siege," *Confederate Veteran* 12 (Feb. 1904): 77–8.

Rowland, Dunbar F., ed., *Jefferson Davis, Constitutionalist: His Letters, Papers and Speeches.* 10 vols. Jackson: Mississippi Department of Archives and History, 1923.

[Ruffin, Edmund,] *Anticipations of the future, to serve as lessons for the present time : in the form of extracts of letters from an English resident in the United States, to the London Times, from 1864 to 1870.* Richmond, Va.: J. W. Randolph, 1860.

Russell, William Howard, *My Diary North and South*, ed. Eugene H. Berwanger. New York: Alfred A. Knopf, 1988.

Scarborough, William Kaufman, ed., *The Diary of Edmund Ruffin.* 3 vols. Baton Rouge: Louisiana State University Press, 1972–1989.

Sherman, William T., *Memoirs.* New York: Appleton, 1875.

Slocum, Henry W., "Sherman's March from Savannah to Bentonville," *Battles and Leaders of the Civil War.* Vol. 4. 1888. Reprint. Edison, N.J.: Castle, n.d., pp. 681–95.

Smith, James Lindsay, *Autobiography of James L. Smith, Including, Also, Reminiscences of Slave Life, Recollections of the War, Education of Freedmen, Causes of the Exodus, Etc.* Norwich, Conn.: Bulletin, 1881.

Stephens, Alexander H., *A Constitutional View of the Late War Between the States: Its Causes, Character, Conduct and Results.* 2 vols. Philadelphia: National Publishing, 1868.

Taylor, Richard, *Destruction and Reconstruction: Personal Experiences in the Late War.* 1877. Reprint. New York: Longmans, Green, 1955.

Taylor, Susie King, *Reminiscences of My Life in Camp with the 33d United States Colored Troops, Late 1st S. C. Volunteers.* Boston: The author, 1902.

Trowbridge, J[ohn] T[ownsend], *The South: A Tour of its Battle-fields and Ruined Cities, A Journey through the Desolated States, and Talks with the People.* Hartford, Conn.: L. Stebbins, 1866.

Two Diaries: From Middle St. John's, Berkeley, South Carolina, February–May, 1865. [Pinopolis, S.C.]: St. John's Hunting Club, 1921.

Walthall, Ernest Taylor, *Hidden Things Brought to Light.* Richmond, Va.: Dietz Printing, 1933.

Washington, Booker T., *Up from Slavery: An Autobiography.* 1901. Reprint. New York: Modern Library, 1999.

Whittington G. P., ed., "Concerning the Loyalty of Slaves in North Louisiana in 1863: Letters from John H. Ransdell to Governor Thomas O. Moore, Dated 1863." *Louisiana Historical Quarterly* 14 (Oct. 1931): 487–502.

Wiggins, Sarah Woolfolk, ed., *The Journals of Josiah Gorgas, 1857–1878.* Tuscaloosa: University of Alabama Press, 1995.

Wiley, Bell Irvin, ed., *Letters of Warren Akin, Confederate Congressman.* Athens: University of Georgia Press, 1959.

Wiley, Calvin Henderson, *Scriptural Views of National Trials or, The True Road to the Independence and Peace of the Confederate States of America.* Greensboro, N.C.: Sterling, Campbell and Albright, 1863.

Williams, Max R., ed., *The Papers of William Alexander Graham.* 8 vols. Raleigh: North Carolina Department of Cultural Resources, 1957–1992.

Wilson, Clyde N., and W. Edwin Hemphill, eds., *The Papers of John C. Calhoun.* 28 vols. Columbia, S.C., 1959–2003.

Winther, Oscar Osburn, ed., *With Sherman to the Sea: The Civil War Letters, Diaries and Reminiscences of Theodore F. Upson.* Bloomington: Indiana University Press, 1958.

Woodward, C. Vann, ed., *Mary Chesnut's Civil War.* New Haven, Conn.: Yale University Press, 1981.

Yacavone, Donald, ed., *A Voice of Thunder: The Civil War Letters of George E. Stephens.* Urbana: University of Illinois Press, 1997.

Secondary Works: Books, Articles, Theses

Alexander, Thomas B., and Richard E. Beringer, *The Anatomy of the Confederate Congress: A Study of the Influence of Member Characteristics on Legislative Voting Behavior, 1861–1865.* Nashville, Tenn.: Vanderbilt University Press, 1972.

Aptheker, Herbert, "Notes on Slave Conspiracies in Confederate Mississippi," *Journal of Negro History* 29 (Jan. 1944): 75–9.

Ash, Stephen V., *Middle Tennessee Society Transformed, 1860–1870: War and Peace in the Upper South.* Baton Rouge: Louisiana State University Press, 1988.

Avary, Myrta Lockett, *Dixie after the War: An Exposition of Social Conditions Existing in the South, During the Twelve Years Succeeding the Fall of Richmond.* New York: Doubleday, Page, 1906.

Bauer, Craig A., *A Leader among Peers: The Life and Times of Duncan Farrar Kenner.* Fayetteville: University of Southwestern Louisiana, 1993.

Beard, Charles, and Mary Beard, *The Rise of American Civilization.* 2 vols. New York: Macmillan, 1930.

Beckett, J. C., *Making of Modern Ireland, 1603–23.* New York: Knopf, 1966.

Bensel, Richard Franklin, *Yankee Leviathan: The Origins of Central State Authority in America, 1859–1877.* New York: Cambridge University Press, 1990.

Berlin, Ira, Barbara J. Fields, Steven F. Miller, Joseph P. Reidy, and Leslie S. Rowland, *Slaves No More: Three Essays on Emancipation and the Civil War.* Cambridge, Eng.: Cambridge University Press, 1992.

Berlin, Ira, *Slaves without Masters: The Free Negro in the Antebellum South.* New York: Random House, 1974.

Blackbourn, David, *The Long Nineteenth Century: A History of Germany, 1780–1918.* New York: Oxford University Press, 1998.

Blackerby, H. C., *Blacks in Blue and Gray: Afro-American Service in the Civil War.* Tuscaloosa, Ala.: Portals Press, 1979.

Bleser, Carol, ed., *In Joy and Sorrow: Women, Family, and Marriage in the Victorian South, 1830–1900.* New York: Oxford University Press, 1991.

Blight David W., *Race and Reunion: The Civil War in American Memory.* Cambridge, Mass.: Harvard University Press, 2001.

Bloch, Marc, *Feudal Society*, tr. L. A. Manyon. Chicago: University of Chicago Press, 1964.

Blum, Jerome, *The End of the Old Order in Rural Europe*. Princeton, N.J.: Princeton University Press, 1978.

Blum, Jerome, *Lord and Peasant in Russia from the Ninth to the Nineteenth Century*. Princeton, N.J.: Princeton University Press, 1961.

Blum, Jerome, "The Rise of Serfdom in Eastern Europe," *American Historical Review* 62 (July 1957): 819–21.

Bolland, O. Nigel, "Systems of Domination after Slavery: The Control of Land and Labor in the British West Indies after 1838," *Comparative Studies in Society and History* 23 (Oct. 1981): 591–619

Boritt, Gabor S., ed., *Why the Confederacy Lost*. New York: Oxford University Press, 1992.

Bowman, Shearer Davis, *Masters and Lords: Mid-19th Century U.S. Planters and Prussian Junkers*. New York: Oxford University Press, 1993.

Brewer, James H., *The Confederate Negro: Virginia's Craftsmen and Military Laborers, 1861–1865*. Durham, N.C.: Duke University Press, 1969.

Brock, W. R., *Conflict and Transformation: The United States, 1844–1877*. Harmondsworth, Eng.: Penguin, 1973.

Brown, William Wells, *The Negro in the American Rebellion: His Heroism and His Fidelity*, ed. John David Smith. 1867. Reprint. Athens: Ohio University Press, 2003.

Butler, Pierce, *Judah P. Benjamin*. 1907. Reprint. New York: Chelsea House, 1980.

Callahan, J. Morton, "The Confederate Diplomatic Archives—The 'Pickett Papers,'" *South Atlantic Quarterly* 2 (Jan. 1903), 1–9.

Carter, Dan T., *When the War Was Over: The Failure of Self-Reconstruction in the South, 1865–1867*. Baton Rouge: Louisiana State University Press, 1985.

Cecil-Fronsman, Bill, *Common Whites: Class and Culture in Antebellum North Carolina*. Lexington: University Press of Kentucky, 1992.

Cimprich, John, *Slavery's End in Tennessee, 1861–1865*. University: University of Alabama Press, 1985.

Connelly, Thomas L., *Autumn of Glory: The Army of Tennessee, 1862–1865*. Baton Rouge: Louisiana State University Press, 1971.

Connelly, Thomas L., *The Marble Man: Robert E. Lee and His Image in American Society*. Baton Rouge: Louisiana State University Press, 1977.

Connolly, S. J., "Eighteenth-Century Ireland: Colony or Ancien Regime?" in *The Making of Modern Irish History: Revisionism and the Revisionist Controversy*, ed. D. George Boyce and Alan O'Day. London: Routledge, 1996.

Constantin, Roland P., "The Louisiana 'Black Code' Legislation of 1865." M.A. thesis, Louisiana State University, 1956.

Conway, Alan, *The Reconstruction of Georgia*. Minneapolis: University of Minnesota Press, 1966.

Conze, Werner, "The Effects of Nineteenth-Century Liberal Agrarian Reforms on Social Structure in Central Europe," in *Essays in European Economic History, 1789–1914*, ed. F. Crouzet, W. H. Chaloner, and W. M. Stern. New York: St. Martin's Press, 1969.

Cooper, William J., Jr., *Jefferson Davis, American*. New York: Random House, 2000.

Cornish, Dudley Taylor, *The Sable Arm: Black Troops in the Union Army, 1861–1865*. 1956. Reprint. Lawrence: University Press of Kansas, 1987.

Coulter, E. Merton, *The Confederate States of America, 1861–1865*. Baton Rouge: Louisiana State University Press, 1950.

Daniel, Larry J., *Soldiering in the Army of Tennessee: A Portrait of Life in a Confederate Army*. Chapel Hill: University of North Carolina Press, 1991.

Davis, William C., *An Honorable Defeat: The Last Days of the Confederate Government*. New York: Harcourt, Inc., 2001.

Davis, William C., *Breckinridge: Statesman, Soldier, Symbol*. Baton Rouge: Louisiana State University Press, 1974.

Davis, William C., *Jefferson Davis, The Man and His Hour*. Baton Rouge: Louisiana State University Press, 1991.

Davis, William C., *Look Away! A History of the Confederate States of* America. New York: Free Press, 2002.

Dillard, Philip D., "Independence or Slavery: The Confederate Debate over Arming the Slaves." Ph. D. dissertation, Rice University, 1999.

Donald, David Herbert, *Lincoln*. New York: Simon and Schuster, 1995.

Donald, David Herbert, ed., *Why the North Won the Civil War*. 1960. Expanded edition, New York: Touchstone, 1996.

Dower, John W., ed., *Origins of the Modern Japanese State: Selected Writings of E. H. Norman*. New York: Pantheon, 1975.

Du Bois, W. E. B., *Black Reconstruction in America*. 1935. Reprint. New York: Athaneum, 1983.

DuBose, John Witherspoon, *General Joseph Wheeler and the Army of Tennessee*. New York: Neale, 1912.

Easterby, J. H., ed., *The South Carolina Rice Plantation as Revealed in the Papers of Robert F. W. Allston*. Chicago: University of Chicago Press, 1945.

Elkins, Stanley M., *Slavery: A Problem in American Institutional and Intellectual Life*. 1959. Reprint. New York: Grosset and Dunlap, 1963.

Emmons, Terence, *The Russian Landed Gentry and the Peasant Emancipation of 1861*. Cambridge, Eng.: Cambridge University Press, 1968.

Escott, Paul D., *After Secession: Jefferson Davis and the Failure of Confederate Nationalism*. Baton Rouge: Louisiana State University Press, 1978.

Evans, Eli N., *Judah P. Benjamin: The Jewish Confederate*. New York: Free Press, 1988.

Faust, Drew Gilpin, *The Creation of Confederate Nationalism: Ideology and Identity in the Civil War South*. Baton Rouge: Louisiana State University Press, 1988.

Faust, Drew Gilpin, *James Henry Hammond: A Design for Mastery*. Baton Rouge, Louisiana State University Press, 1982.

Faust, Drew Gilpin, *Mothers of Invention: Women of the Slaveholding South in the American Civil War*. New York: Random House, 1996.

Fields, Barbara Jeanne, *Slavery and Freedom on the Middle Ground: Maryland during the Nineteenth Century*. New Haven, Conn.: Yale University Press, 1985.

Finley, M. I., *Ancient Slavery and Modern Ideology*. Harmondsworth, Eng.: Penguin, 1980.

Fleming, Walter L., *Civil War and Reconstruction in Alabama*. New York: Columbia University Press, 1905.

Fogel, Robert W., *Without Consent or Contract: The Rise and Fall of American Slavery*. New York: W. W. Norton, 1989.

Foner, Eric, *Nothing but Freedom: Emancipation and Its Legacy*. Baton Rouge: Louisiana State University Press, 1983.

Foner, Eric, *Politics and Ideology in the Age of the Civil War*. New York: Oxford University Press, 1980.

Foner, Eric, *Reconstruction: America's Unfinished Revolution, 1863–1877*. New York: Harper and Row, 1988.

Foote, Shelby, *The Civil War: A Narrative*. 3 vols. New York: Random House, 1974.

Foster, Gaines M., *Ghosts of the Confederacy: Defeat, the Lost Cause, and the Emergence of the New South*. New York: Oxford University Press, 1987.

Foster, R. F., *Modern Ireland, 1600–1972*. London: Penguin, 1988.

Fredrickson, George M., *The Black Image in the White Mind: The Debate on Afro-American Character and Destiny, 1817–1914*. New York: Harper and Row, 1971.

Freehling, William W., *The Reintegration of American History: Slavery and the Civil War*. New York: Oxford University Press, 1994.

Freehling, William W., *The Road to Disunion: Secessionists at Bay, 1776–1854*. New York: Oxford University Press, 1990.

Freehling, William W., *The South vs. the South: How Anti-Confederate Southerners Shaped the Course of the Civil War*. New York: Oxford University Press, 2001.

Freeman, Douglas Southall, *R. E. Lee: A Biography*. New York: Charles Scribner's Sons, 1934.

Furet, Francois, *Revolutionary France, 1770–1880*. Oxford, Eng.: Blackwell, 1992.

Furet, Francois, and Mona Ozouf, eds., *A Critical Dictionary of the French Revolution*. Cambridge, Mass.: Harvard University Press, 1989.

Gallagher, Gary W., *The Confederate War: How Popular Will, Nationalism, and Military Strategy Could Not Stave Off Defeat*. Cambridge, Mass.: Harvard University Press, 1997.

Gallagher, Gary W., and Alan T. Nolan, *The Myth of the Lost Cause and Civil War History*. Bloomington: Indiana University Press, 2000.

Genovese, Eugene D., *A Consuming Fire: The Fall of the Confederacy in the Mind of the White Christian South*. Athens: University of Georgia Press, 1998.

Genovese, Eugene D., *The Slaveholders' Dilemma: Freedom and Progress in Southern Conservative Thought, 1820–1860*. Columbia: University of South Carolina Press, 1992.

Glatthaar, Joseph P., *Forged in Battle: The Civil War Alliance of Black Soldiers and White Officers*. New York: Penguin, 1991.

Goodrich, Thomas, *War to the Knife: Bleeding Kansas, 1854–1861*. Mechanicsburg, Pa.: Stackpole Books, 1998.

Hadden, Sally E., *Slave Patrols: Law and Violence in Virginia and the Carolinas*. Cambridge, Mass.: Harvard University Press, 2001.

Hahn, Steven, "Class and State in Postemancipation Societies: Southern Planters in Comparative Perspective," *American Historical Review* 95 (1990): 75–98.

Hahn, Steven, *A Nation under Our Feet: Black Political Struggle in the Rural South from Slavery to the Great Migration*. Cambridge, Mass.: Harvard University Press, 2003.

Hamerow, Theodore S., *Restoration, Revolution, Reaction: Economics and Politics in Germany, 1815–1871*. Princeton, N.J.: Princeton University Press, 1958.

Harris, William C., "The Hampton Roads Peace Conference: A Final Test of Lincoln's Presidential Leadership," *Journal of the Abraham Lincoln Association* 21 (2000): 31–61

Harris, William C., *Presidential Reconstruction in Mississippi*. Baton Rouge: Louisiana State University Press, 1967.

Harris, William C., *William Woods Holden: Firebrand of North Carolina Politics*. Baton Rouge: Louisiana State University Press, 1987.

Hay, Thomas Robson, "The South and the Arming of the Slaves," *Mississippi Valley Historical Review* 6 (June 1919): 34–73.

Henry, Robert Selph, *The Story of the Confederacy*. Rev. ed. New York: Bobbs-Merrill, 1936.

Hermann, Janet Sharp, *The Pursuit of a Dream*. New York: Oxford University Press, 1981.

Hill, Christopher, *Reformation to Industrial Revolution*. Vol. 2 of *The Pelican Economic History of Britain*. Baltimore: Penguin, 1969.

Holt, Thomas C., "'An Empire Over the Mind': Emancipation, Race, and Ideology in the British West Indies and the American South," in *Region, Race, and Reconstruction: Essays in Honor of C. Vann Woodward*, ed. J. Morgan Kousser and James M. McPherson. New York: Oxford University Press, 1982.

Holton, Woody, *Forced Founders: Indians, Debtors, Slaves, and the Making of the American Revolution in Virginia*. Chapel Hill: University of North Carolina Press, 1999.

Hubbs, G. Ward, *Guarding Greensboro: A Confederate Company in the Making of a Southern Community*. Athens: University of Georgia Press, 2003.

Jensen, Marius B., ed., *The Cambridge History of Japan*, Vol. 5, *The Nineteenth Century*. Cambridge, Eng.: Cambridge University Press, 1989.

Johnston, Richard Malcolm, and William Hand Browne, *Life of Alexander H. Stephens*. Philadelphia: J. B. Lippincott, 1878.

Jordan, Ervin L., *Black Confederates and Afro-Yankees in Civil War Virginia*. Charlottesville: University Press of Virginia, 1995.

Kennedy, James Ronald, and Walter Donald Kennedy, *Was Jefferson Davis Right?* Gretna, La.: Pelican, 1998.

Kimball, Gregg D., *American City, Southern Place: A Cultural History of Antebellum Richmond*. Athens: University of Georgia Press, 2000.

Kinchen, Oscar A., *Confederate Operations in Canada and the North*. North Quincy, Mass.: Christopher Publishing House, 1970.

Kolchin, Peter, "After Serfdom: Russian Emancipation in Comparative Perspective," in *Terms of Labor: Slavery, Serfdom, and Free Labor*, ed. Stanley L. Engerman. Stanford, Calif.: Stanford University Press, 1999.

Kolchin, Peter, "Some Controversial Questions Concerning Nineteenth-century Emancipation from Slavery and Serfdom," in *Serfdom and Slavery: Studies in Legal Bondage*, ed. M. L. Bush. London and New York: Longman, 1996.

Kruman, Marc W., *Parties and Politics in North Carolina, 1836–1865*. Baton Rouge: Louisiana State University Press, 1983.

Lankford, Nelson, *Richmond Burning: The Last Days of the Confederate Capital*. New York: Penguin, 2002.

Lefebvre, Georges, *The Coming of the French Revolution*. New York: Random House, 1947.

Levine, Bruce, *Half Slave and Half Free: The Roots of Civil War*. 2d ed. New York: Hill and Wang, 2005.

Litwack, Leon F., *Been in the Storm So Long: The Aftermath of Slavery*. New York: Knopf, 1979.

Long, E. B., with Barbara Long, *The Civil War Day by Day: An Almanac, 1861–1865*. Garden City, N.Y.: Doubleday, 1971.

Lonn, Ella, *Desertion during the Civil War*. 1928. Reprint. Lincoln: University of Nebraska Press, 1998.

Loveland, Anne C. *Southern Evangelicals and the Social Order, 1800–1860*. Baton Rouge: Louisiana State University Press, 1980.

Lovett, Bobby L., "The Negro's Civil War in Tennessee, 1861–1865," *Journal of Negro History* 61 (Jan. 1976): 36–50.

Luraghi, Raimondo, *The Rise and Fall of the Plantation South*. New York: New Viewpoints, 1978.

McPherson, James M., *Battle Cry of Freedom: The Civil War Era*. New York: Oxford University Press, 1988.

McPherson, James M., *Crossroads of Freedom: Antietam*. New York: Oxford University Press, 2002.

McPherson, James M., "No Peace without Victory, 1861–1865," *American Historical Review* 109 (Feb. 2004): 1–18.

McPherson, James M., *Ordeal by Fire: The Civil War and Reconstruction*, 2d ed. New York: McGraw-Hill, 1992.

McPherson, James M., *What They Fought For, 1861–1865*. New York: Doubleday, 1995.

McPherson, James M. and William J. Cooper, eds., *Writing the Civil War: The Quest to Understand*. Columbia: University of South Carolina Press, 1998.

McWhiney, Grady, *Braxton Bragg and Confederate Defeat*. New York: Columbia University Press, 1969.

Mathews, Donald G., "Charles Colcock Jones and the Southern Evangelical Crusade to Form a Biracial Community," *Journal of Southern History* 41 (Aug. 1975): 299–320.

Meade, Robert Douthat, *Judah P. Benjamin, Confederate Statesman*. New York: Oxford University Press, 1943.

Mohr, Clarence L., *On the Threshold of Freedom: Masters and Slaves in Civil War Georgia*. Athens: University of Georgia Press, 1986.

Moneyhon, Carl H., *The Impact of the Civil War and Reconstruction on Arkansas: Persistence in the Midst of Ruin*. Baton Rouge: Louisiana State University Press, 1994.

Moore, Albert Burton, *Conscription and Conflict in the Confederacy*. 1924. Reprint. Columbia: University of South Carolina Press, 1996.

Moore, Barrington, Jr., *Social Origins of Dictatorship and Democracy: Lord and Peasant in the Making of the Modern World*. Boston: Beacon, 1966.

Neal, Diane, and Thomas W. Kremm, *Lion of the South: General Thomas C. Hindman*. Macon, Ga.: Mercer University Press, 1993.

Nelson, Bernard H., "Legislative Control of the Southern Free Negro, 1861–1865," *Catholic Historical Review* 32 (Apr. 1946): 28–46.

Nevins, Allan, *The Organized War, 1863–1864*. Vol. 3 of *The War for the* Union. New York: Carles Scribner's Sons, 1971.

Nevins, Allan, *The Statesmanship of the Civil War*. New York: Macmillan, 1953.

Nolan, Alan T., *Lee Considered: General Robert E. Lee and Civil War History*. Chapel Hill: University of North Carolina Press, 1991.

Novick, Peter, *That Noble Dream: The 'Objectivity Question' and the American Historical Profession*. Cambridge, Eng.: Cambridge University Press, 1988.

Oakes, James, *The Ruling Race: A History of American Slaveholders*. New York: Random House, 1982.

Oakes, James, *Slavery and Freedom: An Interpretation of the Old South*. New York: Knopf, 1990.

Owsley, Frank Lawrence, *King Cotton Diplomacy: Foreign Relations of the Confederate States of America*. 2d ed. Chicago: University of Chicago Press, 1959.

Parks, Joseph E., *Joseph E. Brown of Georgia*. Baton Rouge: Louisiana State University Press, 1977.

Patrick, Rembert W., *Jefferson Davis and His Cabinet*. Baton Rouge: Louisiana State University Press, 1944.

Perman, Michael, *Reunion without Compromise: The South and Reconstruction, 1865–1868*. Cambridge, Eng.: Cambridge University Press, 1973.

Phillips, Ulrich B., *American Negro Slavery: A Survey of the Supply, Employment and Control of Negro Labor as Determined by the Plantation Regime*. 1918. Reprint. Baton Rouge: Louisiana State University Press, 1966.

Phillips, Ulrich B., *Life and Labor in the Old South*. 1929. Reprint. Boston: Little, Brown, 1963.

Phillips, Ulrich Bonnell, *The Life of Robert Toombs*. New York: Macmillan, 1913.

Polanyi, Karl, *The Great Transformation: The Political and Economic Origins of Our Time*. Boston: Beacon Press, 1957 .

Polk, William M., *Leonidas Polk, Bishop and General*. 2 vols. New York: Longmans, Green, 1915.

Potter, David M., *The Impending Crisis: 1848–1861*. New York: Harper and Row, 1976.

Power, J. Tracy, *Lee's Miserables: Life in the Army of Northern Virginia from the Wilderness to Appomattox*. Chapel Hill: University of North Carolina Press, 1998.

Preisser, Thomas M., "The Virginia Decision to Use Negro Soldiers in the Civil War, 1864–1865," *The Virginia Magazine of History and Biography* 83 (Jan. 1975): 98–113.

Pressly, Thomas J., *Americans Interpret Their Civil War*. 1954. Reprint. New York: Free Press, 1965.

Quarles, Benjamin, *The Negro in the Civil War*. 1953. Reprint. New York: Da Capo, 1989.

Ransom, Roger L., and Richard Sutch, *One Kind of Freedom: The Economic Consequences of Emancipation*. Cambridge, Eng.: Cambridge University Press, 1977.

Reid, Bill G., "Confederate Opponents of Arming the Slaves, 1861–1865," *Journal of Mississippi History* 22 (Oct. 1960): 249–70.

Reidy, Joseph P., *From Slavery to Agrarian Capitalism in the Cotton Plantation South: Central Georgia, 1800–1880*. Chapel Hill: University of North Carolina Press, 1992.

Rhodes, James Ford, *History of the Civil War, 1861–1865*, ed. E. B. Long. 1917. Reprint. New York: Frederick Ungar, 1961.

Richardson, Heather Cox, *The Death of Reconstruction: Race, Labor, and Politics in the Post–Civil War North, 1865–1901*. Cambridge, Mass.: Harvard University Press, 2001.

Rieber, Alfred J., "Alexander II: A Revisionist View," *Journal of Modern History* 43 (1971): 42–58.

Roark, James L., *Masters Without Slaves: Southern Planters in the Civil War and Reconstruction*. New York: W. W. Norton, 1977.

Robinson, Armstead Louis, "Day of Jubilo: Civil War and the Demise of Slavery in the Mississippi Valley, 1861–1865." Ph.D. dissertation, University of Rochester, 1976.

Rose, Willie Lee, *Rehearsal for Reconstruction: The Port Royal Experiment*. New York: Oxford University Press, 1964.

Rosenberg, Hans, *Bureaucracy, Aristocracy and Autocracy: The Prussian Experience, 1660–1815*. 1958. Reprint. Boston: Beacon Press, 1966.

Rutt, Christian Ludwig, *History of Buchanan County and the City of St. Joseph and Representative Citizens*. Chicago: Biographical, 1904.

Sanborn, F. B., ed., *The Life and Letters of John Brown*. 1885. Reprint. New York: New American Library, 1969.

Schott, Thomas E., *Alexander H. Stephens of Georgia: A Biography*. Baton Rouge: Louisiana State University Press, 1988.

Scroggs, Jack B., "Arkansas and the Secession Crisis," *Arkansas Historical Quarterly* 12 (autumn 1953): 180–223.

Segars, J. H., *In Search of Confederate Ancestors: The Guide*. Murfreesboro, Tenn.: Southern Heritage Press, 1993.

Sharp, Buchanan, "Common Rights, Charities and the Disorderly Poor," in *Reviving the English Revolution*, ed. Geoff Eley and William Hunt. London: Verso, 1988.

Shore, Laurence, *Southern Capitalists: The Ideological Leadership of an Elite*. Chapel Hill: University of North Carolina Press, 1986.

Shugg, Roger W., *Origins of Class Struggle in Louisiana: A Social History of White Farmers and Laborers during Slavery and After, 1840–1875*. 1939. Reprint. Baton Rouge: Louisiana State University Press, 1968.

Silber, Nina, *The Romance of Reunion: Northerners and the South, 1865–1900*. Chapel Hill: University of North Carolina Press, 1993.

Simms, J. G., "The Establishment of Protestant Ascendancy, 1691–1714," in *Eighteenth-Century Ireland, 1691–1800*, ed. T. W. Moody and W. E. Vaughan. New York: Oxford University Press, 1986.

Sitterson, J. Carlyle, "The William J. Minor Plantations: A Study in Ante-Bellum Absentee Ownership," *Journal of Southern History* 9 (Feb. 1943): 59–74.

Snitow, Anne Chrisine Stansell, and Sharon Thompson, eds., *The Powers of Desire: The Politics of Sexuality*. New York: Monthly Review Press, 1983.

Spencer, Edward, "Confederate Negro Enlistments," in *Annals of the War, Written by Leading Participants North and South*. 1879. Reprint. Edison, N.J.: Blue and Grey Press, 1996.

Stampp, Kenneth M., *America in 1857*. New York: Oxford University Press, 1990.

Stephenson, N. W., "The Question of Arming the Slaves," *American Historical Review* 18 (Jan. 1913): 295–308.

Sword, Wiley, *Southern Invincibility: A History of the Confederate Heart*. New York: St Martin's, 1999.

Symonds, Craig L., *Stonewall of the West: Patrick Cleburne and the Civil War*. Lawrence: University Press of Kansas, 1997.

Thomas, Emory M., *The Confederacy as a Revolutionary Experience*. 1971. Reprint. Columbia: University of South Carolina Press, 1991.

Thomas, Emory M., *The Confederate Nation, 1861–1865*. New York: Harper and Row, 1979.

Thomas, Emory M., *The Confederate State of Richmond: A Biography of the Capital*. 1971. Reprint. Baton Rouge: Louisiana State University Press, 1998.

Thomas, Emory M., *Robert E. Lee: A Biography*. New York: W. W. Norton, 1995.

Thompson, C. Mildred, *Reconstruction in Georgia: Economic, Social, Political, 1865–1872*. 1915. Reprint. Gloucester, Mass.: Peter Smith, 1964

Watson, Harry L., "Conflict and Collaboration: Yeomen, Slaveholders, and Politics in the Antebellum South," *Social History* 20 (1985): 273–98.

Wesley, Charles H., *The Collapse of the Confederacy*. 1937. Reprint. Columbia: University of South Carolina Press, 2001.

Wesley, Charles H., "The Employment of Negroes as Soldiers in the Confederate Army," *Journal of Negro History* 4 (July 1919): 239–53.

Wharton, Vernon Lane, *The Negro in Mississippi, 1865–1890*. 1947. Reprint. New York: Harper and Row, 1965.

Wehler, Hans-Ulrich, *Das deutsche Kaiserreich, 1871–1918*. Goettingen: Vandenhoeck and Ruprecht, 1994.

Wiley, Bell Irvin, *Confederate Women*. Westport, Conn.: Greenwood, 1975.

Wiley, Bell Irvin, *The Life of Johnny Reb: The Common Soldier of the Confederacy*. 1943. Reprint. Baton Rouge: Louisiana State University Press.

Wiley, Bell Irvin, "Movement to Humanize the Institution of Slavery during the Confederacy," *Emory University Quarterly*, 5 (Dec. 1949): 207–20.

Wiley, Bell Irvin, *The Plain People of the Confederacy*. 1943. Reprint. Columbia: University of South Carolina Press, 2000.

Wiley, Bell Irvin, *Southern Negroes, 1861–1865*. Baton Rouge: Louisiana, 1938.

Wilkins, Joe B., "Window on Freedom: The South's Response to the Emancipation of the Slaves in the British West Indies, 1833–1861". Ph.D. dissertation, University of South Carolina, 1977.

Williams, T. Harry, "Freeman, Historian of the Civil War: An Appraisal," *Journal of Southern History* 21 (Feb. 1955): 91–100.

Wilson, Joseph T., *The Black Phalanx: A History of the Negro Soldiers of the United States*. Hartford: American, 1890.

Wilson, Theodore Brantner, *The Black Codes of the South*. University: University of Alabama Press, 1965.

Winik, Jay, *April 1865: The Month that Saved America*. New York: HarperCollins, 2001.

Wish, Harvey, "The Slave Insurrection Panic of 1856," *Journal of Southern History* 5 (1939): 213–20.

Woodward, C. Vann, *American Counterpoint: Slavery and Racism in the North-South Dialogue*. Boston: Little, Brown [1971].

Woodward, C. Vann, *Reunion and Reaction: The Compromise of 1877 and the End of Reconstruction*. Boston: Little, Brown, 1951.

Wyatt-Brown, Bertram, "Modernizing Southern Slavery: The Proslavery Argument Reinterpreted," in *Region, Race and Reconstruction: Essays in Honor of C. Vann Woodward*, ed. J. Morgan Kousser and James M. McPherson. Baton Rouge: Louisiana State University Press, 1981.

Wyatt-Brown, Bertram, *Southern Honor: Ethics and Behavior in the Old South*. New York: Oxford University Press, 1982.

Yearns, Wilfred Buck. *The Confederate Congress*. Athens: University of Georgia Press, 1960.

INDEX

CPSIA information can be obtained at www.ICGtesting.com
Printed in the USA
BVOW040453180113

310980BV00002B/16/P